Victory
OF THE
West

NICCOLÒ CAPPONI

VICTORY
OF THE
WEST

*The Great Christian-Muslim
Clash at the Battle of Lepanto*

DA CAPO PRESS
A Member of the Perseus Books Group

3/30/07
WN
$27.50

For Francesca and Ludovica,
whose ancestors fought on both sides

First published 2006 by Macmillan an imprint of Pan Macmillan Ltd

Copyright © 2006 by Niccolò Capponi

Cataloging-in-Publication data for this book is available
from the Library of Congress.

First Da Capo Press edition 2007
ISBN-13: 978-0-306-81544-7
ISBN-10: 0-306-81544-3

Published by Da Capo Press
A Member of the Perseus Books Group
www.dacapopress.com

Da Capo Press books are available at special discounts for bulk
purchases in the U.S. by corporations, institutions, and other
organizations. For more information, please contact the Special
Markets Department at the Perseus Books Group, 11 Cambridge
Center, Cambridge, MA 02142, or call (800) 255-1514 or
(617) 252-5298, or e-mail special.markets@perseusbooks.com.

10 9 8 7 6 5 4 3 2 1

Typset by SetSystems Ltd, Saffron Walden, Essex
Maps designed by Raymond Turvey

For Francesca and Ludovica,
whose ancestors fought on both sides

PREFACE

~

'The most noble and memorable event that past centuries have seen or future generations can ever hope to witness': Miguel de Cervantes would thus sum up in a sentence the battle of Lepanto. He could speak with first-hand knowledge, having there lost the use of his left hand. Later, the philosopher Voltaire – with a keener eye for belittlement than historical truth – would dismiss the battle as inconsequential, living as he did in an age when success in war was measured by the amount of captured territory. The nineteenth century would exalt the battle as a victory of Western Civilization over oriental barbarism. Latter-day 'politically correct' historians have reversed these parameters, it being now fashionable to consider Islamic civilizations equal, if not superior, to those based on Christian principles. For these reasons this book's title has been chosen with provocation in mind.

Lepanto was not so much a victory of Western technology, but of the world that had developed it from the so-called Middle Ages onward. This is not intended as a statement of qualitative superiority: Western thinking may be at the root of democratic representation and scientific advancement, but it has also fathered biological racism and weapons of mass destruction. I don't intend to go into complicated explanations of the hows and the whys of this situation

– others have already done so, and better than I could ever hope to do. More simply, for the last 300 years a speculative approach to knowledge has allowed the West to impose its own vision on the rest of the world.

As a result, determinism (whether economic, technological, philosophical or any other) can be an irresistible temptation for any historian dealing with East–West relations. Historical anachronism is also an ever-present trap for those studying the Early Modern age, and so is the habit of dividing the world into 'us' and 'them', as if an insurmountable barrier existed between the two. At the same time it is difficult for those used to a Western view of reality to understand how a polity could be built on religious beliefs, and how much these tenets shaped the life of the average citizen. So while it would be wrong, for instance, to draw parallels between the religiously inspired Ottoman empire and the atheistic former Soviet Union, one must also not forget that the division between East and West in the sixteenth century did follow sacred lines. Individuals were prepared to fight for their beliefs, which were the foundations of their way of life and affected both their physical and metaphysical worlds. The struggles between Muslims and Christians in the Mediterranean were not so much wars of religion as wars fought by religious people.

I don't expect this book to be the ultimate work on the battle of Lepanto, for nothing is definitive in the historical field. Yet, just going back to the original sources, whether printed or archival, has made me rethink a whole set of acquired truths. For one, there was never a battle of Lepanto on 7 October 1571; Lepanto, the modern Nafpaktos, is some forty nautical miles from the site of the clash, and more accuratley the Venetians called the battle after the Curzolaris, a group of islands at the mouth of the Gulf of Patras. For this reason, in the present text Curzolaris has been used instead of Lepanto when referring to the battle. The circumstances surrounding the fight have also been coloured by writers wishing to promote their own version of events, following national and/or political allegiances. After reading some contemporary accounts one is left doubting what and whom to believe, so cross-checking became a necessity as much as a historical duty. Some anecdotes, however, were too good to be left out, even if based on only one source. Like the apocryphal story of George Washington and the cherry tree, they provide spice to what could otherwise become a dull sequence of facts and figures.

Over the last few years I have come to know many of the protagonists in this book through personal letters, direct accounts, related stories or historical hearsay. I have tried to give the Ottomans their due, regretting not being able to use as many Turkish sources as I would have liked. I also admit to having something of a soft spot for the Turks as fighters, my great-great-grandfather, a Crimean War veteran, describing them as the best soldiers in the world. Still, my unstinted admiration goes to the men on every side who fought and suffered in the wars fought in the Mediterranean during the sixteenth century. *Requiescant in pace.*

~

During the research and writing of this book I have been helped by many people, too many in fact for me to give all of them the credit they deserve. My first and foremost thanks go to Dr Marco Morin, for his constant and tireless help in finding Venetian documents, as well as for correcting some of my most glaring mistakes in technological matters. Dr Luca Lo Basso was likewise precious for his advice on galleys and oarsmen, not to mention the many documents he sent by post or email. Admiral Tiberio Moro clarified a number of crucial nautical matters as well as sharing with me his deep knowledge of the Cyprus war of 1570–3. My deepest thanks go to Professor Christine Woodhead for her generous translations of Turkish sources, and for the many valuable exchanges of ideas. Professor Erendiz Özbay-oğlu and Dr Sinan Çuluk helped me in no little way with archival sources in Istanbul, allowing me a better understanding of Ottoman politics at the time. Dr Giulia Semenza's help in the Archivo General de Simancas (Valladolid) was priceless. The late Dr Carlo De Vita was particularly generous in sharing his knowledge about archives in Rome. My gratitude goes also to the director and staff of the state archives of Florence and Venice, to my friends and former colleagues at the Medici Archive Project, and Dr Anna Evangelista for her understanding of logistics.

For books, rare printed matter and manuscripts, I can't thank enough the director and staff of the Biblioteca Casanatense (Rome), the Biblioteca dell'Istituto Nazionale degli Studi sul Rinascimento (Florence), the Biblioteca Marucelliana (Florence), the Biblioteca Moreniana (Florence), the Biblioteca Nazionale Centrale (Florence), the Biblioteca Nazionale Marciana (Venice), the Biblioteca Riccardiana (Florence), the British Institute Library (Florence), the British Library (London), the Kunsthistorisches Institut (Florence), and the Bernard Berenson Library of the Harvard University Center for Italian Renaissance Studies, Villa I Tatti (Florence). In particular, Dr Silvia Castelli of the Biblioteca Marucelliana bent over backwards to find otherwise unavailable printed sources.

My special thanks go to Prince Jonathan Doria-Pamphilij for allowing me to use his family archive, and to Dr Allessandra Mercantini for guiding me through Giovanni Andrea Doria's papers. Countess Floriani Compagnoni and Count Piero Guicciardini kindly permitted me to browse through their ancestors' fascinating documents. I am most grateful to the town hall of Noventa Vicentina, and especially to Dr Cristina Zanaica for allowing me to photograph the frescoes in the Villa Barbarigo.

Among others who helped in no little way with suggestions, references, support or simply by sharing ideas, I would like to thank the titular grand duke of Tuscany HRIH Sigmund v. Habsburg-Lothringen, Professor Gabor Ágoston, Don Nino Allaria Olivieri, Professor Nancy Bisah, Dr Maurizio Arfaioli, Dr Pinar Artiran, Brandon Barker, Professor Jeremy Black, Professor Palmira Brummet, Professor Franco Cardini, Professor William J. Connell, Dr Mary Davidson, Professor Domenico Del Nero, Dr Brooke Ettle, Captain Robert E. Ettle, Melinda Ettle, Dr Roberta Ferrazza, Leonie Frieda, Leticia Frutos, Madeleine Gera, Father Michele Ghisleri OP, Professor John Gooch, Professor John F. Guilmartin Jr., Thomas Harris, Dr Mark Hutchings, Professor Colin Imber, the unforgettable late Professor Patricia Labalme, Professor Thomas Madden, Christine Moritz, Dr Bruno Mugnai, Dr Rosemarie Mulcahy, Dr Rhoads Murphey, Dr Alana O'Brien, Dr Ciro Paoletti, Dr Susanne Probst, Douglas Preston, Dr Gianni Ridella, Andrew Roberts, Dr Brian Sandberg, Professor Richard Talbert, Professor Bruce Vandervort, Professor Roger Vella Bonavita and Dr Marino Zorzi.

My infinite gratitude goes to my agent Georgina Capel and to my editor Georgina Morley. Kate Harvey at Macmillan showed incredible patience in putting up with my mundane questions on minor details ('Do you think Don Juan of Austria's photo should be in black and white?') as well as kindly providing me with some very useful books. I can't thank enough Georgina Difford and Hugh Davis for their help in editing the original manuscript. My gratitude goes to all those who have written before on the subject of the battle of Lepanto, no matter the quality of their work; if in every tenth-rate film there is a shot worth a Rembrandt, then even in the lousiest of history books there might be an intuition worthy of Ranke.

Finally I would like to thank my family for their support during the difficulties I have had to face over these last two years, especially my darling daughters Francesca and Ludovica; just their 'Hello, Papa' after a long day is enough to dispel all troubles.

Florence, 30 April, 2006

CONTENTS

AUTHOR'S NOTE

~

MEASURES

In the sixteenth century no uniform system of weights and measures existed in the Mediterranean, or in the world at large for that matter. For this reason, when possible I have converted all weights into imperial (British) pounds. For linear measures, yards and sometimes metres have been used in the text. Miles at sea are the standard nautical miles.

TIME

In 1571 there were two systems for calculating time: the French, derived from the earth's rotation, and the Italian, which was based on the hours of daylight. The latter system was particularly inaccurate as sunrise and sunset vary according to the seasons. It should also be remembered that the Julian calendar used at the time had caused over the centuries a discrepancy between the astronomical and legal dates. Thus, 7 October in 1571 was actually the 17th, the sun rising at 06.40 and setting at 17.35.

OTTOMAN SURNAMES

Until the 1920s the Turks used nicknames instead of surnames to distinguish one another. Thus Müezzinzâde Ali means Ali son of the prayer caller (muezzin); Sokollu Mehmed, Mehmed from Sokol; and Sari Selim, Selim the Sallow.

LANGUAGE

For Turkish terms I have used the modern spelling, with the exclusion of those words like, for instance, 'muezzin' that have an accepted English form. The spelling of 'Pasha' has also been anglicised, except when part of a proper name or title (Salihpaşazăde; Kapudan Paşa). Place names are usually in their modern form (for example, Zakynthos instead of Zante) unless there is a universally accepted alternative (for instance, Lepanto instead of Nafpaktos). Where an English equivalent exists, it has been retained (Rome and not Roma). I have also tried to use 'Ottoman' instead of 'Turk' (unless for the sake of variety), the latter being a misleading term since by 1571 the Ottoman empire had ceased being ethnically Turkish. I employ the terms 'Muslim' and 'Islamic' as viable alternatives to 'Ottoman', not so much to indicate people's faith (the Greeks serving on the Ottoman fleet were usually Christians), but as a reference to the Porte's political philosophy.

CURRENCY

Until the French Revolution, European countries as a rule followed the old Carolingian monetary system, based on the *libra* ($\pounds$), the *solidus* (*s.*) and the *denarius* (*d.*): $\pounds 1 = s.20$; $s1. = 12\ d$. The names of these currencies varied from country to country, but the subdivisions remained the same. Higher denominations such as the ducat (*ducado, ducato*), or the *scudo* (*escudo* in Spanish) could be worth anything from £3 to £20. The Ottomans used a different system, based on the silver *akçe*. For the sake of clarity, whenever possible I have converted everything in Spanish 'pieces of eight'.

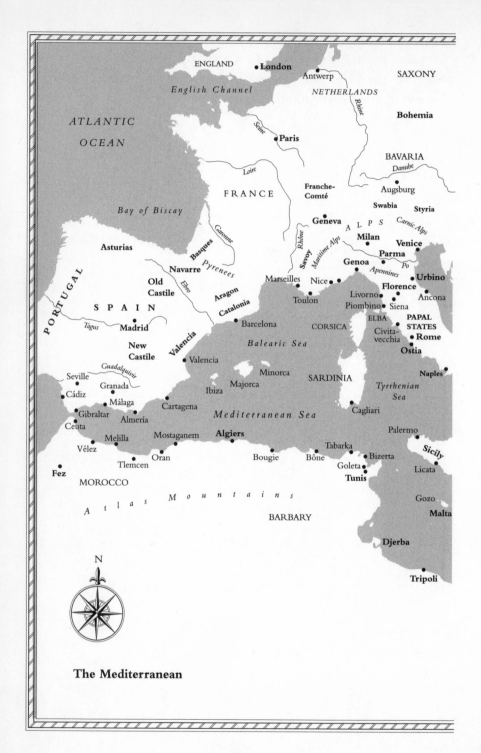

The Mediterranean

POLAND

Silesia

Moravia

Vienna

Szigetvar

Buda

HUNGARY

Mohacs

Slavonia

Croatia

Zadar

Sava

SERBIA

Sarajevo

Dubrovnic

Kosovo

Herce Novi

Kotor

Skopje

Macedonia

Durres

Apulia

Avlona

NAPLES

Otranto

Corfu

Messina

Lefkàs

Reggio

Keffalonia

Zakynthos

Syracuse

Navarino

Modon

Coron

Mani

LITHUANIA

Vistula

Podolia

Carpathian Mountains

Dniestr

Theiss

Transylvania

Temesvar

Moldavia

Belgrade

Morava

Danube

RUMELIA

Edirne

Istanbul

Salonika

Gallipoli

AEGEAN
SEA

Mytilene

Preveza

Evvia
(Negropont)

Patras

Athens

Chios

Andros

Izmir

Tinos

Paros

Naxos

Monemvasia

Canea

Retimo

Iraklio

Scarpanto

MUSCOVY - RUSSIA

Kiev

Kharkov

Cossacks

Don

Azov

Khanate of Crimea

Sea of
Azov

Caffa

BLACK SEA

Varna

Amasya

Izmit

Bursa

Ankara

Sivas

Katahya

ANATOLIA

Karaman

Konya

Tarsus

Atalya

Aleppo

Finike

Famagusta

Nicosia

Tripoli

Rhodes

Cyprus

SYRIA

Adriatic
Sea

Albania

Morea

Ionian Sea

Crete

Mediterranean Sea

Alexandria

Gulf of
Sidra

EGYPT

Nile

OTTOMAN EMPIRE

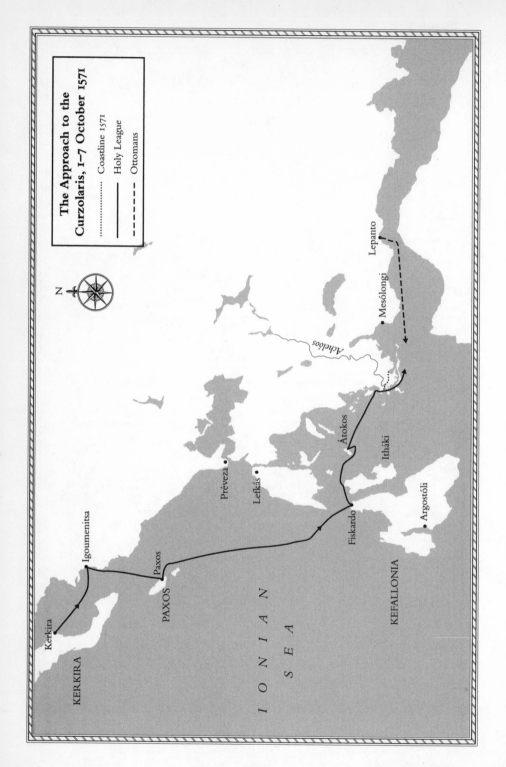

The Approach to the
Curzolaris, 1–7 October 1571

Coastline 1571
Holy League
Ottomans

N

Kerkira

KERKIRA

Igoumenitsa

Paxos

PAXOS

Préveza

Lefkás

I O N I A N

S E A

Fiskardo

Átokos

Itháki

Argostóli

KEFALLONIA

Achelóos

Mesólongi

Lepanto

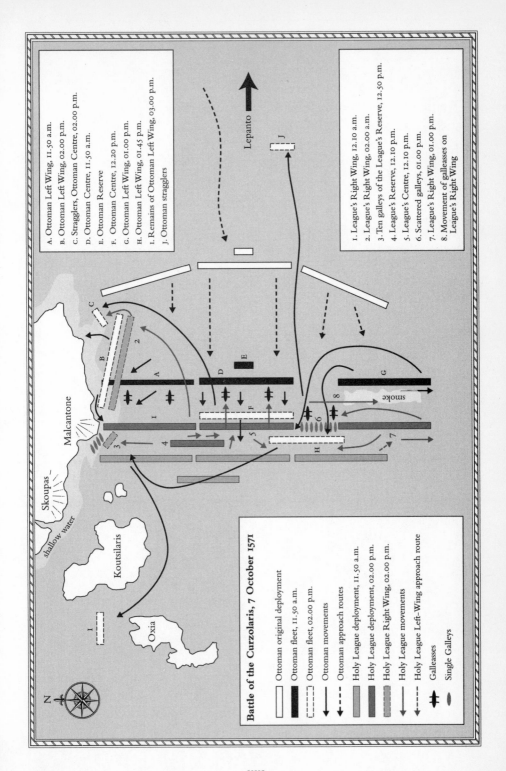

Battle of the Curzolaris, 7 October 1571

A. Ottoman Left Wing, 11.50 a.m.
B. Ottoman Left Wing, 02.00 p.m.
C. Stragglers, Ottoman Centre, 02.00 p.m.
D. Ottoman Centre, 11.50 a.m.
E. Ottoman Reserve
F. Ottoman Centre, 12.20 p.m.
G. Ottoman Left Wing, 01.00 p.m.
H. Ottoman Left Wing, 01.45 p.m.
I. Remains of Ottoman Left Wing, 03.00 p.m.
J. Ottoman stragglers

1. League's Right Wing, 12.10 a.m.
2. League's Right Wing, 02.00 a.m.
3. Ten galleys of the League's Reserve, 12.50 p.m.
4. League's Reserve, 12.10 p.m.
5. League's Centre, 12.10 p.m.
6. Scattered galleys, 01.00 p.m.
7. League's Right Wing, 01.00 p.m.
8. Movement of galleasses on League's Right Wing

Ottoman original deployment
Ottoman fleet, 11.50 a.m.
Ottoman fleet, 02.00 p.m.
Ottoman movements
Ottoman approach routes
Holy League deployment, 11.50 a.m.
Holy League deployment, 02.00 p.m.
Holy League Right Wing, 02.00 p.m.
Holy League movements
Holy League Left-Wing approach route
Galleasses
Single Galleys

Lepanto

Malcantone

Skoupas

shallow water

Koutsilaris

Oxia

smoke

N

DRAMATIS PERSONAE

~

Abd-el Malik Moroccan prince. Fought at the Curzolaris, later ruler of Fez.

Abu Humeya (Hernando de Cordoba y Valor) Leader of the Morisco revolt in Spain 1568–70.

Adrian VI (Adrian of Utrecht) Pope 1522–3. Tried unsuccessfully to unite Europe's rulers to fight the Ottomans.

Ahmed ben Sinan Helmsman of the *Sultana* at the Curzolaris. Later promoted to galley captain as a reward for his bravery during the battle.

Alticozzi, Muzio Captain of an Italian infantry company in Spanish service. Executed for revolt at Igoumenitsa.

Alva, Fernando Àlvarez de Toledo, duke of Viceroy of Naples in the late 1550s and later governor of Flanders. Opposed Philip II's Mediterranean policy.

Álvarez de Toledo, Garcia Viceroy of Sicily 1565–6. Gave advice to Don Juan of Austria about sea battles during the Holy League's campaign of 1571.

Álvarez de Toledo Osorio, Pedro Viceroy of Naples, 1532–3. Father-in-law of Cosimo I de' Medici.

Andrada, Gil de Knight of Malta and captain of the *Real* in 1571. Conducted scouting missions for Don Juan of Austria in the weeks preceding the battle of the Curzolaris.

Antinori, Bernardino Knight of St Stephen. Fought at the Curzolaris. Executed by Francesco I de' Medici in 1575.

Aruj Reis Corsair captain and elder brother of Hayreddin Barbarossa, ruler of Algiers 1516–18. Killed fighting the Spanish at Tlemcen.

Ashkenazi, Solomon Personal doctor of Grand Vizier Sokollu Mehmed Pasha. Sworn enemy of Joseph Nassi and supporter of a peaceful settlement between Venice and the Porte over Cyprus.

Austria, (Don) Juan of Illegitimate son of the Holy Roman Emperor Charles V. Commander-in-chief of the Holy League 1571–3.

Ávalos Aquino, Francisco Fernando d' Marquis of Pescara and viceroy of Sicily 1568–71. Responsible for providing supplies to the Holy League's fleet.

Ávalos Aquino-Gonzaga, Isabella d' Wife of the above, took over her husband's duties during his last illness.

Badoer, Alvise Venetian politician sent to Constantinople in 1540 to discuss peace term between Venice and the Porte.

Badoer, Andrea Venetian politician sent as ambassador to Constantinople in 1573 after the end of the Cyprus war.

Badoer, Giovan Andrea *Provveditore* of the Venetian arsenal, responsible with Marcantonio Pisani for the creation of galleasses.

Baffo, Dimo Christian renegade corsair in Ottoman service, captured and executed by the Venetians at the Curzolaris.

Baglioni, Astorre Military governor of Famagusta, executed by Lala Mustafa Pasha after the city's surrender.

Balbi, Antonio Venetian governor of Korcula. Repulsed an Ottoman attack in 1571.

Barbarigo, Agostino Deputy captain-general of the Venetian fleet in 1571. Mortally wounded at the Curzolaris.

Barbarigo, Antonio Venice's permanent ambassador in Constantinople 1556–8.

Barbaro, Marcantonio Venice's permanent ambassador in Constantinople, 1568–74. Imprisoned by the Ottomans at the beginning of the Cyprus war.

Barbaroszâde Hasan Pasha Son of Hayreddin Barbarossa. Fought at the Curzolaris and later became governor of Algiers.

Barbaroszâde Mehmed Pasha Son of Hayreddin Barbarossa. Fought at the Curzolaris.

Bayezid Süleyman I's second son. Revolted against his father but was defeated by his brother Selim. Taking refuge among the Persians, his hosts eventually handed him over to the Ottomans for execution.

Bayezid I Known as the Thunderbolt. Crushed a crusading army at Nicopolis in 1396 but was in turn defeated and captured by Tamerlane at Ankara in 1402.

Bayezid II Sultan 1480–1512. Bested the Venetians in the 1499–1502 war. Deposed by his son Selim I and died soon after.

Berardi, Alfonso Florentine *bailo* in Constantinople in the 1540s.

Biffoli, Agnolo Knight of St Stephen. At the Curzolaris he commanded the Tuscan galley *San Giovanni*, suffering severe wounds in the battle.

Bonelli, Michele Cardinal, nephew and adviser of Pius V.

Bonelli, Michele Soldier and nephew of Pius V. Fought at the Curzolaris and later became general of the pope's infantry.

Bourg de Guérines, Claude du French diplomat in Constantinople in 1570 and negotiator of a treaty between France and the Porte.

Bragadin, Marcantonio Governor general of Famagusta. Flayed alive by Lala Mustafa Pasha after the city's surrender.

Bressan, Francesco Master builder of the Venetian arsenal. Transformed a dozen large galleys into the first galleasses.

Caetani, Niccolò Known as Cardinal Sermoneta. Uncle and sponsor of Onorato Caetani.

Caetani, Onorato Duke of Sermoneta. Commander of the papal infantry contingent at the Curzolaris.

Canal, Antonio da *Provveditore* of the Venetian fleet in 1571. Distinguished himself at the Curzolaris.

Canal, Cristoforo da Venetian politician, author of *Della Milizia Marittima* and reformer of the Venetian navy in the 1550s.

Caracciolo, Ferrante Count of Biccari, fought at the Curzolaris and later published an account of the Holy League's exploits.

Carafa, Carlo Cardinal and nephew of Paul IV. Tried to gain Ottoman military support during the war of the papacy against the Colonna. Later executed by Pius IV.

Cardenas, Bernardino de Spanish nobleman, killed at the Curzolaris.

Cardona, Juan de Leader of the advance party during the Holy League fleet's approach to the Curzolaris. Later commander of Sicily's galley squadron.

Caur Ali Reis Genoese renegade in Ottoman service. Captured at the Curzolaris.

Cavalli, Giovanni Antonio Brescian nobleman and veteran of the battle of Mühlberg. One of the two *sopracomiti* designated in 1570 to command the galleys armed for Venice by the city of Brescia.

Cavalli, Marino *Provveditore generale* of Crete in 1571. Sent a frigate to inform the Christian fleet of the fall of Famagusta.

Cecco Pisano Mariner in the service of Marcantonio Colonna.

Cervantes Saavedra, Miguel de Spanish soldier, administrator and author. Wounded at the Curzolaris.

Charles V of Habsburg Holy Roman Emperor 1519–56.

Charles VIII of Valois King of France. His invasion of Italy in 1494 triggered off the so-called Italian Wars lasting until 1559.

Charles IX of Valois Son of Henry II and Catherine de' Medici. Opposed to the Holy League.

Clement VII (Giulio de' Medici) Pope 1523–34. His bad political judgement caused Rome to be sacked by Charles V's troops in 1527.

Colonna, Marcantonio Cardinal, cousin and namesake of the papal commander at the Curzolaris.

Colonna, Marcantonio Duke of Tagliacozzo and Paliano. Papal commander at the Curzolaris and later viceroy of Sicily.

Cosimo I de' Medici Duke of Florence and Siena, and from 1569 grand duke of Tuscany. Twelve of his galleys, loaned to Pius V, fought at the Curzolaris.

Dandolo, Nicolò Venetian governor of Cyprus. Killed at the fall of Nicosia.

Dax, François de Noailles, bishop of French envoy in Constantinople 1571–3.

Dervis Pasha Ottoman governor of Aleppo, Syria. Distinguished himself at the storming of Nicosia.

Diedo, Girolamo Venetian officer and writer. Fought at the Curzolaris and later wrote a lengthy account of the 1571 campaign.

Donà, Leonardo Venetian ambassador in Madrid 1570–3. Elected doge of Venice in 1604.

Doria, Andrea Prince of Melfi and knight of the Golden Fleece. From 1529 admiral of Emperor Charles V. Bested by Hayreddin Barbarossa at the battle of Preveza in 1537.

Doria, Giovanni Andrea Knight commander of Santiago, marquis of Tursi and later prince of Melfi. General at sea of Philip II in 1571. Led the Christian right wing at the Curzolaris.

Doria, Pagano Knight of Malta and brother of Giovanni Andrea. Wounded at the Curzolaris.

Dragut *See* Thorgud Reis.

Duodo, Francesco Commander of the Venetian galleasses at the Curzolaris. Later governor of Brescia and *procuratore di San Marco*.

Ebu's-su'ud Chief mufti under Süleyman I and Selim II. Upheld the legitimacy of the Porte's claim over Cyprus.

Elizabeth I Tudor Queen of England 1559–1603. One of the main supporters of the anti-Spanish rebellion in the Netherlands.

Emmanuel Philibert of Savoy Duke of Savoy. Won the battle of St-Quentin against the French in 1557. Sent three galleys to fight at the Curzolaris.

Esdey Mustafa Paymaster-general of the Ottoman fleet in 1571. Fought at the Curzolaris.

Espinosa, Diego Cardinal and bishop of Siguenza. One of the main advocates of the repressive measures enacted by the Spanish crown against the Moriscos, 1567–71.

Facchinetti, Giovanni Antonio Papal nuncio in Venice 1570–3. Later elected pope with the name of Innocent IX.

Farnese, Alessandro Son of Ottavio Farnese, duke of Parma. Fought at the Curzolaris and later became governor of the Spanish Netherlands.

Ferdinand I of Habsburg King of Hungary, king of the Romans and Holy Roman Emperor. Opposed Ottoman expansion in Hungary.

Figueroa, Lope de Commander of the Spanish troops embarked on the *Real* during the 1571 campaign. Wounded at the Curzolaris. Gave detailed report of the battle to Philip II of Spain.

Fisogni, Orazio Brescian nobleman. One of the two *sopracomiti* designated in 1570 to command the galleys armed for Venice by the city of Brescia.

Floriani, Pompeo Military architect and engineer. Fought against the Huguenots in France and against the Ottomans at the Curzolaris. Wrote a number of treatises on strategy and fortifications.

Foscarini, Giacomo Venetian *provveditore generale* of Dalmatia. Took over from Sebastiano Venier as commander of the Venetian fleet in 1572.

Francesco I de' Medici Crown prince and later grand duke of Tuscany. Sent by his father Cosimo I to Genoa to appease Don Juan of Austria.

Francesco Maria II della Rovere Son of Guidobaldo II, duke of Urbino. Fought at the Curzolaris and succeeded his father in 1574. Left a rich correspondence on the 1571 campaign.

Gatto, Angelo One of the defenders of Famagusta 1570–1. Left an account of the siege.

Gianfigliazzi, Bongianni Knight of Malta. Fought at Montechiaro in 1570 and was captured at the Curzolaris the following year. Appointed Florentine ambassador to the Porte in 1578.

Giustiniani, Pietro Knight commander of the Order of Malta. Severely wounded at the Curzolaris.

Giustiniani, Vincenzo Genoese governor of Chios in 1566. Taken prisoner by Piyale Pasha after the island's surrender.

Gómez de Silva, Ruy Prince of Eboli and duke of Pastrana, secretary to Philip II of Spain.

Granvelle, Antoine Perrenot de Cardinal and bishop of Arras, enemy of Marcantonio Colonna. Spanish plenipotentiary in Rome, 1570–1. Later viceroy of Naples and president of Philip II's *Consejo de Italia*.

Gregory XIII (Ugo Boncompagni) Successor of Pius V in 1572. Reformer of the Western calendar in 1583.

Guasto, Paolo dal Venetian officer. Defended Nicosia in 1570.

Habsburg, (Don) Carlos of Son of Philip II of Spain. Given to bizarre behaviour, he was imprisoned by his father in 1568 and died in confinement.

Hasan Bey Commander of the *capitana* of Rhodes at the Curzolaris.

Hayreddin Barbarossa (Hizir Reis) Turkish corsair. Ottoman governor of Algiers in 1519. Commander-in-chief of Süleyman I's navy 1533–46.

Hindī Mahmūd Judge and member of Selim II's household. Taken prisoner at the Curzolaris.

Hürrem Sultan Former slave of Slavic (possibly Russian) origin. Wife of Süleyman I and mother of Selim II.

Ibn 'Ulayyan Leader of the anti-Ottoman revolt in Mesopotamia in 1567. Later Ottoman governor of the region.

Isfendiari Mustafa Pasha Cousin of Süleyman I and commander of the Ottoman army at the siege of Malta in 1565.

János Szapolyai King of Hungary 1526–40. Ally of Süleyman I against Ferdinand I of Habsburg.

Jem Brother of Bayezid II. Escaped to Europe after his unsuccessful bid for the Ottoman throne.

Kara Hodja Bey Ottoman *sancak bey* of Avlona, corsair and former Dominican friar. Killed at the Curzolaris.

Kılıç Ali Pasha Algerian corsair, born Luca (or Giovanni) Galeni. Governor of Algiers in the late 1560s. Commanded Ottoman left wing at the Curzolaris. Became *kapudan paşa* in 1571. Retook Tunis from the Spanish in 1574.

Lala Mustafa Pasha Former tutor of Selim II and commander of the Ottoman army in Cyprus 1570–1. Famous for his savage treatment of Venetian prisoners after the fall of Famagusta. Grand vizier in 1580, following the death of Sokollu Mehmed Pasha.

Landriano, Giuseppe Francesco Count of Landriano and viceroy of Sicily 1571–6.

Loredan, Pietro Doge of Venice at the outbreak of the Cyprus war.

Marignano, Giangiacomo de' Medici, marquis of Milanese nobleman, commander of the Holy Roman Empire's forces during the war of Siena.

Mawlay Hamida Spanish-backed lord of Tunis. Evicted by the Ottomans in 1569.

Maximilian II of Habsburg Holy Roman Emperor from 1564. Refused to join the Holy League.

Mazzinghi, Luigi Florentine knight of Malta. Fought at the Curzolaris and left an account of the battle.

Medici, Catherine de' Widow of Henry II of Valois and regent of France.

Medici, Tommaso de' Commander of the Florentine galley *Fiorenza* at the Curzolaris. Severely wounded in the battle.

Mehmed II Ottoman sultan and conqueror of Constantinople in 1453.

Mihirimah Daughter of Süleyman I and wife of Grand Vizier Rüstem Pasha.

Mocenigo, Alvise Doge of Venice 1570–8.

Monte, Piero del Grand master of the Order of Malta at the time of the battle of the Curzolaris.

Moretto, Ottaviano Captain of the Savoyard galley *Piemontesa*. Killed at the Curzolaris.

Mudazzo, Zaccaria Venetian governor of Kyrenia in Cyprus. Surrendered without a fight to the Ottomans in 1570. Arrested by the Venetian authorities and died in prison.

Müezzinzâde Ali Pasha *Kapudan-i deryâ* from 1567 in place of Piyale Pasha. Killed at the Curzolaris.

Mustafa First son of Süleyman I. Executed by his father on suspicions of treason.

Nani, Federico Agostino Barbarigo's deputy at the Curzolaris. Took command when the former was mortally wounded.

Nassi, Joseph Jewish merchant, duke of Naxos and adviser to Selim II. One of those responsible for the Cyprus war.

Negroni, Alessandro Commander of the Tuscan galley *Grifona* at the Curzolaris.

Noailles *See* Dax.

Nobili, Leonardo de' Florentine ambassador in Spain in 1569.

Odescalchi, Giulio Maria Papal nuncio with the Holy League fleet in 1571.

Orange, William of Nassau, prince of Leader of the Netherlands revolt in 1568. Murdered in 1584.

Orsini, Paolo Commander of Venice's infantry contingent at the Curzolaris. Badly wounded in the battle.

Orsini, Paolo Giordano Son-in-law of Cosimo I de' Medici. Fought at the Curzolaris on the *capitana* of the Lomellini.

Pacheco, Francisco Cardinal and archbishop of Burgos. Spanish plenipotentiary in Rome 1570–1.

Parma, Margaret of Habsburg, duchess of Natural daughter of Charles V and mother of Alessandro Farnese. Governor of the Netherlands 1559–67.

Paruta, Girolamo Venetian governor of Tinos in 1571. Repelled the Ottomans under Piyale Pasha.

Paul III (Alessandro Farnese) Pope 1534–9. Convened the Council of Trent in 1545.

Paul IV (Gianpietro Carafa) Pope 1555–9. Went to war with Charles V and Philip II for their support of Marcantonio Colonna.

Pertev Pasha Second vizier and *serdar* during the in 1571 campaign. Opposed attacking the Christian fleet but was overruled. Wounded at the Curzolaris, he was forced to retire in disgrace after the battle.

Philip II of Habsburg King of Spain 1556–8.

Piyale Pasha *Kapudan-ı deryâ* 1558–67. Commanded Ottoman fleet at Djerba, Malta and Chios. Created vizier by Selim II, he was put in charge of Ottoman naval operations in 1570. Forced to retire for failing to stop Venetian reinforcements from getting to Famagusta.

Pius IV (Giovanni Angelo de' Medici) Pope 1559–65. Closed the Council of Trent.

Pius V (Antonio Ghisleri) Pope 1565–72. The main force behind the creation of the Holy League.

Podocattaro, Ettore Venetian defender of Nicosia. Executed by Lala Mustafa Pasha after the fall of the city.

Porcia, Silvio da Commander of a Venetian infantry regiment at the Curzolaris.

Provana de Leynì, Andrea Savoyard admiral. Fought at the Curzolaris and left a report of the battle.

Querini, Marco Venetian *provveditore generale* of Crete in 1570. Commanded the relief expedition sent to Famagusta in the winter of 1571. One of the deputy commanders of the Venetian fleet at the Curzolaris.

Ragazzoni, Giacomo Venetian merchant, unofficially sent on a peace mission to Constantinople in spring 1571.

Requesens y Zúñiga, Luis de *Comendador mayor* of Castile of the Order of Santiago. One of Don Juan of Austria's advisers during the 1571 campaign. Later became governor of Milan and of Flanders.

Romegas, Mathurin Lescaut dit Knight of Malta and corsair. Captain of Marcantonio Colonna's galley at the Curzolaris. Left an account of the battle.

Roxelane *See* Khürrem.

Rüstem Pasha Grand vizier and son-in-law of Süleyman I.

Saint Clément, François de Commander of the Maltese galley fleet in 1570. Defeated by Uluç Ali at Montechiaro, he was subsequently condemned to death for negligence.

Salihpaşazâde Mehmed Bey Governor of Evvoia. Captured at the Curzolaris and released a few years after the battle.

Santa Cruz, Alvaro de Bazan, marquis of Commander of the

Christian reserve at the Curzolaris. Later defeated an Anglo-French fleet at the Azores.

Scetti, Aurelio Tuscan musician sent to the galleys for murdering his wife. Left an account of the battle of the Curzolaris.

Selim I Known as the Grim. Deposed his father Bayezid II in 1512. Conquered Egypt in 1517.

Selim II Known as the Sallow. Sultan 1566–74. Declared war on Venice over Cyprus.

Sereno, Bartolomeo Papal officer. Fought at the Curzolaris, and later wrote an account of the Cyprus war.

Sermoneta *See* Caetani.

Shah Ismail Founder of the Safavid dynasty and promoter of Shia Islam in the Middle East.

Sokollu Mehmed Pasha Grand vizier under Süleyman I and Selim II. Opposed the latter's decision to go to war with Venice. Murdered in 1579.

Soranzo, Giovanni Venetian plenipotentiary in Rome 1570–1.

Spinola, Ettore Commander of Genoa's state galleys at the Curzolaris. Left a report of the battle.

Strozzi, Piero Florentine exile, arch-enemy of Cosimo I de' Medici. Fought for the French in the Siena war, and later for Paul IV.

Süleyman I Known as the Lawgiver. Sultan 1520–66. Reorganizer of the Ottoman legal system. Fought successfully the Persians, the Habsburgs and the Venetians. Failed to take Malta in 1565. Died on campaign in Hungary in 1566.

Şuluç Mehmed Pasha Governor of Alexandria in 1571. Commanded the Ottoman right at the Curzolaris. Captured by the Venetians, he died of his wounds soon after.

Surian, Michele Venetian plenipotentiary in Rome 1570–1.

Thorgud Reis Turkish corsair, known in Europe as Dragut. An associate of Hayreddin Barbarossa. Conquered Tripoli for the Ottomans in 1551. Killed at the siege of Malta in 1565.

Toledo *See* Álvarez de Toledo Osorio.

Uluç Ali Pasha *See* Kılıç Ali Pasha.

Vallette, Jean Parissot de La Grand master of the Order of Malta. Defeated the Ottoman attempt to take Malta in 1565.

Venier, Sebastiano Commander-in-chief of the Venetian fleet in 1571. Fought at the Curzolaris in the central squadron. Elected doge of Venice in 1578.

Zane, Gerolamo Commander-in-chief of the Venetian fleet in 1570. Disgraced and imprisoned for his failure to relieve Cyprus.

Zaydi Imam Leader of the anti-Ottoman rebellion in the Yemen 1566–7.

Zuñiga, Juan de Venetian plenipotentiary in Rome 1570–1. Later viceroy of Naples.

PROLOGUE

~

On the morning of 7 October 1571 a long procession exited Constantinople, capital of the Ottoman empire, heading west in the direction of the town of Edirne. Forbidding-looking soldiers marched, or rode, alongside turbaned officials, veiled ladies, doctors, pages, clerks, cooks and all the other individuals necessary for the running of a court. In the middle of this human snake, protected by his bodyguard of janissaries and Sipahis of the Porte, rode the flushed, swollen figure of Sultan Selim II, 'Emperor of Rome, Constantinople, Romania, Africa, Asia, Trebisond, Cyprus, Capadocia, Paphlagonia, Cylicia, Panphilia, Licia, Frigia, Archanania, Armenia; Lord of the Greater and Lesser Tartary, with all its provinces of Arabia, Turkey and Russia; Sultan of Babylon, Persia, and of Greater India, with everything that the seven branches of the river Ganges touch; Universal Lord of everything that surrounds the Sun; descendant from Divine Lineage; destructor of the Christian Faith; and dominator of the Universe'. The forty-seven-year-old sultan could feel satisfied as he travelled to his winter palace in Edirne, anticipating a rewarding hunting season. He had reasons to be pleased. After nearly two years of war with the republic of Venice his army had finally conquered the last enemy stronghold on the island of Cyprus, while the Ottoman navy had harassed Venetian-held territories along the Adriatic coast. It was true that

1

now he was facing an alliance of many Western states, but it was common opinion that the league would soon collapse due to internal dissent. This year he had added Cyprus to his empire; the next would see Crete, Corfu, Kotor and – Allah willing – Venice itself.[1]

~

Several hundred miles away in the Gulf of Patras a swift-moving frigate approached a large galley immobile in the water. On the frigate the twenty-four-year-old Don Juan of Austria, illegitimate son of the Holy Roman Emperor Charles V and half-brother of the king of Spain Philip II, was scanning the galley's stern searching for someone: Sebastiano Venier, captain-general at sea of the republic of Venice and a very difficult character. Don Juan and Venier had not been on speaking terms for some days, ever since the Venetian had arbitrarily hanged some rebellious soldiers in Spanish pay; but the present situation demanded personal and national pride be swallowed. 'Must we fight?' shouted Don Juan at the seventy-five-year-old, thick-bearded Venetian leaning over his galley's railing. Venier, turning towards the Ottoman fleet slowly deploying into battle order eight miles to the east, answered with steely determination, 'We must, and can't avoid it.'[2]

~

From his station on the poop deck of his galley, Müezzinzâde Ali Pasha, the grand admiral of the Ottoman fleet, beheld the Christian array in the distance. Early reports that the enemy was on the run had been disproved, and it appeared that the Christians intended to fight. Müezzinzâde Ali, confident of victory only a few hours before, was having misgivings. Admittedly, the Ottomans enjoyed a numerical superiority over the allies, but the latter's fleet was bigger than expected. Everything pointed to a tough battle ahead, but despite everything the *kapudan-ı deryâ* was convinced that his plan would be successful – provided everyone worked in unison. Of his captains and soldiers he was sure, and even of the Greek volunteer rowers, but what about the Christian slaves? Had not one of his subordinates expressed suspicions that they would rebel at the first opportunity? 'Friends,' said Müezzinzâde Ali, turning towards the oarsmen chained to his galley's rowing benches, 'I expect you do your duty today, in return for how I have treated you. If I win, I promise you your liberty. Should the day be yours, then Allah will have given it to you.'[3]

In the allied fleet others were also hoping that victory would give them freedom. On 9 August 1565 the musician and convicted murderer Aurelio Scetti had laid his head on the executioner's block in the city of Arezzo. But instead of feeling on his neck the cold steel of the axe, Scetti was pulled to his feet by the hangman amidst shouts of 'Pardon!' His sentence commuted to life servitude and the confiscation of his property, the musician had since lived with the other criminals condemned to row on the galleys of His Most Serene Highness Cosimo I de' Medici, grand duke of Tuscany. Many a time had Scetti petitioned the Florentine authorities for a reprieve, but to no avail. Now his hopes of being liberated were revived as news of the general amnesty proclaimed by Don Juan of Austria for all those convicts prepared to fight spread through the fleet like wildfire. Dragging himself to his battle station, the lame Scetti could only wish to survive the day without ending up chained to an Ottoman rowing bench.[4]

Like many of his colleagues Salihpaşazǎde Mehmed Bey, governor general of the province of Negropont (the present-day Evvoia) was puzzled by the Christians' behaviour. What did they think they were doing towing to the front of their battle line what appeared to be six large transport galleys? According to intelligence reports the Venetians had modified some *mavna* (as the Ottomans called such vessels) to carry guns, and prisoners taken a few days earlier had confirmed this. But the captives had only admitted to three artillery pieces at the bow and stern – not much in the way of ordnance, and hardly capable of stopping the Ottoman advance. The Christians' move looked like an act of sheer desperation, and as the Ottoman fleet started moving forward the forty-year-old, squint-eyed Salihpaşazâde Mehmed could only assume that the allies were behaving like sheep ready to be slaughtered.[5]

~

From the forecastle of his heavily armed galleass Captain Francesco Duodo watched the Turkish galleys as they loomed ever larger on the horizon, approaching steadily at a speed of about 100 yards a minute. The Venetian commander and his crew welcomed the enemy's arrival. Less than three days had passed since the Christian fleet had received word of the brutal murders in the Cypriot port of Famagusta. Word had circulated of the Turks' treachery after they reneged on their promise of safe conduct for their Venetian prisoners. Among Duodo's crew anger toward the Ottomans ran at fever pitch. Now, in the waters off the western coast of Greece, the Venetians had the chance to exact revenge; their six galleasses, rowing ships of a novel design never before tested in battle, would strike the first blow at the Turkish fleet. Venice had placed all its hopes in these unusually heavy vessels, laden with six times the ordnance of a conventional galley. In a significant tactical and technological shift, the Venetians would rely first on the over-whelming force of their artillery before resorting to hand-to-hand combat at close quarters. Taking in the approaching ships with the eye of an expert mariner, the captain coolly waited until they were only half a mile away.

~

The glow of the early afternoon sun hovered over the city of Rome, shining through the windows of the Vatican palace as Pope Pius V conversed with a group of close collaborators. The sixty-seven-year-old pontiff had many worries: Protestants were busy spreading their heresies all over Europe and the Ottomans' advance in the Mediterranean seemed unstoppable. Pius had done much to

4

counter both perils, even managing to create a league of quarrelsome Christian princes to fight the Muslims. He knew that an allied fleet had been operating for some weeks in the Levant, and all this time the gaunt, deeply religious pope had been fasting and praying for divine aid against the Islamic menace. Suddenly Pius walked towards a window, opened it and stood for some time looking at the sky. At length closing the shutters, he turned towards his treasurer Bartolomeo Busotti. 'It is no time for business,' he exclaimed, his face lit with joy. 'Let us go and thank God, for this very moment our fleet has defeated the Turks.'[6]

1. THE WAXING CRESCENT

~

In early February 1545 Duke Cosimo I de' Medici was busy inspecting the new fortifications of Prato, twelve miles to the north-east of Florence. With him was his wife Eleanor Álvarez de Toledo, who being in the final stages of a pregnancy would have wanted to pay a visit to the Sacro Cingolo (Girdle of the Virgin) in the local cathedral. This sacred relic was believed to be especially beneficial to women who were unable to conceive, or who feared complications in childbirth. Since February was also carnival time the ducal couple managed to combine military and pious duties with the pleasures of the season, including attending a theatrical presentation in the old castle of Prato which involved a mock battle between Christians and Turks. At one tumultuous moment of the show an actor portraying a Turk accidentally exposed his 'larger that usual' privates, which caused everyone in the audience to laugh with great gusto.[1]

But in the circumstances the ducal guffaw rang hollow, for in 1545 the Turks were no laughing matter. Anybody travelling along the coasts of the western Mediterranean could have witnessed the havoc caused a few months before by the Muslim fleet under the command of the redoubtable corsair and Ottoman high admiral, Hayreddin Barbarossa: villages torched, crops and livestock destroyed, thousands of people killed or enslaved. In a Venetian atlas of the same year six Turkish galleys can be seen cruising off the Tuscan coast, ready to strike at the Italian mainland, or at anybody unfortunate enough to cross their path. 'Do you think the Turks will invade this year?' asks one of the protagonists of Niccolò Machiavelli's ribald play *The Mandrake*. 'Yes, if you do not pray,' answers a friar.[2] Machiavelli was poking fun at credulous people and corrupt clergymen, but nobody in his day would have denied that the Muslim menace was very real. Indeed, for many it must have seemed only a matter of time before a final onslaught brought the whole of Europe under the rule of Islam.

By the standards of the time, the speed of the Ottoman expansion in Europe and Asia had been stunning. At the beginning of the fourteenth century a petty Turkish warlord called Osman had controlled some land in the north-west of Byzantine Bithynia; 200 years later his descendants, known as the Ottomans, ruled over territories stretching from Durazzo on the Adriatic to Erzurum in eastern Anatolia. In the following decades the Ottomans would conquer the whole of Egypt, large swathes of North Africa, more than half of Hungary, nearly all the Aegean, a big chunk of the Caucasus, the Crimean peninsula and Mesopotamia down to modern-day Basra. In addition, the Sublime Porte,* as the Ottoman empire was commonly known, extended its rule to the Yemen and the Muslim holy cities of Mecca and Medina, also holding sway over a number of tributary territories, including the whole of Arabia plus the principalities of Moldavia and Wallachia in the Balkans. Through war and treaty, skilfully exploiting the weaknesses of their enemies, the Ottomans had gobbled up piecemeal the Byzantine empire and many other sovereign entities in the Mediterranean. When compelled to

---

* A translation of the Turkish *kapi* or *dergah-ı-ali*, which originally indicated the place where the Sultan heard legal suits and engaged in law-making activities. The term eventually became the common way to describe the Ottoman government, very much as the White House is synonymous with the executive of the United States of America.

give battle, the Ottoman armies usually prevailed thanks to their superior tactics and discipline. A crippling blow was inflicted on the Serbian kingdom at the first battle of Kosovo in 1389, and the Serbs were forced thereafter to accept the Ottomans as overlords before being finally conquered in 1458. At the battle of Nicopolis in 1396, Sultan Bayezid I crushed a crusading army sent to aid the beleaguered kingdom of Hungary.[3] The flower of European chivalry was either killed or taken prisoner, and Bayezid followed up his victory by annexing the whole of Bulgaria.

The Ottoman expansion was not, however, without its setbacks. The death of Sultan Murad I on the field of Kosovo prevented the Turks exploiting their victory in full, while thirteen years later the famous Mongol warlord Tamerlane delivered a nearly fatal blow to the budding empire. Thanks to a series of whirlwind campaigns Tamerlane managed to carve out a huge state in central-west Asia, eventually overwhelming and capturing Bayezid I at the battle of Ankara in 1402. The sultan died in captivity a year later, and everybody reckoned that this was the Ottoman state's death knell. But Tamerlane was not able to consolidate his conquests, and when his empire collapsed after his death in 1405 Bayezid's heirs took the opportunity to reclaim their inheritance. What followed was a civil war among the late sultan's offspring, out of which Mehmed I (1413–21) emerged as the sole victor and ruler, allowing his successor Murad II (1421–51) to resume the Ottoman drives east and west.

But the title of 'conqueror' would appropriately be bestowed on Murad's son, Mehmed II (1444–46, 1451–81), although his first experience as a ruler was well nigh disastrous.[4] His father abdicated in 1444, only to be recalled from retirement by his former viziers when the twelve-year-old Mehmed hesitated in the face of a devastating offensive led by the king of Hungary, Vladislav I, against the Ottoman territories in the Balkans. In a show of daring, Murad crossed the Bosporus with his army – mainly thanks to the active collaboration of the Genoese fleet – and inflicted a crushing defeat on the Hungarians at Varna, killing Vladislav and restoring Ottoman dominance in the region. He then proceeded to suppress a number of internal revolts before overpowering the Hungarians once more at the second battle of Kosovo (October 1448). By the time Murad died three years later, Mehmed had more than learnt his lesson.

From the very beginning of his reign Mehmed's fixed idea was the conquest of Constantinople.[5] By this point the Byzantine empire under the rule of Constantine XI was a shadow of its former self, being reduced to its capital and a few scattered territories in Greece and Asia Minor. However the sultan undertook the war methodically, first by securing his borders through treaty and military force. He then proceeded to block the Bosporus with fortresses, artillery and ships, before laying siege to Constantinople from the land side. The garrison of the city counted 7,000 men, of which 2,000 were foreigners, and thus vastly inferior to the approximately 150,000 Ottoman attackers. Nonetheless, the Byzantines were prepared to fight to the bitter end, and had the advantage of Constantinople's triple circuit of massive walls. For this very reason Mehmed's army had in its train two colossal bombards designed specifically for the destruction of heavy masonry. The city fell after a two-month siege, thanks to intense artillery pounding and incessant assaults. There followed an orgy of rape and pillage, until Mehmed put a stop to it. The fall of Constantinople not only sent shock waves through the Western world, but also provided the Ottomans with a legal and psychological basis for their wars of conquest: by possessing Constantinople they could claim sovereignty over all the lands of the former Roman empire – of which the Byzantines considered themselves the heirs.

Mehmed followed up his victory by conquering the Genoese colonies on the Black Sea, the Greek–Florentine duchy of Athens, the kingdom of Serbia, most of the Peloponnese, and the last Byzantine enclaves in Anatolia. He next turned against the rebel ruler of Wallachia, Vlad III Drakul (whose favourite pastime was impaling Turkish prisoners of war), forcing him to submit to Ottoman rule. Then, after taking over the Genoese island of Lesvos,

Mehmed turned his attention to the kingdom of Bosnia and the duchy of Hercegovina. By 1466 both territories were completely under Turkish rule, resulting in a wave of conversion to Islam among the native populations. While still engaged in Bosnia Mehmed's aggressive policies in Greece and the Balkans caused him to become embroiled in a war with Venice over the latter's colonies in Greece, as well as having to fight the troublesome Albanian lord George Kastriote 'Skanderbeg'. Kastriote was beaten, although not without considerable effort, and driven into exile. The war with Venice lasted until 1479 when the Venetians were forced to relinquish to the sultan a number of important locations, including the islands of Zakynthos and Kefallonia, as well as the strategic port of Avlona at the mouth of the Adriatic. Even more serious for Venice was the fact that the Turks, from their bases in Bosnia, had been able to make a number of devastating inroads into the Venetian home territories, exposing not only their vulnerability but also that of the whole Italian peninsula to a determined attack. Although the European powers would not become aware of Italy's weakness until the French invasion of 1494, Mehmed had already grasped it. While planning his offensive into the heart of the Mediterranean, he was determined to rid himself of a foe nearer home: the Christian-held island of Rhodes – this to be followed by a deep probe into Apulia, the heel of Italy.

Since the beginning of the fourteenth century Rhodes had been the headquarters of the monastic–chivalric order of the Hospital of St John of Jerusalem. Its members, known as Johannites, Hospitallers or Knights of Rhodes, had over the years transformed the island into one of the finest fortresses in Europe.[6] On 23 May 1480 the Turkish army, 70,000 strong with a powerful artillery train, landed on the island under the command of Mesic Pasha, a Greek renegade and kinsman of the last Byzantine emperor. The siege lasted until the end of July, but bombardment and mass assaults did not manage to overcome the defences. Mesic Pasha re-embarked his army, having lost at least 25,000 men killed or wounded, plus enormous quantities of materiel, against a few hundred defenders. Rhodes had been a disaster for the Ottomans, and now Mehmed looked to his Italian campaign to redress the balance.

On 28 July a Turkish expeditionary force of 18,000 men under the command of the redoubtable *sancak* of Avlona Gedik Ahmed Pasha landed in front of the town of Otranto.[7] The ostensible reasons for this invasion were Mehmed's vague claim to Apulia as heir of the Byzantine empire, plus his desire to punish the king of Naples for his military assistance to Skanderbeg. In reality, the expedition's objective was to probe the defences of the kingdom of Naples and, or at least it was rumoured so at the time, even attempt the conquest of Rome.★ Otranto was taken, the Ottomans executing about 800 male prisoners who refused to convert to Islam and enslaving the women and children. But very soon Gedik discovered there was not enough plunder in the area to sustain his army and, in the face of stiffening Neapolitan resistance, the following October he retired across the Adriatic, leaving 800 foot and 500 horse to garrison Otranto. His intention was to come back the following year, and for the whole winter rumours abounded in Italy about the pope being about to leave Rome for fear of a Turkish raid. But Mehmed II's death in May 1481 and his successor's desire for peace after thirty years of constant warfare – leaving the state coffers empty – resulted in Gedik's downfall and subsequent execution. The Ottoman troops in Otranto quickly surrendered to the Neapolitans, some of them even joining the ranks of their vanquishers. Italy was saved, at least for the time being.

~

★ While Mehmed's plans may seem overambitious, it has to be remembered that at the time the south of Italy and the Papal States were seriously depleted of military forces, the king of Naples and the pope being engaged in central Italy against a joint Florentine–Venetian army – the so-called War of the Pazzi Conspiracy. The sultan's decision to strike indicates an awareness of the Italian situation, a tribute to Ottoman espionage.

The speed of Ottoman conquest had been possible thanks to superior tactics, organization and cunning, all augmented by Islamic doctrine. The relevant tenet of this was the notion of jihad, meaning effort, struggle or fight, but implying in general holy war on behalf of Islam. Akin to jihad is *gaza*, meaning a raid (against infidels), and the fact that from the beginning Ottoman rulers adopted for themselves the title of *gazi* shows their commitment as fighters in a religious war. Sharia, Islamic law, in fact stresses jihad against non-Muslims as a specific duty for Muslims as a group; thus a continuous state of conflict is believed to exist between the *darülislam*, the abode of those who have embraced the true faith, and the *darülharb* (literally 'house of war'), the dwelling of the unbelievers. Jihad against infidels is a perpetual obligation until the universal domination of Islam is attained, so peace with non-Muslim polities is but a provisional state of affairs, justified by peculiar circumstances. Given the permanence of holy war, only truces, not authentic peace treaties, are possible with non-Islamic political entities; at the same time any truce may be repudiated unilaterally before its expiration should it be profitable for Muslims to resume the conflict, although notice should be given to the infidel party together with a request to accept Islam. Technically only the 'people with holy books' – Christians and Jews – can refuse to embrace Islam once subjugated; anybody else who rejects conversion may be freely killed or enslaved. However, Trinitarian Christians may be seen as polytheists and thus not protected by the sharia law – the massacre at Otranto being a case in point. Similarly, incursions conducted by Muslim border raiders and corsairs, even in times of peace, may be justified by the legal–religious obligation to wage *gaza* as stated in sharia law.[8]

Gaza, as described above, is taught by the Hanafi Islamic school of religious law, the one followed by the Ottomans.* Thus, by

---

* The other three schools of law within Sunni Islam are the Shafi, the Maliki and the Hanbali.

fighting the Christians the sultans were not only following God's command, but also legitimizing their role as rulers of the faithful. However, although the tenets of Islam did pervade Turkish society and institutions, it would be wrong to see the Ottoman empire as a conquest machine single-mindedly driven by religious beliefs. It had come together by force, but also thanks to the tacit, and often open, acceptance of Ottoman rule by the various conquered populations. This meant that the empire's make-up – indeed its military forces – comprised not just orthodox Sunni Muslims, but Christians and Jews as well. Also important were the more or less heterodox Islamic cults: for example, the *Bektaşi* dervish sect, which combined elements of Islam, Christianity, Buddhism and pre-Muslim Turkish paganism, was particularly popular amongst the elite janissary troops. While it would be wrong to describe this as tolerance in the modern sense, it is however true that the teachings of the Hanafi school – stressing political harmony and the rights of the 'people with holy books' – in general favoured a live-and-let-live policy. As a result, the sultans allowed the various religious communities to run their own affairs, provided this did not lead to unrest. Islamic law thus allowed the Ottomans an opportunistic approach to international politics, but also provided them with an ideological framework to justify their expansionist policy.

Ideology aside, the Ottoman advance had been possible mainly thanks to their army and the administrative system created to support it. The early Ottoman army had consisted mainly of mounted raiders gathered around their leader, conducting a highly mobile and unsystematic type of warfare.[9] As the expanding Ottoman state started developing its own internal organization, it also adopted a more stable and efficient military structure. This process owed as much to specific martial necessities as to the need of the central government to exercise an efficient form of territorial control throughout the empire. Ottoman troops were essentially of four types: 'feudal', permanent, militia and volunteer.

The army derived most of its quantitative strength from the feudal *timar* system,[10] which involved the sultan granting land to individuals in exchange for cavalry service. By the mid-sixteenth century this existed throughout the empire, with the exclusion of a few places such as Egypt and Algeria. Of the military fiefs the smallest was the *timar* proper, considered to be worth up to 20,000 *akçe* per year (the *akçe* being the standard silver monetary unit), followed by the bigger *zeamet*, with a value of up to 100,000 *akçe*; any fief worth more than 100,000 *akçe* was known as a *hass* and reserved for district and provincial governors.

A typical *timar* would consist of a village or a number of villages, with adjoining fields, ruled by a cavalryman, or *sipahi*, who had the right to collect taxes from the local peasants, and exercise 'low justice' – imposing and collecting fines for misdemeanours. Part of the taxes collected in a *timar* went to the imperial treasury, while the remaininder paid for the *sipahi*'s upkeep. The *sipahi* had to maintain his own horse, carry a fixed set of weapons (bow, sword, shield, lance and mace), plus armour if he could afford it, and for every 3,000 *akçe* of revenue provide also a fully armed *cebelü* horseman. At the beginning of the sixteenth century a *sipahi* running a *timar* worth 5,000 *akçe* would bring on campaign a suit of armour, one *cebelü* and a tent.[11] The *timars* of a certain district, or *sancak*, would come under the control of an appointed official known as a *sancak bey*. *Sancak*s were grouped together to form a province (*beylerbeik*) under a *beylerbey*. With the exception of a few hereditary *sancak*s, the sultan appointed district and provincial governors, and the same was true for most *timar* holders.

The *timar* system was possible for two reasons. For one, the vast majority of the land was *miri*, crown property. Second, the sultan's subjects owed their allegiance to him only, prompting Machiavelli's famous comment, 'The Turkish empire is ruled by one man; all the others are his servants,' a sweeping statement, perhaps, but containing a lot of truth.[12] Comprehensive lists indicating *timar* holders, as well as all others enjoying in some way the revenues of a *sancak*, allowed the central government to create accurate muster rolls for campaigns, and enforce when necessary the statutory penalties against unjustified absences. However, the system needed tight control from the centre since only a strong executive could intimidate the fief holders to obey the rules. Luckily for the Ottomans, during the sixteenth century they never lacked strong leaders.

Failure to appear at musters could cause a *sipahi* to lose his *timar*, while the sons of fief holders only inherited the right to acquire one, not their father's actual holding. It could take years of military service for someone to obtain a fief in the first place, and one of the reasons behind the Ottomans' expansionism was the never-ending need to find more land to allocate to the many aspiring *timar* holders, especially those who came from the ranks of the imperial bureaucracy or professional military. By 1525 there were nearly 28,000 such holders, a number that would increase in the following years with the empire's territorial expansion. At the beginning of the seventeenth century such contingents amounted to a paper strength of 100,000 men, albeit not all of them serving at any one time. Thanks to the *timar* system, the sultan could plan a military expedition with a precise idea of the number of feudal cavalrymen at his disposal.[13]

The Ottoman permanent standing army, the *kapıkulu* troops, followed a different pattern. For one its members were recruited in the same way as top government officials, which many, not just in the West, found repugnant. Nonetheless, the system guaranteed professionalism and total loyalty to the Ottoman dynasty, if not to the sultan as an individual. From the beginning the ranks of the sultans' army and administration had been augmented by slaves, captured in war or bought at market. The practice of using slaves as soldiers and administrators was not new in the Islamic world; the *ghulam* or *kul* system, which emphasized the training of slaves in order to make them loyal government agents or soldiers, had allowed the rise of centralized military regimes like that of the Mamluks of Egypt. But even at the acme of Ottoman expansion the capture or purchase of slaves was not sufficient for the state's needs. Alternative ways had to be found to solve the manpower problem, and starting in the mid-fourteenth century the sultans started employing the *devşirme* (literally collection), which meant nothing less than the enslavement of their Christian subjects. This practice went against Islamic law, since non-Muslims living under Muslim sovereignty who pay the prescribed taxes may not be enslaved or have their property confiscated. Nevertheless, the sultans found the *devşirme* too useful a tool, and although certain scholars debated its lawfulness it would survive until the eighteenth century.[14] For the majority of those subjected to it, the *devşirme* was an odious practice; and even if it catapulted some people from impoverished backgrounds 'into arguably the most powerful and refined polity in the world',[15] for most this was hardly a consolation. It was not simply that parents lost their beloved sons; the prospect of the collected youths becoming Muslims was appalling for all Christians.

The *devşirme* appears not to have been applied on a regular basis, but rather when need arose. Once a collection was decreed, officials visited Christian villages, and also by the Bosnians' own request the Muslim ones in Bosnia, where they would select boys between the ages of eight and eighteen at the rate of one every forty households, being careful not to pick only sons, craftsmen, married individuals, people of good social standing or anyone with unacceptable physical or personality traits. The youths thus chosen were sent to Constantinople, where they were inspected by the ağa, or commander-in-chief, of the janissaries, circumcised* and then, according to their physique, intelligence or other qualities, sent off to their final destination: one of the palace schools, the royal gardens or, for the majority, a farm in Anatolia. From now on the boys' careers, indeed their very lives, depended on the sultan's will, and each of them, from the future vizier to the lowest of soldiers, became a *kapıkulu*, a slave of the Porte. Those selected for the military were 'sold' to Muslim farmers, eventually being recalled to

---

* Circumcision was not practised by the Christians but is a mandatory condition for a Muslim. Thus, the removal of the foreskin, if not technically a forced conversion, was at least from a psychological point of view a powerful way to give the collected youths an Islamic imprint, forcing on them a sense of being separated for good from their original family and religious community.

the capital to train for one of the most formidable military corps of all time, the janissaries.

Founded probably by Sultan Orhan in the mid-fourteenth century by recruiting prisoners of war, a practice that was never fully abandoned even after the introduction of the *devşirme*, the *yeniçeri* (new troops, hence janissaries) were educated for several years in spartan conditions. During this period they exercised with every type of infantry weapon and tactics, besides performing a series of manual jobs for the sultan. Some of them were also trained as artillerymen or engineers. Once their schooling was ended the recruits were accepted into one of the *kapıkulu* units. The years of hardship and rigorous training, enhanced by legally imposed celibacy and the soldiers' religious commitment, contributed to the creation of the janissaries' esprit de corps. On more than one occasion battles were won thanks to the determination and resilience of the janissaries, and foreign observers were right to consider them the core of the Turkish army. Tough, disciplined, highly professional and often brutal, the janissaries were amongst the finest troops the world has ever seen.

The janissaries' fame was originally enhanced by their small numbers, which however would markedly increase as the Ottomans found themselves embroiled on more fronts: 10,156 in 1514; 11,439 regulars and apprentices in 1527; 20,543 in 1567, more than a third of them novices; 21,094 seven years later; and finally a grand total of 45,000 in 1597. During this period the proportion of cadets was between a third and a fourth of the total. This allowed for a steady stream of replacements, as the regulars either died or retired, without burdening excessively the Sultan's treasury, given that all *kapıkulu* troops were permanently on the payroll. This said, the janissaries could be very costly in other ways, their habit of meddling with the internal politics of the empire often forcing the Ottoman rulers to appease them with monetary or other gratifications. On the other hand, the idea of the worthy receiving generous rewards was widespread, and woe betide any Ottoman army commander not displaying the appropriate degree of largesse.[16]

The sultans' permanent household troops also included the Six Cavalry Divisions (the Sipahis of the Porte), numbering 5–6,000 men in the sixteenth century, and the 2,000-odd gunners of the artillery, all *devşirme* individuals not selected for administrative duties. Outside the *kapikulu* corps were the less glamorous but nonetheless useful *azab*s, militiamen from the towns, by the 1500s used mostly for garrison duties. In addition, there were the roughly 40,000-strong *akincis*, or Raiders, light cavalrymen from Rumelia (Ottoman-held Europe) who served for booty on a semi-voluntary basis, conducting a sort of permanent warfare along the Habsburg–Ottoman frontier in the Balkans. The corps of sappers, organized in a manner similar to the *timar* system, in 1521 could send on campaign something like 50,000 men out of a pool of 300,000.

Although the sultan could field armies of more than 150,000 combatants the main strength of the Ottoman war machine in the sixteenth century lay in its organizational structure, superior battle tactics and the employment of up-to-date military technology. The individual soldier's direct allegiance to the central government played a part in this, for as the Venetian envoy Daniello de' Ludovisi would report in 1534, 'The Lord Turk can count on good soldiers because they are not mercenaries . . . nor given to him for aid by other princes . . . instead, the troops of the Lord Turk are but his own.'[17] Although Ludovisi was speaking specifically of the sultan's standing army, the same could be said of the rest of his forces including the upper levels of the military. *Sancak bey*s, *beylerbeyk*s, *ağa*s of the janissaries and viziers overwhelmingly came from the ranks of the *kapikulu* and thus owed their loyalty to none but the state. A centralized administrative structure coupled with an efficient road network also guaranteed that armies on campaign received sufficient supplies. The system's major drawback was the need of a firm and efficient controlling hand, and disaster could occur if a top official, for whatever motive, decided to withhold provisions from an army on campaign. Infighting among Ottoman commanders or administrators would be the cause of numerous military failures.

Until the end of the sixteenth century, and despite a few setbacks, the Ottomans ruled supreme on the battlefield. This was partly due to their numbers, a factor emphasized time and time again by European observers, but also their skilful use of technology. Indeed, until after the Peace of Passarowitz (1718) the Turks could boast comparable military know-how to their Western opponents, showing a remarkable capacity to adopt new discoveries.* From the beginning the Ottomans had perceived the importance of firearms, and by the mid-fifteenth century had an impressive artillery park, employing also some of the best cannon makers and artillerymen of the day.† Technological developments tended to spread quickly in the Mediterranean area, but the Turks demonstrated great ingenuity and flexibility in applying them to battlefield situations. For example, they adopted the *wagenburg* from the Hungarians once they had seen it in action, creating a train of mule-drawn carts equipped with hand gunners and light cannons. Despite the fact that Ottoman artillery is usually associated with big siege guns, the sultans' armies made extensive use of easily transportable pieces weighing about 125 pounds. These guns used in coordination with infantry and cavalry were to prove a great tactical asset, real battle-winning instruments, according to some observers.[18]

The main weakness of the Ottoman military machine lay somewhat paradoxically in the fact that in many ways it was still very much a medieval institution, each soldier fighting in formation but always as an individual. The janissaries chose their own weapons,

---

* The Peace of Passarowitz between the Ottomans, Venice and the Holy Roman Empire provided for a twenty-four-year peace and gave to the Habsburgs what remained of Turkish Hungary, Lesser Wallachia and Belgrade with parts of northern Serbia. Venice retained a few of the territorial gains it had acquired in the previous years. Although this is considered to mark the end of Ottoman western expansion, it must be remembered that Belgrade and Lesser Wallachia were recovered once more by Turkey after the Treaty of Belgrade in 1739.

† Mehmed II employed a number of German and Hungarian gunners, lured to Constantinople by high wages. During the 1480 siege of Rhodes a German engineer and artillery expert in Ottoman service by the name of Maister Georg defected to the Knights of St John, only to be executed by them when they discovered that he was passing information to the besiegers about the position of the defenders' guns.

were superb marksmen and unbeatable in a man-to-man situation, but it took years and much expense to train them properly. By the mid-sixteenth century the West was perfecting the musket and pike system, allowing masses of men to be trained for battle in a relatively short period of time. Even more important, these men were easy to replace, but most Ottoman soldiers, in particular the household troops, were not. Europe adopted the opposite view to that of Grand Vizier Lufti Pasha, that troops should be few but excellent, and in the end the Western system of warfare would emerge victorious. To be fair, the Ottoman attitude was not simply blind conservatism, being instead the result of a pragmatic approach to warfare. During the sixteenth and seventeenth centuries the Porte faced simultaneously a number of enemies employing different fighting techniques. Adopting exclusively Western tactics would have put the Ottomans at a disadvantage when facing their easterly foes, and vice versa.

~

Mehmed II's death caused a civil war between his two sons Jem and Bayezid. When the former was defeated and forced to flee, he sought asylum first with the Knights of St John and then with the pope. The following fifteen years would see Jem playing an important, if passive, role in all Mediterranean diplomatic manoeuvrings, with Bayezid always concerned about his exiled brother being exploited by some European state. This situation benefited the Sultan's neighbours: from the very beginning Bayezid was eager to conclude treaties with his former adversaries or ratify existing ones. Until the mid-1490s the Ottoman empire did not attempt any major war against a Western power, this being as much due to Jem's presence as to Bayezid's need to reorganize the state and settle its finances. It is often believed that the Ottoman empire was a 'gunpowder state', not interested in commerce, but the Porte recognized the importance of trade, the treaty with the the Dalmatian city of Dubrovnik (Ragusa) being a case in point. For a token annual tribute of 3,000 ducats the Ragusans obtained extensive commercial privileges in the Levant and the assurance that their territory would not be subjected to the peacetime raids launched by the Turks as part of *gaza*. Moreover, like every Early Modern polity much of the empire's revenue came from custom duties, an inflow of money that could be reduced dramatically in time of war.[19] Bayezid needed peace in order to rebuild the state's financial assets, and places like Dubrovnik were the gates through which strategically important goods and new discoveries, military technology in particular, made their way into the Ottoman empire.

Despite Bayezid's essentially peaceful nature, during the early years of his reign there was no lack of war. The first target was the prince of Wallachia, Karabogdan, attacked for refusing to pay the tribute due to Constantinople, and in the following years the Ottomans slowly brought the lower Danube area under their control. Temporarily distracted by a six-year war against the Mamluks of Egypt, Bayezid had to wait until 1495 before resuming his father's expansionist policy. Jem's death in the February of that year freed the sultan's hands, allowing him to attack Hungary, fight Poland over the control of Moldavia, and finally go to war with Venice. The change from a low-conflict policy, for the sake of which even border raiding was kept to the minimum, to one of open warfare was not only the result of Jem's death; for some years there had been no major campaign and the army, the *kapıkulu* corps in particular, was getting restless. After major riots in Constantinople in the summer of 1496 the government realized that it could no longer keep its professional troops from pursuing glory, booty and rewards.[20] Bayezid needed new *timar* land, and to secure his frontiers in Greece and the Balkans. The war with Venice in 1499 was a direct result of this, although the ostensible motive was the Franco-Venetian alliance – Charles VIII of France having proclaimed an anti-Ottoman crusade – and Venice's financial support for the Sultan's enemies in the Balkans.

The conflict had been brewing for some time, and from 1496 onward the Ottomans subjected the Venetians to continuous provocations in the Balkans and the Adriatic. The Republic of St Mark swallowed one humiliation after the other with little protest, considering the safeguarding of her Levantine trade more important. Partly for this reason war did not erupt immediately, and in any case between 1496 and 1498 Bayezid was too busy fighting in Poland to pay much attention to his western frontiers. However, by the summer of 1498 Venetian merchants in Constantinople were reporting with alarm the Sultan's extensive shipbuilding programme, suggesting there could be only one target for such preparations.[21] These fears became reality the following spring, when, after some further desultory diplomatic exchanges, the Ottomans suddenly attacked and quickly overran most of Venice's territories in Greece with the exception of a few coastal cities. Then a Venetian fleet was roundly defeated at Zonchio, sending the message that not only had the Ottoman navy come into its own but, was also a force to be reckoned with. The Ottomans followed up their victory by taking the key fortress of Lepanto and fortifying the entrance to the Gulf of Corinth. From now on the main Venetian trade route to the Levant could be closed at the sultan's whim. Disastrous as the situation might have appeared in Greece, the rudest shock for the Venetians came from another front. In June a rapidly moving army under Iskender Pasha departed from its bases in Bosnia and proceeded to conduct a massive raid deep into Friuli, with cavalry units arriving at Venice's very doorstep. From the lagoon the terrified citizens could see the flames of the torched hamlets.

In the course of the war the Venetians lost the majority of their coastal cities, managing to hold on only to Nafplio, Monemvasia and Corfu. Their only real success was the capture of the Adriatic port of Levkás. Venice could not throw all of her resources into the conflict, as the republic was also fighting in Italy and desperately seeking allies elsewhere. Eventually, following France's example, the papacy, Hungary and Spain also agreed to join the fray, but Venice had to pay the Hungarians a subsidy of 100,000 ducats for their support. Hungary's contribution was half-hearted, and never really threatened the Ottomans. Venice's other allies also proved a disappointment: in 1501 a joint French–Hospitaller–Venetian expedition against Mytilene (Lesvos) ended in fiasco, mainly because of the indecision of the French commander. In the end Venice had to give up most of her few conquests, retaining Zakynthos and Kefallonia plus a small number of footholds on the Greek mainland. For Bayezid the war had been a triumph; not only had he managed to consolidate his European borders, but now many trade routes between east and west were under Ottoman control. This not only resulted in an increase in revenue but also boosted the sultan's international standing.

From 1503 until 1521 the Ottomans paid little attention to Europe, having to face a new threat that had arisen in the east.[22] The new enemy, and the Ottomans' bane for the next two centuries, was the Persian Safavi dynasty, which in less than ten years, from 1501 to 1510, managed to conquer not only most of Mesopotamia and the whole of modern Iran, but also Azerbaijan and a number of territories around the Caspian Sea. A clash between the Ottomans and the Safavis was pretty much inevitable, not only due to the latter's claim to Turkish lands in eastern Anatolia but also because of their religious beliefs. The Safavis were Shia, considered a heterodox branch of Islam by the Sunni Ottomans, and their leader Shah Ismail was soon actively promoting Shi'ism in Anatolia, thus suborning the allegiance of many of the sultan's subjects, especially the Turcomans of the border regions, ever resentful of Constantinople's rule. Worrying as this might have been, even worse from Bayezid's point of view was Ismail's membership of the dervish *Bektaşi* order. Since the latter was traditionally associated with the janissaries, the sultan risked seeing his standing army going over to the Safavis literally lock, stock and barrel.[23]

Bayezid at first approached the problem with great caution, trying unsuccessfully to close his eastern borders to Shia missionaries and exiling to the Peloponnese a number of Safavi sympathizers. Otherwise he limited himself to sending an army to keep watch on his eastern frontiers, and studiously tried to avoid hostilities with his powerful new neighbour. The sultan's prudence was largely motivated by the desertion rate among Ottoman soldiers in the east, many going over to Ismail, attracted by his religion, ideology and generosity.[24] The sultan watched with apprehension the growth of Ismail's power and Safavis' diplomatic overtures towards Venice and his other potential enemies. From this date the Ottomans would be constantly concerned about possible alliances between Persia and one of the Western powers.

Things came to a head in 1511 when a massive Safavi-sponsored rebellion erupted in western Anatolia. Led by the charismatic Shah Kulu (the shah's slave), the rebels marched north, defeated an Ottoman army, stormed Kütahya and proceeded to advance towards Bursa. News of these events threw Constantinople into a panic, but the government reacted quickly: 4,000 *sipahi*s and *kapıkulu* troops were sent to Asia from Rumelia under the command of Prince Ahmed and Grand Vizir Hadim Ali Pasha. The rebels managed to defeat this force near Sivas, killing Hadim; but Shah Kulu also lost his life, leaving his leaderless followers to seek asylum in Persia.[25] The rebellion discredited Bayezid's regime, causing Prince Selim, who from the beginning had advocated strong measures against Ismail, to revolt against his father. Obtaining the janissaries' support, he forced Bayezid to abdicate in his favour on 24 May 1512. Broken in spirit, the old sultan died two months later.

Despite its sad ending, Bayezid's reign marked a period of great economic growth and administrative consolidation for the Ottoman empire. The war with the Egyptian Mamluks resulted in improved weapons for the *kapıkulu* troops, in particular the janissaries, and during this period the Ottomans adopted smaller field guns. The Mytilene campaign of 1501 taught them also some lessons about the use of naval artillery in amphibious operations, and indeed Bayezid's greatest achievement was the creation of a fleet equal to that of Venice. Although he conquered few territories, these were nevertheless strategically important, and the strengthening of the Ottoman state and its military organization would pay enormous dividends under his successors.

Selim I showed immediately that he came from a different mould than his father, and it is with some justification that he is known as Yavuz (the Grim). After eliminating his brothers Kurkud and Ahmed he proceeded to launch a mopping-up campaign in Anatolia, executing Ismail's followers in their thousands and removing disloyal fief holders. He then attacked the Shah himself. Selim was first careful to obtain a fatwa★ declaring that it was just and mandatory to destroy the heretical Ismail and his followers, and at the battle of Chaldiran, in August 1514, the Safavi cavalry was brought down by the entrenched Ottoman artillery and handgun-armed janissaries. Selim followed up his victory by annexing the mountainous area from Erzurum to Diyarbakir, bringing under his control the local warlike Kurdish tribes. However, at the same time Turcoman tribes from Anatolia emigrated en masse to Persia, where they enlisted to fight for the Safavis.

Selim's next move, and his military masterpiece, was the subjugation of Egypt, one of the biggest grain producers in the Mediterranean basin.[26] Having received intelligence of a possible anti-Ottoman alliance between the Egyptians and the Persians, Selim struck first and, in a two-stage campaign lasting from the beginning of August 1516 to the end of January 1517, conquered the whole of Syria and Egypt. The Turkish takeover of the Mamluk state meant that nearly all the commercial routes to the Levant were under Ottoman control, and now, thanks also to his powerful navy, the sultan could dominate the grain trade of the area. For the rest of the century the resources of defeated Egypt would sustain the Ottomans' expansionism, while many European countries used to tapping into the Mamluks' grain supply found Egypt's new rulers disinclined to grant them such facilities.

Selim would have liked to continue campaigning in the east but discovered that his exhausted troops would follow him no further. Not one to be deterred from new conquests, the sultan turned his attention to the improvement of his arsenal and fleet with the objective of capturing Rhodes. This was as much a matter of necessity as

---

★ A fatwa is a legal opinion based on the Sharia law and is issued by an individual or a body of religious standing within the Islamic world.

of prestige, since while Rhodes remained under the control of the Knights of St John the sea routes between Egypt and Istanbul would never be secure. Besides, the conquest of Rhodes fitted very well with Ottoman expansionist strategy, which stressed, according to one writer, a policy of 'one step eastwards, one step westwards'.[27] By the end of Selim's reign the Ottomans would be able to pursue at the same time extensive maritime and land campaigns against Europe, not just thanks to an extensive shipbuilding programme, but also because by 1519 they had managed to establish their suzerainty over the cities of Tunis and Algiers. On a map the Ottoman empire now resembled the gaping maw of a prehistoric beast, poised to devour the whole of the Western world.

Selim died in 1520, bestowing to his son Süleyman an empire doubled in size. He also left a legacy of war with Persia and plans for future conquests in Europe, and for this reason Süleyman's reign has been described as having a 'crisis of orientation'.[28] Süleyman is justly known in the West as the Magnificent as under him the Ottoman state would reach its apex of splendour and power, but it was also during his reign that the first cracks in the edifice of the empire started to appear.* Selim I may have warded off the Safavi threat, but already a new foe had appeared in the south. Ever since Vasco de Gama had rounded the Cape of Good Hope in 1497, the Portuguese had been threatening Muslim commerce in the Indian Ocean. In 1507 they captured the stronghold of Hormuz, all but closing down the route from Basra to Aleppo. In 1517 they attempted the same in the strategically important Red Sea, only to be rebuffed after a sharp fight off Jiddah, forty miles west of Mecca. But in the long run the Portuguese maritime advance to the east, followed later by the Dutch and the English, would contribute to the disruption of the Mediterranean trade system, of which the Ottomans were one of the greatest beneficiaries.

Likewise, the sultan's aggressive stance towards the West turned

---

* For the Turks he is *Kânûni*, the Lawgiver, since it was during his reign that Ottoman civil law was given an organic and permanent structure.

him into something of a bogey man and effectively stifled the possibility of trustworthy relations between the Ottomans and most European countries. But right from his accession Süleyman was faced with the compelling need to keep his standing army occupied and find new *timar* land for the ever-growing list of postulants from the military and administrative classes, the ultimate buttress of his power. Since the one way for somebody to obtain a fief was to prove his worth on campaign, for the Ottomans war-fed expansionism was almost inevitable. To this should be added the ideology of conquest developed by the Ottomans over two centuries, summarized by Süleyman himself as 'not fighting for gold and treasures, but for victory, glory, renown and the increase of the empire'.[29] For the Ottomans war was as much a political and social necessity as the result of a powerful ideological drive.

Süleyman started his reign by crushing a rebellion in Damascus, before turning his attention to Hungary on the pretext that King Lajos II had imprisoned the Ottoman ambassador. It appears that the Porte had been planning an attack for some time, having decided that of all the possible targets Hungary was the weakest,[30] and in the course of a brief if not totally successful campaign captured the important fortress of Belgrade. His next move involved using Selim I's navy against Rhodes, and at the end of June 1522 a gigantic expeditionary force of 300,000 men, including soldiers, support units and sappers, landed on the Hospitallers' island. After six months of relentless bombardment and assaults, the few surviving defenders, lacking food and munitions, surrendered on the condition they could be allowed to leave the island with their treasure and records. Süleyman could afford to be generous; and as the grand master and his surviving knights set sail from the island on the first day of the following January, the sultan commented gravely, 'Truly I cannot but grieve to see this unfortunate old man, driven out of his dwelling, to depart hence so heavily.'[31] He would soon be cursing his chivalrous attitude.

It took Süleyman a couple of years to make good the losses in men and materiel sustained at Rhodes, giving his neighbours a brief respite while the sultan chose his next objective. He had a number of choices, including a naval campaign against the Portuguese in the Red Sea to protect the spice trade routes. For a number of reasons, mostly logistic, this plan proved difficult to implement, the Porte preferring instead to obtain the same result by striking a deal with the Persians. Thus the only military option left to Süleyman was to advance westward – a decision helped by a revolt of the war-hungry janissaries in 1525 – and specifically once more against the kingdom of Hungary, having first taken care to isolate it politically. The campaign not only succeeded in subjugating the kingdom and satisfying the *kapıkulu* troops, but also secured safer borders. Thus, after attempting to obtain King Lajos' surrender by diplomatic means, an Ottoman army invaded Hungary in the summer of 1526 and on 29 August won a resounding victory at Mohács. Intense fire from the Turkish artillery and the janissaries' muskets broke the badly coordinated Hungarian attacks, killing Lajos and 15,000 of his men. Süleyman followed up his victory by sacking and burning the Hungarian capital of Buda; however, with overstretched supply lines and in the face of reorganizing enemy forces, he decided not to occupy the whole kingdom, preferring instead to retain only the strategically important southern part of the country and retiring his army to its winter quarters in Belgrade.[32]

For the next two years serious troubles in Anatolia kept Süleyman busy, allowing a political crisis to develop in Hungary which would engage him for the rest of his reign. The death of King Lajos at Mohács had produced a power vacuum that the Hungarian Estates attempted to fill by electing the magnate János Szapolyai, a decision contested by the late sovereign's Habsburg brother-in-law Ferdinand who had himself crowned king of Hungary in December 1526. Süleyman decided to throw his weight behind Szapolyai, and in 1529 the disgruntled Ferdinand invaded Hungary and took its capital, provoking the Porte's immediate response. Moving swiftly, Süleyman retook Buda and reinstated Szapolyai, but now as an Ottoman vassal and with a janissary garrison. Keeping up the momentum of his advance, the sultan marched deep into Austria and proceeded to besiege Ferdinand's capital Vienna. Although forced to retreat due to Austrian resistance and the approaching winter, Süleyman's feat sent shock waves through Europe. Nonetheless, Ferdinand's appearance on the scene had considerably complicated the Ottomans' position in Hungary. Now they were facing a serious opponent, the king of Bohemia and brother of the Holy Roman Emperor Charles V, not simply a weak and politically isolated country.

The Habsburg–Ottoman war ground on for another two years until Ferdinand and Süleyman agreed to a truce in 1533, leaving the Hungarian question largely unresolved. The sultan was having troubles with the Safavis, and thus unwilling to fight on two fronts at the same time. The Ottoman campaign in the east lasted until 1536, bringing to the empire Bitlis, Tabriz, Erzurum and the plum city of Baghdad. But Süleyman's Western adversaries were not idle; in 1535 a Spanish amphibious expedition led in person by Emperor Charles V managed to capture the Ottoman vassal city of Tunis. Süleyman realized that despite his considerable fleet, to gain supremacy at sea he needed a skilful strategist and tactician. As a result in 1533 the *beylerbey* of Algiers Hayreddin Barbarossa was summoned to Constantinople and made *kapudan-ı deryâ*, grand admiral of the Ottoman navy.

The choice could not have been better. Born in Mytilene around 1466 to a family of Albanian origin, Hayreddin, then called Hizir, had become a corsair with his older brother Arouj at an early age. The two brothers, known as Barbarossa allegedly because of their red beards, enjoyed a certain amount of success as pirates in the eastern Mediterranean, operating partially with the support of Bayezid II's son Kurkud. With the advent of Selim I and the death of their sponsor, Arouj and Hizir decided to take their business to healthier North African waters. Arouj quickly established himself as ruler of Algiers and on his death in 1518 power passed to Hizir, who by now had taken the nomme de guerre of Hayreddin.[33] Faced with the growing power of the Spanish, the surviving Barbarossa understood that if he was going to survive he needed a patron. In 1519 he submitted to the sultan in exchange for the title of *beylerbey*, and from his base in Algiers became the scourge of the Mediterranean. By choosing him as grand admiral Süleyman was entrusting his fleet to one of the most distinguished sailors Islam has ever produced, while Barbarossa could now count on the immense resources of the Ottoman empire.

Hayreddin wasted no time. In 1534 he launched raids on the Italian coast, leaving a trail of destruction from Latium to Calabria. On the night of 8 August he stormed the town of Fondi, near Rome, intent on kidnapping the internationally renowned beauty Giulia Gonzaga as a gift for the sultan. Warned in time of the impending peril, Giulia escaped in her nightgown, leaving a thwarted Barbarossa to vent his fury on the town. The next year, in revenge for a Spanish expedition against Tunis, he attacked the Balearic Islands, netting 6,000 slaves. In the meantime, to resist growing Habsburg power Süleyman had become an ally of the French king Francis I. The two rulers hatched a plan involving a French attack on the north of Italy, while Barbarossa executed an amphibious assault in the south. In February 1537 a French army crossed the Alps, the sultan waiting with his army in Avlona for the right moment to strike. In mid-July the advance party of Süleyman's army under Lufti Pasha landed on the heel of Italy and, avoiding the strongholds of Brindisi and Otranto, began to advance towards Naples. But the military situation was very different from what it had been in 1480, the south of Italy being now part of the Habsburg Mediterranean system. The Turks only managed to conduct a raid in depth, and in the meantime Francis signed a ten-year truce with Charles V. Faced with the risk of his communication being cut by a joint Venetian–papal–Habsburg naval force, Süleyman was forced to withdraw his forces after only two weeks.[34]

Francis had assured the Porte that the Venetians would remain neutral in the event of a war against Charles V, but for the safety of his communication and supply lines the sultan had to be sure that no surprise would come from Venice's remaining bases in Greece. When the Republic of St Mark hesitated to join the Franco-Turkish alliance, Süleyman initiated hostilities in August 1537 by besieging unsuccessfully the Venetian fortresses of Corfu and Nafplio. The sultan's decision was made after it became clear that the French were not going to invade Italy after all, but Süleyman needed to give his booty-deprived war hounds something to chew on. Predictably, the Ottoman move pushed the Venetians into the arms of the Habsburgs, Venice, Charles V and Pope Paul III creating the first anti-Ottoman Holy League. The following year the league's naval forces were mauled by Hayreddin's fleet at Preveza. Dissent among the allies had hampered coordinated action against the Ottomans, and for the next thirty years the naval initiative in the Mediterranean would be in Muslim hands.

~

The Ottomans had started out as a land-based power, and it had taken them some time to develop an interest in the sea. During the fourteenth century and the first half of the fifteenth Venice had been the undisputed hegemonic maritime power in the Levant, using the dozens of independent political entities in the Aegean Sea as buffers against the Ottomans' advance. Only after the war of 1479 had the Ottomans managed to push the Venetians back towards the western Mediterranean, and by capturing the city of Avlona in Albania they had gained an important post at the entry to the Adriatic for monitoring Venetian, and later Spanish, naval movements.[35]

Ottoman sea policy was to an extent conditioned by Islamic legal thinking. From the earliest days Muslim scholars had distinguished between the high seas, coastal and inland waters, the former being somewhat of a free zone and the others falling under the jurisdiction of whoever controlled the adjacent land. However, according to some Islamic theorists the Mediterranean was not really an open sea, but, as the twentieth-century French historian Fernand Braudel aptly put it, a series of watery plains united by channels of varying width. Thus the Adriatic, the Sea of Marmara, the Black and Red Seas were treated as inland waters, the property of the states that controlled the nearby coasts. This idea gained strength with the taking of Constantinople, since the city was the pivot between Asia and Europe, the Black Sea and the Mediterranean. It was in this same period that Rome took the place of Constantinople as the mythical Red Apple, the capital of the world to be conquered by Osman's descendants, a city that could be taken only by crossing the Adriatic.[36] Still, until Selim I the Ottomans had limited their maritime claims to the eastern seas, an Ottoman Mediterranean vision developing only after the conquest of Egypt and Algiers. According to Selim I, since the 'White Sea' (Mediterranean) was but one big gulf, it was logical that it should belong to one and not many. Süleyman I would claim to be 'Sultan and padişa (roughly emperor) of the White and Black Seas', to which his successors added also the Red Sea.[37]

Starting in the fifteenth century, the Ottoman maritime advance proceeded from east to west, gaining territory piecemeal by the apparently unsystematic conquest of the various islands of the Aegean. However, this was actually the result of a sound strategic scheme, which aimed to isolate major potential objectives, such as Crete, Cyprus and Rhodes, by creating around them a cordon sanitaire of Turkish-held islands. Moreover, the fragmentation of Venetian and to a lesser extent Genoese possessions in the Levant allowed the sultans to occupy one by one the less well-defended islands. Since the Ottomans' ultimate objective was the conquest of the whole West, it was more important to open wide enough gaps in the liquid frontier to allow large forces to pass through without hindrance than to conquer all the islands.

Although not originally a seafaring power, the Ottoman empire could rely on a pre-existing naval tradition. The Seljuk conquest of a substantial portion of Anatolia in the eleventh century had brought the Turks into contact with the sea, and very soon they had a fleet large enough to threaten Constantinople.* But the Byzantine

* The Seljuks were the Turkish dynasty which from the eleventh to the fourteenth century ruled in Anatolia, Syria, Persia and Mesopotamia. From the mid-1200s the Seljuks were reduced to the status of Mongol tributaries and it was the definitive collapse of their rule after 1302 that permitted the rise of the Ottomans, who considered themselves the Seljuks' heirs.

empire was then still a force to be reckoned with, and in a series of campaigns it managed to push the Turks back inland. Following the turmoil that engulfed the Byzantine state after the Fourth Crusade, the Seljuks occupied once more the southern Anatolian coastline around Antalya and quickly took to the sea. Their subsequent capture of Alanya, where they built a superb arsenal, allowed them to extend their range of naval activities down into Egyptian waters. The Mongol invasion of the Middle East in the mid-thirteenth century and the consequent destruction of the Seljuk state favoured the rise of a number of maritime *gazi* emirates. The capture of these polities by Bayezid I did not curb the actions of the sea *ghazi*; instead, by allowing them to enjoy the resources of the empire, the sultans channelled their energies into Ottoman expansionism. In addition, Mehmed II's conquest of Constantinople, Greece and the Balkans had provided the Ottomans with further maritime know-how. Naval entrepreneurship was supported, and to an extent financed, by the state, allowing the creation of a pool of experienced captains – the Barbarossa brothers being the most famous products of this system. More important, the Ottomans could substantially increase their fleet at the drop of a hat by simply commandeering corsair vessels.[38]

The navy's command structure took longer to develop. After 1453 the fleet was usually entrusted to the *sancak* of Gallipoli, probably because the main Ottoman naval base came under his jurisdiction. This, however, was not a fixed rule and on more than one occasion the sultan appointed commanders according to the requirements of a specific situation. During the Otranto expedition of 1480 Gedik Pasha was in charge of both land and sea forces. The position of the naval commander-in-chief, the *kapudan-ı deryâ*, better known after 1567 as the *kapudan paşa*,[39] increased in import-ance with Hayreddin Barbarossa, Süleyman adding to the title the newly created *beylerbeik* of the Archipelago, carved from the coastal *sancaks* of Greece and western Anatolia. High admirals did not always come from similar backgrounds, by-products of the *devşirme* alternating with Muslim-born professionals. Privateers were a permanent and important feature of the Ottoman fleet, Katib Çelebi maintaining that if the admiral was not one of them he should seek their advice 'and not act on his own initiative'. On the other hand, it would appear that in the sixteenth century some Ottoman commanders considered corsairs a somewhat unsavoury lot, the Venetian ambassador Bartolomeo Cavalli stating in 1560 that 'they don't trust them much and employ them in the same way doctors use poison, that is in small doses and intermixed with the rest of the fleet'.[40]

The Ottoman conquest of the eastern and southern Mediterranean meant that their fleet had to face an increasing number of challenges. Since these often required a quick response without recourse to the main fleet in Constantinople, a number of autonomous naval commands were established in the course of the sixteenth century. The northern Aegean was under the responsibility of the captain of Kavala, whose main duty was to escort grain ships from northern Greece to the capital; more to the south, the *sancak* of Lesvos patrolled the waters in the vicinity of his island. After the conquest of Rhodes by Süleyman I a substantial flotilla operated from the former Hospitaller base, guarding the sea routes between Egypt, Turkey and Syria. To this purpose the Rhodes *sancak* was to collaborate closely with the Alexandria squadron, the second Egyptian unit, based in Suez, being responsible for security in the Red Sea. Other flotillas could be found on the Danube and in the Black Sea, while after 1519 the sultan could count, albeit never easily, on the experienced men and fine ships of the North African maritime cities. In addition, the various coastal *sancak*s could be ordered to patrol the seas under their jurisdiction with one or more galleys, and after 1566 it became customary for the eight *sancak beys* of the Archipelago to provide a certain number of vessels for the imperial navy. Thus the sultan had at his disposal a rapidly deployable fleet unequalled in the Mediterranean.[41]

A large navy required a well-tuned organization to function properly, and that meant arsenals. Bayezid I built a large one at Gallipoli in the 1390s, placed in such a position as to control the

Sea of Marmara and facilitate the passage of Ottoman troops from Anatolia to Rumelia. In addition it provided a base for raids on enemy islands in the Aegean and controlled the shipping routes to and from the Black Sea. Despite the construction of a new arsenal at Galata by Mehmed II immediately after the taking of Constantinople, Gallipoli remained the main Ottoman naval base until the beginning of the sixteenth century. Later Selim I and Süleyman considerably enlarged the Galata arsenal, diminishing Gallipoli's importance. Other permanent shipbuilding sites were at Sinop on the Black Sea, Alexandria in Egypt, Suez on the Red Sea, Izmit near Galata and, after 1538, Basra. However, the nature of most sixteen-century Ottoman shipbuilding meant that vessels could be built at ad hoc sites along the coast. This appears to have been standard practice when the sultan needed a large fleet at a short notice.[42]

The Ottomans started probing at Western defences in the Aegean in the 1390s, alternating *gazi* forays with major naval operations, their initial lack of experience resulting in some very hard knocks. In 1416 and 1429 the Venetians trounced them in two battles at the mouth of the Dardanelles. Despite their successes on land, it took the Ottomans most of the fifteenth century to build up confidence in naval matters, and in 1466 they still considered a superiority of at least four to one necessary to tackle the Venetians. The real increase in Turkish naval power came with their territorial conquests during the 1463–79 war. By denying the Venetians and other Western states a number of key havens in Greece and the Aegean, they reduced their enemies' capacity to conduct major operations in the Levant. Likewise, the Ottomans' occupation of certain islands allowed them to control the main sea lanes in the eastern Mediterranean, casting an ominous shadow over the whole region. Even before the battle of Zonchio there was no doubt that the sultans' fleet had become a force not to be dismissed.[43]

The 1499–1503 war also demonstrated an improvement in the Ottomans' ability to launch amphibious operations, and following the French expedition against Mytilene the Turks learnt the use of galley artillery fire to cover the advance of troops on shore. Most of the Greek islands were within striking distance of their bases, allowing the Ottomans to execute surprise attacks against targets vulnerable to gunpowder weapons. But if the Ottoman conquest of most of the Aegean allowed them to push their frontier to the west, the fragmentation of this maritime border also put them in a vulnerable position. It was now impossible for the sultans' fleet to control the thousands of nooks and crannies dotting the eastern Mediterranean, making it an ideal hunting ground for pirates and corsairs. This situation could result in disruption to the trade routes linking Egypt to Anatolia and was one of the main reasons prompting Süleyman to conquer Rhodes, and his son Selim II to do the same with Cyprus.

At the beginning of the sixteenth century the Turks were attempting to protect the main trade routes in the Levant by a system of naval patrols, but it soon became evident that Christian pirates and corsairs still had access to the fresh-water resources of the Greek islands. An extensive control system was impossible to implement except at crippling cost, since small enemy fleets operating from Italy or the centre of the Mediterranean could sneak up nearly to the mouth of the Dardanelles and ambush Ottoman shipping before the local naval defences had time to react.[44] The only way to stop this menace was to push into the western Mediterranean, forcing the Christian states of the area to employ their resources to defend their own coasts. But by concentrating their attention on Europe, the Ottomans were losing a different contest in another part of their empire. By the time of Selim I's conquest of Egypt the existence of the world beyond the Mediterranean was a known fact, and some of the sultan's advisers were pushing for the conquest of India or even China. This would have called for the development of a significant navy in the Red Sea and a consistent policy to sustain it. However, the internal dynamics of the Ottoman regime caused Süleyman I to focus on the conquest of Europe, thus inhibiting the possibility of an Ottoman expansion in the Indian Ocean. Although the sultan was fully aware that the

Portuguese presence in the Red Sea had diverted much of the local tax-producing trade once directed to Egypt towards the Iberian peninsula, faced with a fief-hungry army he preferred to concentrate his attention on *timar* holdings as a source of revenue than engage in a more long-term expansion policy through the control of oceanic trade routes.[45] Besides, land conquests fitted better psychologically with an expanding *darülislam* – always a major concern for the Ottomans – even if Grand Vizier Lufti Pasha warned the sultan that 'however important may be the business of land affairs, those of the sea are far more important'.[46] To the Ottomans' credit, up to the very end of the sixteenth century nobody could have predicted the huge developments in the field of oceanic shipbuilding. In the mid-1520s it made perfect sense to think that, should need require it, the Red Sea fleet could easily grow big enough to tackle the Portuguese with success.

Süleyman was nevertheless forced to act when the slump in the Mediterranean spice trade became too serious to be ignored, although this decision was also influenced by the Portuguese threat to Muslim pilgrims travelling to the holy city of Mecca. Ottoman naval commitments in the Mediterranean caused further delay, and it was only in 1538 that a fleet finally sailed from Suez and circumnavigated the Arabian peninsula, trying unsuccessfully to capture the Portuguese fort of Diu on the north-west coast of India. The Portuguese retaliated by attempting to take Suez three years later, and their control of Hormuz in the Persian Gulf effectively stunted the development of Basra as both an Ottoman military base and commercial centre. In 1552 the Turkish admiral and cartographer Piri Reis tried in vain to take Hormuz, a failure that cost him his life, and despite a number of territorial acquisitions in the region over the next few years, including part of the Abyssinian coast, the Ottomans by now understood that evicting the Portuguese from the Gulf area was impossible without huge human and material investments.[47] But Süleyman had already too many problems to deal with in Europe and the Middle East and never pursued victory in a war fought at the fringes of his empire. It would also appear that at this point expanding the navy was not among Constantinople's top priorities, prompting a Venetian diplomat to comment that luckily the Ottomans were less powerful on sea than on land.[48] The strategic choices made by the Ottoman empire meant that it was destined to lose the race for world domination, as more European countries joined the Portuguese in the struggle for the eastern trade routes, while at the same time the Ottomans were unable to exploit the vast riches of the New World.

~

But this was all in the unforeseeable future, and in the meantime the Ottoman juggernaut continued to press forward. Barbarossa's victory at Preveza caused the Holy League to collapse, and from the subsequent peace treaty between Venice and Constantinople the Ottomans obtained among other things the important bases of Monemvasia and Nafplio in the Peloponnese. Süleyman also managed to annex the south-eastern part of Moldavia, before turning his attention once more to Hungary. The Habsburg–Ottoman arrangement of 1533 had left everyone dissatisfied, and despite Süleyman bestowing the Hungarian kingship on János Szapolyai it was clear that the Porte was just waiting for the right moment to bring the whole country under its direct control. In the meantime the Ottomans slowly increased their military presence in the area, much to Szapolyai's chagrin. As a result, in 1538 the Hungarian ruler and Ferdinand I agreed that on János's death his lands would pass to the Habsburgs, and when this happened in 1540 Ferdinand lost no time making good his claim. Dissent within the Hungarian ruling elite thwarted Ferdinand's attempts to capture Buda, giving Süleyman sufficient time to assemble a strong enough army to defeat the Habsburgs in the field. The sultan annexed the whole of Szapolyai's former lands, as a sop to Hungarian pride nominating János's infant son king of Transylvania, the eastern portion of the old kingdom.[49]

While busy in Hungary, Süleyman was having to face another Habsburg threat. In the late summer of 1541 Charles V launched an attack against Algiers, and the renewal of full hostilities in the Mediterranean brought to the fore the tensions existing within the Ottoman government between those, like Grand Vizier Lufti Pasha, who advocated a more incisive maritime policy, and others committed to land conquest. Süleyman dismissed Lufti Pasha from his post for opposing the Hungarian venture, believing that in order to keep the Habsburgs at bay he had to confront them on their own turf. Besides, such a move would also test the ground for a possible Ottoman expansion in the western Mediterranean. Conveniently, Francis I now decided that the time had come to break the truce he had signed earlier with Charles V and employ Ottoman naval power to try and recapture strategic positions in Italy. Backed by French logistical support, in the summer of 1542 Barbarossa laid waste the coastal regions of northern Italy and Spain, even taking the town, although not the castle, of Nice. He wintered his fleet in Toulon as the guest of Francis I, and then proceeded to raid all the way down the Italian coast before making a triumphant return to Constantinople.[50] This was to be Barbarossa's last campaign, the old admiral dying peacefully in the magnificent palace he had built overlooking the Dardanelles. For years to come Muslim ships sailing through the Bosporus would fire a gun in salute as they passed in front of his mausoleum.*

The peace of 1544 between France and the Holy Roman Empire deprived Süleyman of an ally, but in the meantime both Charles V – who was having trouble with his Lutheran subjects – and Ferdinand were willing to come to an agreement with the sultan over the Hungarian question. A formal five-year treaty was concluded in 1547 confirming the territorial status quo in Hungary, with Ferdinand agreeing to pay a tribute of 30,000 ducats a year for the land under his control. For the sultan the treaty had an added value, since Charles, who did not wish to sign as Holy Roman Emperor, was mentioned in the agreement simply as 'King of

---

* A rather less flattering legend states that he jumped out of his tomb various times, until a necromancer found the solution of burying him with a black dog.

Spain'. Süleyman believed that the document sanctioned for good his right to style himself Emperor of the Romans or Caesar.[51] In addition, Ottoman jurists could now argue that by paying tribute to the Porte Ferdinand had become Süleyman's subject. Even if only psychologically, the horns of the Ottoman crescent had penetrated deep into the heart of Europe.

Peace with the Habsburgs left Süleyman free to deal with the Safavis, returning to the western theatre only in 1550. By then the situation in Hungary had once more erupted into war, this time the struggle being over the control of Transylvania. The Ottomans managed to conquer part of the kingdom including Temesvár (Timişoara), but as usual the sultan had also to deal with the Mediterranean front. In 1550 Charles V's Genoese admiral Andrea Doria conducted a series of operations against Tunisia, capturing a number of strongholds from Thorgud (or Dragut) Reis, Barbarossa's heir as foremost Muslim corsair. The fact that at the same time the Spanish were trying to take over the city state of Siena in the south of Tuscany alarmed the French, who were afraid that the western Mediterranean was fast becoming a Habsburg lake. The new Franco-Ottoman alliance initially resulted in very little, partly because Süleyman was more interested in his Persian campaign, although in 1551 the Turks managed to capture the city of Tripoli, held by the Knights Hospitallers since 1530. By the time peace was signed with the Safavis in 1555, the Ottomans had lost a golden opportunity to take their offensive against the Habsburgs onto the Italian mainland.

At this point Süleyman's anti-Habsburg offensive was not confined to military action. Ever since the Reformation had started in central Europe the Ottomans had followed its progress with interest. Advised by the French, the sultan wrote to the German Lutheran princes, urging them to continue to fight the pope and Charles V and pointing out beliefs shared by Protestantism and Islam. This move was only partially successful, since the reality of the Turkish menace was apparent to both Catholics and Protestants. Moreover, Charles V's need to obtain the financial and military support of the imperial estates for his wars in the end compelled him to grant a certain amount of tolerance to Lutheranism. Thus, while the wars of the first half of the sixteenth century favoured the rise of Protestantism, it is also true that for Charles V France was as dangerous as the Porte. A more serious threat to the Habsburgs was the Ottomans' backing of Calvinism in Europe, since this represented an authentic revolutionary force, hostile to Lutheranism nearly as strongly as it was to Catholicism and not averse to striking a Faustian pact with Islam. For this reason the Calvinist populations of Hungary and Transylvania increasingly looked to the Porte as an ally against the Catholic Habsburgs. Needless to say, the Ottomans were only too happy to oblige.[52]

But religious divisions in France soon deprived Süleyman of his best ally in Europe. The abdication of Charles V as Holy Roman Emperor, and the division of his territorial possessions between his brother Ferdinand and his son Philip, was initially good news for the Porte; the Habsburgs were no longer a united front. But the following year Philip, now king of Spain as Philip II, inflicted a crushing defeat on the French at the battle of Saint-Quentin in Flanders, and for some time it was expected that the Spanish would march on Paris. Faced with the Spanish threat and having to deal at home with the unrest caused by the Calvinist Huguenots, the French king Henry II started peace talks with Philip. In the ensuing treaty of Cateau-Cambrésis France recognized Spain's claims in Italy and Flanders, ratifying what is commonly know as the fifty years of the Pax Hispanica in southern Europe. Philip II then took the war to North Africa, sending an expeditionary force which included contingents from the pope, Malta, Tuscany, Monaco and Savoy to fortify the island of Djerba, halfway between Tunis and Tripoli. In Philip's plan Djerba would together with Hospitaller-held Malta effectively block the sea route from Algiers to Constantinople.

In the event the Djerba expedition was a complete fiasco. The Spanish did indeed manage to capture the island and build a fort, but on 6 May 1560 the Ottoman fleet under the command of Grand Admiral Piyale Pasha caught them as they were re-embarking. Piyale may have been a man of no great intelligence, at least according to the Venetians,[53] but in this action he showed both ability and daring. Running a considerable risk, the grand admiral launched his fleet against the scattered enemy vessels, capturing or sinking thirty of them and killing or capturing around 8,000 men. The beleaguered fort at Djerba resisted until the end of the following July, when lack of munitions and supplies forced the garrison to surrender. While most of Spain's allies had their fleets wiped out by Piyale's exploit, more serious for Philip were his considerable losses in skilled naval personnel, hampering Spain's ability to launch any major naval operations for years to come.[54] Piyale's triumph was crowned by his solemn arrival in Constantinople with the captured galleys in tow on 27 September 1560. Their success at Djerba had offered the Ottomans a vision of future victory, and it appeared only a matter of time before they attempted the conquest of the remaining Habsburg territories in the Mediterranean. But without French support it would have been logistically impossible for Süleyman to launch such an ambitious operation, unless some suitable advance base could be found between Constantinople and Gibraltar. The ideal stepping stone was the island of Malta, between Tunis and Sicily, boasted some excellent havens where a large fleet could find shelter. For the Ottomans the island was a ripe fruit ready to be plucked, provided they could first defeat its masters: old acquaintances of Süleyman and not likely to give up without a fight, the Knights Hospitaller.

Seven years after it had been ousted from Rhodes, the Order of St John had found refuge on the island of Malta. Its new home was a gift from Charles V, who, already burdened with too many commitments, also thought to saddle the knights with the defence of the recently conquered city of Tripoli on the North African coast. Although initially not happy with the bequest, the Hospitallers, now known as the Knights of Malta, quickly resumed preying on Ottoman shipping routes in the eastern Mediterranean. For the sultan the knights represented a constant source of irritation, and while it may be true that it was the insistence of Mihirimah,

Süleyman's daughter, and other members of the Ottoman administration which tipped the Sultan's decision, he hardly needed their prodding to realize that Malta was a problem that urgently needed solving. In October 1564 the *dîvân-ı hümâyûn* (imperial council) debated a possible expedition against Malta. Not everybody agreed on the venture, but in the end the sultan's will prevailed and it was decided to attack the island the following spring.

News of Ottoman preparations quickly reached Hospitaller headquarters, but the order's grand master, Jean Parissot de La Vallette, had no intention of repeating the experience of Rhodes. Determined to make the most of the island's defences, he resolved to resist until the arrival of the Spanish relief force promised by the viceroy of Sicily, Don Garcia de Toledo. La Vallette and Toledo were counting on time, the latter not wishing to risk another Djerba by facing the Ottoman fleet at the height of its strength. The Ottoman commander, on the other hand, hoped to capture the island before autumn weather forced a return to Constantinople.

The Ottomans landed on Malta in the second half of May 1565 with a force of roughly 35,000 fighting men, including about 10,000 *timar* holders and 6,500 janissaries. To put together the force some two dozen *sancak*s had been milked dry of their manpower,[55] extra soldiers being provided by volunteers, plus North African and Anatolian corsairs. A substantial number of artillerymen handled a siege train of nearly sixty guns, some of them huge masonry destroyers. By contrast, La Vallette could count initially on less than 600 members of the order, 400 Spanish troops, 4,000–5,000 Maltese capable of bearing arms and nearly fifty artillery pieces of various sizes. The Ottomans first tried to take Fort St Elmo, but to their chagrin it held out until 24 June, when the remaining defenders were overwhelmed in a massive assault. But in the meantime the Christians had inflicted on the invaders something like 6,000 casualties, many of them *sipahis* and janissaries, against losses of 1,500. The most illustrious victim was the famous corsair Dragut, killed by a cannon shot while directing artillery fire.

As the weeks drew on the Ottoman losses in men and materiel

started to tell, fatigue and diminishing gunpowder stocks lessening the besiegers' efforts and bombardment by the day. It was just the moment that the viceroy of Sicily had been waiting for since May. On 9 September a relief force of 11,000 men engaged the Muslims as they retreated towards their ships. In vain the Ottoman commander Isfendiari Mustafa Pasha tried to rally his troops but nothing could stop the Ottomans after months 'of fighting devils, not men'.[56] As La Vallette led his brethren to give thanks to the Blessed Virgin for her miraculous aid in lifting the siege, the whole of Europe breathed a sigh of relief. But although the Ottomans had suffered a serious defeat they still remained a formidable threat.

2. A HOUSE DIVIDED

~

Grand Master La Vallette was not a man to mince his words. As he watched the construction of the new fortified city which eventually would take his name – he could not but feel a sense of uneasiness. True, the Hospitallers' popularity after the siege had meant the arrival of new recruits and an influx of much-needed cash, but with the Ottoman threat still real it was necessary to build fortifications capable of withstanding another attack. Yet the grand master had constantly to plead and cajole to get the necessary assistance from European sovereigns, venting his anger in a letter to the Duke of Anjou, brother of the king of France, Charles IX. Stressing the risk of an Ottoman onslaught against Malta, La Vallette reminded the duke, 'After what we have passed, we are still weak.' For this reason he was writing to all the Catholic rulers and especially to the king of France, asking for help, stating bluntly that he foresaw 'great trouble against which we cannot hope to preserve ourselves unless we are aided'. He concluded by begging the king and his councillors not to refuse assistance, for the Turkish threat was not directed solely at the order 'but against Christendom'.[1]

The grand master had reasons for concern. At the time of the siege the French, because of their alliance with the Turks, had been reluctant to help the Knights of St John, King Charles IX even preventing a force of French volunteers from joining the beleaguered Maltese. Valois hostility towards the order came from the fact that Malta was a Spanish fief, and there were others in Europe who would have been happy to see the Hospitallers destroyed. Many Venetians, despite some of their fellow citizens being members of the order, were furious that the knights' corsair activities disrupted commerce in the Levant. Undismayed by the Ottoman retreat, the knights' enemies were sure that the following year the sultan would come back with a more powerful fleet to finish the job.[2]

~

This sort of attitude was no novelty; it could be described as standard in Christian Europe. For centuries its various states had been busier fighting each other than trying to stop the Muslim advance. In some cases they had even actively helped it, wittingly or otherwise. To make matters worse, the one force potentially capable of uniting the warring polities was no longer able to do so. The pope, while still considered rather more than just another head of state, was nevertheless often treated as such, and the very secular behaviour of many clergymen did not help. Admittedly the papacy was not in an easy position, needing to be not just a spiritual but also a temporal power in order to maintain its independence. In many ways it was difficult for the pope not to get deeply (sometimes too deeply) involved in the European political game. It should also be remembered that clergymen are part of the same cultural milieu as their lay counterparts, and in this sense the Church has always mirrored the secular world.

By the beginning of the sixteenth century Christendom was in a very sorry state. Gone were the crusading ideals of old; people turned deaf ears to the alarmed utterances of preachers and popes about the necessity of stopping the Turkish advance. For most European governments the Ottoman threat was low on their list of concerns – they were more interested in maintaining their positions in the rich eastern markets – while a few states were quite ready to abet, or at least not hinder, the sultans' expansionist policies for the sake of their own commercial interests. Both the Venetians and the

Genoese on different occasions provided the Ottomans with technology and ships for their campaigns. Some Europeans were even prepared to admire the efficiency of the more centralized Ottoman state, especially when contrasted with the situation in most of western Europe. As much as the Ottoman political and legal system smacked of arbitrary rule, not everyone saw this as a drawback. Indeed, somebody as distinguished as the Florentine jurist and historian Francesco Guicciardini considered it beneficial in more than one way:

> I do not wholly condemn the Turkish method of administering the law in civil matters, though it is sudden rather than summary. For he who determines with his eyes shut may likely enough decide half his cases justly, while he saves the parties time and expense. Our own tribunals move so slowly, that often it were better for him who has right on his side to have the cause given against him on the first hearing, than to win it after all the cost and trouble he is put to. Besides, because of our judges' ignorance and dishonesty, as well as from obscurity in our laws, even with us black is too often made to appear white.[3]

On the other hand, Niccolò Machiavelli in *The Prince* emphasized how the main strength of the Porte was, in the long run, in fact its main weakness. By stating that it was 'difficult to win control of the Turkish Empire' but that once it had been conquered it could be 'held with ease',[4] Machiavelli underscored the fact that the Ottoman state could only function effectively with strong leadership. For once, Machiavelli was right in his analysis. Although administratively less efficient in the short term, the decentralized states of western Europe were much more capable of sustaining the sort of political, military and social blows that nearly brought the Ottoman empire to its knees in the course of the seventeenth century.

In the meantime the West watched with indifference Mehmed II's conquest of Constantinople, although only a few years before the Eastern and Western Churches had decided to end the schism that had divided them since 1055. The effects of this reconciliation were, however, largely nominal; the vast majority of Byzantines hated the very idea of Rome and, according to one source, 'preferred to be ruled by the Sultan's turban than the Pope's tiara'.[5] Many Westerners reciprocated the feeling. One of them after a lengthy stay in the east came to the conclusion that the stories about Ottoman cruelty were nothing but malicious gossip: 'I have found the Turks to be much more friendly than the Greeks,' wrote the Frenchman Bertrandon de La Broquière.[6] In any case, the Ottoman conquest of Constantinople nullified the attempts at a permanent rapprochement between the Churches, the sultan, with the support of his Greek Orthodox subjects, preferring to rule over Christians whose leaders he could control and, following the old Byzantine practice, appoint himself.

Not everybody in Europe was passive in the face of the Turkish onslaught. Aeneas Sylvius Piccolomini, one of the foremost scholars of his day, while convinced that the negative image of the Turk was exaggerated and that some Christians were second to none in committing atrocities, also had a very clear perception of the Ottoman peril.[7] Once elected pope as Pius II in 1458 he immediately tried to unite the rulers of Italy and other parts of Europe for a military expedition in the Balkans. Pius's anti-Ottoman international conference, held in Mantua in 1459, failed miserably, the various European governments studiously avoiding committing themselves. The failure of the conference prompted Pius to write his famous 'Letter to Mehmed II' in which he suggested the sultan become a Christian in exchange for Papal recognition of his present and future conquests. By offering to Mehmed in effect nothing less than the crown of the Holy Roman Empire, Pius was sending a message to European rulers that the only thing the sultan lacked was baptism to be a legitimate sovereign with the material and spiritual means to rule the whole of the Western world. But, as historian Nancy Bisaha has convincingly demonstrated, the letter was never intended for Mehmed, since Pius's lambasting of Islam would have turned the missive into a huge diplomatic faux pas, making it largely useless as an instrument for Mehmed's conversion. The text was probably intended for the edification of Western readers, and indeed it circulated widely in Europe even before being put into print a few years after the pope's death.[8]

Pius's efforts to launch a crusade continued unabated for the rest of his pontificate, and when war erupted in 1463 between the Ottomans and the Venetians he jumped at the opportunity. Wishing to set an example, he declared his intention of leading himself an anti-Ottoman expedition. Faced with such commitment, many rulers promised to send money and troops, the king of Hungary and the duke of Burgundy even expressing the desire to join in person. One head of state who actually did participate was the neo-pagan lord of Rimini, Sigismondo Pandolfo Malatesta, anxious to regain papal favour after Pius had hounded him with sword and pen into submission. Encouraged by all this, the pontiff left Rome for Ancona, where the whole army was supposed to embark on ships provided by the Venetians. But neither the king of Hungary nor the duke of Burgundy appeared, the Venetians sent just a few galleys, and only a handful of soldiers eventually arrived in Ancona. An ailing Pius was still hoping for the promised troops when he died on 14 August 1464, being spared the ultimate disappointment of seeing his crusade fall apart.

As soon as news of the pope's death became public, every government discovered more pressing priorities nearer to home, Philip the Good of Burgundy for one preferring to wage war against the French than the Ottomans. Many historians have belittled Pius's crusading attempts as inane, forgetting that the pontiff did actually manage to put together the skeleton of an expeditionary force, something that many of his predecessors had failed to do.[9] It is legitimate to ask what would have happened if the pope had not died and instead departed for the east. Given the mentality of the time, it would have been difficult for Europe's rulers to avoid supporting the spiritual head of Christendom in his crusading efforts. After Pius II the papacy continued to advocate military expeditions against the Ottomans, but without Aeneas Sylvius's dedication; the popes became too entangled in Italian politics to seriously consider launching crusades. In any case the cosy world of fifteenth-century Italy, with its crafty political games, was soon to be shattered in a dramatic way.

~

The French invasion of 1494 triggered off what are known as the Italian Wars, destined to last until 1559. The term is actually misleading, since the Valois' initiative produced a domino effect that set the whole of Europe aflame. Still, up to 1530 much of the fighting involved Italy, France's attempts to gain control of the kingdom of Sicily and the duchy of Milan being opposed by the Spanish. The game immediately involved all the other Italian states, the Holy Roman Empire, the Swiss Confederation and, albeit on the side, the Ottomans. In a whirlwind of uncertainty, the various participants played a deadly diplomatic and military game, alliances being made or undone yearly.

By 1520 the situation was somewhat clearer: southern Italy was more or less under Spanish control; the Venetians had been humiliated; the Swiss were out of the game; while both Spain and the empire were under the rule of Charles V of Habsburg. Five years later the French suffered a crushing defeat at the battle of Pavia, and in 1527 the Habsburgs brought the papacy to its knees by taking and sacking Rome. After 1530 Florence also fell within Charles's sphere of control, as did most other Italian states.[10] However, the struggle for Italy between the Habsburgs and the Valois would continue for another twenty years, although the actual fighting was somewhat reduced in intensity. Yet there was always the risk for Charles that the French could regain the upper hand, in particular after the alliance between Francis I and Süleyman I. The alliance between the 'Most Christian King' and the heathen Turk may have shocked many at the time, but this would not be the only occasion when political expediency prevailed over religious division.

Religion was one of the main factors at play in sixteenth-century Europe, the struggle between Islam and Christianity overlapping with the latter's internal split. The papacy was a major player in both disputes, although often in an ambiguous manner and sometimes in contrast with basic Christian principles, inevitable for something that was at the same time a metaphysical institution and a political entity. To this should be added the theological confusion characteristic of the period. Since the mid-fourteenth century the intellectual movement known as Humanism had been growing in Europe, emphasizing the importance of the classical world at the expense of the so-called Middle Ages. By stressing the importance of textual analysis the humanists, at the beginning unwittingly, were undermining the very foundations of Catholic tradition. Taken to extremes, humanism bred secularism and scepticism, but most scholars were simply happy that ancient Roman and Greek culture was reborn (hence the term Renaissance). As Europe struggled to find a balance between antiquity and Christianity, few at the time realized that the continent was a religious time bomb ready to explode at any moment.

By now almost everybody in Catholic Europe agreed that a reform of the Church was badly needed. The poor behaviour of the clergy was no novelty – the corruption of clerical mores being as old as the Church itself – and down the centuries ecumenical councils, forceful emperors and reforming popes had often performed drastic religious house cleaning. The corruption of the clergy had always created scandal, but in the past this had been seen as a consequence of churchmen being imperfect human beings, not the fault of the Church as a divine institution. Indeed, in a paradoxical manner, ecclesiastical vices could even be an instrument of eternal salvation. In Giovanni Boccaccio's *Decameron* the Jew Abraham becomes a Christian after visiting Rome and witnessing every single vice in the world. Abraham's logic is that God must really be upholding the Church, since all clergymen, from the pope downwards, 'are devoting all their care, all their intelligence and skill to expunging the Christian religion and ridding the world of it, whereas they are supposed to be its bedrock and mainstay.'[11]

But many Renaissance thinkers spurned such niceties, convinced that the metaphysical beliefs of centuries were less important than the truths to be found by studying ancient texts. Since humanistic ideas and ideals permeated most of the culture of the time, it was logical that many cultivated people, clergymen included, should abide by them. Christianity, paganism, erudition and superstition lived side by side, as Plato, Aristotle, Cicero and the astrologists of old were put on the same level as the Bible and the Church fathers. Pope Alexander VI in his Vatican apartment had a painting with Moses conversing with the third century AD mage Hermes Trismegistus (considered a contemporary of Moses and thus as authoritative) and the Egyptian goddess Isis. Salvation, it was felt, could be obtained through knowledge as well as faith. Yet humanism and classical culture were causing theological confusion. For instance, the philosopher Pietro Pomponazzi, basing his arguments on Aristotle, could happily deny the immortality of the soul and argue the impossibility of miracles. Using textual criticism a humanist like Lorenzo Valla argued that the temporal power of the popes was based on a forgery. By editing, albeit in a rather cavalier manner, and publishing a Greek version of the New Testament, Erasmus of Rotterdam cast doubts on the textual veracity of the Gospels as originally translated into Latin by St Jerome in the fourth century AD. The movement stressing the importance of original texts spilt over into religion, many advocating not just ecclesiastical reform but also a return to the Church's original purity. The Dominican friar Girolamo Savonarola would thunder from Florentine pulpits against vanities and clerical corruption, targeting in particular Pope Alexander VI. The novelty of his preaching was that it advocated the creation of a world based on Christian humanistic values, Savonarola being a biblical scholar who filled his sermons with references to themes dear to the humanists.[12]

It was these factors coupled with the political ambitions of rulers that triggered off the Protestant Reformation in Germany. Started by an Augustinian friar by the name of Martin Luther in 1517, the Reformation quickly took hold thanks to the fact that many German princes considered it a useful way to gain control over the

Church in their domains. Luther's arguments asserting the superiority of sacred scripture over apostolic tradition owed much to the cultural milieu of the time, and so did his selective use of the Church fathers. Also – giving a theological justification to a well-established attitude – Luther upheld the interference of secular rulers in ecclesiastical matters. At the beginning Rome reacted with indifference towards the new movement; it was used to crackpot theologians. Emperor Charles V's approach to Lutheranism was more ambiguous. Although he rightly considered himself the protector of religious orthodoxy, he also saw Lutheranism as a way to enhance his own authority and force the Church to clean itself up.

At the beginning both the reformers and the papacy shared a common fear of the Muslim peril – Pope Leo X (reigned 1513–19) was genuinely concerned with the threat posed by Selim I, in particular after the latter's conquest of Egypt – although the answer of the religious reformers of northern Europe to the Ottoman problem was somewhat uncertain. Erasmus of Rotterdam in his *De Bello Turcico*, whilst recognizing the existence of the Ottoman military threat, maintained that even against the Turks 'war must never be undertaken unless, as a last resort, it cannot be avoided'.[13] Luther initially thought that fighting the Turks was like resisting God, who had sent the Ottomans to punish the Christians for their sins. Later, after the scare of Süleyman's siege of Vienna, Luther would urge the princes of the empire to fight the Turks under the leadership of Charles V.[14] However religious reformers in Germany were now starting to look on Rome and not Constantinople as the main evil threatening Christianity. As Luther himself would write, 'Is there nothing more corrupt, more pestilential, more offensive than the Roman Curia? It surpasses beyond all comparison the godlessness of the Turks.'[15]

Pope Adrian VI, Leo X's successor, would have agreed. Adrian was a pious, stern and thorough man, bent on extirpating clerical abuses, checking Lutheranism, bringing peace to Europe and stopping the Turkish advance. In all these fields he was to be singularly unsuccessful. King Francis I, who considered Adrian a puppet of the

emperor, threatened schism; the Roman Curia, jealous of its privileges, stonewalled the pope in every possible way; and Lutheranism
continued to spread like wildfire, with Adrian's own utterances
against the papal court bolstering the reformers' case. Italians
thought him a miser and a barbarian. His frantic appeals to Christian
rulers to defend Rhodes fell on deaf ears, and the fall of the island
hastened Adrian's earthly demise.[16] He died on 14 September 1523,
nineteen months after his election. The Roman Curia sighed with
relief, and predictably the next conclave elected the Florentine
Giulio de' Medici, Leo X's first cousin, as Clement VII. For many
it seemed that, after an unfortunate pause, it was business as usual.

Alas, this was not to be the case, not least because Clement
proved himself a very bad politician. Although in the past he had
been admired as a skilled negotiator, he showed little diplomatic
ability after his election to the papacy. He was much disliked in his
native Florence, then under Medici control, because of the high-
handed attitude of his henchmen. By mismanaging the dispute over
the marriage between Catherine of Aragon and Henry VIII, he
caused the religious split between England and Rome. To cap this
bleak picture, his dealings with France and the Habsburgs would
prove disastrous for the papacy. Convinced that Charles V represented a threat to papal freedom, Clement allied himself with the
Valois king. It was a huge miscalculation. The French proved
unreliable and in the spring of 1527 an imperial army 30,000 strong,
comprising Germans, Spaniards and Italians, marched through Italy
against scant opposition, when not actively aided by local rulers. On
6 May the Habsburg troops stormed the walls of Rome, Clement
having barely the time to take refuge in the fortress of Castel Sant
Angelo. What followed was a savage sack of the city, 'as if done by
Turks',[17] which lasted days, while the pope watched impotently the
scenes of rape, pillage and murder from the walls of his shelter.* At
the beginning of June he threw in the towel, regaining his liberty

* As sacks went, that of Rome was no worse than others. What shocked people
was that Rome was not only the spiritual centre of Christendom, but also one of
the great cultural hubs of the time.

with a promise to pay a huge ransom. In exchange for the restoration of Medici rule in Florence – the city having revolted against the pope's relatives at the time of the sack – he agreed to crown Charles as Holy Roman Emperor.* With the Turks at the gates of Vienna, Charles was more than willing to reach an agreement with the pope, at the same time trying to convince Clement to call a general council. Yet, despite some timid attempts in the direction of reform, the pope was unwilling to bow to Charles's request, fearing that the council might turn against him.[18]

It was left to Clement's successor to make the first step in this direction. Paul III (reigned 1534–49) was no saint; originally made a cardinal thanks to his sister Giulia being Alexander VI's lover, as Cardinal Alessandro Farnese he had fathered several illegitimate children. Pope 'Fregnese' (thus satirized by distorting his surname into the vulgar term for vagina) would prove to be an unrepentant nepotist, loading his relatives with honours and riches, even carving out independent states for them.† But he was also aware of the need to reform the Church and stop the Ottomans. After many years of preparation and a number of failed attempts at reconciliation with the Lutherans, in 1545 Paul declared the opening of a general council in Trent. It would last for nearly twenty years, on and off, and dramatically change the face of the entire Church.

The pope was not the only one having problems with the Protestants. Charles had managed to stop the Ottomans in front of Vienna by granting concessions to the Lutheran princes of the empire, receiving in exchange money and troops. But Lutheranism had taken on a definite militant and military aspect, a number of powerful German princes in 1531 creating the Schmalkaldic Bund.[19]

---

* Charles until then was only the emperor-elect, although his imperial authority was undisputed even before his coronation.
† Papal nepotism stemmed largely from the popes' need to appoint people they could trust in key administrative positions. While in itself not a negative thing, nepotism was prone to abuse in the hands of pontiffs more interested in the good of their families than of the Church.

Officially a pact of mutual defence, in reality its goal was to consolidate the reformed religion throughout the empire. The Bund had created a substantial military force – 10,000 foot and 2,000 horse – and was openly defiant of the emperor's authority. To make matters worse, the following year it allied itself with France. Since Charles could not afford, militarily or financially, to stop this, he was forced to tolerate the spread of Lutheranism, often by force, in the Schmalkaldic-controlled territories. The creation of a Catholic Bund in 1538 appeared to many the prelude to a showdown between Charles and the Protestant princes, but at the Diet of Frankfurt the following year the two sides agreed to a temporary and uneasy peace since Charles was still busy fighting the allied Franco-Ottoman forces.

Charles bided his time while trying to undermine the Schmal-kaldic Bund by exploiting its internal rivalries. By 1546 he had won over the dukes of Saxony and Bavaria, signed the Peace of Crépy with France, agreed to a truce with the Ottomans – once more distracted by war with Persia – and was busy raising troops to fight his Lutheran enemies. Paul III, also convinced that Protestantism needed to be crushed, sent money and troops. The Bund was slow to react, its army marred by a divided leadership. In April 1547 Charles smashed the Schmalkaldic forces at Mühlberg in Saxony, but his desire to consolidate his victory by restoring Catholicism throughout the empire or alternatively reach some sort of advan-tageous settlement with the Lutherans was thwarted by Paul III's fear of him becoming too powerful. The papal troops were with-drawn from Germany, and Paul started considering the possibility of a French alliance. The situation was exacerbated by the murder by imperialist-backed conspirators of the lord of Piacenza, Pier Luigi Farnese, Paul's son, who with the rest of his family, including the pope, had backed a number of anti-Habsburg plots in various parts of Italy. Charles V's decision to retain Piacenza threw the pope into the arms of Henry II of Valois, Francis I's successor, and by the time of Paul's death in November 1549 negotiations for a league between Rome and France had reached an advanced stage.[20] Paul III had been committed to reforming the Church, but like many of his predecessors his interest in worldly matters made him forget the common good of Christendom. In this sense, the Renaissance papacy had only itself to blame for the spread of Protestantism in Germany.

The German Lutherans had suffered a severe blow at Mühlberg, but once more received aid from the French, the Ottomans and ultimately the pope. Julius III, who succeeded Paul III, was initially well disposed towards the family of his predecessor, confirming its various members in the possessions they had managed to acquire, including the duchy of Parma. In spite of this, relations between the pope and the Farnese soured quickly when the latter got embroiled in a dispute with the Habsburg governor of Milan, Ferrante Gonzaga, who insisted that he needed to control Parma for the defence of his master's territories against the French. As a result, the Farnese appealed to the king of France for protection, much to Julius's chagrin and concern; by placing themselves under Henry II's suzerainty the Farnese were not just committing an act of rebellion against their feudal overlord, but also threatened to cause another war in Italy. Reluctantly the pope was forced to side with the emperor, fearing that otherwise the papal territories would be in jeopardy.

Military operations initially went well for the joint papal–imperial army, and by August 1551 it appeared that the city of Parma was about to capitulate, but a French attack through the Alps forced Gonzaga to rush to Piedmont, leaving the pope to fend for himself. Meanwhile, a Turkish fleet under Dragut raided the coast of Sicily, sacked the Maltese island of Gozo, before swinging south and capturing Tripoli from the Hospitallers. By now Charles V had not only to deal with the French and the Ottomans, but also with the Lutherans. Exploiting the emperor's difficulties, the German Protestants led by Maurice of Saxony unexpectedly attacked the imperial forces, while Henry II occupied the imperial cities of Metz, Toul and Verdun. Charles was forced to conclude the Treaty of Passau with the insurgents in April 1552, agreeing to a high degree of religious freedom for the German princes. With the main theatre of war now in the Low Countries and Charles fully occupied with the French and Turks, Julius, his coffers empty, was happy to make peace with the Farnese, allowing them to keep Parma and all their other territories. The Renaissance papacy had run its course, burnt out by the world it had helped create.

3. MEDITERRANEAN MEDLEY

~

It was cold in Rome in mid-January 1557, and inside the Vatican His Holiness Pope Paul IV's mood only increased the winter bitterness. Less than two months before he had been forced to agree to a humiliating truce with the Spanish commander Fernando Alvarez de Toledo, duke of Alva, whose army was encamped a few miles from the city. The ease of Alva's advance, brushing aside the troops sent to stop him and capturing stronghold after stronghold, had only increased the pope's shame. To add insult to injury, mingled with Alva's forces were those of the hated Colonna family, against which Paul had waged incessant warfare. Individual Colonna had been imprisoned or excommunicated and their property in the papal states confiscated and redistributed among the pope's nephews. Now the soldiers of the rebel Marcantonio Colonna had reoccupied many of these lands, sending the papal protégés running.

Since the expiry of the truce, on 8 January, Paul's forces, reinforced with contingents sent by Henry II of France, had managed to retake the fortress of Ostia, and a French army under the duke of Guise was about to invade the Spanish-held kingdom of Naples. But this was not enough for the eighty-year-old firebrand pontiff, doggedly determined to remove the Colonnna from their inheritance and the Habsburgs from Italy's soil. Thus, on that cold winter day while conversing with Cardinal Giovanni Morone, the pope declared emphatically that he was prepared to seek every possible ally in his just war against Philip II of Spain, even from Protestant Germany if necessary. Morone, who knew the Lutherans well from first-hand experience, cautioned Paul that the Germans hated the papacy. The aged former inquisitor glared at the cardinal, whom he suspected of Lutheran leanings, and hissed, 'The Turks will not fail us!'[1]

Paul IV's comment may come as a shock (and Cardinal Morone was indeed shocked), especially since we imagine St Peter's successors to be unwavering champions of Christianity and not prepared to sell their souls to their worst enemy for political reasons. However, when it came to striking deals with the infidels, Paul was very much of a latecomer.

~

Although by the sixteenth century the Venetians were the only consistent Christian bulwark left in the east, they had never been happy fighting the Ottomans, preferring commerce to crusading activities. According to Paolo Preto, between 1453 and 1797 the Venetians and the Turks were at war with each other only for a total of 61 years, against 273 during which they were on peaceful terms. With pragmatic realism, the Republic of St Mark would pursue war ferociously – often with the help of other powers – to defend its Levantine possessions against Ottoman attacks, but for the sake of its commercial interests would be as determined to stay at peace with the Ottomans once hostilities ended. For this reason, after the end of the 1463–79 war the Venetians steadfastly refused to join the other Italian states in an anti-Ottoman league, prompting accusations of an unholy alliance between Venice and Constantinople. Given the scare provoked by the Turkish occupation of Otranto, the accusations were understandable, but there was another side to the coin: the Levantine trade was what allowed the republic to maintain a fleet large enough to counter the Ottomans' maritime expansion. Venice's dealings with Constantinople coupled with its growing power on the Italian mainland caused considerable concern and hostility in European diplomatic circles; Louis XI of France is said to have once commented that if the sultan agreed to be baptized, he would gladly help him against the Venetians.

Venice's expansionism set her on a collision course with her neighbours and also with some rather more powerful enemies. By the late 1490s the Republic of St Mark had managed to acquire a number of key ports at the heel of the Italian peninsula, fighting Florence and Milan with French backing. Meanwhile, Sultan Bayezid II feared a possible Franco-Venetian attack against Constantinople, especially after King Charles VIII of France trumpeted his intention of launching a crusade. To make matters worse, the Venetians had been giving support to a number of Balkan petty lords hostile to the Ottomans. The Milanese and Florentine ambassadors in Istanbul were busy poisoning Bayezid's ear against the Venetians, counting on the Turks to distract Venice from pursuing further territorial conquests in Italy.[2] A series of incidents at sea involving Venetian corsairs and Turkish merchantmen gave the sultan an excuse to attack, although ostensibly his military preparations were directed against Rhodes.

The war of 1499–1503 was disastrous for the Venetians. Not only were they defeated at sea, but the Ottomans also managed to capture the key fortress of Methoni on the southwest coast of the Peloponnese. The sultan's orders to give no quarter resulted in the massacre of Methoni's soldiers and adult males: they died on the impaling stakes, at the flaying posts or after having witnessed their internal organs thrown to dogs. These grisly details may be exaggerated, but it is certain that between 800 and 1,000 men were executed in the presence of Bayezid and his court. The strongholds of Koroni and Zonchio (near Navarino) then surrendered without a fight, and despite French support when the war ended in 1503 Venice was left with precious few possessions on the Greek mainland.[3]

A few years later all the pieces on the political chessboard had moved. By 1507 Venice's expansion in the Romagna region, traditionally claimed by the papacy, had aroused the ire of the warlike Pope Julius II. To counter the Venetians, the pontiff found allies in France, the Holy Roman Empire and Spain, all of which considered the republic a dangerous competitor in Italy. In the 1509 War of the League of Cambrai, Venice suffered a major defeat at Agnadello, and in the wake of the battle lost nearly all its territorial possessions on the Italian mainland. With the Republic's very existence in peril, the Venetian government took the dramatic step of seeking a military alliance with the Ottomans, a decision which did not come easily. More than one heated debate took place in the council chambers between those who could not swallow the idea of such an impious treaty, fearing it would bring destruction to Italy and the whole of Christendom, and those who were quite prepared to see 'the infidels in Italy' to save Venice. Eventually the hawks prevailed, and secret talks took place with the sultan's envoys for the dispatch of a Turkish expeditionary force. Bayezid, however, was unwilling to get embroiled in a war in Italy, since his truce with Hungary was about to expire, and the Venetians only managed to obtain a few consignments of grain and permission to recruit some units of Ottoman–Albanian cavalry. These troops were actually employed for military operations, but Venetian public opinion was aghast about involving the sultan in an anti-papal campaign. Moreover, Venice had once more regained the initiative in the field, as well as most of the territory it had previously lost, making the Ottoman presence unnecessary. When Venice signed an anti-French treaty with the pope in 1510 the planned alliance with Bayezid was quickly forgotten and the republic attempted a historiographical cover-up on the whole matter.[4]

This volte-face was typical of the Italian wars of the first half of the sixteenth century; to survive Venice had to play a very tricky diplomatic game. After the French defeat at the battle of Pavia in 1525 the Venetians became alarmed about the Habsburg presence on their borders, since it was known that Charles V's brother Ferdinand had set his eyes on Hungary. To counter the threat of encirclement by the Habsburgs, Venice encouraged Süleyman I to invade Hungary, and a formal embassy was sent by the republic to the sultan to congratulate him after his victory at Mohács. Charles V fumed at what he considered this betrayal of the common Christian cause, Venice being a 'poisonous plant' capable only of sowing discord amongst Christian princes and constantly in alliance with the sultan. Charles's ire was more than just a rhetorical outburst, since it was clear to everyone that the Ottomans were fighting Venice's battle against the Habsburgs.[5]

~

As much as the Venetians feared his retaliation, the emperor preferred to wait. The chance to repay Venice came a decade later, at the time of the 1537 Franco-Ottoman operation against Italy. Süleyman was concerned about the vulnerability of his communications between Apulia and Albania, fearing they could be cut by a hostile fleet. A few accidental skirmishes between Venetian and Ottoman ships convinced the sultan that the republic was indeed playing a double game, and these fears were adroitly exploited by Charles V's admiral, Andrea Doria, who started attacking Ottoman shipping in Venetian waters. In vain Venice's envoy in Constantinople protested that his fellow citizens were not responsible. Having failed to conquer southern Italy, Süleyman was unwilling to face the embarrassment of having to go home empty-handed, and war with Venice was exactly what he needed. The sultan also understood that before launching any future expedition against Italy he would first have to take the Venetian island of Corfu, considered the key to the Adriatic, Italy, Dalmatia and north-western Greece. For Süleyman war with Venice was necessary for the advance of the *darülislam*.

The Ottoman attack against the Venetian possessions in Greece was not unexpected, but executed swiftly. The fortress of Butrint was taken by surprise, and Corfu resisted only because the local commander, warned of the impending attack at the eleventh hour, managed to put together an effective defence. As soon as news of these events reached Venice, the republic mobilized its troops, seeking allies in the emperor and the pope with the hope of putting together an army 50,000 strong and a fleet of more than two hundred galleys. Paul III immediately sent his fleet, but Doria, originally from Venice's traditional rival Genoa, replied that he could not move without explicit orders from Charles V. In the meantime Ferdinand of Habsburg started new military operations in Hungary, while Venice managed to take a few coastal towns in Dalmatia. Süleyman's siege of Corfu was leading nowhere, the fortress being state-of-the-art and too hard a nut to crack even for the skilful Ottoman engineers. The same thing was true for the other Venetian strongholds of Monemvasia and Nafplio. After months of assaults and heavy losses, the Sultan decided to throw in the towel. He informed Venice that he was prepared to discuss peace terms provided the republic paid compensation for his losses, threatening otherwise to attack Friuli and Crete. In the face of such effrontery the Venetians decided to continue fighting, although the resolution passed by only one vote in the senate and the doge himself opposed it.

Venice joined the Holy League with the pope and the emperor on 8 February 1538, agreeing to pay two-sixths of its total expenses and contribute eighty-two galleys to the war effort. The Venetians were unhappy that the league's naval forces should be under the command of Andrea Doria, a manifestation of the mutual mistrust which plagued the league from the beginning. Venice feared that the Habsburgs would exploit the alliance for their own hegemonic interests, while the pope and the emperor suspected the Venetians of planning a separate peace with the Ottomans. The continual bickering among the allies meant that the league's fleet did not come together until September. It was late in the campaign season, and Doria was willing to postpone all military operations to the following spring. When the Venetians protested, he agreed to move towards the Muslim fleet under Barbarossa anchored at the entrance to the gulf of Preveza. Doria tried to lure the *kapudan-ı deryâ* out of his protected haven, but the wily corsair bided his time, waiting for the allies to exhaust their provisions. At the right moment he struck, catching the league's fleet as it was retreating towards its supply bases. The allies' losses were light – seven vessels in all – but Doria's caution aroused a storm of criticism, the Venetians accusing him of having deliberately snatched defeat from the jaws of victory for the sake of weakening Venice's position vis-à-vis Charles V. Even more sinister was the accusation that Doria was engaged in secret negotiations with Barbarossa, a charge substantiated by more than just circumstantial evidence.[6] Partly to quash such allegations, the following October Doria captured the fortress of Castelnuovo in Dalmatia, which he proceeded to garrison with Spanish troops. Once more Venice protested, stating that according to the league's terms any conquered territory in Greece previously owned by the Venetians should revert to them. Doria ignored these remonstrations; he was following Charles V's agenda of diminishing Venice's power, and he also needed to disembark thousands of mutinous soldiers. These troops disappeared permanently from the scene when the following year Barbarossa retook Castelnuovo after a siege lasting from March to September, and which Doria made no effort to lift. Indeed, the behaviour of the Genoese admiral proved so desultory that the Venetians became convinced the only option was to seek terms with Constantinople.

This humiliating course of action was forced on the Venetians not only by Doria but also by France. The French ambassador in Constantinople had encouraged the sultan to prolong the war unless Venice agreed to give up Napflio, Kotor and Corfu, hoping thus to force the republic to seek help from the Valois and sever the Habsburg alliance. French envoys were sent to Venice offering substantial aid against the Ottomans, but the Venetians soon discovered these promises to be hollow. Now completely alone, Venice decided to pursue peace talks, sending to Constantinople Alvise Badoer with instructions to secure terms without if possible ceding Kotor, Corfu, Nafplio or Monemvasia. Badoer was given authority to agree to an annual tribute of up to 6,000 ducats and war indemnities up to a maximum of 300,000 ducats.

The Venetian ambassador arrived in Constantinople in April

1540, but to his dismay found the Turks adamantly committed to obtaining Nafplio and Monemvasia as well as an indemnity of 300,000 ducats. What Badoer ignored was that the French envoy in Venice had managed through bribery to obtain copies of the ambassador's instructions delivering them to the Ottomans. The Venetians were forced to give in, only managing to obtain the evacuation from Nafplio and Monemvasia of all those unwilling to live under Ottoman rule. In 1542 the Valois spy ring in Venice was uncovered and the Venetians did not hesitate to besiege the French embassy where a number of those involved had taken refuge, threatening to attack the building if they were not handed over. France complied with the request, having also the decency not to protest at the violation of its ambassador's diplomatic immunity.[7] As for Venice, until the Ottoman invasion of Cyprus it would bend over backwards to stay at peace with the Porte.

~

The Venetians had every reason to be suspicious that Doria was playing a double game; he had a remarkable record for duplicity. It had been the admiral who in 1528 had set Genoa firmly in the Habsburg camp, after decades of the city switching alliances between France and her enemies. Just a few months before finally throwing in its lot with the emperor Genoa had actively assisted the French in their final bid to conquer Naples. A mixed Venetian–Genoese fleet had been providing support to the advancing Valois troops, the Genoese under Andrea Doria's son Filippino even defeating a Spanish naval force off Capo d'Orso on 28 May. But the high-handed behaviour of the French, which included territorial encroachment in Liguria, provoked Genoa's bitter resentment. Protests having no effect, Andrea Doria negotiated for his fellow citizens an alliance with Charles V. Thus, on 4 July the Genoese vessels abandoned Neapolitan waters, leaving their erstwhile allies in the lurch. Doria profited considerably from the deal, obtaining from Charles V, in addition to the Order of the Golden Fleece, 60,000 florins a year for the rent of twelve galleys.[8] Henceforth, a large part of Charles V's Mediterranean fleet included vessels managed by Genoese *condottieri* families. Genoese bankers would also become the major moneylenders to the Spanish crown between the sixteenth and the seventeenth centuries, benefiting greatly from the riches of the Iberian empire.

Given these events, the Venetian mistrust of the Genoese and Doria in particular was understandable. But there were also other factors behind the lack of Genoese military commitment against the Turks. Most of Genoa's overseas empire had been gobbled up by the Ottomans in the course of the fifteenth century with the notable exception of the island of Chios, and for a number of reasons both the Genoese and the Ottomans had an interest in maintaining the status quo. The Porte received a yearly tribute of 12,000 ducats from the Genoese corporation, the *Maona*, ruling Chios, but also had other motives for tolerating an independent and potentially hostile territory near its coasts. The thought of a Habsburg–Genoese fleet using Chios as a base for operations against Ottoman territory in the Levant must have given nightmares to the sultan's admirals; but the Genoese understood that they held Chios on sufferance, and tried in every possible way not to irritate the sultan. The Genoese diplomats in Constantinople were always at pains to justify the actions of the 'citizen' Andrea Doria, and even asked the latter to nominally relinquish the command of his fleet to his great-grandson Giovanni Andrea, so as to deprive the French representatives in Constantinople of any excuse to poison the sultan's ear against Genoa. Because of its alliance with the Habsburgs, by the 1520s the Ottomans' main adversaries in the Mediterranean, Genoa was now one of the Porte's potential enemies. Relations between the two states became even more strained after the Franco–Ottoman alliance, which, among other things, contemplated punishing the 'treacherous' Genoese.[9]

This was easier said than done. Although by the beginning of the sixteenth century Chios was no longer the trade centre it had once been, it still played a significant role in the commercial exchanges between Genoa and Constantinople. By controlling the bulk of tin imports into the Ottoman empire, the *Maona* was in a position to impose severe limitations on the sultan's war effort. The cannon foundries of Constantinople's arsenal depended heavily on English tin, the Mediterranean trade in which was virtually monopolized by the Genoese. The English also benefited from the commerce, keeping a resident consul in Chios until the reign of Mary I, despite the occasional protest over the high taxes imposed by the *Maona*. Merchandise also flowed in the opposite direction, many Genoese having an interest in the Chios trade in gum mastic, alum, salt, pitch and aromatic resin, 'God's gift to the *Maonesi*' according to a contemporary.[10]

How much Andrea Doria was involved in Chios's commerce is unclear, but in any case, as befitted a good Genoese, he must have been concerned with the island's safety. Apart from its economic value, it was considered the republic's 'right eye' in the Levant[11]. Since it would have been very difficult and costly for Genoa to send a relief force to Chios in the event of an Ottoman attack, Doria preferred to safeguard the island by striking a deal with Barbarossa. The Genoese admiral's duplicitous behaviour before, during and after the battle of Preveza, was motivated by pragmatism and economic convenience. A few years later such considerations would cause the Genoese to liberate Dragut, one of the most famous Muslim corsairs of the time, in exchange for the coral-rich island of Tabarka off the Tunisian coast.[12] In addition, it should not be forgotten that at Preveza many of the 'Spanish' galleys were actually the private property of Genoese entrepreneurs on loan to Charles V. In no way could Doria have risked investments worth thousands of ducats unless absolutely sure of a return. Charles V would have agreed, considering also the repercussions of any major damage to Doria's fleet on his Mediterranean strategy. At the time of Preveza a gap existed between the emperor's objectives and those of the Venetians wide enough for someone like Doria to behave with the political adroitness his fellow citizens expected from him. As often the case in the history of the Mediterranean, fighting and friendship went hand in hand.

~

For Charles V the 1537–8 war was part of a greater strategy aimed at containing the Muslim, not just Ottoman, onslaught in the Mediterranean. By the time of Preveza the Habsburgs' southern maritime frontier was porous to say the least. The coasts of Spain, southern Italy and Sicily were especially exposed to the raids of Muslim corsairs, not to mention full-scale Ottoman invasions. This represented a serious challenge for the 'Catholic kings' – as the rulers of Spain styled themselves – even before the advent of the Habsburgs on the thrones of Castile and Aragon in 1516, a challenge destined to consume considerable quantities of Spain's military and financial resources.

By capturing Granada in 1492 Ferdinand VII of Aragon and Isabelle II of Castile had brought an end to the last independent Muslim state in the Iberian peninsula, everything possible being done to ensure that this situation remained permanent. The fall of Granada in no way ruled out another Islamic invasion. Twice before, the *Reconquista* – the reconquest of Iberia from the Moors, starting in the eighth century AD – had been stopped in its tracks by an influx of Muslim warriors from North Africa. No one could guarantee such a thing not happening again. This fear strengthened a very particular Spanish attitude which had taken shape during the centuries of the *Reconquista*, namely the feeling that Spain had a unique and exclusive role in the defence of the Christian faith. For this reason the Catholic kings would always be as much concerned with threats from abroad as with those lurking within their borders. In pursuing their enemies the kings were hampered by Spain at the time being politically and administratively divided – indeed, it was referred to as 'Spains' – the various kingdoms, political bodies and communities of the peninsula being fully conscious of their traditions, rights and privileges. Any failure by the central authorities to recognize these could trigger uprisings, and indeed in 1520 Castile was shaken to its roots by the widespread rebellion of the kingdom's communities, the revolt of the *Comuneros*.[13] Painfully aware of their weakness, the Catholic kings reacted with aggression, both at home and abroad, in order to guarantee the safety of their kingdoms.

Given this situation, it was almost inevitable that all those hostile to the Catholic faith should be perceived as potential enemies, to be dealt with accordingly. The first blow fell on the Jews, who were given the choice between conversion and expulsion soon after the fall of Granada. Next came the Moriscos, the Islamic population of Moorish ancestry left behind by the *Reconquista*. Mainly concentrated in Andalusia but strong also in Castile and Aragon, they made up large and economically important communities. Expelling such a substantial number of people would have been well-nigh impossible for the Spanish rulers of the time, the country's political divisions not allowing the sovereign to muster enough support for such a radical course of action. The alternative was forced conversion, the hope being that the converted Muslims would soon be absorbed into the Christian environment.

By 1502 Islam had been proscribed throughout Castile, although Granada was spared for a few years after 1492 thanks to the moderation of its Christian administrators. However, the archbishop of Toledo Cardinal Ximenes de Cisneros had been heavy-handed with the Granadan Moriscos. This had produced a rebellion in 1499–1501, put down only with great difficulty. A lull followed until 1525, when Charles V extended the policy of compulsory Christianity to Aragon. The Moriscos in Valencia promptly revolted, but were swiftly suppressed by royal troops. After each uprising many Moriscos agreed to be baptized, but many more escaped to North Africa nourishing a burning hatred towards all Christians. Those who remained in Spain as Muslims were subject to a growing number of restrictions, more in the kingdom of Castile than in Aragon, where for a time they were allowed to exercise their religion in private. All these measures were motivated by fear of a Morisco fifth column, capable of giving active aid to a Muslim expedition launched from Africa against the Spanish mainland.[14]

This was not paranoia. The frequent *gazi* expeditions launched by Barbary corsairs against the Spanish coast were actively aided by the Moriscos living in exile in North Africa but still in contact with their brethren across the sea. For the Spanish authorities stopping this sort of exchange was virtually impossible, lacking as they did the necessary forces to control, let alone repress, the large Morisco population in Andalusia. A viable alternative was denying the corsairs use of their African naval bases. As early as 1302 the Spanish had established a presence in Algiers by occupying for some time the Peñon, the island at the mouth of the city's harbour. In 1505 at Ximenes's instigation the stronghold of Mers-el-Kebir was taken, followed in 1508 by the Peñon de la Gomera. In May 1509 Oran fell, and many of its inhabitants were slaughtered. These conquests were followed by those of Bejaia, Tlemcen and Tripoli, and in 1510 the Spanish reoccupied the Peñon of Algiers. This series of victories came to an abrupt end when, the same year, an over-bold Spanish army was ambushed and cut to pieces on the island of Djerba off the Tunisian coast. Over the following years, distracted by the Italian wars, the Spanish were to lose much ground in North Africa.

Unable to challenge the Spanish effectively, the North African rulers looked abroad for aid. Desperate for help, in 1515 the emir of Algiers Selim al-Toumi sent for the Turkish corsair Arouj Reis Barbarossa, who with his brother Hizir, later more famous as Hayreddin, was operating successfully off the Tunisian coast, preying on Christian shipping and ferrying Moriscos to North Africa. Arouj expelled the Spanish from the vicinity of Algiers, although not from the Peñon, had the emir strangled and himself proclaimed ruler of the city. Turning it into a corsair haven, he quickly extended his control over the adjacent region, regaining much of the territory previously conquered by the Spanish. In 1518 Arouj was killed in battle at Tlemcen, and his brother then submitted to Sultan Selim I in exchange for an Ottoman garrison in Algiers. Hayreddin continued Arouj's work, retaking Bône (Annaba) in 1522 and the Peñon of Algiers seven years later after a siege lasting only three weeks. In 1534 he captured Tunis, throwing out its Spanish-backed ruler. Spain's bid for security had paradoxically resulted in Ottoman rule being extended over the greater part of North Africa.

By this date, however, Charles V felt secure enough in Italy to direct his energies against the Muslims in the Mediterranean. His granting of Malta and Tripoli to the Hospitallers in 1530 freed him of the necessity of guarding these two strategically important places, allowing him also to tap into the military and financial strength of the foremost chivalric order of Europe. At the end of May 1535 a joint Spanish, papal, Genoese and Maltese fleet of seventy-four galleys and 330 other ships descended on Tunis. After taking the key fortress of La Goleta, six miles from the city, the expeditionary force marched towards its main objective. Barbarossa's troops were routed, and the former ruler of Tunis, Muley Hassan, restored to his throne. Charles capped his victory by taking also Bône and Bizerte before returning in triumph to Sicily. Six years later, having covered his back by agreeing to a truce with France in 1538, the emperor decided it was high time to deal with Algiers. In the autumn of 1541 an expeditionary force of fifty galleys, 150 transport ships and 24,000 soldiers sailed for North Africa, confident of overpowering Algiers' garrison of 6,000 men. As fate would have it, however, in late October the armada was hit by a devastating storm that wrecked two thirds of the ships and killed thousands.[15] For the next quarter of a century the North African theatre witnessed once more a gradual Muslim resurgence. Despite the small Habsburg success against the Tunisian fort of Africa, north of Sfax, in 1550, Tripoli was retaken by Dragut from the Hospitallers the following year, and Bejaıa in 1555.[16] In both cases the Habsburgs did not react, having more serious and pressing problems to deal with.

~

Once more France and the Ottomans were to prove the main source of trouble for the emperor. What Charles probably had not envisaged, despite the vagaries of Italian politics, was the possibility of an alliance between the papacy and the Porte. No sooner had the Parma war ended than on 3 August 1552 the city of Siena, a Habsburg protectorate, expelled the garrison from the Spanish-built fortress, proceeded to demolish it, and immediately sought the protection of France. For Charles V this was a serious blow; it threatened to create a French-controlled state in the heart of the Italian peninsula and had come when he already had his hands full in Germany, Flanders and Hungary. To make matters worse, a French-backed Ottoman armada under Dragut had been spotted off the Roman coast sailing in the direction of Naples. The Habsburg viceroy of Naples Don Pedro de Toledo had very few men at his disposal to face the expected invasion and sent frantic requests for help to Andrea Doria. The Genoese immediately put to sea a mixed Spanish–Italian fleet, but one contingent under Don Juan de Mendoza was ambushed and destroyed by Dragut off the isle of Ponza on 5 August. Too distant to give any help, Doria preferred to withdraw his ships to Sardinia. Emboldened by their victory, the Ottomans laid siege to the town of Gaeta, but finally decided to sail for Constantinople after waiting for twenty days for the French galleys to arrive. The French fleet eventually appeared in Constantinople a few weeks later, but despite the insistence of Admiral Antoine d'Escalin the Ottomans adamantly refused to resume operations until the following spring.

Charles V, however, was not prepared to wait, and in the winter of 1552–3 started operations in earnest against Sienese territory laying siege to the town of Montalcino, having previously obtained from the pope authorization to march through the papal states. With memories of the sack of Rome still fresh, Julius III was not in a position to refuse. By May it seemed that nothing could save Montalcino, when suddenly the imperialists lifted the siege and departed towards Naples, recalled by the threat of another Franco-Ottoman invasion. The Valois–Ottoman fleet, 150 sails strong, did materialize in the lower Tyrrhenian Sea, but after a few raids on the Neapolitan coast sailed north to the Sienese coastal stronghold of

Porto Ercole in the south of Tuscany. Having embarked there some 4,000 French troops previously been sent to aid Siena, this armada went on a devastating rampage through the Tuscan islands before swinging west towards Corsica. The island was weakly defended, and in addition the population was in a chronic state of revolt against its Genoese overlords. In little more than a month the Franco-Ottomans had occupied the whole of Corsica with the exception of Calvi, being unable to overcome the spirited resistance of the local Spanish garrison.

When the Ottomans retired towards the Levant at the beginning of October the French remained in sole control of the island and proceeded to impose terms: in exchange for Corsica, the Genoese were to abandon Charles V and become allies of Henry II. But the Franco-Turkish military alliance had sent shock waves down the length of Italy, bringing into the Habsburg camp many states until then cool towards Charles V's policies. Cosimo I de' Medici, duke of Florence, was worried that if Genoa fell to the Valois the French would then try to conquer Naples and dominate the Mediterranean together with their Ottoman allies. Although Cosimo had always tried to remain neutral in the fight between the Valois and the Habsburgs, his wife was Don Pedro de Toledo's daughter and the duke also owed his position to Spanish backing. In addition, Cosimo wanted Siena for himself, particularly after in early January 1554 Henry II put the city's defences under Marshal Piero Strozzi, a ferociously anti-Medici Florentine exile. Cosimo played his hand carefully, asking Charles V to be allowed to make war on Siena in the emperor's name, both sides agreeing on the number of troops and the expenses necessary to bring the city back into the Habsburg fold. At this stage Cosimo was not asking for Siena, but only the reimbursement of his expenses.[17]

The duke struck immediately, three columns of Florentine–imperial troops crossing the Sienese border on 26 January under the command of Giangiacomo de' Medici, marquis of Marignano, a Milanese nobleman unrelated to the duke. But despite the capture of a few strongholds in the countryside the invaders failed to take

Siena by storm and were forced to settle down for what promised to be a long siege. Marignano's difficulties were increased by Piero Strozzi's military ability, the Franco-Sienese commander conducting hit-and-run raids deep into Florentine territory. These forced the besiegers to detach forces to engage him and relieve the pressure on Siena. But Strozzi's strategy could ultimately succeed only with substantial French reinforcements, and these did not materialize in time for the marshal to deliver Marignano a knock-out blow. Instead, the Florentine commander caught and soundly defeated Strozzi with a numerically superior army at Marciano, south of Siena, on 2 August 1554. Siena was forced to surrender on terms the following 21 April. A number of exiles from the city joined together in Montalcino, and with French help resisted for another two years.

The Siena war was bitterly fought, both sides committing atrocities seldom seen during the Italian wars. Much of the latter part of the conflict was fought in southern Tuscany, the Franco-Sienese forcing their enemies to capture each stronghold in turn, sometimes more than once. In addition the Florentines had always to contend with the possibility of an Ottoman raid, this threat materializing in July 1555 when a naval force of 104 sail under Dragut attempted a two-pronged attack against Piombino. Luckily for the Florentines their commander in the area, Chiappino Vitelli, intercepted the Ottomans just after they had landed, forcing them back to their ships. The invaders lost 550 killed out of a force of 3,500, all Ottoman prisoners being summarily dispatched by their captors. Dragut then tried to take Portoferraio on the island of Elba, but finding it too tough a target sailed towards Corsica.[18]

By now another front was about to open up in Italy. Pope Julius III died at the end of March 1555, was succeeded briefly by Marcellus II (twenty days) and then by Paul IV. The new pontiff, born Gian Pietro Carafa, a stern and devout man of unbending principles, was nearly eighty when elected. From the early part of his ecclesiastical career he had shown himself zealous in fighting heresy, and had even been entrusted by Paul III with reorganizing the Roman inquisition. During his sojourn in Spain as papal nuncio under Leo X he had also developed a burning hatred of the Habsburgs, the latter fully reciprocating the sentiment. Paul's priorities were the defence of Catholic orthodoxy and diminishing the power and prestige of the Habsburgs, his loathing of Charles V becoming even more pronounced when the emperor, through his brother Ferdinand, yielded to the Lutherans' demands at the Diet of Augsburg (February–September 1555): from then on in Germany it would be up to the local authorities to determine the official religion of their subjects, thus introducing the concept of *cuius regio, eius religio*. By now, Charles, tired and ailing, had lost the will to fight, and between October and August 1556 he abdicated to his son Philip (Philip II) his domains in Spain, Italy, the Netherlands and the Indies, while his brother Ferdinand received the imperial title together with Germany and Hungary.

For Paul, Charles's behaviour towards the Lutherans was nothing less than an open betrayal of those same Catholic principles the emperor was supposed to uphold. Determined to destroy the Habsburgs once and for all, on 15 December 1555 he signed a treaty with Henry II of France − although somewhat uneasy about the Valois alliance with the Porte[19] − for the creation of a Franco-papal army of 20,000 to conquer Milan, Naples and Siena. The French were to keep the conquered territories, minus a large chunk of the Neapolitan kingdom to be incorporated into the papal states, and Siena, which was to go to one of the Pope's nephews. If Venice and Ferrara should decide to join, then they too were to receive territorial compensation, with Sicily being reserved for the Republic of St Mark.[20] The proviso on Siena was probably the most striking element of the treaty; despite all his reforming zeal, Paul IV was very much a chip off the nepotistic Renaissance block. For advice he relied on his pushy nephews, in particular the ambitious and unscrupulous former soldier Cardinal Carlo Carafa. In many ways Paul was a man of the fifteenth century and was fond of recalling the days of his youth, when Italy was 'a musical instrument with four strings' − the Church, Venice, Naples and Milan, Florence not then being part of this idyllic picture – until the French invasion of 1494 had put an end to this 'ancient harmony' and to Italy's liberty.[21]

Paul's plans nearly fell through when in February 1556 the Valois and the Habsburgs agreed on a five-year truce at Vaucelles, near Cambrai, which in essence allowed the French to keep all their conquests in Savoy and the empire. The agreement left the pope to face alone the Spanish army in Italy, but Cardinal Carafa effectively managed to destroy the truce by convincing Henry II to assist the pope in the event of a war with Spain. Strengthened by the promise of French aid, the pope started persecuting all of his subjects with Habsburg sympathies. A number of prominent cardinals and Roman citizens were either imprisoned or put under house arrest, but the full force of the pope's fury was reserved for the Colonna family, their lands in the papal states being confiscated and redistributed among Paul's nephews. When Philip II welcomed Marcantonio Colonna and others of his kin into the kingdom of Naples, the pope excommunicated him with his father Charles V, placing their domains under interdict and absolving their subjects from the oath of fealty. It was tantamount to a declaration of war.

Paul's actions proved costly.[22] Philip II acted rapidly, obtaining Venice's neutrality and securing the support of Florence and Parma by promising Siena to the Medici and Piacenza to the Farnese. When attempts to reach an agreement with the pope met with Paul's stubborn refusal, war became inevitable. On 1 September the duke of Alva, viceroy of Naples after the death of Don Pedro de Toledo, invaded the papal states from the south with an army of 12,000 foot and 1,800 horse, 300 of them provided by Marcantonio Colonna. Advancing through the Roman countryside and occupying a number of strategic places against little resistance, Alva thwarted all attempts to stop him. As the Spanish approached Rome the populace, mindful of the sack of twenty years before, flew into a panic: citizens, priests and friars were sent to work on the walls and additional troops hastily raised. Alva, however, was not interested in taking the Holy City as much as in denying the pope the

chance of receiving French reinforcements from the sea. On 18
November, shadowed by Piero Strozzi's forces, he took the fortress
of Ostia, at the mouth of the Tiber. Having put a stranglehold on
Rome's supply routes, Alva was willing to negotiate from a position
of strength.

Alva and Cardinal Carafa, acting in the pope's name, met near
Ostia on 28 November, but with the exception of a forty-day truce
the parties did not manage to reach an agreement. The pope
steadfastly refused to give in to Alva's demands, which included
restoring to the Colonna their confiscated possessions. Carafa himself was willing to exchange these lands for the lordship of Siena,
but this was something that Philip II was not prepared to concede.[23]
Alva returned to Naples, leaving behind Marcantonio Colonna with
7,000 men. Both contestants needed the respite to reorganize and
augment their forces for the next campaign season; the viceroy was
also concerned about a possible French inroad into the kingdom
of Naples. Cardinal Carafa departed for Venice in an attempt to
convince the republic to enter the fray on the pope's side, but the
Venetians refused to relinquish their neutrality despite Carafa's offer
of a substantial chunk of Neapolitan territory in the event of a
papal–French victory. The pope's nephew hinted darkly that should
the Venetians refuse their support then Paul IV would be forced
not only to bring into Italy so many French troops that it would
then be very difficult to get rid of them, but also, lacking a navy of
his own, the pontiff would have to avail himself of the Turkish
fleet.[24] Carafa was invoking the spectre of an Ottoman invasion of
Apulia, something ultimately capable of putting Venice's very existence at risk.

The cardinal would later state that this had been but a ploy to
convince the Venetians, but this assertion is disingenuous. Already
in September 1556 he had concocted a plan to employ the Ottoman
fleet against Spain's domains in Italy. The following March he
would write directly to Süleyman – probably with the pope's
blessing – asking him to stop waging war in Hungary and instead
concentrate on building a great fleet to attack the kingdom of

Naples. Carafa had already been in correspondence with the sultan some months before, and the cardinal would later defend himself by stating that he had acted on papal orders. Although we may doubt the veracity of Carafa's account, there is no doubt that Paul IV knew about his nephew's dealings. In any case the pontiff's hatred of the Habsburgs overcame any scruples he may have had when it came to choosing his allies.[25]

In the meantime the French had intervened in force, an army of 12,000 foot and 1,200 horse under the duke of Guise marching from Piedmont down the Adriatic coast. Skirting the borders of the duchy of Florence it entered Umbria, although both Guise and Cardinal Carafa would have preferred to attack Cosimo I: the pope's nephew still had his eye on Siena. As a result, Cosimo, who in order to obtain Siena had been toying with the idea of a French alliance, threw his lot with Philip II. The pope, encouraged also by the progress of his own forces against Marcantonio Colonna, was adamant that the main objective should be the kingdom of Naples. Colonna had weakened his position by dispersing his soldiers in a number of garrisons, and Piero Strozzi was quick to exploit the situation. Upon the expiry of the forty-day truce he pounced on Colonna, forcing him to abandon Ostia and retreat towards the south, losing a third of his troops in the process. With the supply routes to Rome reopened and Colonna on the run, the papal army could manoeuvre freely in the Roman countryside, and very soon Vicovaro, Palestrina, Frascati, Grottaferrata, Castel Gandolfo, Marino and Tivoli had been recovered for the Holy See. With the French army approaching fast, the Spanish faced the real risk that Strozzi and Guise would unite their forces, something that in conjunction with the feared arrival of an Ottoman fleet could have put an end to Habsburg domination in the south of Italy. The Ottomans, however, did not materialize, and Guise instead of moving towards Rome entered the Abruzzi region, occupying a few towns and laying siege to the fortress of Civitella del Tronto. The stronghold proved impregnable and in mid-May Guise lifted the siege, unwilling to face Alva's superior forces approaching fast from the south. With the situation under control in the Abruzzi, Alva dispatched 3,000 men to help Marcantonio Colonna. Strengthened by these reinforcements Colonna rapidly went on the offensive, regaining much of the ground lost to Strozzi the previous winter. On 15 August he stormed Segni, sacking the city and putting the garrison and many civilians to the sword. In the meantime Guise remained inactive, the French having become increasingly dissatisfied with the pope since he had not provided the promised troops or the necessary funds. Alva exploited the situation by once more invading the papal states, but acting on strict orders from Philip II limited himself to raiding the Roman countryside up to the walls of the Holy City.

Paul was losing ground fast. On 10 August – the feast of St Laurence, a saint to whom Philip II was particularly devoted – the French under Constable Anne de Montmorency were roundly defeated in Flanders at the battle of St Quentin by a Habsburg army led by Duke Emmanuel Philibert of Savoy, who previously had been evicted by the Valois from his domains. France lay open to invasion, and Guise was hastily recalled from Italy. Philip II had also finally managed to corner Cosimo I by giving him Siena as a Spanish fief, thus making the slippery Medici his vassal.[26] To everyone except the pope it seemed high time for peace. Paul, now completely isolated and desperately short of funds, grudgingly accepted Venetian and Florentine mediation, and on 12 September 1557 signed the Treaty of Cave. The terms were extremely generous for the pontiff: all papal lands were to be restored, in exchange for the lifting of the temporal and spiritual sanctions against the Habsburgs and their followers. Excepted from this pardon were confirmed rebels such as Marcantonio Colonna, the latter getting the muddy end of the stick, since both Alva and Cardinal Carafa had reasons for leaving him high and dry. The pope's nephew knew that Paul would never agree to pardon Marcantonio, and in any case Carafa had benefited greatly from the confiscation of Colonna lands. The viceroy of Naples, meanwhile, was hoping that the Colonna possessions, including the important fief and fortress of

Paliano, would go to his kinsman Don Garcia de Toledo, married to Marcantonio's elder sister, Vittoria.[27] In any case, both Alva and Philip II, always uneasy about waging war against the Holy See, were eager to strike a deal with the pope in order to tackle the Valois undisturbed.

The French were in no condition to continue fighting. Most of their former allies in Italy had opted for neutrality or chosen the Habsburg camp. In Hungary, Ferdinand and Süleyman had agreed some time before on a temporary peace, which, despite a number of border clashes over several disputed fortresses, seemed to be holding. The Ottomans, of course, remained a viable option for Henry II, and indeed in the early summer of 1558 a large Turkish fleet conducted extensive raids on the coast of southern Italy and across the western Mediterranean. As had happened before, lack of coordination meant that the Ottomans never managed to link up with their French allies, who waited in Corsica while the Turks plundered the isle of Minorca. In any case, Süleyman was now facing problems at home, having to deal with the rebellion of his son Bayezid, and thus in no position to aid his Valois ally in any way. Henry II had no choice but to agree in April 1559 to the Peace of Cateau-Cambrésis with Philip II.[28]

By the treaty, France was forced to give back practically the whole of Savoy to Duke Emmanuel Philibert and Corsica to the Genoese, and withdraw all its troops from Italy. The Habsburgs kept for good the southern Italian kingdoms of Naples and Sicily, the duchy of Milan, and Siena. The latter had already been enfeoffed to Cosimo I de' Medici with the exclusion of a few fortresses in the south of Tuscany retained by Spain, although the treaty actually called for the restoration of the Sienese republic. Cosimo got round this through a *fictio juris*: allowing the old Sienese magistracies to survive, but adding others staffed with his henchmen. The Valois retained the imperial cities of Metz, Toul and Verdun, plus regaining certain territories in north-eastern France. In addition, it was agreed that French and Genoese merchants should have free access to each other's ports. All these agreements were to be cemented with a series of dynastic marriages. Finally the parties agreed to employ all means to help reform and reunite the Church, a clause filled with unintended irony since the French by allying themselves with the Lutheran princes in Germany had done everything possible to shatter for good the religious unity of western Europe. They were already being repaid in kind. The Huguenots, Protestants of extreme Calvinist persuasion, had grown to alarming numbers within France itself. The Huguenots included in their ranks commoners as well as a substantial portion of France's nobility, and were rapidly becoming a vociferous, compact and militant force, soon to challenge the very existence of the Valois dynasty. For nearly forty years after Cateau-Cambrésis France would not be able to play any sort of significant military role in Europe, being crippled by religiously inspired civil unrest and war. Having sown the Lutheran wind, the Valois were now reaping the Huguenot whirlwind.

~

Cateau-Cambrésis not only confirmed Spain's hegemony in Italy, it also inserted most of the Italian states, albeit in different degrees, within the framework of the Habsburgs' Mediterranean strategy. This did not mean absolute control on Spain's part. Venice pursued its interests as before; the papacy had its own, variable, agenda; and both Savoy and Florence were, at best, very opportunistic allies. Duke Emmanuel Philibert of Savoy, the victor of St Quentin, had recovered his duchy from the French thanks to Philip II, but continually tried to escape from his patron's suffocating embrace. Nearly completely landlocked, Nice being its only port of significance, and wary of its troublesome French and Swiss neighbours, Savoy preferred to concentrate on its army rather than its navy. Florence was in a different position.

With Siena, Cosimo I de' Medici acquired a coastline extending the length of the upper Tyrrhenian Sea, together with the burden of protecting this watery frontier. It was an unenviable task, Florence having no fleet at the start of the Medici dukedom in 1532, the Florentine republic for financial reasons doing away with its galley squadron at the end of the fifteenth century.[29] The low priority given to naval matters by the Florentines was also due to the fact that up to the 1530s they were little affected by Ottoman expansion in the Mediterranean. This had taken place mostly at the expense of Venice, with whom Florence had a somewhat antagonistic relationship. What changed the Florentines' attitude towards the Porte was the Franco-Ottoman alliance of 1536 and Hayreddin Barbarossa's victory at Preveza two years later, events leading to a series of Muslim raids on the Italian coasts. The situation worsened with Barbarossa's massive raiding expedition across the western Mediterranean in 1543–4, and Florence became seriously alarmed by the possibility of a Franco-Ottoman attack.[30] By 1547 Cosimo I had started reorganizing his state's coastal defences, basing them on watchtowers, galleys and mounted units. This system was intended only for local protection, and until 1550 there were no more than a couple of Florentine galleys cruising the upper Tyrrhenian Sea between the port of Livorno and the island of Elba. It was the war for Siena in 1554–5 that precipitated a dramatic increase of the Medicean fleet – from two to six galleys – after the Florentines were forced to confront a Franco-Ottoman amphibious expeditionary force in southern Tuscany. In addition, the acquisition of Siena by Cosimo meant not only the Florentines having to protect a longer coastline, but also the inclusion of the Medici fleet in the Habsburgs' Mediterranean defences, the enfeoffment agreement stipulating that the Florentine galleys be at the disposal of the Spanish crown in times of need.[31] However, in dealing with the Ottoman problem the military option was but one of a number at Cosimo's disposal, diplomacy being for a long time a viable alternative. Besides, as befitted the descendant of merchants, the duke was interested in establishing strong commercial links with the Levant.

The republic of Florence had a long tradition of economic relations with Constantinople, the first trade concessions being granted by Mehmed II around 1455 and reconfirmed by Bayezid II in 1488. However, Florence's political turmoil after 1494, together with the wars of the sixteenth century, had not allowed the city to establish a stable commercial partnership with the Ottomans. Only with the advent of the Medici dukedom in 1532, coinciding with a more stable political and economic situation, were attempts made to reverse this situation. Despite what has been written by some,[32] the death of the Florentine *bailo*★ in 1530 did not imply the end of diplomatic relations between Florence and Constantinople, the presence of other *baili* being recorded at the beginning of the 1540s. Certainly by 1543, ten years after the accession of Cosimo I, the Florentines were trading actively in Constantinople as well as in Alexandria. The Medici representative in Constantinople, Alfonso Berardi, was instructed to do everything possible to cultivate the powerful Grand Vizier Rüstem Pasha so as to encourage Ottoman merchants to trade with Florence as they had once done. Cosimo was prepared to go to any length and expense: Berardi was ordered to discover what sort of gifts the grand vizier might appreciate.[33] The greatest expansion of Florentine trade with the Ottoman empire took place in the 1550s, and a Florentine diplomat was present in Pera until the middle of the next decade. By then direct commercial links between Tuscany and the Near East had been all but severed, trade giving way to an endemic state of war between the Medici and the Porte destined to last until the eighteenth century. What happened?

The culprit is usually identified as Counter-Reformation religious zeal, which resuscitated the apparently moribund crusading spirits of the Medici and their subjects. While evidence of such a revival can't be ignored, it is also true that beliefs were but one of many factors at play. Cosimo had some very strong dynastic ambitions, entwined with a compelling need to bring under control Tuscany's ruling elites. Immediately after the conquest of Siena, the duke had started to toy with creating a new maritime chivalric

---

★ *Bailo*, a word of Venetian origin, indicated a state's permanent resident at the Porte.

order, with himself in the role of grand master. Cosimo's objective was twofold: provide himself with an experienced pool of naval personnel and create a socio-political patronage system firmly in Medici hands. The order could also channel the energies of potentially unruly members of society towards the noble goal of protecting Christendom against the Muslim onslaught.[34] Cosimo chose to name the institution after St Stephen, pope and martyr (not to be confused with the more famous St Stephen, the first martyr), whose feast fell on 2 August, a date the duke considered particularly auspicious since it coincided with two of his most important military victories, including that of Marciano.

According to Cosimo's intentions, the order was to be self-sufficient, and thanks to its revenues capable of maintaining up to twelve galleys. But the grand duke's dream of the knights having their own fleet quickly foundered in the face of the order's unwillingness to use its considerable fortune to fight the infidels. As a result, the Tuscan fleet, while manned by the knights of St Stephen, was invariably financed by the Medici purse. Only in the 1620s would the order agree to pay a token yearly sum towards the upkeep of the fleet, at a time when the galleys were costing the Medici on average 15 per cent of Tuscany's yearly revenue.[35] Large numbers of Italian, and not just Tuscan, aristocrats swelled the ranks of the order immediately after its creation, and soon vessels flying the red eight-pointed cross of St Stephen became a common and feared sight in the Mediterranean. Even more important, the Medici became firmly associated with the order, a thing that would ultimately condition the Florentine dynasty's foreign policy.

~

Still occupied fighting the Valois, Philip II decided it was high time to reach some sort of agreement with the Porte, concerned that his uncle Ferdinand's agreement with Süleyman over Hungary would leave him to face alone a possible Franco-Ottoman offensive. Around the middle of 1558 Philip sent the Genoese Francesco Franchis to Constantinople to sound out the sultan on the matter, the king's choice of agent motivated by his desire to save face by not appearing to be making the first move. Franchis was also entrusted with the task of establishing an intelligence network in the Ottoman capital.[36] But in Constantinople there were doubts about the Genoese's real mission, Grand Vizier Rüstem Pasha openly accusing him of spying. Only after much persuasion did Franchis manage to convince the Ottoman authorities of the sincerity of his intentions. Like Philip, Rüstem was unwilling to take the initiative, but was prepared to consider informal talks with his Spanish counterparts. Following up on this, the king's secretary Gonzalo Pérez drafted a truce proposal to be submitted to the sultan: it was to last at least ten years, include 'tributaries, subjects and allies' of the two parties, and also contemplated an exchange of prisoners of war reduced to slavery. The following 6 March Philip informed Gonzalo Fernández de Córdoba, duke of Sessa and governor of Milan, that he had decided to send Niccolò Secco to Constantinople as his envoy since he knew well the local situation, having spent many years in the Levant. The instructions to Secco included bribing the grand vizier to obtain the truce from the sultan and also to stop the Ottoman fleet from sailing west that year.[37] Eventually, nothing came of these initiatives, both sides being unwilling to commit themselves to a treaty that might result in a loss of political prestige.

As was often the case, negotiations went hand in hand with military activities. The Peace of Cateau-Cambrésis effectively prevented the Turkish fleet from using French ports during their forays into the western Mediterranean, but for the Spanish the North African corsair bases remained a source of deep concern. Muslim sea *gazi* were an incessant threat to shipping routes, and regularly raided Christian shores. Even more worrying for Philip II was the fact that these bases could be used as logistical stepping stones for a major Ottoman attack on Spain or the Habsburg domains in Italy. Following an established pattern, in June 1559 it was decided to strike at the Muslim corsair bases in North Africa, but the expedition against Tripoli ended in disaster at Djerba the following year. For

Spain and her allies this was a dramatic defeat, the losses in men and equipment being equivalent, if not worse, to those suffered by Charles V at the time of his expedition against Algiers in 1541. More setbacks were to follow. In 1561 the Muslims captured three galleys under Visconte Cigala, one of the few squadrons to have survived Djerba. A few weeks later, Dragut with seven vessels captured the whole Sicilian war fleet of eight galleys. This litany of woes reached its climax a year later when a force of thirty-two galleys under Juan de Mendoza foundered off Malaga, with the loss of twenty-nine ships and 4,000 men.[38]

Ships could be replaced, but to rebuild a significant pool of experienced naval personnel took years. It would be some time before the Spanish could again tackle the Ottomans at sea, and inexperienced crews made amphibious operations very risky. For this reason, when the Ottoman host descended on Malta in 1565, the viceroy of Sicily, Don Garcia de Toledo, did everything he could to safeguard the meagre resources at his disposal, biding his time until it was safe to send a relief force to the island. For Don Garcia, and indeed the Spanish crown, the relief of Malta was as much a matter of sound military strategy as of prestige. By capturing the island the Ottomans would not only have imposed a stranglehold on shipping routes across the Mediterranean, but from Malta and their bases in the Balkans could also threaten the whole of southern Italy. Besides, Philip II was the Hospitallers' feudal overlord, and thus had a compelling duty to give them assistance. Yet Don Garcia knew perfectly well that any hasty move on his part could result in disaster, and preferred to deal with the situation using Fabian tactics. The viceroy knew that the Knights of St John would put up a stiff fight, allowing him to buy time while the Ottomans exhausted themselves in a prolonged and costly siege. Malta's location also meant that the Ottomans had dangerously extended their supply lines, making them vulnerable to a counterstroke delivered at the right moment. But this was not so easy to determine, Don Garcia having to judge exactly when the Ottomans were at their weakest. For this reason he was careful to send enough reinforcements before and during the siege to stiffen the knights' resolve, but not too many to seriously affect his own capabilities if Malta should fall. The viceroy was taking a calculated risk, but his strategy ultimately proved successful.

Don Garcia's tactics provoked a storm of criticism from the Hospitallers and their followers, the viceroy's prudence going as far as forbidding a number of knights gathered in Messina to join their besieged companions. He also ordered that the reinforcements sent in the middle of June should not land in the event of Fort St Elmo having already fallen, there being no way the troop-carrying ships could enter Malta's Grand Harbour without being intercepted by the Ottomans. As it happened, the reinforcements arrived the very day St Elmo's defenders were overwhelmed, but the knights leading the relief force managed to conceal this from the Spanish command-ers on board the galleys and make their way to the town of Birgu from the south, passing undetected through Ottoman siege lines – a feat little less than miraculous. However, it seems Don Garcia was not being excessively cautious, as the loss of the relief force would not only cause Malta to fall, but also put Sicily at grave risk. The island's vulnerability to an enemy invasion would be graphically described a few years later by another viceroy, the duke of Terra-nova: no money, few soldiers, even less sailors for the galleys, lack of provisions and undermanned fortresses.[39]

Don Garcia received continuous news on the progress of the siege from Maltese boats that time after time managed to elude Ottoman patrols. The viceroy also placed lookouts on Capo Passero, Sicily's southernmost tip, to listen to the distant boom of the great Ottoman siege guns. He knew that St Elmo had fallen when the sound ceased, since it would take the Ottomans several days to relocate their artillery and resume firing against the next objective.[40] The slackening rumbles from Malta gave Don Garcia the clue that the Turks were running short of gunpowder, meaning that they would not be able to continue the pounding for long. But even at this point, by deciding to send a large relief force to Malta the viceroy was stretching his luck, for there was always the risk of encountering a numerically superior Ottoman army. Nevertheless the viceroy arrived just at the right moment to inflict the coup de grâce on the Ottoman expeditionary force, although the historians of the Order of St John would like us to believe otherwise.[41] Don Garcia's strategy had certainly paid off, but prudence and procrastination would not always work with the Ottomans.

4. BUILD-UP TO DRAMA

~

On Easter Sunday 1566 there was a palpable sense of uneasiness among the inhabitants of Chios. The day before an Ottoman fleet numbering eighty galleys with 7,000 men on board had dropped anchor just outside their port; and whilst the *kapudan-ı deryâ* Piyale Pasha had refrained from entering the harbour – ostensibly for fear that his presence would disturb the Easter celebrations – this show of sensitivity only increased the Chians' apprehension. The island's governors were perfectly aware that they were personae non gratae with the Ottoman government, and especially with Grand Vizier Sokollu Mehmed Pasha. The latter had more than one reason to be irate with the Genoese rulers of Chios: Genoa was now firmly in the Habsburg camp, while the island was perceived by the Porte as a nest of spies – the Chians constantly keeping Genoa, and thus Spain, informed about the movements of the Ottoman fleet – and a haven for fugitive Christian slaves. In addition, the Maona in control of Chios was always in arrears with the tribute it was supposed to pay to the Sultan.[1]

Visits from large Ottoman fleets were no novelty for the Chians. Given the island's proximity to the Anatolian mainland, Turkish ships often stopping for water and victuals. When Piyale entered the harbour the following Monday he was received with the customary greeting salvos from the fortresses' artillery. The next morning the admiral, having expressed his desire to relax for a few days in the island's orchards, took a boat to the shore in the company of a number of high-ranking officers, *sancaks* and engineers. Piyale enjoyed a pleasant day observing fortifications and gardens. The following day he announced his departure, adding that before going he wished to discuss an important matter with the Chian government. Presently six of the twelve *signori governatori* arrived on Piyale's flagship but he, claiming that this constituted a breach of etiquette, stated adamantly that he would only speak to the whole governing board. The *podestà*, the governor of Chios appointed by Genoa, Vincenzo Giustiniani and the *signori governatori* were in a quandary. Although suspicious of Piyale's motives, they could not afford to offend the admiral by refusing to meet him, fearing that this could lead to a military confrontation. Chios's extensive fortifications would have allowed the city to resist for a short while – given also that the Ottoman army was busy fighting in Hungary and still making good the losses sustained at Malta – but in the long run the distance between the island and Genoa made relief a very unlikely eventuality. Besides, the Genoese were busy putting down yet another revolt on Corsica, and the Spanish had their own problems trying to defend their Mediterranean possessions.

The fates of Chios and Corsica were actually more closely linked than may appear, Corsican rebels, backed by the French, attempting to obtain the Porte's aid in their fight for independence. The Ottomans, unwilling to help directly, knowing that they could not count on the Valois' active support, had provided some undercover aid to the leader of the rebellion Sampietro di Bastelica. When the latter landed on his native island in June 1564, triggering off a revolt that would last until 1569, it had been the Ottomans who had provided the transport for him and his followers, a number of Muslim vessels also helping him in the taking of Porto Vecchio.[2] To the acute embarrassment of the Maona, the notorious Sampietro had stopped for three days in Chios harbour, under the protection of the sultan's banner, when returning from his diplomatic mission to Constantinople.[3] Since the Genoese proved unable to crush the

The *devşirme* or 'collection': Christian youths forcibly enlisted in the Sultan's service

The results of the *devşirme*: the Vizier Lala Mustafa Pasha entertaining janissaries

Europe's bogeyman: Sultan Süleyman I

Unequal to his father: Sultan Selim II

The backbone of the West: Pius V, Pope and Saint

Able diplomat and foresighted statesman:
Grand Vizier Sokollu Mehmed Pasha

Roman Cardinal and
Habsburg courtier: Antoine
Perrenot de Granvelle

The Papal Admiral Marcantonio
Colonna: charming, if an
inexperienced sailor

Giovanni Andrea Doria:
a skilled mariner
and politician

The Florentine Fox:
Grand Duke Cosimo I
de' Medici

Elegance, looks and chivalry:
Don Juan of Austria

The acme of Venetian patriotism: Captain-General Sebastiano Venier

In charge of Venice's secret weapon: Captain Francesco Duodo

Last of the school of Barbarossa: the Beylerbey of Algiers, Uluç Ali Pasha

Victim of treachery: the Governor-General of Famagusta, Marcantonio Bragadin

Brave, humane and unlucky:
Kapudan-ı deryâ Müezzinzâde
Ali Pasha

Timing and opportunity:
Don Álvaro de Bazan,
Marquis of Santa Cruz

Cold steel more than artillery: Müezzinzâde Ali's *Sultana*

Technological cutting edge in 1571: a gun-bristling Venetian galleass

Corsicans themselves, they had to turn to the Spanish for aid, the rebellion thus having the effect of tying down both Habsburg and Genoese naval forces in the western Mediterranean. As far as Chios was concerned, the Ottomans' hands were free.

With the deepest reluctance the island's governors went to Piyale's galley, where they were courteously received by the admiral. His politeness, however, was short-lived. Piyale proceeded to accuse the Maonesi of espionage, giving aid to fugitive slaves and Christian corsairs, failing to pay tribute to the Porte, and providing information to the sultan's enemies. He then informed the governors that it was the sultan's will that they be punished accordingly, arrested them and threatened to torch the city of Chios if the tribute, together with an extra sum of money for himself, was not paid within three days. The Chians quickly got word of what had happened, but Piyale moved swiftly. Thousand of Turks with weapons concealed under their robes had already infiltrated the city over the previous two days, under the guise of buying clothes and other items.[4] As soon as they received the admiral's signal they quickly moved to occupy the fortress, while the populace could only watch in dismay and fear the hoisting of the crescent standard. Piyale disembarked with the rest of his troops, took over the city gates and ordered that under pain of death no injury should be done to the Christians, hanging two soldiers guilty of disobeying his command. But the next day, the admiral had the interiors of the cathedral and of other churches destroyed, seizing the gold and silver vessels, destroying the altars and removing the bells. The cathedral was left to the Christians, but two other churches were turned into mosques, the Chians observing all this vandalism with tearful eyes.

On Friday 19 April Piyale summoned all the Giustiniani – the family whose members ran the Maona – to the government palace, and played a cat-and-mouse game. He promised them his protection but demanded they hand over all the diplomatic documentation between them and the Porte over the possession of Chios. The Maonesi agreed, despite knowing only too well that by doing so they were losing any chance of future legal redress. Next, Piyale announced that anyone wronged by the Maonesi should come forward and receive justice. No one appeared, although the Maona was notoriously corrupt, and over the years tensions had existed between the Catholic and Greek Orthodox communities. Indeed, many Chians asked Piyale to intercede with the sultan on behalf of the Giustiniani. But the admiral's answer came as a shock: an order had arrived from Süleyman to execute the leading Maonesi and exile the others to Caffa on the Black Sea. Frantically, the Chians dipped into their purses to pay for a frigate to carry an appeal to Constantinople. When the ship returned (if it was ever sent – there was a strong suspicion that Piyale had been lying the whole time) the admiral announced that the sultan had decided to exile the *podestà* and the *signori governatori*, while the other Maonesi were to buy their freedom for between 500 and 1,000 ducats ahead. In order to raise this money – which included also the tribute to the Porte – the Giustiniani were forced to 'sell' their property to Piyale. The island's erstwhile governors were then shipped to Caffa together with their families, excluding twenty-one of their children sent instead as *kapıkulu* to Constantinople. Eighteen were put to death a few months later for refusing to embrace Islam, while the remaining three accepted circumcision but eventually managed to escape back to Genoa, where they reverted to Catholicism.

On the sultan's order Chios was turned into a *sancak* governed by the Hungarian renegade Gazanfer Bey. Piyale left a force of five galleys, 500 janissaries and 200 *sipahi*s to guard the island, forbidding anyone to leave without permission or suffer severe penalties.

Piyale followed up his success by sailing across the Aegean Sea towards the western Mediterranean. On 24 June the Turkish armada was sighted by two Spanish galleys some thirty miles south of the isle of Zakynthos. The Ottomans gave chase, but their quarry managed to escape. Both in Madrid and Rome it was feared that Malta would be Piyale's objective, and hastily raised troops were sent to man the island's yet unfinished fortifications. Instead, the sultan's admiral skirted Italy's heel and moved up the Adriatic, dropping anchor in front of Dubrovnik. The Ragusei had already received news of Chios's fate, and, fearing that Piyale would try something similar with them – Dubrovnik, despite being one of the Porte's tributary states, always maintained extensive relations with the Habsburgs and other Western powers – adamantly refused Piyale entrance into the city's fortified harbour, for good measure pointing their guns towards the Ottoman ships. Whether because of this show of force or because he had never planned to take Ragusa in the first place, Piyale limited himself to collecting the sultan's yearly tribute before sailing north towards the Gulf of Trieste. After trying unsuccessfully to deal with some Albanian rebels and raiding the eastern coast of southern Italy, he turned back to Constantinople. On the return voyage he occupied the islands of Naxos, Andros, Kea and Sifnos – all independent states held by Venetian families since the thirteenth century.[5] By the end of the year very few islands in the Aegean Sea were not in Ottoman hands, Venetian-held Cyprus and Tinos being among the exceptions.

As in the case of Chios, all these takeovers went smoothly, and the Porte could be satisfied that it had managed to remove a number of troublesome thorns in its side. Yet Piyale's escapades were not without consequences: Chios may have been a source of irritation to the Ottomans, but while it was in the hands of the Maonesi Constantinople could be sure that the Genoese would be reluctant to aid the Habsburgs should the latter decide to launch a major offensive in the eastern Mediterranean. Worse, Piyale's rapacity destroyed an important commercial community and effectively severed a number of important economic links between the Ottoman empire and the rest of Europe. Chios, as we have seen, was the sultan's main source of English tin, and until the establishment in Constantinople of the English Company of the Levant in the early 1580s the Ottomans suffered from a shortage of this metal.[6] Since tin was essential for the manufacture of artillery, one can argue that the losses incurred by the Ottomans in conquering Chios by far outweighed the gains.

~

Chios was to be Süleyman's last victory. The seventy-two-year-old sultan had aged considerably, battered by lingering ailments and private misfortunes. His beloved wife Hürrem, known in the west as Roxelane, had died a few years before, and family upheavals only increased Süleyman's grief.[7] Suspecting that his first-born, Mustafa, born of the concubine Mahidevran, was plotting to depose him, Süleyman had him executed in 1553. Ottoman historians have long maintained that the flames of the sultan's suspicions had been adroitly fanned by his wife, his daughter Mihirimah, and the latter's husband, Grand Vizier Rüstem Pasha. Indeed, rumours circulating at the time pointed to Rüstem as the main instigator of the prince's downfall, the grand vizier allegedly forging a letter from Mustafa to the shah of Persia. Hürrem had every reason to want Mustafa out of the way, wishing one of her offspring to be the next sultan and knowing all too well that if Mustafa came to the throne he would immediately execute his half-brothers together with their male descendants.* Perhaps Süleyman's bad health made the hatching of palace plots inevitable – by custom, from the mid-fourteenth century all sons of the ruler were equally entitled to succeed their father, making the Ottoman throne 'occupative', rather than hereditary or elective.[8] Mustafa's popularity with the janissaries and other sections of the army made him a very dangerous player. Mindful that his grandfather Bayezid I had been ousted by a conspiracy spearheaded by the janissaries, Süleyman opted for a preemptive strike against his son for both his throne and his life's sake.

The death soon after Mustafa of Hürrem's third son Jihangir left only two other candidates, Selim and Bayezid. Hürrem's own demise in 1558 spared her further tragedies, for the two princes, until then kept in check by their mother, were immediately at each other's throats like a pair of Kilkenny cats, with Süleyman unable to

---

* Fratricide was customary within the Ottoman royal family. Introduced by Mehmed II, it was justified by the need to eliminate any potential pretenders to the throne. The practice of the new sultan killing his brothers and their male offspring was discontinued in the seventeenth century, although this did not stop Ottoman rulers from occasionally executing their siblings.

make up his mind about the succession, the sultan favouring in turn Selim and Bayezid. Their incessant squabbling irritated Süleyman to the point that he threatened to break with all law and custom by bestowing the throne on his sister's son, Osmanşa. He also tried to separate the two brothers as much as possible, dispatching Selim to Konya and Bayezid to Amasya.

Bayezid was not at all happy with this decision, accompanying his departure from his governor's seat in Kütahya with threats of rebellion and calling Selim a coward. His decision to raise an army from discontented *timar* holders, country people and border tribesmen, took him further down the slippery slope to civil war. Selim, on the other hand, showed himself totally submissive to his father's wishes, thus earning Süleyman's favour. The sultan not only provided Selim with troops, artillery and commanders, but also managed to obtain from Chief Mufti Ebu's-su'ud, a fatwa ruling that it was rightful for Süleyman to fight his rebellious son's followers.[9] As it happened, when the two brothers' forces clashed near Konya, Bayezid's 12,000 men were utterly routed. The defeated prince managed to flee to Persia, throwing himself on the mercy of the Safavid Shah Tahmasb. Süleyman embarked on a concerted diplomatic campaign to convince the shah to hand over his guest. Tahmasb procrastinated until he had managed to squeeze the most favourable concessions from the sultan, including a peace treaty, a hefty sum of money and a number of gifts for his family. The hapless Bayezid was then delivered to Ottoman officials, and executed together with his sons.

Selim was now the only heir to the throne but in many ways far from being an ideal candidate for the succession. Despite having a certain amount of experience as a provincial governor, he preferred wine to statecraft. Süleyman could do nothing to correct this situation, only behold the ruin of what had once been his family. As a result the embittered sultan retreated more and more into the privacy of his palace, leaving the day-to-day running of the empire to his ministers, in particular the able Grand Vizier Sokollu Mehmed Pasha. Yet, despite increasing bouts of senility, Süleyman was still the recognized, respected and feared Ottoman leader, and a force to be reckoned with.

The Austrian Habsburgs realized this very soon. The Holy Roman Emperor Ferdinand I died in 1564, and his son Maximilian had initially been willing to renew the truce agreed by his father with the Porte a few years before. But Maximilian still claimed suzerainty over Transylvania, and in 1565, exploiting the fact that the Turks were occupied in the Mediterranean, took the border towns of Tokaj and Szerencs. Süleyman ordered the governor of Buda to make a raid in reprisal, but it was not until the following year that a serious campaign could be undertaken against Maximilian, who was now suing for peace. Unfortunately the grand vizier was bent on teaching the Habsburgs a lesson, anxious also for a success to eclipse the Malta debacle. Operations started in June 1566, and the following month a huge Ottoman army – 300,000 strong according to one source,[10] and with Süleyman himself in command – crossed the Danube, penetrating into Habsburg-held territory and laying siege to the fortress of Szigetvár. The town finally fell to a determined assault on 8 September, but not before the defenders had blown up the walls burying many of the enemy with them.[11] Süleyman could not rejoice over the victory or grieve at his losses: the aged sultan had died two days before, possibly from a stroke, with the grand vizier at his side.

Sokollu Mehmed acted quickly.[12] Süleyman's entrails were removed and buried on the spot and his death kept hidden from the army, lest turmoil should ensue. For good measure, all those of low rank privy to the secret were quietly executed. The grand vizier immediately sent a message with the news to Selim, then in Kütahya, telling him to return to Constantinople in haste. Selim wasted no time doing so, securing the allegiance of all the officials in the capital before departing for the Balkans. He arrived in Belgrade in the middle of October and waited for the arrival of the grand vizier. The latter had in the meantime settled the army's pay, and, with the excuse that the campaign season was coming to a close, dismissed the *timar* troops. On 21 September Süleyman's body was placed in a covered litter as if he were still alive, and only when the army approached Belgrade did the grand vizier reveal what had happened, showing the troops their lord's corpse – a grim sight, even for battle-hardened soldiers. Yet, as much as they grieved over Süleyman's death, the troops wasted no time informing his successor that they expected some sort of monetary gratification, and Selim was forced to distribute generous sums and *timar*s to his unruly military to avoid having to deal with a rebellion.

The new sultan was cast from a different mould to that of his father. In Ottoman history he is remembered as Sari Selim, Selim the Sallow, due to his yellowish complexion, or perhaps to the blonde hair inherited from his mother,* but in the West he was universally known as the Sot, because of his love for alcohol. Perhaps it is not surprising that after what he had witnessed while growing up – including the violent death of his brothers – Selim should have sought refuge in drink, much to his father's displeasure; allegedly Süleyman had one of Selim's drinking pals executed, considering him to be his son's evil genius. The Venetian ambassador Andrea Badoer has left us a rather unflattering description of the sultan, confirming his worst excesses:

> This Sultan Selim is fifty-three years of age, small in size and weak of health. This is due to his intemperance, with women as with wine, drinking great quantities of the latter. He is very ugly indeed, with all his limbs out of proportion, according to everyone more a monster than a man. His face is burnt and ruined, from too much wine and the spirit he drinks to digest . . . Not only is he ignorant about the arts, but also can barely recognize written characters. He is uncouth in his speech, unversed in state affairs and lazy, leaving all the great weight of government to the Grand

* Hürrem was almost certainly of Slavic origin, and some maintain that her original name was Aleksandra Lisowska. However, in Italy there is the tradition that she was the daughter of Nanni Marsili, a Sienese gentleman with possessions in the south of Tuscany, and was kidnapped by Muslim corsairs when little and sold as a slave in Constantinople.

Vizier. He is miserly, sordid, lecherous, unrestrained and reckless in all the decisions he makes . . . What he enjoys doing most is drinking and eating, something he does for days on end; I am told that His Majesty sometimes spends two or three days constantly at the table.[13]

Given that this report was written after the Cyprus War, there is a legitimate suspicion of bias on Badoer's part. Yet the French ambassador to Venice, François de Noailles, would describe Selim as 'the biggest fool ever to run a state',[14] and another Venetian diplomat, Costantino Garzoni, would comment on the sultan's stubbornness and lack of character.[15] It is also true that Selim delegated most government tasks to the grand vizier, but in his defence it should be noted that his father had never bothered to train him properly in the art of statecraft. Being the third son, he had never expected to become sultan, anticipating rather that he would be executed once Süleyman died. Yet Selim was not devoid of qualities, being a skilled archer, an accomplished poet and a discriminating patron of the arts – so much for Badoer's comments.[16] He was also lucky to have some very capable advisers, and although he looks unimpressive next to Süleyman, many of the political decisions made during his reign, if ultimately flawed, were based on sound strategic reasoning.

The advent of Selim II meant a reshuffle within the Ottoman hierarchy. Sokollu Mehmed remained grand vizier, but would soon find himself in the imperial council in the unwelcome company of Selim's old tutor, Lala Mustafa Pasha. An ambitious intriguer, Lala Mustafa had been relegated by Grand Vizier Rüstem Pasha to the political backstage, first as a provincial governor and then, with the object of ruining him for good, as tutor (lala) to the then Prince Selim. In this position Mustafa had proved himself once more to be a troublemaker, being one of those responsible for igniting the rivalry between Selim and Bayezid.[17] Sokollu had little love for Lala Mustafa, and initially managed to get him transferred once more to a provincial governorship in what would prove to be a vain attempt to get him out of the way. In settling other old scores the grand vizier was more successful, for instance convincing Selim to execute the chief treasurer, Yussuf Ağa. Piyale Pasha was also added to the imperial council, being promoted to vizier after having been demoted from the position of *kapudan-ı deryâ*, allegedly for having kept most of the Chios booty for himself. His place as *kapudan paşa*,[18] the title from then onwards bestowed on an Ottoman admiral-in-chief provided with a *beylerbeik*, was taken by one of Sokollu's protégés, the former *ağa* of the janissaries, Müezzinzâde Ali Pasha.[19] Very soon two factions would emerge in the *dîvân*, one headed by Sokullu advocating the continuation of Ottoman expansion in Hungary, and another, its chief proponents being Lala Mustafa and Piyale, insisting instead on pursuing a Mediterranean policy. The latter group could count on the support of an influential person working behind the scenes of the Ottoman power system: Joseph Nassi.

Nassi is an enigmatic figure, his real influence on Ottoman politics being still a matter of debate among historians.[20] He was born João Miquez into a prominent Castilian *marrano*★ family who had left Spain for Portugal in 1492, moving then to Antwerp, Venice and Ferrara. Around the mid-1550s, the Nassi made Constantinople their final abode, reverting to the Judaism of their forefathers and engaging in a number of successful business enterprises. Joseph's relocation to the Ottoman capital, however, was as much due to his behaviour as to commerce, having been banished from Venice for the abduction of one of his cousins. His wealth allowed him to live majestically in a palace in the district of Ortakoy, where in a richly furnished library he would discuss politics with the French ambassador, ornithology with the local rabbi and astrology with the Greek Orthodox patriarch. Something of a proto-Zionist, as early as 1563 he tried to establish a Jewish settlement on the banks of Lake Tiberias in Palestine, attempting to obtain the money for the venture from the king of France.[21] Although this

★ *Marrano* was applied to those Iberian Jews who converted to Christianity.

project failed, by becoming one of Selim II's drinking pals he managed to obtain Naxos, together with the title of duke, as a fief from the sultan, Piyale Pasha obligingly evicting the island's legitimate ruler Giacomo Crispi. Harbouring a deep hatred of Venice, Nassi was considered by the Venetians the evil genius behind the sultan's drive to extend his rule over all the islands of the Aegean Sea.

But the sultan had more compelling problems on his plate before attempting expansionist enterprises. The war in Hungary was occupying the Ottoman army just when its presence was badly needed on other fronts. Zaydi Imam of the Yemen had revolted against the sultan's rule, expelling the Ottomans from most of the province, and to make matters worse the Arabs living in the marshes north of Basra had also rebelled. In order to avoid getting bogged down – literally – in Mesopotamia, Sokollu employed carrot-and-stick tactics to deal with the Arab uprising. In 1567 Ottoman troops launched a river-borne expedition against the rebels' bases, forcing their leader Ibn 'Ulayyan to submit. This show of force was immediately followed up by the sultan bestowing on the defeated Arab the title of governor, thus securing his loyalty in a key region on the border of Safavid Persia. In Hungary, after Süleyman's death there had been some desultory fighting, but by and large the two sides were happy to play a waiting game. Maximilian wanted peace and so did Sokollu; the former because the war was draining his financial resources, while the latter needed a free hand to deal with the Yemen problem. In September 1567 three Habsburg ambassadors arrived in Constantinople and were treated to an amicable audience with the sultan. The next five months witnessed much hard bargaining between the two parties, the ambassadors trying to win the grand vizier's favour, as well as that of other important officials, with rich monetary and material gifts. Finally, on 21 February 1568, an eight-year peace treaty between Maximilian and Selim was signed, apparently more or less restoring the situation in Hungary to the status quo ante; in reality, by recognizing Maximilian's rights to certain parts of Hungary, the pact turned out to be more favourable to the Habsburgs. Three days after the agreement the grand vizier made some extra requests, in particular asking that France be included in the treaty. This was a result of the French ambassador in Constantinople's attempt to put a spanner in the diplomatic works, fearful that peace between Maximilan and the Porte would encourage the former to try to recover Metz.[22] The Habsburg envoys politely refused Sokollu's demands, and the grand vizier gave in without insisting further. Both parties were satisfied with the pact, no one at this stage wanting to upset the apple cart.

With his hands free in Europe and Mesopotamia, Sokollu could now tackle the Yemen problem, also with an eye to palace politics. He skilfully managed to get Lala Mustafa appointed commander of the expedition, hoping he would discredit himself. Sure enough, no sooner had Lala Mustafa arrived in Egypt than he managed to get into a fight with the local governor-general, Koja Sinan Pasha, over the provisioning of the army. Lala Mustafa was dismissed from his post, returning to Constantinople apparently in disgrace, and Sinan appointed in his stead. Selim, however, continued to favour his old tutor, saving him from execution and appointing him vizier in 1569, thus thwarting Sokollu's plans.[23] Meanwhile, Sinan conducted a successful campaign in the Yemen, in 1568 capturing Taiz, and then Aden with a brilliant amphibious and overland attack. The following year he took Zaydi Imam's fortress of Sana'a and by 1570 the whole of Yemen was once more under the sultan's control. The conquest of this unruly province would shortly have a number of momentous consequences.

~

While the Ottomans were busy fighting in Hungary and in the Arabian peninsula, a new foe had arisen in Europe. On 7 January 1566, following the death of Pius IV the previous December, Cardinal Antonio Ghisleri was elected pope, taking the name Pius V. Destined to become one of the most celebrated pontiffs in the history of the Catholic Church, he was an incredibly strict yet extremely charitable man, born in 1504 of a noble but impoverished family from Alessandria in Piedmont. He joined the Dominican order, taking the name of Michele, and was ordained a priest in 1528. Striving to spread the authentic spirit of St Dominic among his brethren, Father Michele, as he then was, was the first to give an example: he fasted, did penance, meditated and prayed for long hours during the night, matters of God being constantly on his lips. His religious commitment brought him to the attention of Paul IV, who in 1556 made him bishop of Sutri and inquisitor for Lombardy. This promotion was followed in quick succession by a cardinal's hat, the title of inquisitor general and the diocese of Mondovì, where he made a name for not tolerating any breaches in ecclesiastical discipline. He often clashed with Paul IV's successor, Pius IV, not approving of the latter's worldly and nepotistic attitudes. As soon as he was elected pope, a position he accepted with reluctance, he made it known that he did not intend to favour his relatives in any way.[24] Many of his family who arrived in Rome with hopes of preferment were told that, if not really indigent, their connection to the pope was richness enough. Bowing to considerable pressure from the College of Cardinals, who thought it inappropriate that the pope should not create one of his nephews cardinal, he finally elevated to the purple his sister's son, Michele Bonelli. A few other deserving relatives over time were given administrative or military positions within the papal states. However, the pope did not hesitate to demote and banish one of his nephews on discovering his illicit love affairs.

Once elected, and despite the burdens of his office, Pius practised the virtues he had previously displayed as a friar and a bishop, praying constantly, visiting hospitals and tending personally to the needs of the sick. He also strived to impose greater standards of morality on the clergy, no matter the rank. Indeed, bishops now had to prove themselves spiritually, morally and intellectually qualified for the job and were obliged to reside in their dioceses. Pius was a giant in a century of giants.[25]

The pope was actually doing nothing more than putting into practice the dispositions and decrees of the Council of Trent.

Convened originally, as we have seen, by Paul III in 1545, the council had suffered up to 1560 a number of interruptions, postponements and relocations from its original meeting place. Despite this, it had managed to pass some fundamental doctrinal measures, including that on the correct interpretation of Holy Scripture, and one on justification by faith – incorporating some Lutheran elements. The delays which had occurred to the council's work were due mainly to the opposition of the various Catholic rulers of Europe, each of whom had his own political agenda and was unwilling to support a reform process – although officially in favour of it – that threatened to remove the Church from the control of secular powers. For instance, when Pius IV reconvened the council in 1560, the Holy Roman Emperor Ferdinand I attempted to have all decisions on matters of dogma deferred in order not to alienate his Protestant subjects. Nonetheless, the council worked with alacrity between 1562 and 1564, issuing proclamations on such matters as clerical celibacy, Holy Communion, relics, sacred images, the intercession of saints, the Church's independence vis-à-vis rulers, catechism, the mass, ecclesiastical benefices and discipline. All these matters were the subject of lively – and often heated – debates within the council. The obligation for bishops to reside in their dioceses was opposed by some members of the Roman Curia, in one case by arguing that the removal of so many bishops from Rome, together with their households, would ruin the city's economy. Many secular rulers opposed through their delegates ecclesiastical independence, and much negotiation was necessary before a document on this matter could be agreed upon. Yet, when Pius IV formally approved the council's decrees on 26 January 1565 nobody could doubt that, finally, the Church had done some very thorough house cleaning.[26] The clear language used in the official documents – something lacking in those of the later Second Vatican Council – meant that from then on Catholics would know where they stood, what they believed, what could be discussed and those articles of faith that could not. As for the Protestants, they were able to develop a clear sense of their own religious identity, the Council of

Trent having done away with the doctrinal ambiguity of the early years of the sixteenth century.

Notwithstanding their force, the Tridentine rulings risked becoming yet another of the many disregarded documents with which the history of the Church is littered. The peril was very real, given that most European states greeted the council's decrees unenthusiastically at best. The Italian states not under direct Spanish rule accepted them, and so did Poland. Spain acknowledged only those decrees that did not affect royal authority. The French crown, wishing to uphold its ecclesiastical privileges and not enrage its numerous Calvinist subjects, declined to accept Trent's rulings, and the Emperor Maximilian I decided that their official adoption would be imprudent. Protestant countries like Sweden, Scotland, England and Lutheran Germany simply ignored them. Yet the Council of Trent, secular opposition notwithstanding, boosted a movement within the Catholic clergy and laity for widespread religious renewal and reform which was destined to yield substantial results in the years to come. While many in the upper echelons of society were aping pagan practices, apparently not interested in the Church's plight, at the grass roots of Catholicism a renewed spirituality was in the making. For some decades the religiosity of orders like the Jesuits, the Theatines and the Capuchins, impeccable for their way of life and theological beliefs, had been progressing silently but steadily within the body of the Church.* By the 1550s an increasing number of high-ranking clergymen, including many of those who would attend the final sessions of the Council of Trent, shared this spiritual outlook. The reform movement within the Church was given a huge boost by Pius V, who in the six years of his pontificate strived incessantly for the implementation of the Tridentine decrees within the Catholic world.

But there were also other tasks facing the pope. In northern Europe and France Calvinism had gained significant footholds; in

---

* This despite the fact that one of the first Capuchin leaders, Bernardino Ochino, turned Protestant and escaped to Calvinist Geneva.

the Mediterranean the Ottomans appeared increasingly menacing. Practically from the day of his election Pius V started to canvass the creation of an anti-Muslim league with the Catholic rulers of Europe. The moment for such an alliance was favourable, the impending war in Hungary seen as a chance to bring together the forces of Spain and the Holy Roman Empire to inflict on the Ottomans a decisive blow.[27] Pius was hoping that France and Venice would also join the fight, but the Valois had too many problems at home – and in any case their alliance with the Porte was not up for discussion – while the Venetians were adamantly opposed to anything that might damage their Levantine trade. Philip II, always with an eye towards North Africa, expressed his interest in the venture, provided he could get enough money to finance an army and a fleet. Pius was only too happy to oblige, granting the king of Spain the renewal of the five-year subsidy, known as the *quinquennio* or *subsidio*, first granted by the Holy See in 1560. This was to be levied on the clergy of Castile and Aragon, and was supposed to finance a combined force of forty Spanish and sixty papal galleys.[28] Since the money ended up being handled by the Spanish treasury, in reality it could be used at Philip's discretion. The measure of Pius V's personal uprightness and sincerity can be seen by the fact that, unlike his predecessor, he did not ask for a single penny for himself or his relatives in exchange for the *subsidio*. As it happened, Sultan Süleyman's death, together with the end of hostilities in Hungary, lessened considerably Philip's interest in an anti-Ottoman crusade, the king considering such an enterprise fruitless and damaging if undertaken by Spain alone. Philip instructed his ambassador in Rome, Luis de Requesens, to obtain as much money possible from the pope, but to adopt a dilatory attitude every time the subject of military alliance against the Ottomans was broached.[29] In any case, Spain was distracted by another matter, which Philip considered far more important than fighting the Ottomans.

For some time trouble had been brewing in Flanders, where high-handed Spanish policies had ignited a general revolt. The causes of the uprising were many, but chief was the attack on the ancient liberties of the Flemish aristocracy. This was closely linked to the huge inroads made by Calvinism among the local population, resulting in widespread attacks on Catholic clergymen, buildings and religious objects. The regent of Flanders Margaret of Parma, illegitimate daughter of Charles V, had managed to restore a modicum of order by playing off the various Flemish factions against each other, but her tolerance of religious dissent did not go down well with Philip. In an attempt to restore royal authority and also implement the Tridentine decrees in the province, the king made the mistake of sending to Flanders the duke of Alva with a large army and extensive military powers. 'I don't know for what purpose,' commented the count of Egmont, a leading dissident noble, to Margaret. 'It is not possible to kill 200,000 people.'[30] Philip, who was planning to visit Flanders in person, was convinced that only by decisive action could bloodshed be averted, and to this purpose he gave Alva instructions to arrest and chastise the rebel leaders before his arrival. Not known for his subtlety, Alva did exactly that. Dissidents, both Catholic and Calvinist, were arrested, tried and executed, including leading nobles like the counts of Egmont and Horne. Another prominent dissident, William of Nassau, prince of Orange, saved his neck by escaping to Germany, where he immediately started organizing anti-Spanish resistance. In all, some 1,700 people lost their lives during the repression, and instead of solving the Flanders problem Alva's ham-fisted behaviour managed only to alienate everyone in the region, including those previously favourable to Habsburg rule. By the end of 1568 armed revolt was widespread in Flanders, Alva's army several times having to fight forces advancing from Germany and France under the sponsorship of William of Orange. Although the Spanish proved victorious on each occasion, they would be stuck fighting in Flanders for the next eighty years. Ultimately, the Flemish revolt, with all its international implications, would prove a ruinous drain on Spain's finances.[31]

Knowing from the beginning that Flanders would be a costly enterprise, Philip started pressuring the pope for more money. Pius, however, was initially unwilling to grant any more subsidies, having already authorized the *quinquennio*. What irritated the pope most was that despite all the funds he had managed to collect for the maintenance of the Spanish fleet (500,000 ducats, three-quarters of its costs),[32] the king was delaying sending his galleys to protect the coasts of the papal states, with the excuse that he had to defend his own extensive maritime frontiers.[33] In the end, Pius was forced to yield to the king's requests, concerns about the spread of heresy in Flanders playing a decisive role in the pope's decision. The king was given the right to collect a five-year tax, known as the *excusado*, diverting from the Church's revenues a tithe on every third house of each parish in the Iberian peninsula. The purpose of this levy was not just to help pay the army about to go to Flanders, but also to cover the expenses incurred by Philip in defending Christendom against the Turks.[34] Yet, in the face of Spain's procrastinations over defending the papal territories against Muslims raids, Pius was forced to look elsewhere for protection, his position and prestige allowing him to play at more than one table in the international gaming room. In any case, he had now a willing partner: Cosimo I de' Medici, duke of Florence and Siena.

Philip II's bestowal of Siena on Cosimo I had tied the latter to Spain in an unequivocal manner: not only was Cosimo now a Habsburg vassal, he also had to provide free of charge his galleys and a substantial number of troops (4,000 foot and 400 horse) every time the Spanish-ruled duchy of Milan or the kingdom of Naples came under attack. In addition, the duke was effectively denied the ability to make alliances with other states without Spain's approval.[35] Cosimo had tried to escape the suffocating Habsburg embrace, by upholding the independence of his Florentine territories and then by creating the knightly Order of St Stephen with the open support of Pope Pius IV. Philip disliked the new order,[36] correctly perceiving that by founding a knightly organization, canonically subjected to the Holy See,* the crafty Florentine was attempting to pursue an independent military policy. But Cosimo could not count on Philip for defence – Spain having already too many commitments – and the duke was aware that the security of his states depended on advancing his sea borders to the North African coasts.³⁷ This ambitious policy involved considerable costs which Cosimo could ill afford, and the duke tried to have it both ways by loaning in the mid-1560s ten galleys to Philip II for a five-year period. The terms of the contract (*asiento*) were heavily stacked against Cosimo, who for all intents and purposes had handed over his entire fleet to the king's discretion.³⁸ But the duke needed time to build up the Order of St Stephen's strength and reputation, and so for the moment was content for his own sea forces to acquire some useful experience by working with a well-established navy. In any case, at its foundation the Order of St Stephen had received a gift of two galleys from the duke, the *Lupa* and the *Fiorenza Nuova*, thus allowing it to operate independently from the Spanish fleet.

Maritime skill was something not to be acquired overnight, as the duke would learn to his expense. Eager to show his flag, in 1560 Cosimo had sent four galleys to join the Djerba expedition, only to lose two in the ensuing disaster. These losses were somewhat compensated for by the capture a month later of three Muslim galliots,³⁹ but significant results were to be obtained only through trial and error. In July 1563 a Florentine force was sent to aid the Spanish force engaged in the relief of Oran, then besieged by Dragut. En route the *Lupa* lost its mainmast, forcing the galley to head back alone to the port of Livorno for repairs. No sooner had the *Lupa* distanced herself from the rest of the squadron, than she

---

* The Order of St Stephen was closely modelled on the Spanish Order of Santiago, whose members were not monks but laymen who took vows of chastity within marriage and obedience to the grand master – the king from the end of the fifteenth century. Within the framework of canon law the Order of St Stephen can be conceived as a papal institution 'entrusted' to a ruler for a specific purpose, in this case the defence of Christendom. For the Order of St Stephen as an institution of canon law, see: N[ERI] CAPPONI: 39–54.

was jumped by two Muslim galliots. The *Lupa*'s makeshift crew managed to swim ashore, leaving the knights of St Stephen on board to fend for themselves. Many of them died during the battle that followed, while others were taken prisoner and enslaved.[40] For the budding order it was a serious blow, and during the following years the knights preferred always to operate in conjunction with the Spanish. Only in 1569 did the order gain its first significant victory, a force of four galleys catching and defeating in a seven-hour battle an enemy squadron of five commanded by the redoubtable corsair Kara Ali. The Florentines managed to capture two of the Muslim vessels, securing 310 prisoners and freeing 220 Christian slaves with the loss of 70 killed and 90 wounded. The Florentine ships also suffered much damage, and on their return to Livorno people commented that they looked more the vanquished than the victors.[41]

Despite their grievous losses, Cosimo could be satisfied with the knights' success, since it gave the Medici some much-needed international prestige. It also allowed the duke to take a more independent stance towards Spain in the Mediterranean. In any case, Cosimo was deeply unhappy with Philip II's attitude towards him, the king for instance refusing to pay for two Florentine galleys sunk in a storm while transporting Spanish troops from Italy to the south of Spain. The duke tried to corner the king by informing him that in such circumstances it was impossible for him to observe the terms of the *asiento*, and offering to renegotiate it on terms more favourable to himself. In exchange, Cosimo was prepared to arm up to fourteen galleys for Philip's service, but the king answered curtly that the matter would be discussed once the present contract expired. Philip was short of money, and continually pestering the pope for the renewal of the *cruzada*, which, with the *quinquennio* and the *excusado*, formed what were known as the Three Graces. Based on the sale of bulls of indulgence, the *cruzada* had first been granted in 1482, yielding, according to a seventeenth-century source, 800,000 ducats a year.[42] The pope was reluctant to renew the *cruzada*, and not just because he had already subsidized in abundance the always money-starved Spanish crown. One of the decrees of the Council of Trent had clearly stated that indulgences should be granted with moderation, 'less ecclesiastical discipline be too easily weakened'.[43] Since the sale of indulgences had been the spark that had set alight the powder keg of the Reformation, it is more than understandable that Pius V was reluctant to grant the *cruzada*. Cosimo, on the other hand, had every interest in Spain's coffers being full, but at the same time perceived that the pope could give him much more than the Habsburgs.

Cosimo was painfully aware of being a newcomer on the international scene. Not only was his ducal title recent, but also it had been originally bestowed on the Medici by the Florentines themselves. Only later had Charles V confirmed the title, and Cosimo had done much to better his own situation by marrying Eleanor of Toledo, daughter of the viceroy of Naples. But nobody ever allowed the duke to forget his family's merchant origins – his cousin Catherine's marriage to the second son of Francis I was considered by the French very much of a *mésalliance*,[44] – and Cosimo's frustration was increased by the fact that he was from a secondary, impoverished, branch of the Medici. There was also the question of precedence, in European courts the ambassadors of the dukes of Savoy, Ferrara and Mantua always preceding their Florentine colleagues during audiences or official events.* Cosimo's attempts, with the backing of pope Pius IV, to see his dominion elevated to an archduchy were rebuffed by Emperor Maximilian II, his Habsburg relatives having no intention of seeing an Italian upstart become their equal. In the face of this refusal, Pius IV had intended before his death to bestow himself a title on Cosimo.

His successor Pius V was initially much less favourably inclined

---

* While for us such matters may appear trivial, they were hugely important in the sixteenth century. Ambassadorial precedence was not only a matter of prestige, but also determined who would be first to get a ruler's ear. Since at the time in Italy there were no independent kingdoms (the papal states were not considered such, being an exception in every way) the fight for precedence involved duchies, marquisates, counties, lordships and republics.

towards the duke of Florence, since the latter was known to harbour one of the leading Italian Protestants, the former secretary of Clement VII Pietro Carnesecchi. Cosimo had up to then managed to protect Carnesecchi from the inquisition, but now for reasons of political expediency agreed to turn him over to the pope's envoys. Predictably, and notwithstanding his former protector's pleas for clemency, Carnesecchi was found guilty and executed in October 1567. But Cosimo now could count on Pius's benevolence, and the duke repaid this attitude by taking a decisive stand against the reformed religion, to the point of sending an expeditionary force to fight in France against the Huguenots. The pope then gave Cosimo what he most coveted: an elevation in rank by granting him the title of grand duke of Tuscany in September 1569. From a strictly legal point of view Pius was acting beyond the limits of the law – Tuscany being part of the Holy Roman Empire – but since Maximilian had given his tacit consent, although he never formalized it so as not to displease the duke of Ferrara, the pope considered he was acting within his prerogatives, which included conferring titles of sovereignty.[45]

Pius's move provoked uproar in all the European courts. Cosimo immediately tried to distance himself from the quarrel, maintaining that the grand ducal title was nothing but honorific – not desiring for one thing to accept any overlord for what he regarded as his own Florentine territories. Maximilian was furious. Philip II threatened to reclaim Siena for his half-brother Don Juan of Austria. The king of Spain was also miffed by Cosimo's attempts to woo France, something that risked igniting anew the Italian wars. Philip would have been even more enraged if he had known at the time that since 1562 the Medici and the Valois had agreed to a pact of mutual support in the face of the Habsburgs' overbearing presence.[46] Yet Cosimo had no desire to favour a French return to Italy, in September 1570 writing to the dowager queen of France Catherine de' Medici that on the matter of the grand ducal title he did not wish her 'to take on any burden in this affair', adding that the emperor knew that Cosimo was 'the same servant to Him, as my actions have always proved'.[47] Moreover, by this date many things had changed in the Mediterranean theatre, allowing Cosimo greater opportunities for diplomatic manoeuvring.

~

As much as Philip may have desired to punish his disloyal ally, he had plenty of worries in Spain. First there had been the death of his deranged son Don Carlos, whom the king had been forced to lock up because of his bizarre behaviour. To make matters worse, the royal authorities attempted to conceal the whole matter behind a thick veil of secrecy, allowing Philip's enemies to speculate wildly on the circumstances surrounding the unfortunate prince's fate.[48] Philip soon received another blow, his wife Elizabeth of Valois dying a few months later after delivering a stillborn child. The king was stricken with grief, but could ill afford to let sorrow interfere with his duties as head of state. In fact, he was about to face an emergency within the Iberian peninsula requiring his full attention.

Despite attempts by the Spanish authorities over the years to enforce Christianity on the Moriscos, the majority had remained practising Muslims. The decrees of 1526 forbidding their ancient customs had been largely ignored, in particular after the payment of a large sum of money by the communities of Granada and Valencia. In many cases the Moriscos adopted *taqiyya*, or dissimulation – a practice allowed by Islamic law to Muslims living in a religiously unfavourable environment. By the mid-sixteenth century the situation of the Spanish Islamic community was very bad. Restrictions imposed by the central authorities on their traditional silk trade had left many Moriscos impoverished, and in addition they were subject to increasing attentions from the inquisition. Still, many local nobles in Spain favoured a policy of tolerance towards their Islamic subjects, since they were an important source of labour and revenue. However, a number of clergymen, in particular the bishop of Siguenza and future cardinal Diego Espinosa, president of the Council of Castile, adamantly opposed this lenient attitude, demanding that vigorous measures be employed to stamp out Morisco language, customs and dress.

The crown started doing this at the beginning of 1567, despite the protests of a number of Andalusian landlords, headed by the captain-general of Andalusia Iñigo López de Mendoza, count of Tendilla, who correctly foresaw trouble. While religious intolerance undoubtedly played a part in this repression, people like Espinosa feared that differences in belief would lead to social unrest. Espinosa was also closely linked to Pedro de Deza, whose family had a running feud with the Mendozas, and had Deza himself appointed to enforce the ban against Morisco practices. It is also true that the Iberian Muslims were seen as more than just a potential threat to internal security; in the eventuality of a Muslim inroad, in no way could the Spanish be sure that they would not side with the invaders. In 1565 the discovery of an alleged Morisco spy ring revealed a plan to seize the coast of southern Spain while the Ottomans attacked Malta. There was also fear about supposed Huguenot infiltration of Catalonia, and the Catalans' reluctance to pay the *excusado* in the name of their ancient liberties was seen as an indication that the region was about to turn Protestant. With the spectre of an imminent Muslim invasion aided by a Morisco – and maybe also a Huguenot – fifth column looming over their heads the repressive measures of the Spanish authorities were more than an exaggerated manifestation of religious zeal.[49]

Rumours that an uprising was planned for Holy Thursday 1568 provoked increased police measures by the government against its Islamic subjects; but these only served to postpone the rebellion to the following Christmas Eve, when many Muslim communities rose up in arms, sacking Christian houses and churches, and putting many people to the sword. From an estimated 4,000 at the beginning of the uprising, the insurgents' numbers swelled rapidly, reaching a strength of 30,000 by the summer of 1569. Unable to take Granada immediately due to bad timing and inclement weather, the rebellious Muslims retreated into the mountains to conduct a guerrilla war. All the elements of Morisco culture were resurrected, in particular ancient religious and civic practices. Their leader Hernando de Cordoba y Valor, who had reverted to his Muslim name of Abu Humeya, was proclaimed king in the course of an elaborate traditional ceremony. The rebels did not limit themselves to purely exterior manifestations of sovereignty; the capture of a number of small ports in the south of Spain allowed them to establish political and military links with the Islamic states of North Africa, and a request for help was sent to Constantinople.[50] The fear of an Ottoman attack against the south of Spain was a real concern for Philip's officials, at one point the Spanish ambassador in Paris reporting that three Jews from Salonika had arrived in the French capital with the secret news that the Ottomans were putting together a fleet to help the Moriscos. The sultan, as we shall see presently, had other plans, but nonetheless sent orders to the governor of Algiers Uluç Ali Pasha to aid the Spanish rebels with men and materiel, and indeed Muslim volunteers would fight at the side of their beleaguered Iberian brothers. But arms remained always a scarce commodity for the insurgents, to the point that in the Andalusian coastal town of Sorbas a Christian slave could be exchanged for a gun or a few edged weapons.[51]

The Spanish authorities acted quickly, relying on the man on the spot, the count of Tendilla, to crush the revolt. The Habsburg war machine needed time to get moving, and in any case few royal soldiers were available in Spain, most regular troops having been sent to Flanders. Tendilla did the best he could with his meagre forces, managing to obtain some results by using force coupled with diplomacy. In particular he advocated a policy of tolerance and mercy, maintaining that it was the best way to solve the problem quickly. The king, however, fearing that the rebellion could spread to other parts of Morisco Spain, opted for a more muscular approach, replacing Tendilla with his own half-brother Don Juan of Austria.

The change of commander initially did not produce much in the way of military success. Don Juan was young and inexperienced, and in the meantime the Moriscos had reorganized their forces. As a result, the royal troops suffered a number of reverses. On 3 May the marquis of Los Vélez was roundly defeated while trying to capture the port of La Ragua. The war, already displaying all the brutality of a religious struggle, was destined to become more savage as time went by, many atrocities being committed by both sides. In February 1570 royal troops took the town of Galera, putting the whole population of 2,500 to the sword, razing the settlement and pouring salt over the ruins. Massive influxes of soldiers and weapons from Italy helped to turn the tide in favour of the Habsburgs, and by mid-1570 it was clear that the Moriscos could not hold out much longer despite the help of some 4,000 Turks and North African Muslims. In order to whip up support and cash for the crown, Philip himself had made an extensive, and in many cases triumphant, visit to the south of Spain in the winter and spring of the same year. The rebels were left with no other option than to seek terms, and by the end of November the revolt was over. The aftermath was to be more tragic than the war itself. Fearing future uprisings, the authorities deported some 80,000 Moriscos from Granada, scattering them all over the Iberian peninsula. Nearly 15,000 died during the process; others were enslaved under the pretext that, although baptized, they had abandoned Christ for Muhammad.[52]

The period 1568–70 had been *horribilis* for the Spanish Habsburgs, and not just for the Morisco and Flemish rebellions. The rulers of Tunis had for a long time been closely controlled by the Spanish, who held the key fortress of La Goleta at the mouth of the city's harbour. In 1568 the lord of Tunis was Mawlay Hamida, who in his twenty years of rule had managed to alienate practically everybody. With the Spanish fully occupied with revolts in Flanders and at home, Uluç Ali, *beylerbey* of Algiers, decided to act. In October of the same year he led a force of some 5,000 crack troops overland towards Tunis, the ranks of his army augmented during the march by numerous volunteers picked up en route. Mawlay Hamida's regime collapsed practically without a fight, and the deposed ruler saved his skin only by taking refuge with the Spanish in La Goleta. On 19 January 1569 Uluç Ali made his formal entry into Tunis, busying himself over the following two months with the reorganization of the city's administration. When he departed for Algiers at the end of March he left behind a large garrison, paid by the citizenry, under the command of one of his lieutenants.[53] The Spanish presence in North Africa was now confined to a small number of scattered and beleaguered outposts, which could count on little assistance from Philip II in the event of a determined Muslim attack. The Ottomans were indeed about to strike, but luckily for the Habsburgs they were not to be the objective.

5. CYPRUS

~

As Piyale Pasha was preparing to sail for Chios in the spring of 1566, the authorities in Venice received some very alarming news: in a letter of the previous 13 January, the Venetian *bailo* in Constantinople Vettore Bragadin had informed them of the existence of an Ottoman plan to invade Cyprus.[1] Venice and the Porte had been at peace since 1540, and the republic was concerned that after Süleyman's death its possessions in the Levant would be in danger. Now it appeared that the storm would burst even before the aged sultan was lowered into his grave. Luckily for Venice, the losses incurred by the Ottomans at Malta and during the war in Hungary did not allow them to pick a target bigger than Chios. The Venetians watched anxiously the unfolding of events in the months following the transition from Süleyman to Selim II, and were relieved to receive in July 1567 the news that the new sultan had confirmed the previous peace treaty between the two states. Selim, however, had added to the treaty a clause to the effect that all captured Ottoman pirates should be handed over to the Porte for punishment. The Venetians accepted the clause, although it was difficult to implement, prompting the papal nuncio in Venice to comment that the sultan had 'an open door to break the treaty should this suit him'.[2]

But the Venetians remained uneasy about the Ottomans'

intentions towards Cyprus, and with good reason. Between 1567 and 1570 Venice's efficient secret services received a series of warnings about Ottoman espionage activities on the island.[3] The number of reports indicates the Ottomans having accomplices among the local population and it was known that many Cypriots were dissatisfied with Venetian rule, some even asking the sultan in writing to take over the isle.[4]

A real scare for Venice came in September 1568, when a fleet of sixty-four galleys under Müezzinzâde Ali Pasha dropped anchor off Cyprus. When the island's officials boarded the Ottoman admiral's galleys for the ritual courtesy visit, Ali proved to be most inquisitive about the new fortress being built at Nicosia. He objected that there was no need for such a fortress, Venice being at peace with the Porte, and in the unlikely event of a Spanish attack – the Habsburgs were always considered potential enemies by the Venetians – the sultan would surely aid his friends. The admiral appeared to be satisfied with the officials' answer that the construction was a way to provide employment for the island's needy inhabitants. The Ottomans then sailed into the harbour of Famagusta and were graciously received by its captain Marco Michel, who, out of courtesy and because there was no viable alternative, showed them the city's fortifications.

The Turks exploited their time on Cyprus to do some thorough spying, even using the excuse of finding ancient columns for one of the sultan's palaces. Müezzinzâde Ali, however, did not attempt the same trick Piyale Pasha had used in Chios, returning instead to Constantinople to report his findings to the sultan.[5] It was too late in the season to start a campaign, and in any case the war in the Yemen was absorbing most of the Ottomans' military potential. But during the course of the following year rumours of an imminent Ottoman attack abounded, although there was much debate over whether the fleet being prepared in Constantinople was intended instead to aid the Moriscos in Spain. But the Venetians knew that Selim's Jewish adviser Joseph Nassi had visited Cyprus with the Ottoman fleet, and by the end of December the Venetian *bailo*

Marcantonio Barbaro was pretty sure that the objective of the Porte's military preparations could only be Cyprus.[6]

The Venetian's deductions were not based on rumours as much as on an understanding of the Ottomans' geo-strategic goals. Cyprus was, even more than Chios, a thorn in their flesh. Not only did its harbours provide havens for Western corsairs and pirates, but the island was also within striking distance of the Anatolian coast. Every time the Ottomans went on campaign, troops and ships had to be left behind against a potential attack from Cyprus. There was also the contraband problem. By the mid-sixteenth century, the Near East, once the granary of the Mediterranean, produced only enough grain to satisfy local consumption. The Porte reacted by repeatedly banning the export of grain, knowing perfectly well that hunger is a ready trigger for social disorder. Cyprus was a nest of grain smugglers and a danger to the commercial route between Constantinople and Alexandria in Egypt.[7] The Ottomans' campaigns in the Yemen after Selim II's accession were motivated by their desire to chastise a rebellious province, but also derived from the need to protect the Red Sea trade routes, the Portuguese by now having become a permanent and aggressive presence in the area as well as in the Indian Ocean. Süleyman's attempts to evict them from Hormuz had ended in failure, and Ottoman vessels soon proved to be no match on the high seas for the square-rigged Lusitanian ships. At the same time all Portuguese attempts to establish bases in the Red Sea had been repulsed, but in order to face any future challenges from this sector it was important for the Ottomans that there should be no obstacle to the transfer of military resources from the north to the south of their empire. Cyprus was one such obstacle, and to make matters more serious it was also a threat to the pilgrims taking the sea route from Constantinople to Mecca and Medina. In 1517 the Ottomans had declared themselves the protectors of Islam's holy cities, and no sultan who wished to be considered a pious Muslim could allow pilgrim ships to come under attack.[8]

Cyprus was also a hindrance to the development of the Porte's grand strategy, which required a coordinated effort in the Mediterranean and in Asia. The need to rapidly switch military resources to curb the activities of their various enemies and the desire to find alternative trade routes had caused the Ottomans to look at the possibility of building canals to unite the rivers Don and Volga, and to connect the Red Sea to the Mediterranean. These two engineering projects would have allowed the Ottomans to bypass the Safavid empire and rapidly deploy military and economic resources as far as the Persian Gulf. For such plans to be implemented in full, Cyprus had to be Ottoman, by treaty or by force. In 1569 the capture by pirates of the ship carrying the *defterdar* (treasurer) of Egypt dispelled any of Selim's residual doubts. On hearing the news he flew into a rage, and from then the conquest of Cyprus became central to the Porte's political agenda.[9]

In November 1569 Selim went hunting, accompanied by the members of the *dîvân*, specifically to discuss the takeover of Cyprus. As the chase proceeded, the various ministers rode up in turn to the sultan's side to give their opinion on the matter. Sokollu Mehmed tried to dissuade Selim from going to war with Venice, pointing out that it would be damaging for the economy, since the Ottomans benefited substantially from trade with the republic. He felt it would be more fruitful in the long run to aid the Moriscos, not only for reasons of religious brotherhood, but also to keep the Spanish busy. Finally, there was always the risk that the invasion of Cyprus could produce an anti-Ottoman alliance, with unpredictable results. Piyale Pasha and Lala Mustafa Pasha, who both hated Sokollu as well as having a vested interest in the Cyprus enterprise, hotly upheld the necessity of war. Piyale was hoping to regain his position as *kapudan paşa*, and Lala Mustafa wanted command of the invasion army in order to restore his tarnished military reputation. The two viziers underscored the military and geographical problems involved in aiding the Moriscos. On the other hand, Cyprus was near and a Venetian relief force would have to cross half the Mediterranean before reaching the island. The divisions among the Western powers made the creation of an anti-Ottoman alliance unlikely in the short run, and Cyprus was expected not to be too hard a nut to crack. Selim was swayed by these arguments, although it is possible that he had already been convinced by Joseph Nassi, who later would be seen as the villain of the piece, the evil genius behind Selim's decision to go to war against Venice.* He certainly played a part in convincing the sultan, and not just out of hatred for the Venetians. He had extensive economic interests in the Aegean wine trade and held the monopoly on the importation of timber for wine barrels. Nassi supported the Cyprus enterprise because the island's large wine production promised considerable profits.[10]

Besides distance, the Ottomans had other reasons to believe that Venice would be incapable of defending Cyprus. On the night of the 13–14 September 1569 the explosion of a powder magazine in the Venetian arsenal ignited a general conflagration. Nearby houses and churches were destroyed or severely damaged, but luckily the lack of wind hindered the spread of flames. In the end, apart from four galleys, in the arsenal only the buildings used to store munitions and a section of the wall surrounding the compound were destroyed – not an excessive loss in monetary terms. The Venetian authorities launched an inquiry to ascertain who could have been responsible for the conflagration. Almost immediately rumours started that Ottoman agents or saboteurs in the pay of Joseph Nassi had caused the explosion, but investigations in this direction proved inconclusive. When news of the blaze reached Constantinople, the Ottomans believed that the Venetians had suffered greater damage than in reality they had. This gave extra fuel to the arguments of the war party, who asserted that Venice was in a state of military paralysis.[11] Even if the real facts had been known, it would probably have not made much of a difference to the warmongers. It would take some time for Venice to replenish its ammunition stocks, and while this was in no way crippling the Venetians in the meantime could react but slowly.

---

* According to von Hammer, Selim promised to make his friend king of Cyprus, and Nassi created for himself a coat of arms with this title (HAMMER: 195).

Sokollu was still trying to stem the tide of war, knowing that the only possible way to do so was to convince the Venetians to cede Cyprus peacefully. At the end of January 1570 he agreed to meet Marcantonio Barbaro, worried about rumours of an imminent Ottoman attack on the island. It was known, for instance, that the previous October Lala Mustafa Pasha had informed the French ambassador in Constantinople about a planned assault on Cyprus. Mustafa had also suggested that maybe the king of France or the duke of Savoy might advance their claims to the island and become tributaries of the Porte, something that the Ottomans would consider economically more convenient than direct rule.[12] As much as we may doubt Mustafa's sincerity, the episode is nonetheless indicative of the attempts of the war party in Istanbul to isolate Venice diplomatically before striking. Both the French kings and the dukes of Savoy possessed ancient claims to Cyprus – a relic of the crusades – but neither were in a position to assert their rights over the island. Still, by dangling Cyprus in front of their noses, the sultan could hope that they would be more reluctant to take up arms against the Porte.

When Barbaro met Sokollu he protested that the Venetians had always been friends with the Porte, having systematically refused in the past to join anti-Ottoman alliances. Sokollu, who previously had told Barbaro that the Ottomans intended to aid the Moriscos, answered that he was sorry about what was happening, but there had been many examples of the Venetians violating the terms of the peace treaty. Now the affair was in the hands of Muslim doctors of divinity, and since it had become a 'matter of religion' there could be no going back. Sokollu then asked the distance between Venice and Cyprus. Slightly baffled by the question, Barbaro answered that it was about 2,000 miles. To which Sokollu retorted, 'What do you think you can do with such a distant island, that gives you no profit and causes only trouble? It will be better off in our hands, since we have so many possessions nearby.' The sultan was determined to have Cyprus, and it would be better not to waste time, men and money defending it. The only comment that Barbaro could offer in response was that 'dignity and reputation' compelled states to defend their possessions.[13]

When Sokollu had spoken about matters of religion he had not been dissembling, for the war party had managed to obtain the support of Chief Mufti Ebu's-su'ud. By this stage the chief mufti, the *şeyhü'l-islam*, had acquired considerable influence in matters of state policy; although not a member of the imperial council, he had obtained the right to nominate candidates for the best-paying professorships and judicial posts, and continually engaged the state administration in struggles over jurisdiction. The grand viziers hotly resented the mufti's meddling, provoking from one of them the outburst that instead of intervening in state affairs, the *şeyhü'l-islam* should keep himself busy by 'seeking answers to religious questions'.[14] Yet it was precisely because of his authority in divinity matters that the mufti had become a permanent presence in Ottoman political life. He was the highest interpreter of divine law, and thus no official, not even the sultan himself, could disregard his opinion. Given the importance of religion in Ottoman and all other cultures any fatwa issued by the *şeyhü'l-islam* carried enormous weight. At the same time, when it came to questions regarding matters of state any mufti with political sense would know exactly what sort of opinion was expected from him. When the sultan delivered to Ebu's-su'ud the question of whether it was legitimate to break a peace treaty in order to restore to the true faith a country that once had been under Muslim rule – Cyprus having been under Arab domination from the seventh to the tenth century – the mufti, quoting Islamic sacred texts, had no problem stating that any treaty with the infidels could be broken should this bring advantage to the universal community of the true believers.[15] This sort of religious carte blanche was exactly what the war party needed, and an invasion became pretty much inevitable.

The mufti's ruling was mainly intended for internal consumption, the Ottomans being too politically savvy to use it in the international arena. Instead, in denouncing the treaty with Venice they protested the many violations of the pact committed by the

Venetians over the years: building castles and villages in border regions; protecting pirates and allowing them to use Cyprus as a logistic base; executing captured Muslim pirates. It was true that during the previous few years there had been a number of violations of the Venetian–Ottoman treaty, but these were not limited to one side. The Venetians had indeed rebuilt the border castles destroyed during the previous war, and worse were using them as raiding bases against Ottoman territory. On the other hand, Muslim corsairs had been attacking ships in the Adriatic with the complicity of the local Ottoman authorities. The commander of the Egyptian squadron Şuluç Mehmed Pasha had captured a Venetian ship, imprisoning the crew, and the same had happened to a number of Spanish soldiers on board two other Venetian vessels arbitrarily taken by the Ottomans. Venice, however, habitually executed any Islamic corsair it managed to catch rather than sending the culprit to Constantinople for punishment.[16] As often happens in history, fault is born an orphan and dies a spinster.

The sultan's representative, the çavuş Kubad, brought all his master's grievances to Venice at the end of March 1570, accompanying them with an ultimatum that only by giving up Cyprus peacefully would Venice retain the Porte's friendship. Sokollu Mehmed also sent a letter, repeating the same arguments and inviting the Venetians to be reasonable, given the costs of a war and the difficulty the republic had in finding allies. The Venetians had been expecting this for some time, and over the previous months had quietly strengthened their overseas defences, recruited soldiers and mariners, and built new ships. Doge Pietro Loredan dismissed Kubad, saying that justice would give the Venetians the sword to defend their rights, and God would aid them to defeat the sultan's unjust violence. An official reply in the same tone was sent to Selim, together with a covering letter to Sokollu Mehmed ending with the words, '[the sultan] will be an example to all princes how much they can trust his promises'. [17]

On his way back to Constantinople Kubad stopped in Dubrovnik, divulging the news that Venice had declared war. Immediately, the Ottoman forces in the area launched a series of raids across the border, remaining a menace to Venice for the rest of the conflict. Kubad arrived in Istanbul on 5 May, and informed his master of the doge's decision. Selim may have expected his answer but was apparently irritated by the fact that Loredan addressed him simply as 'The Most Serene and Excellent Lord Emperor of the Turks', omitting all his other titles. What really enraged the sultan, however, was another episode. Two months before Kubad's arrival in Venice the French diplomat Claude Du Bourg de Guérines had arrived in the city accompanied by Mahmud Bey, the sultan's ambassador to the king of France. The two men intended to proceed to Paris to formalize a treaty negotiated between Du Bourg and the Porte, although the former had by now incurred Charles IX's displeasure. Du Bourg left soon after, leaving behind Mahmud Bey as a guest of the French ambassador in Venice. Suspicions soon arose about the Ottoman envoy's real mission, and on 6 March he was arrested and locked up with his entourage by the Venetian authorities. No justification was given for this action, but it was common knowledge that Mahmud had been sent by the sultan to spy on the Venetians. When Selim heard the news, he ordered the arrest of all the Venetian diplomats in the Ottoman empire, Marcantonio Barbaro being consigned to the fortress of Alcasabach. Initially his confinement was not too strict, with only a small number of janissaries to watch him. Later, the Ottoman authorities would tighten the screws, sealing all doors and windows of Barbaro's quarters. Nevertheless, he still managed to send information to Venice by circuitous routes with the aid of Sokollu's Jewish doctor Solomon Ashkenazi, a sworn enemy of Joseph Nassi. Barbaro was aware that Sokollu was intercepting all letters to and from Venice, although reading them was a different matter as they were mostly in code. In any case, the *bailo* and the grand vizier depended on each other: the former to get information to Venice; the latter to keep a diplomatic channel open with the Republic of St Mark.[18]

Military activities picked up in mid-spring with an Ottoman attack on the island of Tinos, south of Evvoia and one of Venice's strategic outposts in the eastern Mediterranean. Piyale Pasha, the vizier senior to the *kapudan paşa* in charge of naval operations, believed the island to be easy prey and its conquest the first step to restore his reputation. But the governor of Tinos, Girolamo Paruta, expected mischief and had taken adequate countermeasures. Piyale moved down the coast of Evvoia, arriving at his objective in the early hours of 5 May. Hoping to catch the Venetians napping, he landed 8,000 men and sent them to assault the island's main stronghold. Paruta, warned of the impending Ottoman arrival, managed to bring most of the inhabitants within the walls and then proceeded to engage the attackers with a brisk cannonade. Frustrated in their attempt at surprise, the Turks brought forward their artillery and opened fire on the fortress, hoping to create a breach in its walls. Getting nowhere, Piyale settled his men down for a siege, in the meantime conducting systematic raiding operations across the island. After ten days, having torched houses, destroyed churches and killed livestock, Piyale left for Rhodes with little more than his losses to show for the attack. The first round had gone to the Venetians, but a long and gruelling match lay ahead.

Even before war was formally declared, the states of Europe had had their eyes fixed on the Levant. The Venetians, who until then had snubbed every proposal for an anti-Ottoman alliance, suddenly became very concerned about the Ottoman threat to Christendom. Initially the republic showed some reluctance in joining forces with the Spaniards, fearing not only the Habsburgs' hegemonic designs over Italy, but also that it might be asked to defend Spanish possessions in North Africa.[19] Towards Rome they had a different attitude, everybody knowing Pius V's willingness to create a league to stop the Muslim advance. But the pope was at loggerheads with Philip II, still fuming because Pius had bestowed the grand ducal crown of Tuscany on Cosimo I de' Medici. Apart from resenting what he considered to be the pope's unjustifiable interference in matters outside his jurisdiction, Philip's chagrin had been increased by the presence at Cosimo's coronation of Marcantonio Colonna and Paolo Giordano Orsini. That Colonna was the hereditary high constable of the kingdom of Naples was particularly annoying, and the fact that Orsini's family had always been pro-French made the king suspect mischief. Indeed, some of Philip's ministers were convinced that Pius's attempts to create an anti-Ottoman alliance involving the Italian states would weaken the Habsburgs' presence in the peninsula, and were 'the true way to throw us out of Italy'.[20]

It was in this climate of suspicion that Pius met the Spanish ambassador Juan de Zuñiga at the beginning of March. The pope informed Zuñiga of the imminent Ottoman war against the Venetians, adding that the latter would be willing to conclude a defensive alliance with the Spaniards. Zuñiga answered that the Venetians were always out for themselves, and once the Turkish peril had passed would happily resume relations with Constantinople. In any case, any alliance was conditional on the pope's renewal of the *cruzada*, since without it the king could not possibly defend his territories let alone fight the Ottomans. Zuñiga was following Madrid's orders, and in another meeting with Pius a few weeks later he again expressed his scepticism about Venice's real intentions, stating that the Venetians would probably try to strike a deal with the Ottomans. However, he suggested to Philip that it would be better to send his galleys to Sicily, the Ottomans' real objective being still unclear, and that an alliance like the one envisaged by the pope could turn out to Spain's advantage in the long run.[21]

Pius decided to approach Philip in person, and in mid-March sent Monsignor Luis de Torres to the Spanish court. Torres arrived in Cordova on 19 April 1570 and two days later had a long interview with Philip. The king proved not ill-disposed towards the idea of a league between the papacy, Spain and Venice, adding however that since it was a serious matter it needed to be thought through. Two days later Torres dined with Cardinal Espinosa, who informed him that the king was prepared to send all his available galleys to

Sicily and also that he would write to the viceroys of Naples and Sicily ordering them to provide victuals for the Venetian fleet.[22] Philip was willing to do something to 'please the Pope and provide always for Christendom's needs' – as he would write to his naval commander, Giovanni Andrea Doria.[23] The king, as we have seen, had his own reasons for sending his fleet to the south of Italy, and intended to obtain as much ecclesiastical money as possible before formally committing himself to an alliance. Philip was aware that without papal subsidies any Spanish funds spent on the Mediterranean theatre would have to be diverted from Flanders, something the duke of Alva virulently opposed. In any case, as the king himself would write to the pope, there were also the Islamic powers of North Africa to consider, not just the Turks; he therefore had instructed his representatives in Rome – Zuñiga, with Cardinals Granvelle and Pacheco – to discuss the terms of a possible treaty. To these Philip sent word that negotiations had to include some sort of agreement about the subsidies, and in any case Spain was not prepared to send more than sixty galleys.[24]

It was common knowledge that Philip's main targets in the Mediterranean were the Barbary states, and for this reason he would try – as the Venetians feared – to avoid fighting in the Levant. This became immediately apparent when the delegates from Spain and Venice met on 2 July, two days after Pius had delivered a vibrant sermon exhorting them to conclude an agreement to fight the Ottomans. Granvelle and Pacheco presented Pius with the request for subsidies and tried to badger the Venetian ambassador Michele Surian into accepting the inclusion of North Africa among the league's potential targets. Spain's initial proposal in fact included a permanent alliance against all infidels, which for Philip also meant the Protestants. Surian retorted that just saying 'the Turk' would be sufficient, Venice not wanting to be involved in some far-flung venture in the western Mediterranean, let alone Flanders. The cost of the league was another bone of contention, the Spanish being unwilling to pay more than half of the total expenses and the Venetians a quarter. The pope pointed out that his annual revenues amounted to just 400,000 ducats, and the most he could give was 35,000 a month for the upkeep of twelve galleys. Besides, Spain was already drawing funds from ecclesiastical sources, had a large empire, and by using the league's army could save on the cost of garrisons. As for the commander-in-chief of the alliance, Philip, as the main financial contributor, insisted on one of his men. The Venetians, unsurprisingly, wanted one of theirs, since they would be providing most of the ships; besides, the war concerned primarily the republic's possessions. In the end it was agreed that Don Juan of Austria should be the leader of a group made up of Venetian, Spanish and papal generals, with the pope as supreme arbiter. The final agreement, however, would be delayed for many months, due to incessant bickering among the delegates. The suspicion that Venice was trying to strike a deal with the Ottomans was always present, despite the fact that the new doge, Alvise Mocenigo – Loredan having died in April – was considered a hawk.[25]

The Pope was determined to help the Venetians, no matter what. On 11 June he nominated Marcantonio Colonna, duke of Paliano, captain-general of the papal fleet, sending him to Venice to hammer out the details of an agreement between the republic and the Holy See. After the death of his arch-enemy Paul IV and the subsequent downfall of the Carafa, the Roman nobleman had been restored by Pius IV to his former possessions and since then had enjoyed papal favour and protection. But Colonna's promotion was ill received by the Spanish delegates in Rome. Both Zuñiga and Granvelle were his enemies, in part because Colonna was a protégé of their rivals at Philip's court. Besides, despite being a Habsburg subject because of his possessions in the kingdom of Naples, Colonna had accepted the pope's naval commission without first consulting Philip. In addition, Granvelle considered the newly appointed captain-general incompetent in naval matters, Colonna's only real experience at sea being his participation in an anti-corsair expedition a few years before.[26]

The pope did not have a navy worth mentioning, and one of the reasons behind Colonna's mission to Venice was to obtain ships and men for his master. The Republic of St Mark duly obliged, providing Pius with four galleys – albeit not the best of vessels, Venice having her own priorities – to be added to another eight, for which the Venetians had provided the shells, being completed in the papal dockyards of Ancona. Venice also provided a minimum of ordnance for the galleys, their other needs not allowing them to equip Colonna's vessels with full gun batteries. The Venetians were less than satisfied with the pope's choice of Colonna, despite the fact that the latter managed to get on extremely well with his hosts. Venice had agreed to place its own galleys under the pope's command, and while the duke of Paliano may have been a charming person his inexperience was a cause of major concern. For this reason the doge wrote to Venice's captain-general, Girolamo Zane, instructing him to be respectful towards Colonna, but retain his independence in matters of importance.[27]

At this point the Venetians' main worry was money. During the last few years fortifying Cyprus had cost the republic enormous sums, and it was an accepted fact that in wartime military expenses went through the roof. In order to raise cash Venice employed the usual expedients of any money-starved Early Modern state: selling offices, increasing the public debt and extraordinary taxation. Although these methods brought in some funds, they were but a drop in Mars' bucket, and by the time the war ended in 1573 Venice would have spent nearly ten million gold ducats.[28] The Venetians were hoping that the pope would cover some of their expenses, but Pius had his own financial problems, and in order to ameliorate these it was rumoured that he had asked for contributions of 30,000 ducats from sixteen newly created cardinals. The pope also deprived his nephew of the office of chamberlain, bestowing it on Cardinal Alvise Corner in exchange for 68,000 ducats.[29] Pius had never been a nepotist in the first place, and believed that his family should share in full the burden of war.

The king of Spain, as we have seen, was always short of funds, and in serious need of those ecclesiastical subsidies that the pontiff had until then denied him. Philip by now understood that it was useless to try and stop Pius from aiding the Venetians, and endeavoured to turn the situation to his advantage. On 15 July he wrote to Colonna informing him that he had ordered Doria to join him with the galleys gathered in Sicily, adding that the Genoese admiral was to obey the papal commander. A letter to the same effect was sent to Pius, and the delighted pope now expressed his willingness to grant the requested subsidies.[30] Pius would have been less elated if he had known the king's secret orders to Doria. Philip had no intention of risking his galleys in what he considered a rash venture, and instructed his commander to 'preserve the galleys as much as possible' sailing with 'all the prudence necessary'. These directives were deliberately ambiguous, in practice giving the admiral carte blanche to decide the best course of action.[31] Doria was not happy with the king's vagueness, and on 8 August confided to his father-in-law the prince of Melfi, 'The king commands and wishes that I should serve him and guess [his intentions]. Yet the more I read his letter, the less I understand it; and the more I squeeze it, the less juice I pull out of it. Thus, I have no other choice but to go, but slowly and with the expectation that another courier may arrive with clearer orders.'[32]

But Doria would wait in vain, despite all his pleadings. Three days later he would write to the king asking his permission to quit the combined fleet by September, and also for precise instructions on what to do, including disobeying Colonna's orders, to ensure the safety of Spain's galleys. He concluded his letter by stressing the opportunity for a strike in North Africa, adding that the Venetians were probably already trying to reach an agreement with the Ottomans. The possibility of a raid against the Barbary states was always present in the minds of those serving the Spanish crown. On 28 July Philip's ambassador in Genoa had written to his master pointing out that it was the right moment to attack Algiers, its governor-general Uluç Ali having gone to sea leaving only a few troops to guard the place. Only a few years before Don Garcia de Toledo had recaptured the Peñon de la Gomera, and a similar operation against Algiers seemed a more viable option than fighting for distant Cyprus. Doria was as determined as Philip not to hazard the galleys under his command, twelve of them being his own property, just to please Colonna and the Venetians. He intended to procrastinate until the season was too advanced for any sort of military operation in the Levant, and attempt instead to convince the allies to attack Tunis. Doria was also worried about the possibility of encountering Uluç Ali, and with good reason.[33]

Immediately after the siege of 1565 the Knights Hospitallers, which by this point had acquired for good the title of Knights of Malta, had resumed their anti-Muslim naval activities. Piero del Monte, grand master after La Valette's death in 1568, willingly responded to the pope's appeal to send his galleys to join the allied fleet to aid Venice against the Ottomans. On 26 June the Maltese contingent of four galleys under the French knight François de Saint Clément sailed from Malta towards Sicily, where it joined Doria's squadron. It was a small unit, yet highly professional and boasting some of the best fighters in the Mediterranean. However, Saint Clément decided to return to Malta after loading his galley with choice wines and provisions, despite having been warned that Uluç Ali was in the area with a fleet of about twenty galliots. Brushing aside all objections, the Maltese commander set sail from the port of Licata on the evening of 14 July.

Twenty miles off the island of Gozo the Maltese squadron stumbled upon Uluç Ali's ships in the early-morning light. The galleys immediately turned tail, heading for the Sicilian coast. Initially Ali hesitated to act, fearing the four vessels to be the vanguard of Giovanni Andrea Doria's fleet. But once he realized that his enemy was on the run, he gave chase. For many hours the Maltese, aided by a favourable breeze, managed to keep their pursuers at a distance. But the wind suddenly dropped, and the swifter Muslim galliots rapidly gained on their quarry by force of oars. The Maltese squadron now split in two, the *Santa Maria della Vittoria* and the *Sant'Anna* heading for the open sea while the flagship and the *San Giovanni* made for the Sicilian coast. Uluç Ali in turn divided his forces, sending seven galliots to chase one pair of galleys, while he with twelve vessels went after the other. Seeing two of the pursuing galliots struggling to keep up with the rest, the *Santa Maria della Vittoria* and the *Sant'Anna* attempted to take on the remaining five in a daring counter-attack. But during the difficult manoeuvre the *Sant'Anna* was immobilized when her sails got tangled. Separated from her companion, the *Sant'Anna* was surrounded and attacked by the whole pursuing force. The Maltese put up a stiff fight for several hours, and only at sunset did the Muslims manage to board the enemy vessel full of dead and dying men. The *Santa Maria della Vittoria* managed to extricate herself and find refuge in Agrigento.

Meanwhile, disaster had also struck Saint Clément's force. Sensing freedom at hand the Muslim slaves on the Maltese galleys had deliberately rowed slowly, allowing Uluç Ali to catch up. The first to go was the *San Giovanni*, surrounded and captured after a brief, ferocious fight. The Maltese flagship could have been saved, had Saint Clément not failed to spot the nearby port of Licata. Desperately trying to escape his pursuers, the commander ran his galley aground near the tower of Montechiaro. At this point the Muslim slaves managed to free themselves and attack their erstwhile masters with hatchets. Retreating ashore to the summit of the tower, the Maltese watched impotently as Uluç Ali refloated and towed away the stranded galley, which he subsequently used as his own flagship. Saint Clément also committed the unpardonable crime of trying to save his own gold and silver, forgetting the banner of the Order of St John. A quick-witted galley clerk by the name of Michele Calli with the help of the knight Bongianni Gianfigliazzi managed to pull down the standard and bring it to safety.

Initially Saint Clément intended to commit suicide, and then decided instead to expiate his sin by becoming a hermit. But in Malta they were not prepared to let the matter drop. Sixty knights and hundreds of Maltese soldiers and sailors had been killed or taken prisoner, and popular opinion demanded that the culprits be brought to justice. The Maltese were particularly enraged that the grand master had tried to blame the disaster on the local seamen, hanging the flagship's pilot. To avoid a revolt, Piero del Monte put all the survivors from the flagship on trial. Saint Clément got wind of this and went to Rome to ask the pope to intercede in his favour, but Pius V, scrupulously fair, answered that it was his duty to go back to Malta and face the consequences of his actions. When the reluctant knight landed on the island he was barely saved from being lynched by the irate populace, who greeted him with 'Kill, kill; die, die!' The subsequent inquiry revealed in full Saint Clément's criminal negligence. He was deprived of his habit, tried by a secular court, condemned to death, strangled, and his body cast into the sea at night-time.*

The capture of three galleys by Uluç Ali was a crippling blow for the Hospitallers and a serious loss for the allies. Philip II immediately sent the order two new galleys from Messina and one from Naples, with an extra gift of sixty criminals condemned to the oars. Still the lack of sailors and rowers meant that the knights could fully arm only two ships. By the beginning of September the renewed Maltese squadron was ready to sail, its numbers augmented by the return of the *Santa Maria della Vittoria*.[34] But by now events had taken a turn which would force the allies to reconsider their strategy.

~

The Ottomans had wasted no time putting together their expeditionary force against Cyprus. On 1 July a squadron under Piyale Pasha landed troops near Limassol, intending to sack the town. Thrown back into the sea by an energetic Venetian counter-attack, the Ottomans sailed along the coast to the salt mines south of Nicosia, and undisturbed managed to establish a beachhead of about 10,000 men, mostly infantry. During the following days a

---

* Since Saint Clément was a member of a religious order, he first had to be 'reduced to the state of a layman' before being tried by a secular court, the only ones which could inflict penalties involving loss of life or limb.

number of skirmishes occurred between the invaders and the Venetians, but without the latter attempting seriously to tackle the main enemy force. This was largely due to the overcautious attitude of the *luogotenente generale del regno* Nicolò Dandolo, who, despite the urging of his subordinates, preferred to wait behind the walls of Nicosia for the Ottoman attack.* This allowed Lala Mustafa Pasha to return on the 18th with a fleet of about 400 vessels of various types and sizes. Half of his 160 galleys were modern and well furnished with troops, harquebuses and cannon; the rest were in bad shape, lacking also men and equipment. Many more soldiers were embarked on the scores of vessels, big and small, that made up the armada. Each galley carried two horses, while the remaining equines, including many mules, travelled on a number of transport ships. The mounted troops totalled 4,000; the janissaries 6,000, the remaining soldiers being artillerymen, auxiliary infantry, sappers and support units. In total the army was between 70,000 and 100,000 strong, drawn from half a dozen *beylerbeik* and boasting a train of some 200 artillery pieces.[35]

The Turkish commanders debated whether to attack first Famagusta or Nicosia. With Malta in mind Lala Mustafa decided on Nicosia as the initial objective, being not only the key to Cyprus but also an ideal place to establish winter quarters. Isfendiari Mustafa Pasha's failure to take Mdina, in the centre of the island, during the Malta campaign had forced the Ottomans to withdraw at the end of the summer, and in addition the garrison of Mdina had proved a constant thorn in the besiegers' side.[36]

It took Mustafa some time to disembark his troops, advancing towards Nicosia four days after his arrival. He proceeded slowly and cautiously, fearful that the Venetians' lack of activity was a ruse to lead him into a well-prepared trap. Dandolo, however, was busy

---

* The title 'lieutenant general of the kingdom' derived from the fact that Cyprus had been a realm since the Middle Ages. Caterina Cornaro (or Corner), widow of the last king of the house of Lusignan, had surrendered to Venice her sovereignty over the island in 1489.

strengthening Nicosia's defences, counting on 24,000 men, 250 guns, abundant powder and provisions to withstand the siege. But portable firearms were in short supply – no more than a thousand harquebuses being available – while citizens and militia made up most of the city's garrison. Yet Dandolo, 'a man of weak judgement' – chosen for having previously served in a number of administrative military positions, was confident that Nicosia's state-of-the-art fortifications would more than compensate for any deficiency deriving from his men's inexperience or lack of weapons.[37] The famous military architect and engineer Giulio Savorgnan had completely rebuilt the city walls between 1567 and 1568, although he considered the work of little use since Nicosia could not be relieved from the sea and stood in a valley surrounded by hills.

To strengthen the city's defences he had reduced its perimeter to four miles. The old medieval walls and ditch, being outside the new ramparts, were levelled so as not to provide shelter to an attacking force, and the stones used to build the updated fortifications. Since there was not enough building material for the planned eleven bastions, these had to be constructed with earth and faggots faced with stones. Savorgnan was recalled to Venice before he could finish his project, leaving its completion to Dandolo. Another military engineer, Bonaiuto Lorini, would describe the new fortifications as: 'The best and most intelligent work (although made of earth) . . . that could be found'.[38] Yet even such modern fortifications were inadequate if unsupported by a field army. Relying exclusively on fixed defences was a mistake that the French would repeat four centuries later, when they counted on the concrete forts of the Maginot Line to repel the attacking Germans.

Mustafa arrived within sight of Nicosia on 28 July, pitching his camp to the south-east on high ground. His headquarters boasted Spanish tents taken by Uluç Ali at Tunis a few months before, and captured Habsburg banners were planted in front of his own pavilion.[39] The various *beylerbey* with their military contingents placed their tents in front of the four southern bastions: Davila, Costanzo, Tripoli and Podocattaro. Mustafa immediately ordered the building on the hills of Santa Margherita and San Giorgio of two redoubts surrounded by ditches to house his artillery. From there he commenced firing against Nicosia's walls, ordering also the diversion of the stream that fed the city's moat, sending his sappers to do the work under the cover of darkness and the siege guns. The Ottomans built two other makeshift fortresses to provide more covering fire for their engineers, and shielded by these batteries occupied the half-filled mediaeval ditch. From there the besiegers advanced to within 150 yards of the ramparts, pushing forward zigzag trenches which the defenders could not enfilade. Here the Ottomans set up another line of batteries and engaged in a four-day bombardment of the southern bastions. The walls, however, had been reinforced with further earthworks, and the artillery barrage produced few results except an expenditure of ammunition. More effective were the Ottoman harquebusiers sent forward by Mustafa to protect his engineers. The janissaries were crack shots, and their accurate fire hindered the defenders' attempts to stop the Ottoman sappers.[40] Trenches were pushed up to the counterscarp, protected against enfilade fire with earth and brushwood ramparts nearly as high as the city walls. In this way the Ottomans were able to reach the angles of the bastions and they began to cut away at the masonry in order to prepare a sloping approach for assault troops.

The Venetians attempted countermeasures, at one point building a wooden parapet with loopholes to allow their harquebusiers to fire at the Ottoman sappers without being hit by enemy marksmen. But the besiegers destroyed the device with well-directed artillery fire, killing a number of defenders in the process. Meanwhile, Dandolo, unnecessarily concerned about a shortage of powder, ordered his soldiers not to return fire, his behaviour arousing in many a suspicion that he was working for the enemy. Far from being a traitor, Dandolo was simply unimaginative, although, given the inexperience of many of his soldiers, his caution if excessive was not irrational.

On 5 August Mustafa launched his first assault against Nicosia's defences and nearly managed to capture the Costanzo bastion, the defending troops taking to their heels. Only the timely intervention of Paolo dal Guasto's company averted a major disaster, and the Ottomans were forced to retreat with considerable losses. As the besiegers' bombardment resumed, the frustration of the besieged increased. Since Dandolo refused to allow sorties against the enemy's siege works, some of the defenders took matters into their own hands. On the night of 10 August 300 men rushed the Ottoman trenches facing the Davila bastion, throwing back the enemy in disorder. Informed of the action, Dandolo refused to send reinforcements, allowing the Turks to counter-attack successfully under the cover of their artillery. Undaunted by this failure, a number of officers in Nicosia organized another raid behind Dandolo's back. On 17 August, as the Ottomans were resting in the midday heat, a large force of about 1,000 men silently exited the Famagusta gate and fell on the enemy siege works. Two batteries were captured, but once more Dandolo, having discovered what was happening, stopped other troops from joining the fray by ordering the closure of Nicosia's gates. Left to their fate, the attacking Venetians nevertheless managed to retreat into the city, but with the loss of many officers and men.

The demoralized defenders gave up the idea of future sallies, concentrating instead on building inner lines of defence across the four threatened bastions against the Ottomans managing to gain footholds on the walls. There was still hope that a Venetian relief force would arrive in time to lift the siege, and in any case provisions and munitions allowed for a prolonged resistance. All of Mustafa's proposals for an honourable surrender were rejected, but this show of bravado belied the gravity of the situation. By the beginning of September the defenders' numbers had been dangerously depleted by death and sickness, the professional soldiers being reduced to a few thousand, and many sections of the walls were barely manned. Artisans, hitherto exempted from military service, were forced to stand sentry to relieve the exhausted soldiers.

Mustafa tried to induce the garrison to give up by putting pressure on the civilian population. Arrows with messages urging surrender were shot over the walls while Ottoman gunners targeted the city's houses and, on Sundays, churches. During a truce the besiegers tried to talk the defenders into surrender, mocking their hope of relief from the Venetian fleet. It was still in port, they said, its crews riddled with disease. The garrison ignored the taunts, and Mustafa ordered a renewed artillery barrage followed by an assault against the walls. Once more the attackers were repulsed, but it was clear that the defenders could not hold out much longer. Colonel Podocattaro begged Dandolo to mine the bastions against the possibility of the Turks capturing them. Dandolo refused.

Mustafa had his own problems. Despite the fact that according to the standards of the time the siege was proceeding well, the Ottoman commander could not keep up the pressure against Nicosia indefinitely. Venetian mounted troops from Famagusta had been harrying his rear, and the bombardment was taking its toll on the besiegers' supplies of powder and shot. Manpower was another of Mustafa's concerns. Dandolo may not have shown much imagination, but his policy of relying on fixed defences was causing considerable losses to the besiegers. The janissaries were unhappy about being in the fore of each assault fearing the bastions to be mined as at Szigetvár. In a few weeks the campaign season would be over, and if Nicosia had not been taken by then the whole Ottoman enterprise would be at risk. After another fruitless attempt to convince the Venetians to surrender – threatening to put the stormed city to the sack – and desperately in need of troops, Mustafa sent an urgent request to the Ottoman naval commanders to send him at least 100 men from each of their galleys. Müezzinzâde Ali Pasha and Piyale Pasha were concerned about weakening their ships' strength in case the allied fleet appeared, but also recognized that the success of the campaign hinged on the capture of Nicosia. Müezzinzâde Ali arrived in person at Mustafa's camp on 8 September, bringing with him some 25,000 men. With these reinforcements Mustafa felt confident of success, and to encourage his janissaries he promised abundant rewards to those first over the walls.

By now Dandolo was at the end of his tether, dithering and desperate. The defence of Nicosia fell to his subordinates, who on 6 September tried to execute another sally to dislodge the Ottomans from their siege lines. The timing was bad, the raid a failure, and with less than 3,000 professional soldiers available Nicosia's defenders could not afford to risk any more of their troops, only wait for what appeared to be the inevitable outcome. In the early light of 9 September the Turks crept up to Nicosia's walls, concentrating most of their troops below the much-damaged Podocattaro bastion. At a signal the Ottoman force rushed the walls, engaging the defenders in a furious hand-to-hand struggle. Eventually numbers started to tell, despite the last-minute reinforcements sent by Dandolo to the beleaguered bastion. At this point, having ordered the blowing up of the remaining gunpowder should the Ottomans prevail, the *luogotenente generale* prudently retired to his palace.

By now the Ottomans had captured Podocattaro and were swarming along the walls to attack the remaining defenders from the rear. The Costanzo and Tripoli bastions were taken after desperate fights, the Venetian survivors retreating into the city chased by the victorious Turks. The defenders gathered for a last stand in the square where Dandolo's palace stood, engaging the Ottomans fiercely at close quarters. From the Tripoli bastion, Derviş Pasha, the governor-general of Aleppo, fired three guns, loaded with canister shot, towards the square, cutting down friend and foe alike. Fumbling for a solution that would save his skin, Dandolo tried to negotiate terms with the assailants. He ordered Tuccio Costanzo, who was leading the resistance, to take a letter to Mustafa offering surrender in exchange for the defenders' lives and property. It was all too late. Costanzo was immediately taken prisoner, and the remaining soldiers retreated into the palace. There Dandolo was confronted by the Venetian patrician Andrea Da Pesaro, who accused him of treason. As Pesaro pulled out his sword, he was slain by two of Dandolo's bodyguards.

Death, confusion and despair held sway in Nicosia. Men,

women and children ran panic-stricken through the streets. Here and there small groups of Venetians attempted last stands, only to be overwhelmed by the enemy. The Ottomans opened the Famagusta gate, allowing their cavalrymen to pour into the city, mercilessly cutting down anyone who stood in their path. Captain Paolo dal Guasto, still holding the bastion of San Luca, turned his guns on the city in a desperate attempt to stem the Ottoman tide. For eight hours the fighting continued, until the last of the garrison had been killed or captured. In the house of the count of Tripoli, Colonel Ettore Podocattaro resisted until nightfall, finally surrendering on condition that all those with him be spared and allowed to buy their freedom, leaving all the goods in the house to Mustafa's discretion. Earlier, the Ottomans had convinced Dandolo to capitulate on terms. The *luogotenente generale* had opened the gates of the palace but unaware of the negotiations a party of janissaries which had managed to enter through a side door attacked and killed Dandolo. Seeing this, the survivors in the building resumed fighting; they were pushed back, resisting room by room. Only a few score were left when the Ottomans broke through the windows, killing all who remained.

Mustafa entered the city in the afternoon and immediately ordered all fighting to cease providing the remaining defenders laid down their weapons. To some extent he managed to restore order, but there was little he could do to stop his battle-maddened troops from engaging in an orgy of murder, rape and pillage. Women, no matter their age or standing, were ravished, churches and houses sacked, and anyone who dared to resist was killed on the spot. This sort of behaviour was not confined to the Ottomans, many other armies throughout history displaying the same brutality.* The

---

* Among a few examples of savage sacks through history one should mention: Brescia (1509), Rome (1527), Antwerp (1576), Magdeburg (1630), Drogheda (1649), Badajoz (1812), Warsaw (1944), Berlin (1945). It should also be remembered that according to sixteenth-century conventions of war if a town was taken after having refused to surrender, the lives and property of its inhabitants were at the victor's mercy.

victorious troops, in particular the janissaries, quarrelled over prisoners and booty, and further bloodshed ensued. The Ottomans captured 160 good artillery pieces, together with much powder and shot, and Mustafa's share of the plunder amounted to 50,000 ducats. Breaking his word, the Ottoman leader also enslaved Colonel Podocattaro with all his family. When the Venetian officer protested, threatening to lodge a formal complaint with the sultan, Mustafa had him beheaded.[41]

The next day the prisoners were auctioned off, while a choice batch of women and boys, together with much treasure, was loaded onto three ships to be sent to Constantinople. Unfortunately, due to the negligence of the crew or, according to Venetian sources, the action of a female prisoner, one of the vessels exploded, engulfing the other two in its flames. Eight hundred young girls perished, and only a few sailors managed to swim ashore.[42] These deaths should be added to the 20,000 Venetians who died during the siege and storming of the city. Ottoman casualties were also high, amounting to perhaps 30,000 men.

Following the capture of Nicosia, Mustafa sent messengers to all the other Venetian strongholds on the island with requests to surrender in exchange for life and liberty for the garrisons. The governor of Kyrenia, Zaccaria Mudazzo, asked for time to make his mind up, adding that no decision could be made without the approval of his superiors. He then sent a letter full of bravado to the governor of Famagusta, Marcantonio Bragadin, who ordered Kyrenia to resist to the last man. But Mudazzo was not made of heroes' stuff, and after consulting with the fortress's military governor surrendered Kyrenia to Mustafa on 14 September, not even waiting for Bragadin's answer. The Venetian authorities were infuriated by this craven behaviour, given that Kyrenia's defences had recently been updated at a cost of 150,000 ducats.[43] True to their word, the Ottomans transported Mudazzo and his men to Crete, but on his arrival in Venice the governor was arrested, ending his days in jail.

Famagusta proved more resilient. Mustafa sent a request of surrender, accompanied by Dandolo's head on a plate, offering generous terms. These included life, freedom and property for all, with the possibility of becoming Ottoman subjects. He added that resistance was useless, since no relief force could arrive in Famagusta without first battling Piyale's fleet. But Bragadin and the military governor Astorre Baglioni were made of stronger stuff than Mudazzo, and sent back a defiant answer. Mustafa had no choice but to settle down for another siege, hoping the city would fall quickly. In this he was to be disappointed.

~

The allied fleet had failed to come to Nicosia's assistance for a number of reasons. When war appeared inevitable Venice had flexed its naval muscles, managing by June 1570 to deploy some 125 galleys, eleven galleasses and twenty-two other vessels. In addition, another fifty galleys, four galleasses and twelve further ships were being built in the Arsenale. The quality of the existing vessels was mixed, some of them being old and not particularly seaworthy. Crews were another problem. Despite the fact that Venice had been busy recruiting troops at home and abroad, by April less than 12,000 soldiers were available for naval service, a meagre seventy-five for each vessel. Their numbers eventually rose to 15,000, still an insufficient force for the task they were supposed to perform.[44] Rowers were also in short supply; Venice, like the Ottomans, relying mostly on free men, not slaves or convicts, to operate its ships' oars.

The Venetian fleet concentrated in the port of Zara (Zadar), sailing for Corfu on 12 June. Its commander Girolamo Zane arrived there on the 23rd with seventy galleys, not bothering to wait for the slower ones. Corfu's *provveditore*, the crusty Sebastiano Venier, asked Zane to provide him with troops to capture the Ottoman-held fortresses of Margariti on the nearby coast. However, the commander of the Venetian naval infantry, Sforza Pallavicino, decided that this was too daring a venture, preferring instead to ravage the enemy countryside. Venier, who with fewer men had captured a few days before the strategically important castle of

Sopot, was incensed by this behaviour, forcing Pallavicino to justify himself to the doge. In any case, the Venetians had more pressing needs than conquering strongholds. Most of the galleys had to be refitted and repaired once they reached Corfu, and moreover the crews had been hit by an epidemic, probably typhoid fever, which was reported to have killed in a few weeks some 20,000 men, 'including many gentlemen, galley owners, and others of the highest condition'.* The lack of proper medical supplies worsened the situation. Those left alive took weeks to recover, preventing Zane from sailing to Cyprus.[45]

Not all the Venetian forces were inactive. The *provveditore* Marco Querini with twenty-one galleys was stationed in Crete to prevent an Ottoman descent on the island. Having received orders to join the main fleet in Corfu, en route he decided to strike the fortress of Mani in the Peloponnese. Managing to hide in a small haven, at nightfall he landed with his men and proceeded to surround the enemy stronghold. The Ottomans managed to retreat to the keep, but their resistance was cut short when Querini brought forward his artillery and bombarded the walls ferociously. The Ottomans surrendered and were immediately sent to the oars. Querini had the fortress razed with mines before sailing for Corfu, reaching his destination on 1 July.[46] It was a small success, but nevertheless an important boost for the Venetians' flagging spirits. Zane immediately sent Querini to recruit men in the nearby islands, whilst he remained in port waiting for his surviving crews and soldiers to get back into fighting shape. Finally, on 23 July he set

---

* Natale Conti would variably impute the disease to 'evil air', 'God's displeasure' or 'someone's carelessness' (CONTI: II, f. 9r). However, Pantero Pantera, an experienced naval commander writing a few decades later, would place the blame squarely on the 'avarice' of those officials who had supplied the fleet with rotten victuals (PANTERA: 95). On 7 April 1571 the Venetian senate would write to the deputy captain-general of the fleet Agostino Barbarigo, accusing the commanders of the 1570 expedition of having kept the galleys in totally unhygienic conditions: 'From which it may be understood the disease and deaths that hit our fleet . . . causing an offence to God our Lord and great damage and misfortune to the public good.' ASV, *SM*, reg. 40, f. 21r.

sail for Crete, where he joined up with Querini in the first days of August.

Meanwhile, Marcantonio Colonna had travelled with his refitted galleys from Ancona to Otranto. His flagship was a great quinquereme, built some forty years before by the humanist naval architect Vettor Fausto.* Arriving in the Apulian port on 6 August, he found a letter from Philip II informing him of the imminent arrival of Giovanni Andrea Doria with a squadron of forty-nine 'Spanish' galleys. The king added that Doria had received instructions to obey the papal admiral's decisions, but the letter's closing lines had an ominous ring for Colonna:

> I trust and pray that in battle you seek Giovanni Andrea's full advice, having been told that it will be most useful. This will contribute to the success of the operation, given his experience and practice in naval matters, and in any case be sure to inform us about any needs you may have. However, if the Turkish armada should pursue a different direction from what it is said to have taken, and should attack our states, then I confide that you will hasten to come to their assistance with all your galleys.[47]

Effectively, Philip was saying that Doria was to obey Colonna at his discretion, and was also reminding the papal admiral of his duties as hereditary constable of the kingdom of Naples.

Colonna had to wait two weeks for Doria, who in a deceitful letter of 16 August blamed the weather for his delay. Eventually the Spanish and papal squadrons were united on the 21st, and the two commanders held a conference to decide what next. The lanky, pointed-featured Doria contrasted starkly with the medium-height, roundish Colonna. The Genoese was not slow to point out the problems facing the allies: the strength of the Ottoman forces, the late season and the poor condition of the Venetian fleet. He suggested to remain in the Adriatic and also recall the Venetians from Crete, reminding the papal commander that his first duty was

* A quinquereme is a rowing vessel with five oars to each bench.

to preserve the king's galleys. Colonna was adamant about the need to join Zane, and Doria in the end gave in. In a letter intended for the viceroy of Sicily, the Genoese stated, 'I will try to preserve this fleet, but without some good excuse it will be difficult for me to avoid the accusation of not wanting to fight'.[48] The two squadrons departed slowly from Otranto, Doria not wishing to tire his crews and deliberately neglecting to take advantage of the favourable wind. Ten days later the allies joined forces in Souda, where Zane immediately summoned a war council. He informed his fellow commanders about the urgent need to relieve Nicosia, adding that the Ottomans could field only 150 galleys against the 200 of their enemies; besides, the firepower of the eleven Venetian galleasses was far superior to that of any Ottoman vessel. But Doria had already perceived that Zane was not a man of decision, and adroitly exploited the Venetian's doubts. His arguments for not engaging the enemy were the same he had used with Colonna, adding also that from Crete onward there were no havens where the fleet could find refuge. He asked for a rapid decision on the course of action to take, wanting to be in Sicily by the end of September.[49]

Doria was clearly employing delaying tactics, but had his reasons for doing so. Not only had Philip II ordered him not to put his galleys in harm's way, but the Genoese also had no intention of risking his own fortune in some reckless enterprise. Doria's twelve galleys were leased to the king of Spain for a yearly 72,000 ducats. In theory, Philip was supposed to pay one sixth of this every two months, the interest rate for any delayed payment being 14 per cent;[50] but the Spanish were notoriously cavalier with their debts, and Doria knew that he would have to meet any losses out of his own pocket.* In any case, the allies may have had an advantage in

---

* This situation was in fact more favourable than it may appear. Doria, like many Genoese naval entrepreneurs, exploited the king's lack of cash to get himself repaid in other ways: the concession of lucrative fiefs in southern Italy, enjoyment of custom revenues, commercial advantages and titles. I thank Dr Luca Lo Basso for this information.

ships, but the Ottomans were superior fighters. By recruiting or, as one contemporary put it, chasing men 'like hares'[51] in the Aegean islands, the Venetians had managed somewhat to make good their lack of personnel, but they were still woefully short of infantry. Colonna had 1,100 and Doria roughly 4,000 infantry, each of the Spanish and papal galleys boasting something less than 100 soldiers each, but on the Venetian vessels the fighting contingent numbered only eighty, many of them sailors. The Genoese admiral even accused the Venetians of misleading their allies about their real strength by constantly moving men from one galley to another. Zane was forced to disarm five galleys, distributing the men among the rest of his fleet. The Venetians were still battling with the epidemic that had hit them in Corfu, Zane complaining to his superiors in Venice about the fleet's desperate condition.[52]

The war council was split between those supporting Doria and others determined to seek battle with the Ottomans. Colonna had the support of the leader of the Neapolitan contingent, one of the most distinguished Spanish mariners of all time. Born Álvaro de Bazán in 1526, he had gone to sea at an early age, in 1544 fighting his first battle against a French corsair squadron. An expert in Atlantic as well as Mediterranean warfare, Bazán had participated in every major anti-Muslim expedition, including Malta and the Peñon de la Gomera. Given command of the Neapolitan squadron, in a short time he had made it a model of efficiency, and in 1569 Philip II in reward for his services elevated him to marquis of Santa Cruz.[53] With such support, Colonna had a field day belittling Doria's objections: the allies had numerical superiority, the Ottoman fleet being scattered along the coast of Cyprus; the season might have been advanced but there was still enough time to engage the Turks and return home; the Venetians had made good their losses, and in any case their rowers being free men could participate in a battle; as for havens, there were many in Cyprus, starting with Famagusta; finally, aiding the Venetians was not just obeying the pope and the king's will, but also a matter of honour.[54] The main parties involved in the debate did not limit themselves to spoken words, being also careful to circulate, in manuscript or print, their own version of events.★ If not in agreement about how and when to fight the Ottomans, the allies were united in waging propaganda war against each other.

The debate about what to do was still raging in the middle of the month when Marco Querini, who had been sent to seek news of the situation in Cyprus, reported that Nicosia was still resisting and the Ottoman fleet dispersed amongst the island's havens. Forced to agree with his more bellicose colleagues that something had to be done to relieve Nicosia, Doria raved in a letter to Fernando d'Avalos, viceroy of Sicily, that Colonna was behaving 'as if he was born Venetian, and caring little for the king of Spain's fleet'. He added that if something was not accomplished by the end of the month he would return home – God protect him in the meantime – although he feared the weather more than the enemy.[55] On the 17th the allied fleet set sail towards the east, numbering 179 galleys, eleven galleasses, one galleon, and fourteen transport ships.† En route they received the dramatic news that Nicosia had fallen, and immediately a war council was convened to decide what to do. It was clear that with Nicosia taken the Ottomans would have many more soldiers on board their galleys, ruining the allies' chances of an easy victory. The mariners were also fearful of encountering bad weather out of reach of a haven sufficiently large to contain the whole fleet. Overruling Zane, who wished to continue on to Famagusta or at least try to capture some of the Ottoman fortresses in the area, the other commanders unanimously decided to return

---

★ For instance, Doria's account dated 16 September on the uselessness of going to Cyprus enjoyed wide circulation. I have used the copy preserved in: AGF, *Miscellanea*, II, n. 24.

† The strength of the allied fleet varies according to source. Santa Cruz estimated that on 5 September the total number of galleys was 187: 126 Venetian, 49 Spanish, 12 Papal. AGS, *SE*, 1058, n. 108 (marquis of Santa Cruz to Philip II, 5 September 1570, from Crete). Yet, by the time the fleet set sail twelve days later, the Venetians had been forced to disarm a number of vessels; some sources also give Doria 45 and not 49 galleys. My estimate follows the breakdown given in: CONTARINI: 16r–19r. Give or take a few vessels, it is safe to say that the armada numbered roughly 200 ships of all kinds.

immediately to Crete.[56] As ill luck would have it, during the return journey the armada was hit by a storm, with the loss of a papal and a Venetian galley. Once again Doria aroused suspicions by insisting on keeping his own ships out at sea, and his colleagues acidly insinuated that he was seeking an excuse to return home. The Genoese retorted that he feared being bottled up, should the Ottoman fleet suddenly appear, but more likely he was concerned about the risk of infection from the Venetian crews.[57]

Doria was not just being difficult, for the Ottomans were well aware of the allies' plight. Around 20 August Piyale Pasha had sent five galliots to find out the Christians' whereabouts, and by interrogating some prisoners captured on the Cretan shore the Ottoman commander learnt of the epidemic that had hit the Venetian crews.[58] At the time the Venetians were still waiting in Corfu for their allies to appear, and on the strength of this intelligence Piyale felt confident enough to provide Lala Mustafa with the necessary troops for the storming of Nicosia. Doria feared a replay of Preveza and Djerba, and during the next war council he made known his intention to return home as soon as possible. When Colonna reminded him who was in command, the Genoese answered that he obeyed the king of Spain. During the subsequent verbal scuffle the Neapolitan Don Carlo d'Avalos insulted Colonna, who answered that henceforth he wanted nothing more to do with the Spanish contingent. Doria, who would later accuse Colonna 'of wanting to acquire honour in Cyprus with my goods',[59] was only too happy to oblige, although careful to keep his ships close to the rest of the fleet to avoid accusations of cowardice. The Genoese was partially vindicated when the allies ran into a violent squall while navigating towards Souda. More than twenty galleys ran aground, four of them belonging to Doria and two from the papal squadron. A number were eventually refloated, but it was clear that the autumn weather prevented any further major naval operations that year.

After spending a few days in Candia (Irakleio) Doria departed for good on 5 October, to everyone's chagrin and relief. Zane met Sebastiano Venier, recently arrived from Corfu, to discuss what to do next. Venier, following his usual bellicose approach, asked for a galley squadron, 4,000 men, equipment and 200 barrels of gunpowder to take to Famagusta. Zane, by now dispirited and sick, showed little inclination to grant his subordinate's requests, restricting himself to sending some ships to gather intelligence before retreating with the rest of his squadron towards Corfu. Marco Querini and Venier were left in Crete to put together the relief of Famagusta. Once in Corfu, Zane reviewed his fleet, disarming some thirty badly damaged galleys. He also sent a report to Venice justifying his actions over the last few months and asking to be relieved due to age and poor health. Venice was notorious for its ruthlessness when dealing with failure. Zane found himself dismissed from his post, arrested with a number of his subordinates, thrown into jail and put on trial for incompetence and corruption. He would die in prison two years later, still awaiting the final sentence.[60]

Piyale Pasha left Cyprus on 26 October in search of the allied fleet, capturing on his way one of the galleys sent by Zane to gather news on the Ottoman whereabouts.[61] Luckily for the allies, Piyale's ships were hit by a fierce north-west wind, forcing him to turn towards Constantinople. Colonna joined Zane in Corfu, where he gave back six of his galleys to the Venetians (now short of ships) before sailing up the Adriatic coast towards Ancona. Bad weather turned the voyage into a nightmare, forcing Colonna to spend weeks in port. Topping everything, while in Kotor his flagship, Fausto's quinquereme, was struck by lightning and blew up. Colonna managed to save his men, including those chained to the rowing benches, the papal standard and his papers, being the last to leave the burning galley. With what remained of his fleet he set sail again, only to be driven ashore by adverse winds three miles from Dubrovnik. The Ragusei helped him and his crew, refusing to turn them over to the Ottomans. Colonna returned to Rome at the beginning of February.[62] Due to indecision, divisions, disease, bad weather and ill luck, 1570 had been disastrous for the Christian cause, and given the discussions still going on in Rome it seemed that 1571 would be no better.

6. A LEAGUE OF MISTRUST

~

The allies' failure to relieve Nicosia produced a stream of bitter recriminations from all sides. Giovanni Andrea Doria was the target of criticism and accusations, Marcantonio Colonna writing to Philip II that the Genoese admiral had purposely distorted for his own personal interest the meaning of the king's orders in order to preserve the Spanish galleys. Pius V refused to receive Marcello Doria, who had arrived in Rome to plead on his relative's behalf. Instead, Pius sent Pompeo Colonna, Marcantonio's cousin, to Madrid to protest with Philip about Doria's behaviour. The king, however, diplomatically chose to approve Marcantonio's handling of the allied fleet, at the same time continuing to place his trust in the Genoese admiral. Colonna had managed to bring back only three of the papal galleys, a fact that his enemies were not slow to exploit. Cardinal Granvelle, for one, did not mince his words. He had been furious when informed about Philip's decision to place Doria under Colonna, 'saying very extravagant and inconsiderate things about the king and his ministers'. Granvelle felt vindicated by Colonna's mismanagement of the papal fleet, and when reminded of Philip's trust in the Roman nobleman, he ironically commented that the king could confide in his own sister but not for this reason entrust her with military affairs.[1]

Doria had also started his own propaganda campaign, his target being not just Colonna but also the Venetians. Although the Genoese felt he had done his duty towards Philip and his native city by behaving with the utmost caution during the campaign, his reputation was now at stake. What rankled with him most were the accusations of cowardice, negligence, self-seeking and ineptitude in naval matters which he suspected originated from Colonna and Santa Cruz. To counter such charges, in letters to various Spanish officials he would stress Colonna's systematic disregard of his advice which had put the Spanish fleet at risk to please the Venetians. Somewhat hypocritically he stated that the latter were to blame for the loss of Nicosia, having wasted time in Crete.[2]

By now it was common knowledge that Doria was the main culprit for the failure of the expedition, but the Venetians received their own share of criticism. An anonymous treatise of the time enumerated the mistakes committed by the Republic of St Mark in handling the war: incompetent diplomacy, disregard of Barbaro's warnings, faulty strategy, bad tactics, awful leadership, inadequate fortifications coupled with an insufficient number of professional soldiers; all these had allowed the Ottomans to take Nicosia and virtually the rest of Cyprus while Venice had lost men, artillery pieces and the substantial revenues from the island's salt pans. The treatise ended on the pessimistic note that the change of Venetian commanders was not likely to solve much, given that both Venier and his deputy Agostino Barbarigo were inexperienced in military and naval matters.[3] The author of this tirade was informed only to a point, but the circulation of such writings did nothing to help the Christian cause.

On the diplomatic front there had been little progress since the summer. The Spanish were still insisting that the pope grant the requested ecclesiastical subsidies before committing themselves to a formal alliance with Venice. They also had other requests, deriving from their suspicions about Venetian trustworthiness. Everyone knew that despite his confinement Marcantonio Barbaro was in contact with the Ottoman authorities, and that the Venetians, worried by the increasing costs of the war and the loss of trade with the east, were ready to reach an agreement with the Ottomans at the drop of a hat. The Spanish therefore asked that the treaty of alliance also stipulate automatic excommunication for any member who should agree to a separate peace with the Turks. The Venetians vigorously rejected this request, arguing that such a clause would give the impression that loyalty to the Christian cause derived only from fear of ecclesiastical censure. They also opposed as unnecessary the Spanish request that fifty galleys be permanently stationed off the Barbary coast to protect Spain's territories, since an attack on one of the allies would cause the others to come to his aid. Finally, the Venetians asked that all grain destined for the allied fleet should be exempt, at least in part, from taxation. Philip's answer to the Venetian points was mixed. He agreed that the excommunication proviso was inappropriate but at the same time insisted that Tunis, Tripoli and Algiers were legitimate targets. After all, the Spanish had sent their galleys to the Levant, so it was only right that now the Venetians should help Spain against the Muslim states of North Africa. As for the grain, the king promised to price it in such a way as to limit his treasury's losses.[4] The negotiations had reached a dead end, and this situation appeared unlikely to change at any time in the near future.

These developments – or the lack of them – in Rome were followed with extreme interest in European diplomatic circles. Ever since receiving his grand ducal title from the pope, Cosimo I de' Medici had been trying to get back in the Habsburgs' graces and have them recognize his new status. Devious as always, Cosimo was playing a risky triangular game between Madrid, Paris and Rome. By using the veiled threat of switching his allegiance from Philip II to the French king Charles IX, he hoped to get the Spanish to intercede in his favour with the Holy Roman Emperor. France's recognition of him as grand duke of Tuscany certainly pleased Cosimo, yet he had to tread carefully so as not to alarm Spain too much, lest Philip should decide to curb by force of arms his recalcitrant vassal's ambitions. The grand duke fully understood France's wish to play once more an active part in Italy's affairs, but was also aware of the perils of a Valois embrace, not least because many in Florence considered his cousin Catherine de' Medici to have a better claim to the city's lordship – something Catherine herself never forgot.[5]

The negotiations to create an anti-Ottoman league provided Cosimo with a golden opportunity to increase his prestige on the international scene by making himself indispensable to one of the parties. But Venice, although eager for allies, was not interested in the Medici. The duke of Savoy was out of the game, Emmanuel Philibert having too many problems with his own Protestant subjects. Besides, the Spanish were concerned that any assertion of the house of Savoy's old claims on Cyprus would upset the Venetians. Emmanuel Philibert, however, denied he wished to assert any such claim and agreed to put his three galleys at the league's disposal. Venice tried to gain the support of the Holy Roman Emperor, since having Maximilian II in the league would force the Ottomans to concentrate their military efforts in Hungary rather than Cyprus. But Maximilian was still fuming over Cosimo's title and had no sympathy for Pius V, whom he described as 'the impertinent bishop of Rome'. Indeed, he was so incensed by the pope's behaviour, considering it an infringement of his rights to contemplate an invasion of Italy with the backing of Germany's Protestant princes, Maximilian himself having an unabashed liking for the reformed religion. He had no intention of going to war with Selim II, having just signed the Peace of Edirne, and knew perfectly well the difficulties involved in raising a sufficiently large army. Besides, he calculated that a league made up of states with such diverse interests would not last long. Still, as the nominal head of Christendom he could not openly refuse to join the alliance without losing face, maintaining nevertheless that it would be unbecoming to renege on the solemn treaty just signed with the infidels.[6] However, in the early months of 1571 the Venetians were still hoping that Maximilian would change his mind, although worried that the inclusion of Tuscany in the alliance would sabotage their efforts at the imperial court.

Cosimo knew that he could not count on Philip II's support, the king being firmly opposed to his presence in the league. But Cosimo was also aware of Philip's need to obtain ecclesiastical subsidies, and that Tuscany possessed a commodity that Pius V desperately needed but had difficulty in obtaining – namely a fleet. The grand duke had been trying to renegotiate with Philip a more favourable *asiento* for his galleys, but now offered them to Pius V. Cosimo was careful to ask for Madrid's approval before agreeing to a deal; and since the pope himself had requested Tuscany's galleys, he could claim he was only acting in the interests of Christendom.[7]

Pius had already tried unsuccessfully to obtain a functioning fleet elsewhere, but with no result. Finding galleys as such was no problem – many states could provide those. But keeping ships running involved considerable logistical capabilities that the papal states did not have. All the pope's attempts to find 'cash-and-carry' galleys had failed thanks to Spain's meddling. Philip needed Pius to depend exclusively on him for his fleet, in order to obtain the *cruzada* and the other subsidies, there being no greedy papal nephews to whom to give pensions in exchange for the pontiff's favour. As a token of goodwill – and to stop anyone else from doing the same – Philip had ordered his half-brother Don Juan of Austria to keep a few galleys at the pontiff's disposal in the papal port of Civitavecchia, north of Rome. Unfortunately, the revolt of the Moriscos and fear of an Ottoman invasion had forced Philip to concentrate his fleet in the western Mediterranean, leaving the Roman coast open to Muslim attacks. Knowing that the pope would look elsewhere for a fleet, the king tried to convince him to conclude an *asiento* with Genoa or the Hospitallers, both firm Spanish allies. But Pius rejected the Genoese, believing that they armed galleys only for commercial reasons; as for the Knights of St John, the distance between Malta and Rome was a serious handicap.[8] For his fleet, the pope now could only turn to Venetians, who had their own problems, or Florence.

It was clear by now that Philip only favoured an alliance which catered to Spain's needs, but the king had to act carefully lest the pope decide to move ahead without the Spanish – Pius being quite capable of doing so – and, God forbid, refuse to concede the renewal of the Three Graces. Philip was trying not to irritate the pope but also buy time so that, should the planned league see the light of day, it would be too late to implement the dreaded 'general enterprise' – as the king called the expedition to the Levant. It would take a long time to prepare the ships and the men for such an expedition, and the protracted delays could eventually result in a military expedition in North Africa. There was also another reason for being cautious: the insistent rumours of peace negotiations between Venice and the Porte.[9]

~

At the start of 1571 the Venetian fleet in Corfu was in a miserable state. Many ships were still under repair, the typhoid epidemic had not yet abated, and to make matters worse the new captain-general Sebastiano Venier was bedridden with phlebitis. But in Crete things were moving, thanks to the energy of the *provveditore* Marco Querini. Discovering that the Ottoman fleet was wintering in Constantinople, with only a dozen galleys remaining to support the army besieging Famagusta, Querini decided that now was the best time to strike. Taking thirteen of the galleys left by Zane to guard Crete the previous year, the *provveditore* set sail for Famagusta on 16 January accompanied by four round-ships loaded with men and munitions. En route one of the galleys had to be sent back because its disease-ridden crew could not keep up with the others, but this did not deter Querini. On the 26th he came in sight of Famagusta, moving his galleys near to the shore before ordering the round-ships to make a dash for the harbour. When eight Ottoman vessels stationed in Costanza, six miles north of Famagusta, tried to inter-cept them, they were hit in the flank by Querini's galleys. Taken by surprise the Ottomans made for the shore, losing three galleys sent to the bottom, the shot-up survivors seeking refuge under the cover of the guns of a makeshift fort Laca Mustafa had built to protect Costanza. The victorious Querini entered Famagusta harbour with the round-ships in tow, to the rejoicing of the local populace. Not satisfied, the *provveditore* spent the next few days in raids, destroying the fort of Costanza and capturing various enemy vessels. He departed on 16 February, the reinforcements of men, munitions and victuals helping to boost the defenders' morale despite the fact that the quality and quantity (1,319) of the new soldiers left much to be desired. Now Famagusta's garrison numbered 8,000 infantry, including professionals and militia, and 100 horse.[10] With these forces and plentiful supplies Marcantonio Bragadin felt that he could resist until a bigger relief force arrived the following spring.

When news of Querini's exploit reached Constantinople, heads rolled – literally. Like the Venetians, the Ottomans were not inclined to forgive those who had failed. *Pour encourager les autres*, the bey of Chios was beheaded and that of Rhodes deprived of his command. Piyale Pasha shared the latter's fate, although he retained his place in the *dîvân*, and responsibility for all naval operations was assigned to the *kapudan paşa*, Müezzinzâde Ali. The Ottoman admiral, winter notwithstanding, immediately dispatched one of his subordinates with twenty galleys to Cyprus with orders to stop any other Venetian attempt to relieve Famagusta. Ali himself departed a month later, gathering reinforcements for Lala Mustafa. Once in Cypriot waters, he organized a ferry system to transport men and munitions from the Anatolian mainland to the island.[11] Everything was ready for resuming military operations against Famagusta, the Ottoman commanders hoping the city would fall like Nicosia to the sheer weight of their army.

Things were also moving on the diplomatic front. Querini's expedition had proved that the Venetians were not lacking fighting spirit, and with Nicosia in Ottoman hands the grand vizier considered it appropriate to start negotiations. For the Ottomans the war was not proceeding as expected, while for the Venetians it represented a colossal expense. In Constantinople Sokollu did not discount the worrying possibility that the Christian states might set aside their petty quarrels and ally themselves against the Ottomans.

An added risk for the Ottomans was that after the death of the *voivode* of Transylvania John Sigismund, war could erupt again in central Europe. The last thing the grand vizier wanted was another front before the Cyprus question was closed for good. He may also have considered that the peaceful surrender of Famagusta would enhance his prestige and damage that of his rival Lala Mustafa. Sokollu desired peace, and the Venetians needed it. Their fleet lacked rowers, fighting men and victuals. The famine which had plagued the republic's territory for the previous two years was causing serious manpower problems, and forcing Venice to raise the wages of those soldiers destined for the Levant 'so that being able to provide to their needs with greater ease, they will more willingly and readily serve us'.[12]

To attain his objective the grand vizier played his hand skilfully, counting also on his French allies. The Valois had everything to gain by brokering a settlement between the Venetians and the Porte, and much to lose if the pope, Venice and Spain consolidated their alliance. The French, particularly Catherine de' Medici, feared that the league would strengthen the Habsburgs' grip on the Italian peninsula. Many saw Spain as the only real bulwark against the Ottomans, a belief that Philip II had no interest in changing by reducing the Turkish threat. Given that Venice was the only completely independent polity left in Italy – if one excludes the papal states – it was in Spain's interest to see the republic weakened by a prolonged war with the Ottomans. France wanted the exact opposite, and in an effort to separate Venice from her potential allies Charles IX even promised to supply the republic with military aid should the Ottomans refuse to make peace. Predictably, the Venetians were unconvinced, aware of the strong political and commercial ties between Paris and Constantinople.[13]

The grand vizier chose to make the first move, banking on the Venetians' exhaustion and their suspicion that the league Pius so much desired would never come into being. Since the need to save face made it impossible for Sokollu to start direct peace talks, another way had to be found. Conveniently enough, a Jew had arrived in Constantinople from Venice, bringing with him some useful news. At the outbreak of hostilities a number of Ottoman subjects in Venice – Muslims and Jews residing there for commercial reasons – had been rounded up, imprisoned and their merchandise seized. One of the prisoners had managed to escape – perhaps with the help of the Venetian authorities, as skilled as Sokollu in dancing the diplomatic tango – and on his arrival in Constantinople had petitioned the sultan to secure the release of his unfortunate colleagues.[14] This was exactly the excuse that Sokollu needed to approach the Venetians, and he acted on it immediately.

Around the end of January Sokollu's envoy, the dragoman Mateca Salvego, arrived in Venice accompanied by Marcantonio Barbaro's personal administrator (*maestro di casa*). Officially his mission was to obtain the liberation of those Ottoman subjects held in custody by the republic in exchange for the Venetians detained in Constantinople, but in reality he had come to start unofficial peace talks. When Mateca in his master's name asked the republic to send a negotiator to the Porte, the Venetians reacted with caution, but like Sokollu wasted no time in sending an envoy to the enemy capital. The man chosen for the job was Giacomo Ragazzoni, who possessed the double advantages of being a merchant and the brother of the bishop of Famagusta. Ragazzoni's task was to negotiate the exchange of the imprisoned subjects of the two states, but he also had secret instructions to sound out Sokollu about a possible peace treaty. Ragazzoni's mission immediately became the subject of much diplomatic gossip, and even if its real objective was only a matter of speculation, an acute observer like the papal nuncio Facchinetti rightly suspected monkey business on the Venetians' part.[15]

Ragazzoni departed from Venice on 11 March, arriving in Constantinople six weeks later. Sokollu received him on 29 April, the two men engaging in a diplomatic fencing match. The Venetian stated that he had only come to settle the matter of the imprisoned subjects and wished to brief Barbaro about it before negotiations could start. Sokollu, who had been informed by his intelligence service about the true nature of Ragazzoni's mission, answered by reminding him of Venice's mistake in wanting to fight. He added that now the sultan also wanted Crete and Corfu 'since the Muslims believe the prophecy that they must be the lords of Rome, it was necessary for the Turks to conquer Venetian territories that would allow [them] to get nearer [to that city]'. As for an exchange of their respective subjects, some Ottoman Jews had protested that the Venetians had sold their confiscated goods for low prices to finance the war. Sokollu also commented obliquely that for such matters it was not necessary to inform the *bailo*, unless Ragazzoni's real purpose was to seek peace between Venice and the Porte. Should that be the case, the grand vizier would be happy to mention it to Selim.

The Venetian envoy stuck to his guns, insisting that he could decide nothing before speaking to Barbaro, adding also that all Ottoman subjects had been well treated by the republic and that the money gained from the sale of perishable goods (with the owners' approval) was in safe storage. Sokollu then went back to the topic of the war, asking how the Venetians could hope to win against the sultan's military machine. Ragazzoni retorted that the Ottomans had started hostilities with no justifiable reason and that Venice had the means to fight back; besides, the republic was about to sign an alliance with other Christian sovereigns and this united front could very well turn the tide of war against the Ottomans. This was the last thing Sokollu wanted to hear, and he angrily called the Venetians fools to place their trust in a league that would most certainly founder. In any case, he retorted, the Ottomans would win because God was on their side. Diplomatically, the envoy answered that any victory was the Almighty's doing. The conference broke up, apparently without accomplishing anything; but Ragazzoni returned to his lodgings convinced that the grand vizier was 'most inclined to peace'.[16]

On 2 May Ragazzoni went to visit Barbaro in Pera, being treated en route to the sight of the Ottoman fleet in full array. The grand vizier had organized the spectacle in an attempt to cow the

Venetian, but the latter appeared unimpressed by the show of force. Ragazzoni and Barbaro agreed to ask Sokollu for another audience to discuss the exchange of prisoners and, possibly, the preliminaries for a peace agreement. On 7 May the meeting took place, this time with Barbaro in attendance, followed by another on the 16th. On both occasions Sokollu ably alternated honeyed words with threats, while the Venetians adroitly avoided being cornered. It became clear that peace between Venice and Constantinople would not be accomplished easily. Sokollu was adamant in demanding the whole of Cyprus – Ragazzoni having proposed the Venetians keep Famagusta as a trading base – plus an indemnity of 750,000 ducats; otherwise the Venetians should carefully watch their other territories, including their capital, because the Ottomans would surely conquer them.[17]

The grand vizier's obduracy was partially due to Selim's stubbornness and the intrigues of the war faction at court, but also to the Transylvanian crisis having evaporated, and with it the peril of Maximilian II and the Poles siding with the Venetians. The Ottomans now had their hands free to deal with Cyprus. Venice was also in a belligerent mood. On 7 May the senate wrote to Barbaro and Ragazzoni about the developments in Transylvania and the arrival in the city of Marcantonio Colonna to advocate the conclusion of the Christian alliance. The Venetians were also elated by the news of anti-Ottoman revolts in Albania, allowing them to capture Durazzo (Durrës). Given the militarily favourable situation, the two envoys in Constantinople were in no mood to cede Famagusta, nor agree to any sort of peace settlement without Venice's authorization.[18] Ragazzoni would receive such instructions only on 17 June while about to depart for home, but by then events had moved at a quicker pace than diplomatic messengers. Neither the Porte nor Venice now had much interest in a peace settlement, each expecting the situation to change in its favour. As for Ragazzoni, having negotiated the exchange of prisoners there was supposedly nothing more for him to do in Constantinople. In this endeavour at least he had been successful, although the sultan, apparently encouraged by Joseph Nassi, insisted that the Venetians be the first to free their detainees and ship them with their goods to Dubrovnik or Zara. On the 18th Ragazzoni took his final leave of Sokollu, leaving Barbaro to wait out the rest of the war in confinement.

~

While the Venetian envoys were busy negotiating in Constantinople, things had moved ahead in Rome. Philip II had already made sure – should the alliance ever materialize – that the general of the Christian fleet would be Don Juan of Austria, and at the beginning of 1571 the king's half-brother was officially designated commander-in-chief of the coalition's forces. Yet many had reservations about the choice, worried by the appointee's age, inexperience and above all his known rashness. The twenty-four-year-old Don Juan, son of Charles V and the Bavarian beauty Barbara Blomberg, was a dashing, almost reckless individual blessed with culture and grace. Educated in Spain on his father's orders, he was a model of sportsmanship and gallantry. He had been received into Philip's court at twelve, growing up with the heir to the throne, the unfortunate Don Carlos, and the future duke of Parma Alessandro Farnese, destined to become one of the greatest military leaders of the sixteenth century. Philip had restrained with difficulty the then eighteen-year-old Don Juan from joining the Malta relief force in 1565, and the king was weary of his relative's energy and audacity. These traits coupled with exceptional good looks made Don Juan a great favourite with the ladies; the prince fathered a number of illegitimate children. No wonder then, when Philip appointed him commander of his Mediterranean fleet in 1568, he kept Don Juan on a tight leash. Even now the king would ensure that the new commander of the allied fleet was surrounded by cooler, more experienced heads. After all, Don Juan's military experience was limited to the Morisco campaign, and the Ottomans were a rather more formidable foe.[19]

The selection of a second-in-command proved more problematic. The Spanish representatives tried to impose someone of their king's choosing, but Pius and the Venetians would have none of it. The problem was not just one of national prestige; since the first of the planned league's objectives was ostensibly the relief of Fama-gusta, the Venetians wanted someone committed to this venture. The pope wanted his trusted Marcantonio Colonna for the job, but this was anathema to Cardinal Granvelle. Philip II, not wishing to alienate Pius, sent to Rome a list of acceptable candidates, including Colonna, topping his roll with Alessandro Farnese, the duke of Urbino, the marquis of Pescara and the duke of Mantua. It was a clear, not to say unsubtle, attempt to force Pius to change his mind, but the aged Pontiff didn't budge: it would be Colonna or nobody. Granvelle and Pacheco, already dragging their heels, slowed down the negotiations to a snail's pace. Determined to have their way, they asked Cardinal Colonna, Marcantonio's cousin and namesake, to convince the pope to be more malleable: if Pius insisted on Marcantonio's candidacy, then the league had no future; the pontiff should agree that his protégé be appointed instead as commander of amphibious operations in the event of Don Juan's absence. Cardinal Colonna politely told his colleagues to get lost, adding that it was not his business to advise Pius on military appointments.[20] The pope's obstinacy was a source of much irritation in Madrid, Cardinal Espinosa acidly commenting that the pontiff should limit himself to prayers and encouragements and not meddle in military matters – a fine example of the pot calling the kettle black. Pius, however, was flexible enough to agree that Philip appoint Colonna as Don Juan's deputy, on condition that the Roman nobleman enjoy the supreme commander's full authority in his absence.[21]

Deciding the chain of command was but one problem, the road towards final agreement being fraught with every kind of difficulty. By mid-March 1571 it even appeared that the league might be stillborn, Granvelle insisting that the Spanish fleet would not be ready for operations in the Levant until the following year. The cardinal's objective was clear: to force the pope and the Venetians to agree to an operation against Tunis some time late that summer, when the Ottoman fleet would not be in a position to interfere. Even more enraging for the other negotiators was the Spanish representatives' brazen proposal that Venice provide and pay for all the ships necessary for the enterprise against subsequent reimbursement.[22] Given Spain's notorious record of insolvency, the Venetians felt insulted and threatened to break off negotiations.

The Spanish representatives' constant duplicity has an immoral ring to it, but one should sympathize with Philip II's reluctance to commit himself to the Cyprus enterprise. Spain considered its Mediterranean frontier to coincide with an imaginary but relatively defensible line running from Corfu to Tripoli; anything east of that mattered little, unless directly affecting southern Italy, Malta or the Iberian peninsula. Besides, as we have already seen, Philip's strategic–religious priorities lay elsewhere, and these were becoming a source of increasing worry to him.

Tensions with England were growing, the English resenting Spain's policy in Flanders for a number of reasons. Elizabeth I had become a champion of Protestantism, giving refuge and assistance to Dutch rebels, and the English trading community considered the Flemish market vital to its interests. In London there was also concern about the rise of a hegemonic power on the other side of the Channel, something England has always resolutely tried to avoid. By the end of the 1560s Elizabeth was already a nuisance, seizing Spanish ships in English waters and attempting to disrupt Habsburg trade in the New World. Retaliation followed, as resentment on both sides grew. But despite Philip commenting in 1570 that England and Spain were 'nearly in a state of war',[23] he was trying not to alienate the English to the point of throwing them into the arms of the French. For this reason he was angered by Pius's decision that same year to excommunicate Elizabeth, although the pope had correctly perceived that by then the queen was committed to the Protestant cause. The troubles brewing in northern Europe were a greater concern to Spain than the war in the eastern Mediterranean, and Philip was all too aware that a prolonged

Levantine campaign would be a serious drain on his military and monetary resources.[24]

However, neither the pope nor the king wanted the alliance negotiations to fail. If Pius was primarily motivated by religious zeal, Philip was anxious not to lose face and, even more important, the long-awaited ecclesiastical revenues. Philip reiterated an old offer to provide 50,000 troops plus the necessary munitions and supplies for the sea expedition, promising also to have some eighty or so galleys ready by the end of May. Venice was asked to provide the greater part of the remaining ships. The Venetians were unconvinced by these proposals, not trusting the king to deliver by the agreed time. The Spanish, for their part, knew about the Venetians' talks with the Ottomans, and the pacifist lobby within the Venetian senate was growing by the day. Unless something concrete was accomplished soon, the only treaty to materialize would be a humiliating deal between the Republic of St Mark and the Porte. Nuncio Facchinetti was doing his best to convince the senate about the perils of an agreement with the Ottomans, fully aware that the Venetians were sitting on the fence. Many senators were convinced that, even if the alliance should happen, the Spanish galleys would not be ready in May. In the meantime a deal could be reached with the Porte, using the league as a bogey; alternatively Venice could threaten an agreement with the Ottomans to obtain better terms in Rome.

To add extra weight to his diplomatic endeavours, in April Pius sent Marcantonio Colonna to Venice. Initially the Roman nobleman's pleadings cut little ice with the senators, to the point where the pope decided he would call his envoy back at the end of the month, 'remitting to the Lord God's will the decisions that the other princes will make'.[25] Undaunted, Colonna pressed on, using his personal connections to bring the senators over to his side one by one. He was also not slow to remind the Venetians that he, unlike Doria, had not abandoned them during the previous campaign. In the end his efforts were rewarded, on 23 April the senate voting to continue negotiations for the league. But the Venetians wanted guarantees before going ahead, telling Colonna that they wished the pope to allow them to tax ecclesiastical property to help their war effort. Philip was, among other things, to provide the promised fully equipped eighty galleys by the end of May and open a surety account somewhere in Italy to contribute to the alliance's financial needs.[26]

The Spanish knew the Venetians would need their support for any major enterprise in the Levant. The same was also true of Pius, and Colonna's mismanagement of the papal galleys meant that the pope would have to rely on someone else for his fleet. This played squarely into the hands of Cosimo I de' Medici. The grand duke was still trying to get involved in the putative league, counting on the support of Cardinal Pacheco to overrule Madrid's objections. But the Spanish were dead set against Cosimo's participation, although Philip wrote to Zuñiga to act prudently and not irritate the Florentine. Instead he should stick to vague promises about allowing Cosimo into the alliance some time later without attempting to prolong the negotiations further. The grand duke was himself anxious that the league should see the light of day, instructing his ambassador in Madrid Leonardo de' Nobili to insist to Philip that he speed things up. Should the Turks get wind of the league, they would react by assembling more troops and ships; and seeing no move coming from the Christians, would use these forces to attack the West. Worse, should the Venetians get tired of Spain's procrastination, they were sure to strike a deal with the Porte, leaving the Muslims to turn their attention to Italy.[27] Cosimo, of course, was trying to convince Philip that since the Ottoman peril threatened everyone, it would be illogical to exclude Tuscany from the league.

Not being able to enter by the front door, the grand duke used the back one. He had already offered his galleys to the pope the year before, obtaining Philip's approval on condition that the ships be employed only in the Levant. Pius, however, wanted them also to guard his coasts – something the Spanish had failed to do – but for prudence's sake Cosimo would initially not agree to this without

Philip's approval. In the end, not receiving any answer on the matter, the grand duke decided to go ahead. The negotiations between Florence and Rome over the galleys took three months, the main discussions between the Tuscan and papal plenipotentiaries concerning the price to be paid per vessel, their captains and the appointment of the squadron's deputy commander. Thanks to the mediation of Marcantonio Colonna it was agreed that Cosimo would nominate ten of the twelve captains and provide all other officers, oarsmen and sailors. Colonna would provide the soldiers, something that the papal admiral, with an eye to his own authority within the fleet, was more than willing to do. The choice of second-in-command proved more difficult, Pius wanting to reserve the decision to himself. In this he was backed by the Spanish and Colonna himself, for different reasons both wishing to diminish as much as possible Cosimo's control over his galleys. The grand duke proved amenable to the pope's request, keen as he was to conclude the *asiento*. Although the main points of the treaty had been settled by the end of April, more weeks would pass before the final agreement. Pius and Cosimo were waiting to see if the negotiations over the league would be fruitful, otherwise Madrid would not approve the leasing to the pope of the Tuscan galleys. Punctilious as always, Pius promised to ask Philip to pay for them should that happen. The *asiento* was finally signed on 11 May, the pope obtaining twelve galleys from Cosimo but with the obligation to pay for only six. Pius still had to meet the cost of the soldiery on board, and certain logistical details took further months of discussion.[28] Still, both parties had gained what they desired: the pope, a fleet costing him only 3,250 ducats a month (500 ducats each for five galleys and 750 for the flagship); Cosimo, an unofficial place in the league.

Pius's acquisition of the Tuscan galleys and Venice's endorsement of the league cornered Philip. The pope had already threatened to revoke all existing concessions on ecclesiastical revenues should the Spanish continue with their delaying tactics – a serious blow, and not just financial, for the king. If losing hundreds of thousands of ducats was a nightmarish prospect, the loss of face for the champion of Christendom would be even worse.[29] The Venetians, however, were stretched to the limit and badly needed Spain's help to protect their remaining Levantine possessions. The Florentine envoy in Rome Piero Usimbardi was convinced that the Venetians had run out of resources and were eager for peace with the Ottomans, fearful of losing Crete as well as Cyprus.[30] There were still to be disagreements, but once the delegates reconvened in Rome at the beginning of May, everyone had the feeling that the league was a done deal. Cardinal Granvelle's absence − in the meantime he had been sent to Naples as viceroy − eased the process considerably. Up to the very end the Venetians haggled over their monetary contribution, while the Spanish moaned that, given their other military commitments in Europe, they were already financially overstretched.[31] By the 19th everything had been settled, and two days later the pope granted the much-desired Three Graces. Although neither Philip II nor the doge would sign it for a couple of months, on 25 May the treaty establishing the Holy League was signed by Pius V for the papacy, Cardinal Pacheco and Don Juan de Zuñiga for Spain, and Michele Surian and Giovanni Soranzo for Venice.

According to the terms of the agreement the league, with its declared aim of fighting the Ottomans and their allies Tripoli, Tunis and Algiers, was to be maintained in perpetuity. Its military forces were to comprise 200 galleys, 100 other ships, 50,000 infantry, 4,500 light cavalrymen, artillery, munitions and other war materiel. Strategic objectives were to be designated each autumn for the following spring, the traditional start of every campaign season. The pope was to provide twelve galleys, 3,300 infantry and horse and one-sixth of all expenses; should the Holy See be unable to meet its bill, this would be divided between Spain (three-fifths), with Venice providing the remaining two-fifths by arming twenty-four galleys. Victuals were to be provided in abundance by each of the participants at an 'honest price'. Articles VIII to XII dealt with the possible use of the league's forces against North Africa or to defend its members' lands against enemy attack. In addition, the Spanish obtained the right, in the absence of any threatening Ottoman naval or land force, to request fifty fully equipped Venetian galleys to use against the Barbary states. As a quid pro quo, Venice could ask for the same support from the Spanish for operations on the Adriatic coast. All strategic and tactical decisions were to be taken by the commanders of the three fleets and executed by the commander-in-chief Don Juan of Austria or, in his absence, by his deputy Marcantonio Colonna. However, 'for any particular enterprise' it would be up to Don Juan to designate the officer in charge. Pius was made arbiter of all future disputes, and the allies promised to uphold Dubrovnik's neutrality 'unless for some reason the pope should judge otherwise'. No member could make a separate peace with the Porte without the knowledge and consent of the others. The last article was an invitation to the kings of France, Poland and Portugal to join the league, together with 'all the Christian princes'.[32]

To a greater or lesser degree the treaty satisfied everyone. The Spanish had obtained the inclusion of North Africa among the league's targets, while the Venetians could be happy that the main effort would be directed against the Ottomans. They also got the pope to grant them 100,000 ducats per year for five years of the tithes owed to the Church by the Venetian clergy. Yet some matters remained vague. For instance, Article V stated that the league's forces should receive priority in the distribution of victuals, but that the king of Spain had the right to look after his own states, plus the needs of the island of Malta and La Goleta. It would be easy for Philip to exploit such a loophole to blackmail the other members, the famine that had hit Italy the previous two years making many states dependent on Spanish and Sicilian grain. As we shall see, the provisioning of the allied navy would be one of the bones of contention.

The ink on the treaty was hardly dry when problems started. Philip had taken badly the pope consorting with the Medici, and as soon as the negotiations for the league were over he delivered an official protest over the concession of the grand ducal title to Cosimo. The Spanish move blighted the enthusiasm and rejoicing that had followed the league's proclamation, creating considerable tension between Madrid and the Holy See as well as arousing Pius's ire. The pope believed that Philip had deceived him, first extorting the ecclesiastical subsidies and only then issuing his protest. Pius even threatened to withdraw from the league, adding that Don Juan's arrival in Italy was probably to wage war on Tuscany and not on the Ottomans. In the end, thanks also to the mediation of Cardinal Ferdinando de' Medici, Cosimo's son, Pius agreed to receive Zuñiga with his sovereign's protest.

The Tuscans clearly had every reason to pour oil on the troubled diplomatic waters, concerned as they were that Philip might wish to reclaim Siena by force. To be on the safe side, an embittered Cosimo fortified his territories, raised professional troops and called up the militia. He even threatened to switch his allegiance from Spain to France, but it was clear to everyone that, given the Valois' internal problems with their Protestant subjects, this was not a real possibility. Cosimo also attempted a more conciliatory approach to Philip through his friend Pacheco. However, when, at the end of July Don Juan arrived in Genoa the Florentines' fear of Spanish invasion reached fever pitch, aided by a prophecy circulating at the time that the Medici would lose Florence that year.[33] But Philip had no interest in starting another Italian war, preferring to humiliate his slippery vassal in some other less expensive way and avoid the repercussions that a military action against Tuscany would most certainly provoke.

~

The alliance's immediate ostensible objective was the relief of Famagusta, where the beleaguered Venetian garrison was putting up a stiff fight.[34] The Ottomans had tried to take the city immediately after the fall of Nicosia, but Marcantonio Bragadin and his deputy Astorre Baglioni* were determined to resist. Famagusta's state-of-

* Since in the sources of the time he is also called Baglione, it should be pointed out that individuals were often identified by the singular version of their surnames.

the-art fortifications, designed by the celebrated architect Sammi-cheli, allowed for a prolonged siege. The walls, nearly three miles long, were reinforced with bastions, towers and earthworks, and surmounted by forts known as 'cavaliers' that dominated the seafront and the surrounding countryside. In addition, the city was ringed by a deep, water-filled moat. An initial bombardment had produced little effect, the distance of the Ottoman guns from the walls not allowing for concentrated fire. Moreover, since Famagusta was built close to the sea mining proved a difficult task, and turned out in addition the besiegers were constantly harassed by sorties from the garrison. In the first three weeks of October the Venetians executed a number of attacks against the still-incomplete Ottoman siege lines, destroying trenches and redoubts before retreating to Famagusta with minimal casualties. But with the arrival of more enemy troops these sorties became more difficult to perform, forcing the defenders to limit their attacks to Ottoman troops caught in the open. At the beginning of November, having failed to obtain the city's surrender by a show of force, Lala Mustafa decided to postpone any further assault to the following spring, hoping that dwindling supplies would force the defenders to give in without too much fighting.

Provveditore Querini's daring relief expedition in January stiffened the defenders' resolve and subverted Mustafa's plans. He had placed his camp to the south-west of the city, strengthened his siege lines throughout the winter and executed some probing attacks to keep the garrison under pressure. The Venetians stood their ground, on one occasion inflicting considerable losses on the enemy by luring them into a well-prepared trap. The Ottomans were made to believe that the defenders had left en masse with Querini's fleet, only to be subjected to a hail of bullets, coupled with a cavalry charge, when they approached the walls. But everyone was aware that the Turks could easily make good their losses, having the double advantage of practically unlimited supplies of men and the proximity of their supply bases. As for the defenders, they could only hope that the relief force, should there be one, would arrive in time.

At the end of March the Ottomans received considerable reinforcements together with some extra artillery pieces from Nicosia.
Preparing for the inevitable, Bragadin and Baglioni did everything
they could to husband their meagre forces. Their first move was to
expel from the city all 'useless mouths', their number varying,
according to the source, from 3,500 to 5,500. The Ottomans,
seeking to undermine the resolve of the city's defenders, allowed
these people safe passage through their lines after providing them
with victuals. The Venetian commanders' decision had been taken
mainly for reasons of morale; the suffering of women, children and
the aged would have imposed additional psychological strain on the
defenders and perhaps hastened capitulation. All foodstuffs were
listed and a strict rationing regime introduced.

Mustafa was hoping that the daunting size of his army – 240,000-
strong according to Angelo Gatto★ – would induce the garrison to
surrender. On 17 April he organized a general review of all his
forces some three miles from the city in full view of the defenders.
The Ottomans believed to be out of range of Famagusta's artillery,
but Mustafa had not reckoned with the Venetian gunners; Baglioni
ordered two 120-pound pieces to be loaded and aimed at the enemy
mass. Just as the Ottoman commander was riding in front of his
arrayed army, the guns fired. A number of shots landed among the
packed troops, doing considerable damage and bringing the review
to an abrupt end. The biggest loss was Mustafa's face, making him
even more determined to solve the Famagusta problem as soon as
possible.

This was easier said than done. Over the following months the
Venetians displayed an uncanny ability to thwart the Ottomans'
attempts to bring the siege to a rapid close. Following standard
practice, the Turks dug trenches, built artillery redoubts and slowly
advanced towards the walls, harassed by the defenders' sorties and

---

★ An Ottoman hostage gave this number to Gatto at the time of the negotiations
for the city's surrender. GATTO: 54–7. The Ottomans were known for their
ability to field and supply large forces, so we should be careful not to dismiss the
figure as fantasy.

constant shooting. Scores of besiegers died each day, but inexorably the Ottomans advanced to the fortress counterscarp. Under cover of loopholed earthworks they sniped at the Venetians on top of the walls. Gun emplacements were built to house some eighty artillery pieces, including a couple of giant 180-pounder 'basilisks'. On 19 May the Ottomans subjected the city to an intense cannonade, to which the Venetians answered with equally forceful counter-battery fire. Since the attackers were firing over the walls with the intent of sapping the Famagustans' morale by destroying their houses, the defenders were able to direct their fire unimpaired into the enemy redoubts, destroying earthworks, silencing a number of guns and killing many Turks. Yet in the long run the Ottomans' advantage in men and materiel meant that Mustafa was able to rebuild during the night what the Venetians destroyed during the day, while the defenders were rapidly consuming their powder supplies. By the end of the month the shortage of powder had forced Bragadin to slacken his fire. Soon the number of shots per gun was reduced to eight a day, and the Ottomans, sensing the defenders' problems, increased their pounding.

To make the Venetians' plight worse, the attackers had now found that it was possible to dig mines under certain sections of the southern wall. The main Ottoman attack was directed against Fort Andruzzi, below which stood another bastion known as the Rivellin. As the Ottomans advanced above and below ground, they used the earth from their tunnels to fill the city moat and build assault gangways. The Venetians dug counter-mines and targeted the enemy with explosive devices; the Ottomans answered in kind by throwing over the walls lighted sacks full of gunpowder and metal fragments. These tactics, together with cannon and musket fire, daily reduced the number of defenders, as the enemy prepared to deliver the final blow. On 21 June a mine was exploded under the tower of the arsenal, bringing down a large section of the walls. With great shouts the Ottoman army surged forward, attempting to carry the breach before the smoke and dust produced by the mine had settled. For five hours the battle raged, the Venetians trying to contain the enemy attack with enfilading artillery fire. At one point the accidental ignition of an explosive device being carried by a group of soldiers killed or wounded 100 Venetians but the Ottomans hesitated, thinking that the explosion had been caused by a mine placed on the walls. The respite was enough for the defenders to pour reinforcements into the breach, forcing the Turks to retire.

Undaunted, on the 29th Mustafa exploded another mine under the Rivellin. The crumbling masonry filled the moat, and the breach was subjected to an intense cannonade to keep the defenders' heads down. The Turks rushed to the attack, one column charging the ruins of the Rivellin, another the fortifications of the arsenal. As the land troops moved forward Ottoman galleys attempted to force their way into Famagusta harbour, only to be repulsed by Venetian artillery fire. Bragadin and Baglioni sent as many reinforcements as they could spare to contain the enemy attack, and after six hours of fighting once more the Ottomans were pushed back with heavy losses. Feverishly the defenders set to work to repair as best they could the ruined walls, Bragadin even commandeering all the bales of cloth stored in the city's warehouses to make earth-filled sacks. However, seeing the impossibility of mending the Rivellin, he ordered it to be mined. The Ottomans built a redoubt in front of the arsenal, targeting the breaches day and night. By now Venetian numbers were dwindling fast, many infantry companies being reduced to two dozen men at most.

As if all this were not enough, Bragadin now had to face serious internal dissent. Victuals were being used up; what wine was left went for fifty ducats a barrel; poultry, used to feed the wounded, three or four ducats apiece; horse or donkey flesh, four or five ducats a pound. The incessant Ottoman bombardment had also destroyed many of the buildings within the city, forcing the still substantial civilian population to seek refuge within the fortresses, placing an extra strain on the combatants. At last the Famagustans petitioned Bragadin to surrender. Relief was unlikely, the Ottomans were stronger than ever, and if they should take the city by storm everyone would lose their possessions, the men their lives and the women and children their honour. The governor and Baglioni used all their powers of persuasion, begging that resistance continue for another two weeks. There was still hope of relief, duty and honour requiring that every effort be made to hold Famagusta as long as possible.

But the end was arriving fast. On 8 July the Ottomans unleashed a violent artillery barrage, 5,000 shots falling on the unfortunate city. The next day another assault was mounted, the Turks concentrating their efforts against the Rivellin. The intensity of the fighting was such that the Venetian guns overheated and were unable to continue firing. Inexorably, the Ottomans pushed the defenders back, occupying the Rivellin. Captain Luigi Martinengo gave the order to explode the mine previously prepared for just such an eventuality. The whole bastion went up, burying under the falling masonry some 1,500 Turks and a few hundred defenders. Again the Ottomans hesitated, fearing the presence of other mines. The respite allowed the Venetians to bring up reinforcements and once again push back their attackers. This pattern was repeated at every assault, each time the Ottomans losing hundreds of men but inflicting losses that the defenders could ill afford. The savage fighting did not spare those women and children left in the city, many of them being killed while bringing food or munitions to the troops, or, harquebus in hand, trying to repulse the advancing enemy. On the 29th the Ottomans launched a series of massive assaults lasting two days. Again and again they were thrown back, losing, among many others, Mustafa's own son, but by their end the Venetian soldiers left standing numbered only 700, too few to oppose another determined enemy onslaught.

The city had resisted for longer than the two weeks requested by Bragadin, but now the population was determined to give up. Food was virtually finished and powder reduced to just seven barrels. Bragadin and Baglioni could do nothing more, and now risked facing enemies within as well as outside the city. Months before, Bragadin had complained – maybe unfairly – to the doge that Nicosia had been lost thanks to 'the slumbering laziness, and extreme cravenness of the defenders'; he also did not want to behave like those of Kyrenia, 'who without a murmur went over to these dogs having always promised to do the opposite'.[35] One of the biggest problems for the Venetians in Cyprus was the local population, for the greater part Greek Orthodox and opposed to Catholic rule.

Mustafa's spies within the city evidently managed to inform him of what was happening, for the Ottoman commander immediately sent an envoy with a proposal that the garrison surrender on terms. The Ottomans were also exhausted, and Mustafa feared the arrival of an allied fleet. Under popular pressure Bragadin agreed to a parley, but refused to have anything to do with it, delegating all negotiations to Baglioni. Observing the death and destruction around him, the governor exclaimed, 'Oh God, why did I not die on these walls?'[36]

The cry was destined to become tragically prophetic.

7. THE CUTTING EDGE

~

Unaware of the situation in Famagusta, the allies were busy preparing their next Levantine expedition. The ports of Barcelona, Genoa, Livorno, Civitavecchia, Naples and Messina were hives of activity, filled with soldiers, artillerymen, slaves, free rowers and mariners – a multitude from all parts of Europe, speaking a babel of tongues, following different religions and, in the words of a near contemporary, 'for the most part lawless and unfriendly to God'.[1] Accompanying them on the expedition would be an army of clerks and sutlers, plus the servants of the many officers on board each vessel. The combination of all these individuals allowed the operation of the primary weapon system of Mediterranean warfare: the galley.

Powered by wind and, more important, by human muscle, the late-sixteenth-century galley was the descendant of a long line of ships that from the classical age onward had dominated southern European seas. Forty-one metres long, five to six metres broad, displacing approximately 200 tons and with two lateen sails, the standard galley (*galera* or *galea* in Italian, *galia sottile* in Venetian) was an elegant vessel. A narrow central deck, flanked by others at port and starboard, standing above the rowing benches, allowed the men on board to go from bow to stern. Galleys from the western Mediterranean sported at the bow a forecastle (*arrembata* in Italian,

179

arrumbada, in Spanish), which also housed the ship's main artiller battery. Instead of the *arrembata*, Venetian galleys had an elevated fighting platform, which was lower and less easy to defend. At the stern stood the poop deck, often richly decorated and reserved for senior officers.

A galley's main propulsive force were the rowers sitting on twenty-four to twenty-six benches along each side of the ship. Galleys built as flagships (in Italian *capitane*, singular *capitana*) or deputy flagships (*padrone*, singular *padrona*) – known collectively as *lanterne* or *fanò* from the large lamps they carried astern – were usually but not invariably the significantly larger *bastarde*, which in some cases reached fifty-five metres in length, seven across, and sported up to thirty-six benches.★ Smaller versions of the galley were the galliot (thirty to thirty-eight metres and sixteen to twenty-three benches), the *fusta* (twelve to fifteen benches) and the *bergantine* (eight to eleven benches). Apart from the size, the main differences between a galley and its smaller cousins consisted in a higher freeboard, greater amount of ordnance and tactical employment.

To say 'galley' is very much like saying 'World War II fighter plane'. In 1940, for instance, the British and the Germans had mainly monoplanes, while the Italians, for political and industrial reasons, by and large fielded biplanes.[2] Likewise, each Mediterranean country of the sixteenth century had its own galley-building philosophy, developed according to its strategic and economic needs. Besides, different building skills meant that no two galleys were alike, the judgement and ability of individual master builders playing a crucial part in the construction of each vessel. There were, however two basic types of galleys: the *ponentina*, employed by Genoa, Savoy, Tuscany, the papacy, Malta, Spain and her Italian dependencies, and the *levantina*, used by Venice and the Ottoman

★ In modern Italian *bastardo* has taken on the English colloquial meaning of scoundrel or villain. In reality its proper meaning is that of love child, or mongrel. Thus a *galera bastarda* was conceptually a cross between a normal galley and a *galera grossa*, or large galley, the ancestress of the galleass and built for commercial purposes.

empire. North African states normally built vessels of the first type, although adapted to the requirements of the hit-and-run warfare practised by Barbary corsairs. The terms *ponentina* and *levantina* indicated also a system of galley management, the former relying more on slave labour. Ottoman and Venetian galleys drew less water than *ponentine*, being also swifter under oars. On the other hand, when it came to sailing *levantine* did not perform as well as their western cousins, the latter also having larger sails.

Until recently it has been fashionable to consider the sixteenth century galley an anachronism, and to assert that by the 1600s the south of Europe had become a technological and military back-water. The survival of galleys in the Mediterranean up to the beginning of the nineteenth century has often been used as evidence of backwardness, ignoring the fact that there were sound strategic, tactical and economic reasons for keeping oar-powered vessels.* In fact the meteorological and geographical conditions of the Mediterranean favoured galleys much more than sailing ships. In ideal circumstances square-rigged sailing vessels could travel an average of forty or fifty miles in twenty-four hours. In good weather and provided the hull was in reasonable repair, a galley under oars could normally sustain a cruising speed of three to three and a half knots, reaching a maximum of seven to seven and a half for short periods. Although their human engines made galleys far less susceptible than sailing ships to the presence or lack of wind, captains would exploit any favourable breeze to allow their rowing crew to rest. It has been estimated that a galley under sail could reach a top speed of twelve knots, but something in the range of nine or ten appears more reasonable. Sails and oars were often used together, for instance if a galley was giving chase or trying to flee from an enemy. Moreover, until the advent of steam engines, rowing vessels guaranteed that distances could be covered in a fixed

* For instance, a small state like Tuscany would try in the first half of the seventeenth century to create a sailing fleet akin to those used in the Atlantic, only to find that galleys were better suited, and much less expensive, for waging war in the Mediterranean. N. CAPPONI (2002).

time.[3] The ability to move without wind, their fighting complement and formidable ordnance allowed war galleys to remain an important component of all Mediterranean fleets up to the mid-eighteenth century.

The sixteenth-century galley did have significant drawbacks, and in the end, despite a number of improvements over the next 200 years, these would eventually prove fatal. For one, with a freeboard of only about half a metre amidships the galley could not cope with winter swells, thus limiting its operational season to March–October, at best.[4] This was not invariably true, as demonstrated by Marco Querini's relief expedition to Famagusta in January 1571; but navigating in the winter was always risky. Even during the summer galley captains preferred to travel with the coast in sight, beaching their ships when hit by inclement weather.

Inactivity during winter months was a straight financial loss for a galley owner. Even if unable to store any cargo of significant size or weight, galleys often transported precious merchandise, such as silk or bullion.[5] They were also used extensively to carry letters of credit, diplomatic dispatches and other mail of importance, a galley being able to make the return trip from Genoa to Barcelona (460 nautical miles) in ten or twelve days. All this was difficult if not impossible in rough seas, while galley rowers always needed to be fed and clothed. The solution, of course, was to build bigger galleys, capable of carrying more freight and navigating all year round. By the mid-seventeenth century galleys were large enough to brave day-long storms without sinking or having to find shelter.[6] However, increased size meant greater overall production and maintenance costs, as well as larger, more expensive, rowing crews.

In the sixteenth century a normal galley was still relatively simple and cheap to produce. Building material and skilled workers permitting, a new vessel could be constructed and outfitted in two months, even if Giovanni Andrea Doria was rumoured to have once done it in the record time of twenty-seven days. The Venetians, on the other hand, considered it took a year to properly build a normal galley, with a squad of twenty men permanently at work.[7] Several types of wood were used, the stern, where the captain's quarters were located, being made of walnut. The deforestation around the western Mediterranean and indeed in the whole of Europe – forcing many governments in the seventeenth century to implement tree-planting programmes – had resulted by the 1550s in a shortage of construction timber. For this reason western Mediterranean galleys were built to last, while the Ottomans, having forests in abundance, appear to have been less concerned with the quality of their construction material.

Turkish vessels appear overall to have been cheaper to produce. In 1591, after the Ottoman empire had been hit by a serious economic crisis and the *akçe* dramatically devalued, the average cost of a completely outfitted galley was 30,000 *akçe*, equivalent approximately to 3,750 pieces of eight. By contrast, a Florentine estimate of 1558 calculated that some 4,800 local ducats, or nearly 6,000 pieces of eight, were needed for a galley shell, and more than double that amount for outfitting and arming the vessel. However, it would be dangerous to use exchange rates indiscriminately, other factors such as the costs of living and labour in a given place, the availability of construction materials and the complexity of a specific vessel playing their part. In 1650 a galley shell built in Genoa was sold for 4,565 pieces of eight, the workers' wages amounting to one third of the price; in the same period the cost of labour for a galley built in Istanbul was 80,000–90,000 *akçe* (roughly 1,000 pieces of eight).[8]

Different economic and strategic needs dictated different approaches to galley building. Since the Ottomans pursued war essentially for the sake of territorial conquest, in many ways their fleets functioned as an auxiliary branch of the army. Ottoman galleys, in the words of John Guilmartin, were designed 'to get the siege forces to their objective and to prevent interference with their activities by enemy naval forces once there'.[9] We can thus understand why the Ottomans did not care too much about the quality of their oared vessels. Besides, their many outposts in the Aegean needed to be constantly supplied all year round and the short distances between the various islands made sailing relatively safe even in wintertime. It made no economic sense to invest too much money in high-maintenance galleys, as demonstrated by the fact that in 1590 the subsidy given by the sultan to a *reis* (captain) for building a galley was just 400 ducats (48,000 *akçe*).

In 1558 the Venetian *bailo* Antonio Barbarigo reported that the sultan could easily put 130 galleys to sea every year, since it was customary to build them with green timber, 'sometimes the construction taking place in the very forest where the trees are felled'. As a result the life span of a Turkish galley was extremely limited – 'little more than a year' – Barbarigo adding that at the end of the sailing season it broke one's heart to see them 'so derelict and ruined'. Four years later Marcantonio Donini, secretary to the *bailo*, would report that the Ottomans could deploy 170 galleys 'for long voyages' and up to 200 'for short ones', plus those privately owned by corsairs. Donini also noted that the quality of Turkish galleys had improved markedly 'compared to what happened previously, and that only because of the slackness of those in charge'. What really rankled the secretary was that these improvements were due to the presence of 'Christian' shipbuilders, many of them Venetian subjects. Be that as it may, it is certain that on the eve of the Cyprus war Ottoman construction techniques were nearly as good as those employed by their Western counterparts. In 1580 the supervisor of the Venetian arsenal Andrea Quirini had in his care twenty-eight Turkish galleys captured nine years before, of which he thought only one should be scrapped as useless. Galleys employed by Ottoman or North African corsairs were of good quality, given the job they had to perform, although an Ottoman captain relying on state subsidy to build his galley would try to economize on building materials in order to pocket as much as possible – one wonders how, given that the subsidy covered only one sixth of the total building costs. In any case it would be wrong to believe that the use of unseasoned wood was something unique to the Ottomans, the Spanish also having problems with the quality of their timber.[10]

By the mid-sixteenth century the development and diffusion of firearms had significantly affected European naval warfare, even if it would take another century for gunfire to become the determining factor in maritime engagements. Artillery had been a permanent feature on war galleys at least since the 1470s, and a century later Western oared vessels mounted an impressive weight of ordnance. A Western galley's main hitting power was concentrated in its bow pieces, capable of delivering a murderous amount of metal. The main gun was a centreline muzzle-loading piece mounted on a recoiling sleigh, weighing between 2,500 and 6,000 pounds and throwing a shot of between fifteen and sixty pounds. By its side stood a pair of seven- to twenty-pounders (1,400–1,800 pounds), usually flanked, at least on Venetian galleys and on *bastarde* in general, by two other shorter pieces of variable calibre. In addition, a galley mounted up to twenty-five smaller breech- or muzzle-loading guns for close-quarters fighting. (See Appendix 2.)

Yet there was never any such thing as standard galley armament, ordnance varying according to tactical necessity or simply what was available. In 1566 the artillery on board one Venetian galley was one fifty-pounder cannon, three six-pounders, two three-pounders, and fourteen smaller breech-loading pieces. Seven years later another Venetian galley deployed one fifty-pounder culverin, three six-pounders, one three-pounder, and twenty smaller guns. In these two cases the armament was respectively completed by twenty-four and sixty-eight *archibusoni* – large muskets placed on fixed stands. By contrast, an inventory of two Spanish galleys dated 1588 lists for the first a 5,400-pound centreline piece, a pair of 1,465-pound *moiane*, four 300-pound *mortarete* swivel guns and five large harquebuses, and for the second a 5,200-pound main gun, a pair of 750-pound *moiane*, and four 300-pound *mortaretes*.[11]

There is evidence that Genoese galleys mounted less ordnance than their Venetian counterparts. In 1582 the vessels of Doria's squadron had on average a 4,500-pound centreline cannon, two 900–1,200-pound *moiane* and four 250–380-pound swivel guns.[12] This relatively light armament can be explained by the need to sacrifice artillery for speed, Doria's galleys travelling continually between Genoa and Barcelona, or Genoa and Messina. The 1575 inventory of the Genoese Lomellini squadron, present at the battle of the Curzolaris, is even more telling in this respect. Like the Doria, the Lomellini, another Genoese family of maritime entrepreneurs, loaned the vessels to Spain as a matter of course.

The names and sizes of the various types of artillery pieces were different across the Mediterranean. The Venetians fielded (in local weight) the one-pounder *moschetto da zuogo*, the three-pounder *falconetto*, the six-pounder *falcone*, the twelve-pounder *aspide* and *sacro* (both having a calibre of 95–100 millimetres, the *sacro* being a foot longer); larger pieces were the fourteen-to-sixty-pounder *cannone* (cannons) and *colubrine* (culverins), the latter being a third longer than the former. Gunpowder produced in the sixteenth century burnt more slowly than its modern equivalent, and as a result the pressure it created in the barrel lasted longer. Thus a shot fired from a culverin would travel a greater distance than one fired from a cannon of the same calibre and loaded with the same amount of powder. Experiments conducted by the Venetians at various times in the sixteenth and seventeenth centuries confirm this: on a straight trajectory a shot from a fifty-pounder culverin would travel for approximately 600 metres, compared to the 480 of a fifty-pounder cannon. A charge three times as big was needed for a cannon to reach the same distance as a culverin and there were

TABLE 1. GUNS OF THE LOMELLINI GALLEYS (1575)[13]

Galleys Guns	*Capitana*	*Padrona*	*Lomellina*	*Furia*
Cannons	1 (46-pdr)	1 (44-pdr)	1 (23-pdr)	1 (21-pdr)
Sacri	2 (1-pdr)	2 (2-pdr)	2 (2-pdr)	2 (2-pdr)
Swivel guns	2	4	2	2

Each galley had twenty-four rowing benches.

TABLE 2. RANGE OF DIFFERENT GUNS AT FIXED MUZZLE ELEVATIONS (METRES)[14]

Elevation Gun	0°	7.5°	15°	30°	45°
60-pdr culverin	650	3,215	5,465	7,330	7,715
60-pdr cannon	520	2,600	4,430	5,940	6,255
50-pdr culverin	600	3,040	5,170	6,935	7,300
50-pdr cannon	480	2,430	4,135	5,550	5,840
40-pdr culverin	570	2,865	4,875	6,540	6,880
40-pdr cannon	470	2,345	4,000	5,175	5,630
30-pdr culverin	550	2,780	4,725	6,395	6,675
30-pdr cannon	450	2,260	3,930	5,150	5,422
20-pdr culverin	520	2,600	4,430	5,945	6,255
20-pdr cannon	430	2,170	3,690	4,953	5,170

As can be seen, even the slightest muzzle elevation (*un punto di squadra* or one point of the gunner's quadrant) emphasized the clear advantage of culverin over cannon loaded with a thirty-pound powder charge. Interestingly, twenty-pounder culverins appear to perform as well as sixty-pounder cannons. In fact, the Venetians would slowly reduce the weight of their galley artillery, concluding that against a light-framed target a twenty-pounder would do the same damage as a bigger gun.

limits to the amount of powder a gun could take without exploding.[15]

The Spanish used different names for their pieces, such as *medio sacre* instead of *falcone*, while, confusingly *sacro* was sometimes used to denote a cannon. *Ponentine* galleys often carried two *moiane*, shorter versions of the *sacro*.* Finally, there were the stocky ten-to-twenty-pounder *petrieri* (*petreros* in Spanish), so called because

---

* All the artillery types were named after animals. *Aspide*, for instance, is an asp, while a *sacro* is a kind of falcon.

designed to fire stone balls; they were used with or in lieu of the *falconi*.[16]

Galley guns were not intended to be fired in volleys. Centreline pieces were used for long-range shooting, while for close-quarters engagements the preferred weapons were large calibre *petrieri* loaded with grapeshot.[17] Crewmen employed similarly loaded swivel guns to sweep decks, repulse enemy boarding parties or assist their own. Centreline pieces once fired could slide back on the main deck to the mainmast, but the flanking guns could only recoil the length of the gun platform. Weight and technical constraints dictated the amount of ordnance a galley could carry.

The comparative swiftness under the oars of a well-kept Muslim galley was also due to its light ordnance load; indeed, at least by Venetian standards, Islamic rowing vessels appear to have been undergunned, around the 1580s a normal Ottoman galley (*kadırga*) sporting a maximum of thirteen pieces of all types. Reporting to the Venetian senate after his return from Constantinople in the summer of 1571, Giacomo Ragazzoni stated that Ottoman galleys carried only three artillery pieces, 'and many just one'. This was also true for the galleys employed by North African corsairs, who preferred to employ boarding tactics. A 1573 inventory of a captured Turkish galley lists a main five-piece gun battery equivalent in every way to what one would expect to find on a western Mediterranean vessel: a centreline cannon weighing 4,300 pounds, two *sacri* of 1,830 pounds, and a pair of *falconetti* swivel guns of 870 pounds; additional evidence points to this galley being a thirty-two-bench *bastarda* and lacking the small pieces typical of western Mediterranean vessels.[18]

Apparently Ottoman naval artillery was nothing to write home about, although 'naval' is a misleading term here since at the time most guns could be employed differently on land and at sea. In 1572 the officials of the Venetian arsenal informed the Council of Ten, at the time responsible for managing the republic's ordnance, of the 'bad quality' of 115 captured Turkish pieces. Their suggestion was to recast the lot, adding a certain amount of good metal. Similar reports about the inferior quality of Ottoman guns appear in Venetian documents up to the end of the seventeenth century, and an inventory of eleven Ottoman pieces taken in 1571 shows them to be lighter in weight than Venetian ones of the same calibre.[19] This would appear to disprove Gábor Ágoston's statement that notions of Ottoman technological inferiority 'are hardly tenable',[20] but could also be evidence of sound tactical reasoning. Galley warfare did not call for prolonged artillery duels, ships exchanging only a few shots before engaging in close-quarters fighting. The Venetians recognized this when they decided to mount on their galleys fifty-pounders 'with little metal', weighing between 2,600 and 3,000 pounds, since 'even during important engagements they do not need to shoot so many times and as often as when used in fortresses'.[21] For both the Venetians and the Ottomans it made no sense to risk losing good pieces in maritime operations. Besides, the pool of experienced fighting personnel at the Ottomans' disposal inclinded them to rely more on hand-to-hand fighting than long-range gunfire.

By the time of the Cyprus war naval gunnery, particularly in seafaring states like Venice, had become an art in itself. The importance attached by the Venetians to artillery is underscored by their galleys carrying six bombardiers, compared to the two normally embarked on a *ponentina*.[22] Although the theoretically effective range of smooth-bore pieces of any size was limited to a few hundred metres, in ideal conditions expert artillerymen with intimate knowledge of their weapons could do great damage even at a considerable distance. According to one study, the possibility of a smooth-bore muzzle-loading gun hitting a target was about 10–15 per cent of the range for all shots fired. This meant that at 1,000 metres all shots fell within an area 100–150 metres across. At such a distance the chances of hitting a small target, like a galley bow or stern, were therefore slim, especially when firing from a pitching vessel. But it was a different matter when shooting at an extended line of men or ships.[23] At short or even medium range the destructive power of galley guns could be devastating, especially if directed against light-framed vessels. Paolo Giovio paints a clear picture of the effect of galley artillery on timber and flesh in his description of the battle of Capo d'Orso, fought in 1528 between a Genoese squadron under Filippino Doria and a Spanish one led by Don Ugo de Moncada:

> Count Filippo [Doria] who in this [artillery fire] placed every attention, as well as being a crack shot, discharged against the enemy his large artillery piece called the Basilisk.★ The terrible ball, smashing through the ram and the forecastle [of Moncada's galley] with horrible slaughter of men, travelled from bow to the stern across the bridge with such violence that, having already killed more than thirty between soldiers and sailors, it slew many honourable people on the poop deck . . . so that the Marquis of Vasto and Don Ugo were spattered with their blood and guts.[24]

Artillery shot was usually made of cast iron or stone, the latter, much favoured by the Ottomans since its shattering on impact produced a shrapnel effect. Most naval gunners employed straight-trajectory firing, but some preferred what in Italian was known as *il tiro di ficco*, i.e. shooting the ball into the sea at a certain angle to make it bounce and hit the enemy vessel at the waterline. It was a method favoured by the Portuguese, although some criticized it by pointing out that bouncing caused the ball to lose too much speed and hitting power to cause much damage to ships of even medium size.[25] However, a ball fired in this way could still inflict consider-able punishment on light-framed craft such as a galley, provided the target was reasonably close.

~

Western reliance on firepower would be at the centre of one of the most revolutionary developments in Mediterranean naval warfare.

★ A basilisk was originally a gun made of wrought-iron hoops. By the 1530s it was a cast piece of the culverin type.

From the 1520s the Venetians had been experimenting with new galley designs in an attempt to create a battle-winning vessel combining manoeuvrability with heavy ordnance. Much ink was spilt in the debate on how to build the perfect oared ship, some arguing that classical examples should be followed, others opting for a less erudite approach. Vettor Fausto's already-mentioned quinquereme was the product of the first school of thought; and while ultimately disappointing it showed that bigger galleys were necessary to carry the desired amount of ordnance. However, the galley's low freeboard meant that artillery could only be placed on the foredeck – excluding a few swivel guns on the gunwales – even if some of the larger vessels carried a few medium-sized pieces at the stern. More artillery meant slower galleys, while there was also an absolute limit to the weight of ordnance a galley could carry; sometimes guns had to be recast into lighter pieces before being taken on board.[26]

On the strength of their experience with Fausto's quinquereme, the Venetians came up with a brilliant solution. Up to the end of the fifteenth century the typical Mediterranean transport ship had been the fifty-metre-long large galley (*galia grossa* in Venetian), known also as a *maona*.* By the 1550s a rise in crew costs had made such ships largely unprofitable, and many were scrapped or left to rot in dock. The Venetians, marrying expediency with scientific theory, realized that they could be turned into excellent gun platforms, and that is precisely what happened. Under the supervision of the *provveditore* of the arsenal Giovan Andrea Badoer and his successor Marcantonio Pisani, the master builder Francesco Bressan between 1568 and 1571 completely refurbished a dozen or so large galleys, turning them into gun-bristling warships. This was done through a feat of engineering genius which involved building a forecastle strong enough to carry half a dozen heavy pieces without

---

* The *maona* (*mavna* in Turkish) is often described as being without oars and having square sails. There is enough evidence, however, to show that *maona* was an alternative name for *galia grossa*. See: ANDERSON (1919): 282.

affecting the vessel's stability. The engineer and inventor Arturo Surian went a step further, devising a system to stop the pieces on the ships' side from recoiling into the rowing benches.[27]

The firepower of these galleasses, as they would soon be called, turned out to be formidable indeed.* A Florentine document of 1572, reporting Venetian practice, gives the following breakdown: forty-four guns in total, including a powerful battery of two fifty-pounder culverins, four thirty-pounder culverins, and four thirty-pounder cannons; there were also twelve cannons or culverins shooting balls weighing between fourteen and twenty pounds, plus twenty-two smaller pieces.[28] About ten large and medium pieces were placed at the prow on an elevated forecastle; fourteen, medium and small, stood on the upper deck at each side of the ship, with the remainder mounted aft. Swivel guns are not mentioned, but their number must have been considerable. Whatever its ordnance, a galleass was able to deliver a devastating artillery barrage from all sides, and in addition its height made it impervious to boarding. The following table gives an idea of the punch these ships could pack.

The galleass sported three tall masts with lateen sails, but like the galley its main propulsive system was provided by a *ciurma* (roughly, rowing crew) of 165 men sitting on twenty-seven benches placed below the upper deck. Given the size of the vessel the number of oarsmen was inadequate to enable galleasses to keep up with the faster galleys, and consequently they had to be towed by smaller vessels. But the Venetian senate had decided that galleass rowers were to be all free men, not slaves or convicts, and the difficulty of finding an adequate number of oarsmen meant having only three men to each bench.[29]

~

---

* Interestingly enough, for a long time Venetian shipbuilders would refer to galleasses as *galere alla faustina*, thus acknowledging Vettor Fausto's influence in their creation. CONCINA: 152–3.

TABLE 3: ARTILLERY ON BOARD THE VENETIAN GALLEASSES DURING THE 1571 CAMPAIGN[30]

Artillery Captain	60cl	50cl	30cl	20cl	14cl	50cn	30cn	20cn	16cn	12s	6fl	3fn	30p	3p	1mb	1mz	Total
F. Duodo	0	2	0	2	6	0	2	6	0	0	0	2	0	8	0	0	28
J. Guoro	2	0	2	0	4	0	4	6	0	0	0	0	0	5	0	0	23
A. da Pesaro	0	0	0	2	0	2	0	8	0	4	0	0	2	8	0	0	26
An. Bragadin	0	2	2	0	4	0	2	4	1	0	2	6	0	4	6	0	33
Am. Bragadin	0	2	2	0	4	0	4	4	2	0	2	12	0	0	8	0	40
P. Pisani	0	2	2	0	4	0	4	4	2	0	3	0	0	2	8	4	35
Total	2	8	8	4	22	2	16	32	5	4	7	20	2	27	22	4	185

The numbers in the upper row indicate the weight of the shot, and the letters the type of gun; thus 60cl stands for 60-pounder culverin. Legend: culverin (cl), cannon (cn), *sacro* (s), *falcone* (fl), *falconetto* (fn), *petriere* (p), *moschetto da braga* (mb), *moschetto da zuogo* (mz). In 1570, when this list was drawn up, Pietro Pisani's galleass was commanded by Vincenzo Querini. The captain of a galleass was called a *governatore*.

Finding galley rowers was a problem all over the Mediterranean during the Early Modern period.[31] By the beginning of the sixteenth century rowing, once a respectable profession, had become more and more a socially degrading job. The resulting shortage meant that experienced oarsmen could now command higher wages. In addition, the constant state of war in Europe led to a veritable arms race, each state spending enormous sums on expanding armies, fleets or both. More galleys meant having to find extra rowers, but this was becoming increasingly difficult given the ever-shrinking recruiting pool. To make matters worse, the same period saw a change in rowing methods, producing an even greater demand for manpower.

Around the 1530s maritime states as well as private galley owners started experimenting with rowing *a scaloccio* (a term possibly derived from the Italian word *scala*, ladder) instead of the traditional *alla sensile* (from the Spanish *sencillo*, simple). The latter required each oar to be pulled by one man, each bench accommodating three rowers (but sometimes four or five), a standard trireme galley *alla sensile* having a complement of 144 to 164 rowers. In contrast, *a scaloccio* entailed a single large oar for each bench handled by three to five men. This brought an increase in the number of rowers – to a maximum of 240 for a twenty-five-bench galley. It may appear perverse that with fewer oarsmen available a rowing system requiring more of them should be introduced; yet with the *a scaloccio* method it was possible to crew a galley without large numbers of trained men, as expert rowers could be interspaced with green ones. One reason for this change lay in the lack of shipbuilding timber, another result of the aforesaid arms race. Since a normal galley *a scaloccio* needed approximately fifty oars instead of the 150 of one *alla sensile*, the result was a drastic reduction in wood, resulting in lower fitting-out costs. In addition, the bigger *a scaloccio* oars broke less frequently. On the other hand, at the time of the Cyprus war the Ottomans, having adopted the *a scaloccio* method, had only three men to each bench manning thin oars 'since this tires the crews less'.[32] It took some time for the new rowing method to take hold, and at the beginning of the seventeenth century experts were still arguing about which of the two systems was best.

The increased demand for rowers meant finding an alternative to volunteers, but luckily for galley captains the grim life led by many people coupled with the endemic violence of the age meant that there was no lack of criminals roaming the streets – ideal candidates for a rowing bench. By the mid-sixteenth century all the Mediterranean states, including the Porte, had introduced laws prescribing galley work for a number of felonies and misdemeanours: murder, robbery, theft, sexual offences, fraud, forgery, coinage counterfeiting, blasphemy and vagrancy. In the Ottoman empire drinking alcohol in public was added to the list.[33] Sending convicts to the oars had the twin merits of removing unwanted members of society and allowing galley fleets to function adequately. States without sea coasts habitually sold their convicts to maritime governments or to private individuals in need of a constant influx of muscle. The small republic of Lucca, with no port of any significance, introduced the penalty of the galley in 1532 following a suggestion by Andrea Doria, and from then onwards *Lucchesi* convicts were always present in the Doria fleet. This did not mean that volunteers disappeared entirely from galley benches, many needy individuals – cold and hunger being very effective recruiting agents – or those with a twisted sense of adventure choosing the oars as their trade. In some states like Venice or the Ottoman empire, where rowing on a galley did not carry any sort of social stigma, recruiting volunteer rowers was not too difficult. Still, most governments or private shipowners preferred forced labourers since their maintenance costs were half those of *buonevoglie* (Italian, loosely freewillers) and they were 'on the whole better rowers'.[34] The following tables, which refer to two *ponentine* galley fleets, one private and another state-owned, demonstrate the overwhelming preponderance of forced rowers over volunteers.

From a superficial glance at the numbers, it would seem that Doria's galleys were still being rowed *alla sensile*, the Genoese entrepreneur changing to the *a scaloccio* system starting from around 1562. At that date he had two galleys employing the new rowing

TABLE 4. GIOVANNI ANDREA DORIA'S *CIURME* (EARLY 1560s)[35]

Oarsmen Galley		Convicts	(%)	Slaves	(%)	*Buonevoglie*	(%)	Total
Patrona	(27)	81	(42.4)	98	(51.3)	12	(6.3)	191
Monarcha	(23)	67	(44.4)	73	(48.3)	11	(7.3)	151
Temperanza	(22)	63	(40.9)	82	(53.2)	9	(5.9)	154
Donzella	(22)	89	(57.8)	56	(36.4)	9	(5.8)	154
Vittoria	(24)	74	(49.3)	66	(44.0)	10	(6.7)	150
Fortuna	(23)	85	(55.9)	54	(35.5)	13	(8.6)	152
Perla	(23)	69	(44.5)	76	(49.0)	10	(6.5)	155
Doria	(22)	84	(54.5)	63	(40.9)	7	(4.5)	154
Marchesa	(22)	77	(50.3)	65	(42.5)	11	(7.2)	153
Aquila	(23)	63	(40.4)	81	(51.9)	12	(7.7)	156
Signora	(15)	80	(52.3)	73	(47.7)	0	(0.0)	153
Total	(246)	832	(48.3)	787	(45.7)	104	(6.0)	1,723

The numbers in the first column refer to the *uomini de cavo* (*gente de cabo* in Spanish), a term covering the fighting men other than soldiers normally part of a galley complement. Their numbers, like those of the *buonevoglie*, appear suspiciously low, so it is possible that the inventory was done when the galleys were in *scioverno*, winter quarters.

system 'with only three men at each bench'.[36] It should also be underscored that although the overall number of *buonevoglie* in the Tuscan galleys was less than 20 per cent of the total, in the *Elbigina* they represented the largest single group within the *ciurma*. The case of Naples is interesting. In 1571 on thirty Neapolitan galleys out of a total of 5,241 rowers *buonevoglie* were 2,220 (42.5 per cent), convicts 2,469 (47.2 per cent), but slaves a mere 552 (10.3 per cent). Thirteen years later out of 4,310 oarsmen on twenty-four galleys, volunteers numbered just 955 (22.2 per cent), while 2,449 convicts

TABLE 5. *CIURME* OF THE TUSCAN GALLEYS (1570)[37]

Oarsmen Galley	Convicts	(%)	Slaves	(%)	*Buonevoglie*	(%)	Sick	(%)	Total
Capitana	186	(69.1)	83	(30.9)	0	(0.0)	0	(0.0)	269
Padrona	139	(64.4)	54	(25.0)	17	(7.9)	6	(2.7)	216
Fiorenza	106	(52.2)	53	(25.7)	39	(19.2)	5	(2.9)	203
Santa Maria	45	(39.4)	13	(11.4)	42	(36.8)	14	(12.4)	114
Toscana	ND	-	ND	-	ND	-	ND	-	ND
Vittoria	94	(45.8)	47	(22.9)	54	(26.4)	10	(4.9)	205
Elbigina	74	(33.9)	56	(25.6)	82	(37.6)	6	(2.9)	218
Pisana	140	(66.6)	44	(21.0)	20	(9.5)	6	(2.9)	210
Grifona	116	(52.2)	59	(28.0)	27	(12.8)	8	(4.0)	210
Siena	115	(54.2)	53	(25.0)	36	(17.0)	8	(3.8)	212
Pace	59	(40.1)	29	(19.7)	21	(14.2)	38	(26.0)	147
San Giovanni	60	(44.7)	9	(6.7)	28	(20.9)	37	(27.7)	134
Total	1,134	(53.0)	500	(23.4)	366	(17.1)	138	(6.5)	2,138

made up nearly 60 per cent of the total crews; slaves amounted to just 19 per cent.[38] In 1571 one might speculate that the Holy League's religious and material incentives had helped to recruit volunteer oarsmen. The presence of relatively few slaves was typical of those states, like Spain, France, Savoy or the Holy See, that did not conduct corsair activities on a large scale.

Slaves and prisoners of war – often both, although not invariably the same thing – clearly constituted an important source of galley manpower. Muslims captured at sea or during coastal raids were regularly sent to the oars by the Christian powers, and vice versa. Yet religion was not as discriminating a factor as initially may appear. French and Greeks figured among the rowers on board Florentine galleys in 1555: Christians, but subjects of states then at war with the Medici.[39] However, the use of enslaved oarsmen varied across the Mediterranean. The Hospitallers employed them extensively, together with large numbers of *buonevoglie* – an indication both of the predatory activities of the knights, and the sea being the primary economic outlet for the Maltese. Contrary to popular Western belief, the Porte did not make massive use of slaves to man its ships. In 1562 Marcantonio Donini calculated that only forty of the sultan's galleys had slave oarsmen.[40] The situation was different in the galleys of the various maritime *beylerbeik* and those owned by Ottoman corsairs, in this case slave rowers being abundant. The same was true of the Muslim states of North Africa. In July 1560 three 'Turkish'* galliots beached on the Tuscan coast had on board 300 chained Christians.[41] Large numbers of slaves or convicts represented a considerable security risk, and captains had constantly to guard themselves against possible rebellions. For this reason the Ottomans preferred to mix slave crew members with free men taken from the annual maritime levy. The statutes of the Order of St Stephen specifically called for no more than one slave per bench, a rule that could not always be implemented.[42]

The Porte and Venice were the two states that made most use of conscription to man their galleys. The Venetians had followed this practice since the Middle Ages, and in 1545 created a specific magistracy, the *Milizia da Mar*, for a more efficient handling of the levy, which covered the city of Venice, its immediate hinterland and all subject cities. The system devised by the Venetian authorities called for a general muster roll, and also specified the number of men each community or social body had to contribute to the crewing of fifty galleys. In the mid-sixteenth century the city's guilds were supposed to supply a total of 2,622 rowers, the *Scuole Grandi* (charitable associations, members of which were both merchants and workers) 1,200, the neighbouring communities 2,340. Within the cities of the Venetian dominion the pool of conscript

* The adjective 'Turkish' (*Turco* or *Turchesco* in Italian) in the sixteenth and seventeenth centuries was applied to anything Muslim. 'Becoming a Turk' was synonymous with converting to Islam.

rowers amounted to a theoretical 10,062 men, all liable to be called up – names to be chosen by lot, although substitutions were permitted – in times of emergency.[43]

The Ottomans employed a similar system. Every *sancak* was divided into a series of different administrative sub-districts, each of which had to contribute one rower every twenty-three households, together with one-month's wage: 106 *akçe* for Muslims and 80 for Christians. Households could opt to contribute a sum of money (*bedel*) instead of the oarsman, to cover the cost of recruiting and maintaining a substitute. Only people from the *reaya* class (non-military, tax-paying subjects) could be levied, and from existing records it appears that conscript crewmen (*küreçi azab*) came from the most distant provinces of the Balkans and Anatolia. The Ottomans also employed volunteers, known as *mariol* – vagabonds, tavern aficionados, the unemployed, Greeks exiled from Venetian territories, all ready to take on any job for a bit of money. More than just a bit, as a matter of fact: in 1558 the Venetian *bailo* Antonio Barbarigo would complain that Venice's Greek subjects were enlisting in droves as rowers in the Ottoman fleet, 'for they are very well treated and paid'.[44]

Given the available pool of free rowers, conscripts and volunteers, one understands why it took the Venetians longer than anyone else to introduce convict oarsmen. This was mostly done at the instigation of Cristoforo da Canal, who advocated the introduction of the crewing methods used in *ponentine* galleys after seeing them in action during the Preveza campaign. In his work *Della Milizia Marittima* da Canal cited considerable evidence to back his thesis: convicts rowed more efficiently for fear of punishment and cared more about personal hygiene, resulting in a lower mortality rate; nor could they run during sea fights. Galleys could be built to travel efficiently under either oars or sail, and the presence of convicts allowed for more soldiers on board. Finally, non-free oarsmen – being chained to their benches and thus unable to stand erect and move back – could adopt a rowing style known as *a rancata*, which used short, quick strokes that allowed galleys to move at greater speed.[45]

Many historians have accepted da Canal's treatise as a bona fide document, but a comparison with existing archival sources shows he manipulated the evidence to support his case. Firstly the assertion that murderers, thieves and robbers rowed better for fear of the lash is unproven. Secondly, free oarsmen were cleaner than convicts, and were trained to fight. As a matter of fact, convicts and slaves tended to suffer greater battle casualties precisely because they were unable to move from their benches. Thirdly, galleys crewed with forced oarsmen were less efficient under oars, since the rowers tended to do the least work possible. As for embarking more soldiers, galleys, due to their structure, could allow on board only so many men – one wonders where da Canal got his idea about convict galleys having extra space. To top everything, rowing *a rancata* exhausted crews more rapidly than other styles involving slower, longer strokes.★

Despite all these contraindications in 1545 the Venetian Senate introduced *galie sforzate*, rowed exclusively by convicts.† It is doubtful that the senators, many of whom had extensive naval experience, did this because convinced by da Canal's arguments. More likely, the reasons were economic and social. Convict galleys cost 7.5 per cent less than those rowed by free men, and in addition allowed the authorities to empty the jails. Moreover, recourse to criminals put less pressure on the aforementioned social bodies to provide conscripts, which had always been an unpopular solution. However, it became immediately apparent, despite da Canal's opinion to the contrary, that galleys manned by chained oarsmen were not the best fighting machines, and to ameliorate the problem it was suggested to alternate convicts with free men on the benches. Initially da Canal's reform seemed to work, so that on the eve of the Cyprus War Venice had twelve galleys entirely crewed by convicts. Yet it was already evident they were qualitatively inferior to those

★ It should be noted that in modern Italian one of the modern meanings of the verb *arrancare* is trudge.

† The use of the letter 's' in front of certain Italian words can mean different things, depending on the area. For instance, in sixteenth-century Tuscan a galley convict was a *forzato*, while *sforzare* meant to force or even to rape.

manned by free men, not least because their commanders had no interest in running them efficiently. One of the main differences between a Venetian *sopracomito* (captain) and his *ponentine* colleagues consisted in his administrative and not just military responsibilities. Commanding a galley not only brought with it prestige but could also be very profitable.

In theory enlisting for the oars in Venice could be quite remunerative, volunteer *galeotti* (free and non-free rowers – in Venice free ones were known as *galeotti di libertà*) receiving a recruitment bounty of at least twenty-five Venetian ducats – between thirty-two and thirty-five pieces of eight in the late sixteenth century. Sometimes this sum was doubled or even tripled, a considerable incentive for individuals coming from the lower strata of society. In any case, even if rowing was hard work, in Venice it was considered an acceptable profession, no worse and sometimes better than toiling in a mine, a field or a workshop. Moreover, for free men life on a Venetian galley was not as hellish as popular imagination would have it. Volunteers were not chained to their benches; unlike what happened in *ponentine* galleys, they enjoyed legal rights and a considerable amount of freedom when in port. The yearly pay of roughly twelve ducats was comparable to that of an unskilled worker, and supplemented by the assurance of food and clothing. Yet, despite all these incentives, it was never easy for the Venetian authorities to find men willing to enlist for galley work.

To begin with, not all the promised bounty was given to the oarsman, but kept instead by the captain against future expenses. Every galley had an account book recording not only each *galeotto*'s earnings and expenses, but also details of his illnesses, dismissal, desertion or death. From the man's original credit were deducted the costs of clothing, medicines, extra food, any money he might owe to other members of the crew, and so on. In any case the *galeotti*'s earnings were calculated in the virtual and largely devalued *moneta d'armata*; but his expenditures in real money. Galley accountants often would also surreptitiously transfer the debts of the deceased and deserters to the remaining members of the crew. Very soon the original credit nearly always became a debit, turning the free man into an indentured labourer. Galley captains sold their men's debts to colleagues in need of rowers, and whole crews could be transferred by means of legal contracts from one galley to another. On the other hand, a *galeotto*, even if a convict or slave, was usually allowed, despite rules to the contrary, to engage in trade and other economic activities when in port, or work for his captain for extra money. It should also be remembered that in Venice *galeotti di libertà* were supposed to fight alongside the soldiers during sea battles, and thus had the opportunity to acquire enough booty to buy back their freedom and retire with more than a few coins in their pockets. Enlisting for the oars was a game of chance, and in Spain, its Italian dominions and Genoa this was more than just a metaphor. Recruitment officials would put up betting stalls, advancing money to penniless individuals who then would gamble for their freedom; losers were immediately sent to the rowing benches until they had repaid their debts.

The lot of the convict or enslaved oarsman was usually worse than that of his free colleague. Venetian law did not allow anyone to be sentenced to the galleys for life, the maximum being twelve years, although this rule did not apply to those criminals acquired from abroad. But even Venetian *forzati* were forced in to the spiral of debt that afflicted the *galeotti di libertà*, and galley accountants would resort to every possible trick not to liberate unencumbered convicts who had served their terms, often 'accidentally' increasing the length of sentences in their books. Muslim slaves appear to have been used only when Venice was in a state of war with the Porte, and were supposed to be liberated once peace was signed. Since most *ponentine* states in the Mediterranean were always more or less at war with their Islamic neighbours, slaves on western Mediterranean galleys generally rowed for life or until ransomed. Convicts on *ponentine* galleys served from a few months to life, or *a beneplacito* – at the discretion of their governments, a rather vague and sinister concept.

The sort of chained humanity which could be found on a western Mediterranean galley can be understood by the following examples taken from an inventory of the Florentine fleet in 1555.

> Bernardino from Bibbiena for having taken three wives, sent for five years . . . Ercole di Benedetto from Pisa, cheese maker, with a three year sentence for sodomy . . . Ser Lorenzo di Bernardino Niccolucci from Modigliana, sent by the inquisition for life as a heretic . . . Senso di Giusto from Monterchi, sentenced for life for having raped and deflowered a thirteen-year-old girl . . . Mustafa, Turk from Anatolia, 45 years of age, tall and white-skinned, branded in the face with His Excellency's [Cosimo I de' Medici] arms, captured in the Gulf of Salerno by Don Pedro de Toledo . . . Salem, moor from Tunis, branded on the right cheek with an M, and with an S on the left, lame, bought in Naples . . . Abdul of Tripoli, blackamoor, known as *Cazogrosso*, tall and lanky with a mark near the hair, lacking two upper teeth . . . Saim, Granadane [now] from Algiers, aged 35, can't row being blind . . .[46]

Information like this evokes images of sweating, gaunt men, constantly subjected to the lash of their overseers. But the way the crews were treated depended on the individual captains, and only very foolish ones would unnecessarily overwork their rowers: forced oarsmen, convicts or slaves, were expensive, costing anything from forty pieces of eight upward in the mid-sixteenth century.[47] Likewise, the entrenched belief that galleys stank to high heaven is only partially true. Some captains had little care for hygiene – with potentially disastrous results, as shown by the fate of the Venetian fleet in 1570 – while others insisted on washing men, decks and benches every other day.

Nonetheless, the life of a galley oarsmen was tolerable at best and at worst hellish. When not at the bench non-free oarsmen, and in the western Mediterranean also *buonevoglie*, stayed in special places called *bagni*, corral-like structures with courtyards surrounded by rooms or cells. In Christian ports there was usually only one *bagno*, while in places like Algiers, Tripoli or Tunis there could be several, housing not only oarsmen but also many of the other slaves of which these cities were filled. Rowers could be recognized by their shaved heads – although Muslim slaves had a small knot of hair in the middle of the skull – and the iron ring on their right heels. In Livorno they wore a shirt, baggy trousers and a floppy red cap. A recognized hierarchy based on seniority existed among slaves and convicts, one functioning as spokesman for the others. Many paid their overseers for the right to exercise some sort of commercial activity or avoid being selected for the heaviest tasks – in Algiers, for instance, working in the local stone quarry. Suicide was a regular occurrence among *bagni* inmates, many being unable to withstand the imprisonment and constant bullying. Yet *bagni* were also meeting places with shops and taverns, in Algiers the latter being run by Christians but frequented also by Muslims. Everywhere official or tacit religious tolerance was practised, Christian clergy being allowed to say mass in Algiers, and in Livorno the Islamic slaves had their own mosque inside the *bagno*. Contrary to what is commonly believed, slaves both in Christian and Muslim countries were not under constant pressure to change their religion, although the Algerians would try to convert to Islam prisoners with particular skills in exchange for their freedom.[48]

Given their hard not to say harsh life, it not surprising that many galley convicts, slaves or even *buonevoglie* took to their heels when they had the chance. Those who enjoyed greater freedom and privileges would also attempt to escape, like a certain Maestro Pedro, who after many years in captivity managed to seize a boat and sail to Valencia, despite having in Algiers his own house with a chapel.[49] Escape rings, sometimes run by unscrupulous locals, existed in every port, together with officially recognized bodies whose purpose was to ransom fellow countrymen or coreligionists. Escaping was always risky and fugitives could expect savage treatment if apprehended. In Algiers recaptured runaway slaves could expect mutilation, severe beatings and even death. Cosimo I de' Medici ordered the ears and noses of two recaptured Turks to be cut off 'as an example for the others'.[50] These instances of extreme brutality coexisted with examples of great chivalry. Courage, generosity and sticking to one's principles were qualities everyone admired, and allowed for courteous behaviour between otherwise bitter enemies. Illustrative of this is the letter sent in 1576 by the Ottoman corsair Cara Assam Reis to the grand duke of Tuscany Francesco I de' Medici.★

> A few days ago arrived here a Turq asked [i.e. called] Sinan of Mythilene, once a slaiv on the Grand Duke of Tuskany's galleys. The said Turq has made himself yours reccomendation for which we thanck you verry particullarle the Captain Caraasam. Iff you shuld need anythung from here I am willings to serve you. Iff you shuld disere to do me a favour helping theis *rais* for which we would consider donne it to ush beeng an old man. Nothung else; if you should neid something in Barbary or Turquey I am entirrely at your servise. God keep you in health.[51]

Such civility was customary between gallant and worthy foes, particularly people of rank, and transcended the fact that important captives were a source of ransom money. The well-known exchange between Dragut and La Valette when the former was a prisoner of Giannettino Doria (La Valette: 'Mister Dragut, custom of war.' Dragut: 'Yes, and reverse of fortune.')[52] is only one of many examples. La Valette himself had just been released from the captivity of a Muslim galley, and so could appreciate Dragut's plight. The fact was that both Christians and Muslims were confident in their beliefs allowed them to treat their religious enemies with assurance.

~

Even before its official ratification all of the Holy League's signatories had started enlisting soldiers on a grand scale. Recruitment officials were busy everywhere in search of suitable candidates for

★ The original Italian is full of misspellings and lacks punctuation. My translation tries to capture the flavour of the document.

the colours: feudal lords ordered their retainers out; states levied military contingents from subject communities; aristocrats from all over Europe – including some French, thus defying their government's veto – eagerly joined the anti-Ottoman expedition, some leading parties of soldiers, others simply as volunteers. If it had not been for the looming war, the gathering of the league's fleet would have been the most fashionable event of the season. Reasons for enlisting were many, ranging from lofty crusading ideals to rather more prosaic motives: Knight of St Stephen Luigi della Stufa joined the allied fleet to redeem himself from some sort of misdemeanour that had cost him two years of exile from Florence.[53] But everyone, whatever their motives and whether from the top echelons of society, the petty nobility or the lower classes, aspired to glory and money – 'in the name of God and good profit', as the Florentines would say. Their goals and aspirations were similar to those of their Muslim counterparts and typical of a world in which religion was integral to daily life.

Francesco Maria della Rovere was born 1549, the son of Guidobaldo II duke of Urbino and Vittoria Farnese, granddaughter of Pope Paul III. His father, like many Italian princes, soldiered by profession, and Francesco Maria received an education befitting someone of his station, physical activities going hand-in-hand with humanistic culture. At the age of sixteen he asked to be allowed to join the Holy Roman Emperor's forces, then busy fighting in Hungary. Guidobaldo agreed, but being then in the service of Philip II had first to seek his employer's permission. The king, wishing to keep Italy under his thumb, insisted that Francesco Maria go to Madrid. The young heir to the dukedom of Urbino arrived there at the beginning of 1570 after visiting every court in northern Italy. In Spain he befriended a number of important people, including Don Juan of Austria, but soon tired of courtly life. Having been refused permission to visit France, he decided to return to Italy and when in Genoa was the guest of Giovanni Andrea Doria. His desire was to gain experience in statecraft, 'but since his father showed no desire to employ him, he went back to his long-neglected studies'.

On hearing about the Holy League, he rushed to join Don Juan of Austria in Genoa, leaving behind his newly wed wife Lucrezia d'Este, sister of the duke of Ferrara.[54]

Not from a royal family but nonetheless someone who could boast Pope Boniface VIII among his ancestors was Onorato Caetani. Born in 1542 to Bonifazio, duke of Sermoneta, and Caterina Pio di Carpi, Onorato, like Francesco Maria, received the typical education of a Renaissance gentleman – designed to fortify the intellect as much as the body – under the direction of his uncle Cardinal Nicola, known as Cardinal Sermoneta. Sermoneta would be a crucial element in Onorato's life. Made a cardinal when only nine by his kinsman Paul III – whose mother was Giovannella Caetani, Nicola's great-aunt – he was notorious for his lechery, but nonetheless a religious reformer and a friend of the Jesuits and the Oratory of St Filippo Neri. Onorato himself was a supporter of the Oratorians and committed to his religious beliefs. Since Cardinal Sermoneta was one of those who had worked most assiduously behind the scenes for the Holy League,[55] it was not difficult for him to obtain a prestigious commission for his nephew, who happened also to be Marcantonio Colonna's brother-in-law. Onorato, one of the few Roman nobles with any naval experience, was made captain-general of the pope's maritime troops.[56]

Although Pius V had confirmed Colonna in the post of high admiral, his disappointing performance during the previous year's expedition required someone competent in maritime matters be appointed to assist him. For the sake of Colonna's dignity and the Holy See's prestige it was necessary to find someone neutral, but of recognized international standing. Pius had no doubt about the right person for the job, and on 12 June 1571 wrote to the celebrated knight of Malta Romegas, inviting him to join his fleet. Romegas did not hesitate for a minute, and ten days later climbed aboard Colonna's flagship with the rank of superintendent of the papal galleys.[57]

Fra Mathurin Lescaut, *dit* Romegas from the name of one of his family's estates, was already a legend. Born in 1528 to a French noble family connected with the great house of Armagnac, he joined the Hospitallers around the age of fourteen in 1542, being dubbed a knight four years later after completing the prescribed period of religious and military apprenticeship. Quickly making a name for himself as a redoubtable sea fighter, Romegas seemed blessed with incredible stamina. When in 1551 his galley was overturned by a waterspout, he managed to survive underwater for twelve hours clinging to the keel with his head in an air pocket. The incident severely affected his nervous system, to the extent that his hands never stopped shaking and he could not drink from a glass without spilling some of the contents. It is unclear if the event affected also Romegas's character, for he is reputed to have been exacting with his men and harsh with prisoners. What is certain is that he was totally committed to the defence of the Catholic faith, fighting with unbounded zeal Protestants and Muslims alike. Considered by all one of the greatest mariners of his age, he knew intimately every nook and cranny of the Mediterranean.[58]

Equal to Romegas in maritime skill but on the Ottoman side was the *beylerbey* of Algiers Uluç Ali Pasha. Originally Luca (or possibly Giovanni Dionigi) Galeni, he was born in Le Castella in Calabria, the tip of Italy's boot, around 1511 into a family of fishermen, reputedly becoming a Dominican friar. Captured by Barbary corsairs and chained to a rowing bench, he converted to Islam – according to one unconfirmed story, his decision motivated by the wish to hide under a turban the ringworm on his head – managed to obtain his freedom and married the daughter of his former master. After fighting at the battle of Preveza he became one of Dragut's associates and soon one of the most feared men in the Mediterranean. It was thanks to his advice that Piyale Pasha decided to attack the Christian fleet at Djerba in 1560, and in June of the same year during a raid against Villafranca Uluç Ali nearly managed to capture the duke of Savoy Emmanuel Philibert. As a reward for his services the sultan made him commander of the Egyptian fleet based at Alexandria, and after Dragut's death at the siege of Malta Uluç Ali succeeded him as governor of Tripoli. Two years later he became *beylerbey* of Algiers and in 1570 captured Tunis for the Ottomans. Of average height, well built with a thick beard, reputed to be at the same time 'most cruel and inhuman' and 'indefatigable and very generous', he was universally recognized as one the ablest naval tacticians of his day.[59]

Equally experienced if not as famous was the commander of the Egyptian fleet Şuluç Mehmed Pasha, better known in Christian Europe as Maometto Scirocco. Another of Dragut's associates, he had been at sea since his teens, operating mainly against the Genoese in Liguria and Corsica. Present at the siege of Malta, after the fall of Fort St Elmo he was given the task of relaying the good news to the sultan in Constantinople. Promoted to governor of Alexandria, during the Cyprus campaign he commanded the Chios and Rhodes squadrons after their commanders' disgrace following Querini's exploit at Famagusta. The Venetians had a particular grudge against Scirocco for his 'insolent' attitude towards them even before the outbreak of the war. Skilled in naval affairs and a devout Muslim, Şuluç was a foe to be reckoned with.[60]

Religion also motivated others. Pompeo Floriani, born in Macerata in 1545, at seventeen had gone to France with the expeditionary force sent by Pius IV to fight the Huguenots. Having risen to company commander, Floriani, a skilled architect and engineer, was once more facing battle against the infidel under his old colonel Paolo Sforza, count of Santa Fiora. Knight of St Stephen Bernardino Antinori came from an old Florentine family with a military background; his cousin Amerigo had fought under Henry VIII of England and the Emperor Charles V. Bernardino, a cultivated man and a poet in his own right, was the son of one of Cosimo I's most trusted servants and had entered the Tuscan order in 1567, following in the footsteps of his older brother Alfonso. After the statutory period of religious and military training, which included the study of history, astronomy, navigation, geometry, arithmetic, drawing and the art of war, fencing with a variety of weapons, shooting with the harquebus, crossbow and the 'Turkish' bow, and wrestling, he went to sea hoping to gain sufficient reputation and seniority to allow him to enjoy the revenues of one of the order's commanderies.[61]

Seeking glory and fortune was also an obscure figure, later destined to overshadow nearly all other participants in the expedition. Miguel de Cervantes y Saavedra was born in 1547 in Alcalá de Henares, a small town near Madrid, into a family with some pretensions to nobility, even if his mother may have been descended from converted Jews. His father, Rodrigo de Cervantes, was an apothecary-surgeon of little means and often in debt, so much of Miguel's childhood was spent moving from town to town with his constantly work-seeking father. Educated by the Jesuits in Cordova and Seville, Miguel later studied under one Juan López de Hoyos in Madrid. Forced to flee from Spain to Rome at the end of 1568 for wounding another man, he entered the service of Cardinal Giulio Acquaviva in 1570. But the same year Cervantes, wishing like many young Spaniards to try his luck in war, joined a Spanish infantry regiment destined for the Levant.[62]

Men of letters could be found on both sides. The scribe Hindī (Dark) Mahmūd was born in Afyon Karahisar, in western Anatolia, to a family of local standing. Thanks to the good offices of a *kadi* (judge) uncle he managed to gain access to Prince Selim, securing employment in the latter's household. Following his master to Konya, Hindī gained experience in both clerical and diplomatic affairs. During this time he also managed to visit Mecca three times as a pilgrim, something which contributed to his rising status. Steadily advancing in the prince's service, his career took a leap forward when Selim became sultan, Mahmūd being given judicial responsibilities in the town of Diyarbakir.[63] Like all administrators, Hindī Mahmūd also had military duties, and in this capacity was on board one of the Ottoman ships.

Leaving aside slaves and convicts, not all those climbing aboard the league's galleys were there spontaneously. Venice's maritime levy required all subject communities to provide galley rowers, and the inland town of Brescia had to contribute a quota of 378 men. However, the various political and social bodies in Brescia and its territories started quarrelling among themselves over how many men each of them should provide, with the guild of notaries claiming exemption because of ancient privileges. After two months of quibbling and haggling with the Venetian authorities, in May 1571 Venice peremptorily ordered Brescia to send without further delay 338 rowers, sufficient to man two galleys, promising to resolve at a later date the matter of the forty men owed by the notaries. Given the unpopularity of naval conscription, Venice attempted to sweeten the pill by allowing galleys crewed with levied rowers to have local commanders and officers. On 3 March Brescia's city council had elected Giovanni Antonio Cavalli and Orazio Fisogni to the role of *sopracomiti*. Of the two, the fifty-year-old Cavalli was the more experienced, having participated in various naval and land campaigns, including the battle of Mühlberg. Both men started immediately to recruit sailors and other naval personnel, completing their task by the 24th of the same month.[64]

Unlike many others, the Tuscan convict oarsman Aurelio Scetti was not keen to go east. A musician by trade who had performed at various Italian courts, on 20 August 1565 'inspired by a diabolical spirit' he had killed his wife with a razor, managing to break a leg while attempting to escape by jumping out of a window. Condemned to death for murder, his friends in Florence managed to get Cosimo I to commute the sentence to life service on the galleys. Because of the lameness deriving from his broken limb, Scetti spent little time at the oars (as a matter of fact certain contradictions in his memoirs arouse the suspicion that he rowed not one day) and at some point was given some sort of minor clerical post. Endlessly complaining about his self-inflicted miserable condition, Scetti beheld the Tuscan galleys leaving port with a mixture of fear and anticipation.[65]

Besides artillery, the fighting capability of a galley was provided by its complement of soldiers. A normal galley had the capacity to carry up to 100–150 soldiers, up to 400 in the case of *bastarde*. With the exception of Venice, few states had troops specifically assigned to serve at sea, and crewmen other than rowers, called by the Spanish *gente de cabo* (artillerymen, sailors and galley guards), were considered combatants for all intents and purposes.[66] As we have already seen, in Venice conscript and volunteer rowers were also expected to fight in sea battles while in *ponentine* galleys convict rowers, or even *buonevoglie*, received weapons only in extreme circumstances. Spain had lost the cream of its experienced naval fighters at Djerba, and from then onward deputed regular infantry to serve on its galleys. Venice employed marines (known as *scapoli* or *uomini da spada*, swordsmen)★ in large quantities, usually but not invariably recruiting them from the costal areas of eastern Italy, Dalmatia, Albania and Greece. The main difference between *scapoli* and the other soldiers to be found on Venetian galleys was that the former were intended to serve exclusively at sea.[67]

Tuscany attempted to recruit marines by introducing a levy in its coastal areas, but the resulting yield in men was never more than 650 and often less. The grand dukes could tap into the well-trained and efficient Tuscan militia for galley troops, but during the 1571 expedition the *asiento* between Cosimo I and Pius V placed the responsibility for troops squarely on the pope's shoulders. As a result, the rank and file on the Tuscan galleys came mostly from the papal states or served under papal officers. Many of the gentlemen rankers (*venturieri* in Italian, *particulares* in Spanish) and junior officers were Tuscan, approximately 100 coming from the Order of St Stephen. The Ottomans had fewer problems finding the necessary military manpower for their fleets, employing for this purpose *timar* and *kapıkulu* troops and normally only sixty per galley. In addition, the

---

★ Sir John Hale aptly describes *scapolo* as 'a chameleon-like term', appropriately translating it as marine. HALE (1983): 312. Yet *scapolo* in the rest of Italy usually meant what it still means today, bachelor. Thus in Tuscany an order to select *scapoli* for galley service from the ranks of the militia meant choosing unmarried men. See for example: ASF, MM, 370, ins. 40, segn. 46, nn.ff. 'Ragguaglio della spesa della Banca al tempo del Gran Duca Francesco, Gran Duca Ferdinando, e del Gran Duca Cosimo' (1620).

sailing crews and free rowers were expected to fight alongside the professional combatants.[68]

With war raging in the eastern Mediterranean, Spain and Flanders, raising enough soldiers to serve on the league's galleys was not easy. For those recruiting for the papal fleet difficulties were increased by Pius V's order 'not to enroll any beardless boy', and scores of soldiers already enlisted had to be dismissed. Many of the Spanish troops were green, Don Garcia de Toledo commenting that they hardly knew how to fire their harquebuses, and that if he had to fight the seasoned Ottoman soldiers he would much prefer to have some veterans from Flanders. Yet the Ottomans, although daunting enemies, were not as formidable as Don Garcia painted them. Their galleys had been at sea since the spring and badly needed maintenance. Ill feeling was rampant among the *sipahis* and janissaries allotted to serve with the fleet, many of whom had been on campaign for more than a year and seen scores of their comrades die in Cyprus.

Venice had similarly serious problems, many of its subjects recruited the year before having fallen victim to the epidimic which had ravaged the republic's fleet. The solution, of course, was to enlist foreigners. But the recruitment campaign produced disappointing results, the Venetians paying through the nose for often inferior and untrustworthy soldiers. To make matters worse, 4,000 men destined for the galleys would not reach them due to an Ottoman foray into the Adriatic that July. As a result, the Venetian vessels were undermanned – Caetani calculating just sixty to eighty fighting men each – forcing their commander Sebastiano Venier to accept Don Juan of Austria and Colonna's offer of extra manpower.[69]

Soldiers were supposed to come with their own weapons, but every galley kept stocks of arms to equip soldiers, sailors and other members of the crew. The 1562 statutes of the Order of St Stephen stated that on each galley there should be seventy-five sets of body armour plus fifty helmets and fifty bucklers, one hundred pikes or 'short weapons' and as many harquebuses. The previously

mentioned 1588 inventory of two Spanish galleys lists fifty harquebuses, sixty-six edged weapons including sixteen pikes, a two-
handed sword and forty-six helmets. Similar weapons in type and
number, with the addition of some fifty breastplates for each ship,
were also stored on the Lomellini galleys in 1575. The evidence
points to a reduction in the number of pikes versus firearms in the
latter part of the sixteenth century, following the universal trend in
this direction. Indeed, a memorandum directed to Don Garcia de
Toledo in the early 1560s stated clearly the need that all the soldiers
on a galley 'should be harquebusiers'.[70]

The harquebus used a matchlock mechanism and fired a lead
ball of approximately half an ounce capable of killing an unprotected
man at 200 yards, even if it would take an exceptional marksman to
hit a target at more than sixty. Another of the harquebus's drawbacks
was its slow rate of fire, although a skilled individual in ideal
circumstances could shoot three times in a minute. Maintaining a
steady rate of fire was considered more important than accuracy, the
tactical employment of firearms calling for formations a number of
lines deep delivering massed volleys. Around the 1590s the Dutch
would realize that rotating the ranks of their soldiers, moving them
to the rear to reload after shooting, could increase the volume of
fire.[71] But this was nearly impossible to do on a narrow galley
bridge, and even the galley's forecastle was too cramped to allow
for such manoeuvres. Seeking ways to keep the bullets flying, navies
came up with some ingenious solutions. One is described in a 1570
report by Giovan Francesco Morosini, Venetian ambassador at the
court of Savoy:

> In addition to the sixty sailors on each of His Excellency's
> [Emmanuel Philibert] galleys, there are also eighty to one hundred
> soldiers. Each of these carries two harquebuses with fifty charges,
> powder and shot being tied together in a piece of paper. Thus
> once the harquebus has been fired, nothing remains to do but
> load it up again by placing the paper wrap in the barrel with
> unbelievable speed. And if need be should warrant it. This operation

is done by one of the oarsmen on each bench specifically assigned to this task. In this manner, while the soldier fires his piece, the rower has already loaded and primed another one, so that shots rain without interruption and much damage for the enemy.[72]

Ottoman janissaries, as we have already seen, also made extensive use of firearms, but for the *sipahi*s matters were different. Due to a misguided sense of honour and military conservatism, for a long time the *timar*-holding cavalrymen spurned firearms, relying on their traditional weapons even when serving dismounted on galleys. This was less of a disadvantage than may at first appear, since the Turks made extensive use of the composite recurved bow. Often seen as an anachronism by those who believe in technological progress at all costs, in the sixteenth century the bow was still a formidable weapon. An Ottoman bowman could deliver something like six aimed arrows a minute, even more when employing barrage shooting against a dense mass of men or ships. The effectiveness of composite bows is proved by the fact that the Venetians were still storing them on their galleys after the Cyprus war. The bow's main defect was that it needed brawn and lengthy training to function effectively, its draw force of approximately 150 pounds draining a man's energy with each arrow fired. Besides, it took several years for a bowman to learn to handle his weapon properly, while a good instructor could train a reasonably able harquebusier in a few days.[73] With the benefit of hindsight, it is easy to assert the clear superiority of firearms over other types of projectile weapons, yet at the time of the Cyprus war this was far from a foregone conclusion. The effectiveness of the harquebus against Ottoman troops was more a consequence of the latter's use of light or no body armour than the firearm's intrinsic qualities; a harquebus ball could easily pierce the coats of plate or mail worn by those *sipahi*s who could afford them. On the other hand, the cuirasses, breastplates and helmets worn by Western infantrymen gave considerable protection against arrows, unless they happened to strike an exposed part of the body such as the face. It is also true that many harquebusiers or even pikemen wore open helmets and no body armour except for leather or quilted cotton jackets.[74] Arrows could easily pierce these sorts of garments, and soldiers would try to exploit the protection of the thick planking typical of the high gunwales found on Western galleys.

Arming a galley fleet was a hugely expensive and lengthy operation. As Grand Vizier Koja Sinan Pasha would write in 1589, 'One can launch a campaign on land by a mere command: everybody mounts his horse and sets off. A naval expedition is not like that . . . however great the material investment and human efforts made, it can only be realized in seven to eight months.' Rulers across the Mediterranean would have agreed. Efficient states like the Ottoman empire had developed elaborate logistics systems to feed their armies on campaign, and alternatively soldiers could always live off the land.[75] Naval warfare, on the other hand, required considerable forethought, since once at sea a fleet could not replenish its supplies, with the exception of water, until it reached a friendly port. In addition, even a small fleet could be a considerable burden on a country's budget. The few galleys that the Medici put to sea every spring cost around 15 per cent of Tuscany's annual revenues. During the Cyprus war arming and manning ninety-six galleys consumed 13–14 per cent of Spain's income including that of Naples, Milan and Sicily, plus the monetary yield of the Three Graces.[76]

Since galleys relied at least as much on human as on natural power, the oarsman's diet had to provide him with the necessary strength to do his work properly. The basic component of every rower's meal was biscuit, of the hard tack variety, often broken up and mixed with water to create a kind of bread soup. But biscuit only provided carbohydrates, and an oarsman's dietary needs also included sufficient protein. Tuscany, like other Mediterranean states, recognized this by regulating the daily amount of food each crew member was to receive.

> Three pounds [a Florentine pound was 339 grams] of black bread a day, or alternatively two and a half pounds of biscuit. On Sundays, Wednesdays and Fridays, three pennies of rice for their

soup, or six of beans with five ounces of oil. At Easter, Christmas and Carnival they receive an extra allowance of one pound of fresh meat, half a measure of pure wine, and a soup. When required to perform extra efforts, half a ration of biscuit and half a measure of pure wine; as an alternative, half a measure of acid wine and two pennies of oil for each bench.[77]

The relatively small allocation of meat was not unusual, flesh not being a normal component of the diet of the poorer classes at the time. Oarsmen on Savoyard galleys received thirty-six ounces of bread a day, often selling the excess to buy wine, while those in Giovanni Andrea Doria's fleet received only thirty ounces. The dietary situation was not as grim as might appear, since crewmen could easily supplement their daily ration with the fish readily obtainable all over the Mediterranean. The *gente de cabo* on Spanish galleys, in addition to their bread ration, also got bacon, cheese, fish and beef. Soldiers received similar allowances. Fresh meat was provided by the livestock carried on board, chickens, rams and calves, slaughtered according to need [78]

All this resulted in galleys being veritable money and food sponges. In 1571 the twelve belonging to Giovanni Andrea Doria received from the Spanish Crown 40,000 pounds of biscuit, 9,000 litres of wine, 3,100 pounds of salted meat, 1,535 pounds of dried herrings, 2,940 pounds of cheese, 4,600 pounds of oil, 810 litres of vinegar, 2,400 pounds of fava beans and 240 pounds of salt, costing in total nearly 1,000 pieces of eight. But all these supplies were sufficient only for a fortnight, just the biscuit consumption of the rowing crew of an ordinary galley being in the range of 7,500 pounds a month. In other words, the victuals consumed by twelve galleys during a three-month cruise would cost more than 6,000 pieces of eight, keeping in mind that food prices fluctuated according to the availability of certain agricultural products in a given place. However, such sums did not represent a straight loss for galley owners, since oarsmen, crewmen and soldiers were supposed to pay for their living. This could be cripplingly expensive for those concerned. In 1615 a Venetian *galeotto di libertà* spent more than three quarters of his wages on the necessary drink 'to sustain himself during efforts'. In 1572 a soldier on a Tuscan galley received a monthly salary of twenty-one Florentine lire (three and a half pieces of eight), but spent nearly nineteen just on food. No wonder so many of those serving on galleys descended into chronic debt, especially when employed by governments, like the Spanish crown, notorious for being bad paymasters. On 18 March 1571 Giovanni Andrea Doria was informed that two companies of Spanish infantry he had left in Palermo the year before were owed eight months' pay, and that the little money they had received in the meantime had barely covered the debts incurred to buy food during the previous three months.[79]

The galley's main logistical problem, and one of the reasons it generally hugged the coastline, was its constant need to replenish its water supply. A normal galley needed between 230 and 280 men to function properly, two thirds of them rowers.[80] Given that rowing is extremely dehydrating work, the men at the oars needed a constant intake of liquid. Water was also used to prepare the soup that constituted the main meal of oarsmen, sailors and soldiers alike. But a galley had limited storage space and also had to accommodate all sorts of stores, ropes, gunpowder, weapons and ammunition. This meant that every few days a galley had to interrupt its progress to land parties of men to search for water, a time-consuming operation which was also fraught with danger if undertaken in enemy territory. For such reasons a galley captain's reputation rested not so much on his success as a tactician – albeit an important factor – as on his ability to keep his vessel in operational order. A galley in good shape, with adequate provisions, well-maintained ordnance and a trained fighting complement was a formidable war machine, one destined to dominate Mediterranean warfare even after the appearance of the great men-of-war from the Atlantic.

8. BRAGADIN'S HIDE

~

As the long line of seventeen galleys approached the mouth of the port of Naples on 24 June 1571, shots rang out in salute from the nearby fortresses. People of all social classes gathered on the shore to behold this living theatre of gilded wood, muscle and metal. Two galleys were from the Neapolitan squadron, but from the mainmasts of twelve others fluttered the papal banner, and the remaining three proudly sported the white cross of the Order of Malta.

The papal high admiral Marcantonio Colonna had departed from the port of Civitavecchia three days before at the head of His Holiness's fleet (courtesy of Cosimo I de' Medici), picking up the other galleys on the way, having spent the previous two weeks raising men and gathering victuals. In fact the infantry companies on board were under strength, but Colonna, remembering what had happened the previous year and fearing that the long voyage between Civitavecchia and Cyprus could result in the death of many men, had correctly calculated that he could fill his ranks by recruiting in Sicily.

The viceroy of Naples Cardinal Granvelle had come to the port in person to greet the papal commander, but the animosity between the two men, thinly disguised under a veil of courtesy, prompted the papal admiral to refuse the viceroy's invitation to stay in his palace. Colonna's intention was to wait in Naples for Don Juan of Austria, but on receiving fresh instructions from Rome he departed for the Sicilian port of Messina, reaching it on 20 July. In Naples he had managed to replace a dilapidated Maltese galley with a new one, but otherwise his stay could hardly be described a success. No sooner had he arrived that a brawl erupted between some papal soldiers and the Spanish of the local garrison; this quickly escalated into a battle with dead and wounded on both sides. The pontifical troops even broke into Granvelle's palace, and only Colonna's timely arrival avoided more violence and bloodshed. Tempers were still running high, however, and following another scuffle in Messina between Spaniards and Italians, Colonna was forced to send the culprits to the gallows or the oars.[1] It was not the ideal start for what was supposed to be a long-term collaboration between Christian princes against the infidels.

The Venetians reached Messina three days later. Captain-General Sebastiano Venier had arrived in Corfu in April, and after receiving the banner of command from the hands of Agostino Barbarigo had immediately set to work to get his fleet in fighting condition. By all accounts the seventy-five-year-old Venier was the quintessential man of action, often to the point of rashness. Born in 1496 into one of the most distinguished patrician families of Venice, Venier, a lawyer by training, had an impressive record of public service. Governor of Crete from 1548 to 1551, he later administered the cities of Brescia and Verona, plus holding a number of other posts. Created *procuratore di San Marco** for his services to the republic, the outbreak of the 1570 war found him in charge of Venice's fortresses, and in March of the same year he was elected governor of Corfu. Designated governor of Cyprus in place of Niccolò Dandolo, he was unable to reach the island due to illness and Doria's delaying tactics, and after Girolamo Zane's disgrace stepped into his shoes as captain-general of the Venetian fleet.

---

* *Procuratore di San Marco* was the highest dignity of the Venetian republic after that of doge, and was likewise for life. It was bestowed on prominent individuals with a distinguished record of public service.

Although inexperienced as a warrior, he was a first-class adminis-trator and an aggressive commander, both much-needed qualities in the spring of 1571. Venier was also a staunch patriot, old enough to remember Venice's golden days before her humiliation during the war of the League of Cambrai. The anti-Ottoman conflict of 1537–39 had fostered his mistrust of the Habsburgs and the Genoese, the latter Venice's traditional enemies, his animosity towards the former growing stronger while serving as one of the delegates to the inconclusive mid-1560s Venetian–Habsburg talks over a dis-puted border in Friuli. It would emerge time and again during the 1571 campaign.[2]

To counter Venier's lack of military expertise, not to mention lack of diplomacy, the Venetian government had installed as his deputy Agostino Barbarigo. Twenty years younger than Venier, Barbarigo also came from an illustrious family, one of his relatives and namesake having been doge at the beginning of the sixteenth century. More important, he had considerable experience both in diplomatic and seafaring matters, having among other things served on an ambassadorial mission to France in 1557 and navigated on galleys since his youth. As *provveditore generale da mar* he was sub-ordinate to the captain-general, but due to Venier's abrasive char-acter destined to become the main representative of Venice's inter-ests within the allied fleet.[3]

Venier had been dissatisfied with what he had found in Corfu. There were twenty-eight galleys in the harbour, all of them in bad condition and lacking provisions. The fortress's defences and artillery also left much to be desired, but Venier could do little to improve the situation until the arrival of reinforcements from Venice. The captain-general was not a man to remain idle, and in the meantime busied himself by reinforcing the garrison of Sopot and trying in vain to take the Ottoman port of Durazzo (Durrës). The Ottomans were successful in repulsing the sallies of Sopot's garrison, on one occasion killing or capturing twenty Venetians.

At length more ships arrived from Venice, together with orders to reinforce with thirty galleys the squadron stationed in Cretan waters. On 6 May Venier received an urgent request for help from Famagusta, the message stressing that the Ottomans had only 100 galleys available to support the besiegers. The captain-general wanted to depart immediately, confident that his ninety-four galleys – including those in Crete – would be sufficient to force the Turkish blockade, but his war council opposed the decision. Paolo Orsini in particular objected that such an enterprise required a fully equipped fleet of at least 130 galleys, ten galleasses and ten transport ships. Venier bowed to the majority will, although later he would complain that had his idea been accepted, Famagusta would have been saved and Venetian territories spared from Ottoman depredations. However, Orsini and the others were probably right to be cautious, since Venier himself admitted that he did not even have forty *scapoli* on each galley, even after the disarming of three of the worst galleys had put at his disposal 386 sailors, marines and rowers. In fact, to reach the barely acceptable number of sixty *scapoli* per galley he would have needed some 800 extra men. Given the shortage of manpower, tackling the Ottoman fleet without the aid of the heavily armed galleasses would have been extremely risky, not to say suicidal.

In any case, the captain-general already had his hands full trying to defend Corfu and the other Venetian possessions in the area, especially after an expeditionary force of 3,000 men was repulsed by the Ottomans near Kotor with heavy losses. To make matters worse, at the end of June Venier received news that Ottoman galleys had ravaged Crete and were moving towards the Ionian Sea. Realizing that he risked being bottled up in Corfu, he sent orders to the Cretan squadron to meet him in Messina, overruling his war council's proposal that the fleet should move to Brindisi instead. As he awaited Barbarigo's return from a scouting mission, six galleasses under Francesco Duodo arrived in Corfu and on 11 July Venier departed for Messina with fifty-eight galleys and the six galleasses. The latter's slowness – being rowed *alla sensile* with only three men to each bench – meant not only that they had to be towed by galleys, but also that the whole fleet's cruising speed was much reduced.[4] Once Venier arrived in Messina twelve days later he immediately set to work with Colonna's aid to recruit soldiers, although managing to find half of the number he needed. To save on provisions he paid his soldiers extra, which in the long run proved a wise decision since the arrival of the allied fleet in Messina sparked a dramatic rise in food prices. Having joined hands, the only thing Colonna and Venier could do was wait for the arrival of the Spanish and their allies.[5]

Don Juan of Austria departed from Madrid on 6 June, but despite the pope's urgings that he reach Italy with the utmost haste Philip II's half brother took nearly three months to reach Messina. This was partly due to the many ceremonies and receptions he attended en route – a necessary component of any royal progress of the time. But many suspected that once more the king of Spain was employing delaying tactics to block any expedition to the Levant, the pope and the Venetians in particular taking Don Juan's endless delays as a sign of the king's lack of commitment.[6] Their distrust was not unfounded, since Philip's aim was to put off the fleet's departure without increasing the Venetians' already strong suspicions.

In Barcelona Don Juan received a letter from Philip ordering him to listen to Giovanni Andrea Doria's advice and on no account to risk battle without the unanimous consent of Doria, the *comendador mayor de Castilla* Luis de Requesens y Zuñiga and the marquis of Santa Cruz.[7] Given Doria's well-known prudence, ordering Don Juan to pay heed to his advice was tantamount to telling him to avoid battle at all costs. Besides, both Doria and Requesens were tied to the duke of Alva, and thus not in favour of a sustained Spanish commitment in the Mediterranean.[8] By stressing the need for unanimity, the king was also curbing the aggressive Santa Cruz. Don Juan took these instructions as a personal affront, and in two letters – of 8 and 12 July, the first to Philip's secretary Ruy Gómez de Silva, the other to the king himself – complained about his brother's lack of trust in him, even suggesting to Gómez that he was ready to resign from his position but telling Philip, 'I will obey, as far as possible, whatever they may be, the orders which Your Majesty may give.'[9] This was rather less petulant than it may at first appear. Once the league's fleet was at sea, it would be up to Don Juan to interpret the king's instructions according to the changing situation. In any case, the king must have been aware that should the league's other military commanders decide to fight, it would be difficult for the Spanish to refuse to do so without losing face. From Philip's point of view, the best way to avoid risking his ships was to delay as much as possible his brother's arrival in Messina.

Despite Don Juan's best intentions, it would be almost another month before he left Barcelona. No move was possible until the arrival of the Cartagena squadron under Santa Cruz, and that of Mallorca commanded by Don Sancho de Leyva. Besides, the galleys needed provisions and troops, and finding both kept Don Juan busy until the middle of July. Gathering victuals for a fleet was never an easy task in Early Modern Spain, as Miguel de Cervantes would later discover at his own expense when acting as royal purveyor at the time of the 1588 Armada. Communities were supposed to provide food, drink and other goods, and suppliers were expected to pay for what they solicited or seized. In reality, general mistrust, administrative delays, legal obstructions and the frequent lack of ready cash hindered the work of the purveyors, who resorted to bullying, cajoling, pleading and negotiation to obtain the necessary supplies.

In any case, transporting victuals to ports was never an easy task, particularly in the Spanish crown's domains. On 30 July the viceroy of Sicily's wife wrote on behalf of her ailing husband to Giovanni Andrea Doria that it would take eight to ten days to load foodstuff on the galleys once they arrived in Palermo, all victuals being still 'in the mountains' lest they rot in the summer heat. A few days later the count of Landriano informed Doria that since he had no way of collecting these provisions, Colonna and the Venetians should send some galleys to Palermo. Eventually, Colonna allotted four of his galleys for the task, gathering extra supplies in the port of Milazzo.[10]

Don Juan sailed from Barcelona on 20 July, arriving in Genoa on the 26th. He spent the next five days attending parties given in his honour and receiving delegations from various Italian states. For some governments Don Juan's arrival was a source of apprehension; they feared that 'the stateless prince' had no intention of sailing on to Messina, but instead would use his forces in Italy. Tuscany had mobilized its militia and reinforced its fortresses, anticipating a possible Spanish invasion. Instead, Don Juan's reception of Crown Prince Francesco de' Medici, sent by his father to pay homage to the league's commander, turned out to be of the outmost cordiality, doing much to allay Cosimo's worries. Don Juan dispelled many fears by announcing that he intended to move on to Naples as quickly as possible, stopping in Tuscany only to pick up soldiers from the Spanish–held fortress of Porto Ercole.[11] True to his word, Don Juan left Genoa on 31 July accompanied by, among others, Doria, Alessandro Farnese and Francesco Maria della Rovere. Santa Cruz had already departed for Naples with his own squadron to deal with a number of logistical matters. Don Juan arrived in Naples on 9 August, and on the 14th, after the now usual festivities in his honour, solemnly received the banner of the Holy League from the hands of Cardinal Granvelle. The need for extra soldiers and supplies caused further delays, and eventually Santa Cruz had to be left behind to complete the task. Don Juan reached Messina on the 23rd, a month after the arrival of the Venetian fleet, greeted by the guns of the fortress and of the other galley squadrons.

The next day a meeting to assess the situation was held on the Spanish flagship. Don Juan stated that he had eighty-four galleys including those, still to arrive, of Doria and Santa Cruz, plus 20,000 good Spanish, German and Italian infantry. Colonna had only twelve galleys, but all in excellent order. Venier was not so enthusiastic. He was still waiting for the rest of his ships, had few men, and had been hindered by the viceroy of Naples in his recruitment and victualling efforts. However, he was expecting the 5,000 troops promised him by Pompeo Colonna and other captains, and in any case his need for soldiers was not as pressing since

Venetian rowers were trained to fight. Don Juan offered to make good with his own troops any gaps in the Venetian ranks, and volunteered to help solve the supply problem. It would have been better for Venier had he been more economical with the truth, since those hostile to the Venetians immediately circulated his frank statements in a distorted fashion. The young inexperienced Francesco Maria della Rovere would write to his father the duke of Urbino:

> We found the papal and Venetian fleets in this port, but both in bad shape and in particular the Venetians. They have forty-eight galleys, six galleasses, and three round-ships, but without soldiers and few, sad, crewmen. Sixty galleys from Crete are expected, but up to now their whereabouts are unknown. Our fleet is very well equipped with men and everything else, being of eighty-one galleys and twenty round-ships, with 20,000 infantrymen on board.[12]

Colonna's galleys were certainly not as run-down as della Rovere, a friend of Doria and his clique, would like us to believe. Moreover, the poor condition of Venier's ships was not due to the commander's sluggishness. Ever since his arrival in Messina he had done everything in his power to bring his squadron up to scratch, only to be systematically stonewalled in his victualling efforts by the local authorities. In frustration he had sent Barbarigo with six galleys to the nearby port of Patti, while he in person with thirty other warships sailed to Tropea in Calabria, being told he could find soldiers and supplies there. Tropea had no harbour, but given the summer season the captain-general considered it safe to anchor his ships near the shore. No sooner had he arrived than a sudden storm threw his galleys against the coast, wrecking six of them. The same ill wind also hit Barbarigo's squadron, sending one of his vessels to the bottom. As ill luck would have it, another two galleys and as many round-ships loaded with supplies were captured by the Ottomans near Corfu. Venier managed to recover all the artillery, masts and other equipment from his foundered ships, but many crewmen, having already endured enough, deserted, thus contributing to Venier's despondency.[13] Francesco Maria della Rovere's patronizing attitude towards the Venetians was ignorant and unjust, to say the least.

The allied commanders having made their points, it was decided that future discussions about the campaign should be postponed until the arrival of Santa Cruz, Doria and the galleys from Crete. At the same time two galleys under Knight Commander Gil de Andrada, captain of Don Juan's flagship, were sent to discover the Ottomans' whereabouts. Don Juan's advisers, ever mindful of Philip's instructions about not risking his ships, welcomed the decision to wait. Requesens was firmly reminded in writing by Don Garcia de Toledo of the king's orders, the former viceroy stressing the importance of not accepting battle unless under totally favourable circumstances, and not to trust the Venetians, 'more used to saying, than doing' – an unfair and dishonest comment. Don Garcia's advice to Don Juan was not very different concerning the Venetians: since they were unreliable it would be better to give them the vanguard of the fleet should they request it; at the same time it would be wise not to inform the Venetians that the vanguard was up for grabs, lest they become suspicious and decline it. But Don Garcia also offered the young prince some very sound tactical suggestions. Remembering Barbarossa's formation at Preveza, he recommended the Christian armada be divided into three squadrons, all sailing in one line but with sufficient distance between them to allow room for manoeuvring.[14] Don Juan, as we shall see, would profit considerably from this advice.

The Spanish also tried to isolate the Venetians by bringing Marcantonio Colonna over to their side. The papal admiral was in a particularly difficult position, being grand constable of the kingdom of Naples and, more important still, a candidate for a number of prestigious posts within the Spanish domains in Europe. A wrong move on his part could jeopardize any chance of future preferment. In distress, he would write to his friend Francisco Borgia – general of the Jesuits, future saint and great-grandson of the lecherous

Alexander VI, for this reason subsequently known as the revenge of the Holy Spirit – about the letters he had received from Philip II, 'always putting before me the obligations which bind me to his service'. He added that he had given the king no offence, yet 'having last year saved the honour of his fleet, and this year helped to conclude the league, I find myself called upon to write a justification of my conduct'. He also expressed the intention of giving up his command, but would wait and see how the situation in Messina evolved. The reference to the 'honour' of the Spanish fleet was a thinly veiled criticism of Doria's dithering behaviour the year before, disingenuously omitting the fact that the Genoese admiral had preserved his master's ships. Luckily for Colonna, Don Juan was itching for action, despite the contrary opinions of his increasingly irritating advisers. In fact the prince found in the papal admiral a precious ally, both men being anxious to accomplish some memorable enterprise which would increase their prestige. At the same time, Colonna's excellent rapport with the Venetians would prove an immense asset for Don Juan in the weeks to come.[15]

~

The Ottomans, meanwhile, had not been idle. Like Venice, the Porte possessed an extensive and elaborate espionage network, and by February of 1571, despite the fact that the league was not yet officially concluded, the Ottomans were taking active steps to stymie a possible allied offensive in the Levant to relieve Famagusta. In mid-February twenty galleys were sent to reinforce the Rhodes squadron, in charge of watching the Venetians in Crete, and all the naval forces in the area put under the command of the governor of Alexandria Şuluç Mehmed Pasha. On 21 March Müezzinzâde Ali Pasha left Constantinople with thirty galleys, reaching Cyprus at the end of the month. He remained in those waters until mid-May, disembarking troops and supplies for the army besieging Famagusta, before sailing towards the port of Karystos (Castelrosso), located at the southern tip of Evvoia, with a force of fifty-five vessels. There he met the second vizier Pertev Pasha, who had left Constantinople at the beginning of the month with 124 galleys and the title of *serdar*. At the same time an army under the third vizier Ahmed Pasha was assembling in Skopje, in Macedonia, ready to operate in conjunction with the fleet against Venetian possessions in Greece. Müezzinzâde Ali spent a few weeks in Karystos, repairing his vessels and waiting for reinforcements. Eventually, with the arrival of Uluç Ali together with a number of Anatolian corsairs, he would have approximately 250 oared vessels of various types, with another twenty left to cover the siege operations in Cyprus. The *kapudan paşa* also carried with him orders 'to find and immediately attack the Infidel's fleet in order to save the honour of our religion and state'. With Famagusta still holding out, the last thing the Ottomans wanted was another Querini-style relief expedition.[16]

Müezzinzâde Ali's next objective was Crete. A raid on the settlements at Souda Bay netted a number of prisoners, and from them he managed to find out the exact strength of the Venetian naval forces based on the island. Boldly, the *kapudan paşa* split his forces into two divisions: one to attack the ports of Chania and Irakleio, while the second, under Uluç Ali, was given the task of capturing the fortress of Rethymno. On 20 June Müezzinzâde Ali tried to take Irakleio by surprise, but the alertness of *provveditore* Querini foiled his plan, forcing him to call off the assault after sustaining losses. Another attempt against the fortress of Turlurù was equally unsuccessful, and to make matters worse a sudden squall drove twelve of his galleys against the shore reducing three of them to splinters. Uluç Ali was more fortunate, sacking and burning Rethymno and capturing twenty-two artillery pieces. Gathering his fleet, the *kapudan paşa* proceeded to pillage the islands of Kythira, Zakynthos and Kefallonia, before making for Corfu.[17]

Deciding that Corfu was too tough a target, Müezzinzâde Ali opted for an amphibious operation to recapture Sopot. The Venetian garrison put up a stiff fight but was eventually forced to surrender to overwhelming numbers. The Ottomans, angered by their losses, put most of the garrison to the sword. Uluç Ali in the meantime was busy operating in nearby waters, capturing the

Venetian *Moceniga* with 800 soldiers destined for Corfu, after a battle lasting eleven hours which resulted in the death of more than half of those on board. After this success the *beylerbey* of Algiers sailed towards Dubrovnik, chasing into the harbour a Venetian galley that had happened to cross his path. The Ragusei, appealing to their neutrality, refused to hand over the ship but nonetheless provided the Ottoman commander with information concerning the league's fleet. Sometime later Uluç Ali was joined by the *kapudan paşa*, who in conjunction with Ahmed Pasha had been busy capturing Venetian fortresses on the Adriatic coast. The capture of Ulcinj (Dulcigno) was considered particularly important, and was the occasion for much rejoicing in Constantinople. Still, the taking of Dulcigno had been costly in terms of manpower, the fortress resisting for a fortnight. In addition many Ottoman naval personnel had deserted, leaving the galleys undermanned.[18]

Once the Ottoman forces were reunited the commanders agreed to pursue a dual course of action: Müezzinzâde Ali with the bulk of the fleet would retreat to Herceg Novi for some much-needed caulking, while the *beylerbey* of Algiers and the famous corsair Kara Hodja were given the task of penetrating deeper into the Adriatic to harass Venetian lines of communication. Kara Hodja and Uluç Ali had much in common, including the fact that both were allegedly former Dominican friars, veterans of the battle of Preveza and the siege of Malta. The two redoubtable Ottoman naval commanders were also famous for their daring and guile. Five years before, Kara Hodja had come with a galley and a *fusta* to Pesaro, on the Adriatic coast of Italy, telling the local inhabitants that he simply wanted to trade. His plan was to attract as many people possible on board and then sail off with an easy catch of slaves. The scheme was thwarted by the arrival of a Venetian galley, forcing the corsair to leave empty-handed. As a token of thanks to their protector St Terence, the citizens of Pesaro commissioned an ex–voto painting, still to be seen in the cathedral.

Cunning was not confined to one side. During his foray into the Adriatic Uluç Ali first attacked Korcula (Curzola), but retreated after being tricked by local commander Antonio Balbi into believing that the garrison was more numerous than in reality it was; Balbi used the old ruse of dressing women in military dress and parading them on the walls. Next, the *beylerbey* and Kara Hodja attacked Hvar (Lesina), capturing the island but losing 300 men in the process. At the same time the Ottoman army tried to take the important coastal town of Zara (Zadar), but the Venetian garrison managed to repulse the attackers. The Ottomans were now within striking distance of Venice, as the city frantically prepared itself to beat off the imminent invasion. Citizens were called up and troops raised; a force of fifteen galleys was made ready and other vessels pressed into service; the forts at the mouth of the lagoon were filled with men, artillery and munitions.[19] The Ottoman fleet was not strong enough to capture Venice, but its actions effectively disrupted Venice's war efforts. In particular, the attack against Crete forced the Venetians back on the defensive and stymied any future attempt Querini might have made to relieve Famagusta. From the strategic point of view, there was no doubt that the Ottomans had the upper hand.

It was now too late to save Famagusta.[20] With no relief in sight Marcantonio Bragadin agreed to exchange hostages and discuss terms for the city's capitulation. The Venetians asked for safe conduct and enough ships to transport to Crete all those who so desired; the Italians should not be harassed but allowed to embark to the beat of the drums, with colours unfurled, taking with them their arms, artillery, families and possessions; those Greeks and Albanians who wished to depart should be free to do so, and likewise those Italians who wished to remain; no Greek should suffer loss of freedom, honour or property, and if after two years he decided to leave, the Ottoman authorities should not hinder his departure, but instead provide safe passage to his final destination. Mustafa agreed to everything except the removal of the artillery, although he apparently allowed the defenders to take away five guns, together with three of their finest horses. The treaty signed, the Ottomans sent ships into the harbour and started embarking the defenders. Everything seemed to be going smoothly in the harbour, but for the Famagustans things were getting ugly. No sooner had the Ottomans entered the city than they started misbehaving, looting homes and churches, robbing people and billeting themselves on households. This would be taken as another example of Ottoman treachery, but more likely it was simply a case of soldiers running amok after months of hardship and slaughter.

Worse was in store. On 5 August, following Mustafa's request for a formal surrender ceremony, Bragadin left the city followed by numerous gentlemen, including Baglioni, and accompanied by an escort of harquebusiers and halberdiers. Bragadin was clad in crimson, as befitted his senatorial rank, and over his head stood a parasol, a symbol of authority. The defenders of Famagusta marched between two lines of angry Turks hurling insults at them, but once they arrived at Mustafa's pavilion the Pasha showed nothing but courtesy, the unsuspecting Venetians oblivious of the tragedy about to befall them. The various accounts of what followed conflict on a number of details, but all agree on the final outcome of the exchange between Mustafa and Bragadin.

According to the Ottoman historian Peçevî Ibrahim Effendi the Pasha asked that the young Antonio Querini remain as a hostage until the ships with the Venetians had returned, to which Bragadin is supposed to have answered, 'You can't order a *bey* or a dog for that.' The reply enraged Mustafa, who demanded the restitution of fifty Muslim pilgrims captured by the Venetians at the beginning of the war. When Bragadin answered that they had all been killed, the Pasha ordered his arrest and that of all those with him. Venetian historians instead maintain that Mustafa had never intended to keep to the terms of surrender and that the pilgrims' alleged execution was not the real reason for his ire; rather, the Pasha was enraged by the number of his casualties and the scantiness of the booty left by the Venetians in Famagusta.[21] Interestingly, Mustafa's report to Pertev Pasha (intercepted and translated by the Venetians), while emphasizing Bragadin's killing of prisoners and his refusal to deliver hostages, stresses that his order to arrest the Venetian commander was triggered by the latter's statement, 'that if I [Mustafa] wished to abide by the articles of surrender, it would be fine with him; but if otherwise, he did not care if they were revoked'.[22] Thus, from a legal point of view Mustafa believed that he was within his rights to act as he did, given that Bragadin himself had broken the truce with these words.

It is quite possible that Mustafa – by all accounts a nasty piece of work – had been waiting for such a chance. Although some historians have justified the Pasha's request for hostages as an accepted practice,[23] by asking for something not mentioned in the surrender terms he was behaving like a loser overturning the poker table in the middle of a game. In any case, Mustafa's subsequent behaviour was nothing short of unwarranted savagery. All those with Bragadin, including Astorre Baglioni, were bound, taken out of the pavilion and beheaded on the spot. The Venetian soldiers shared their officers' fate, and caught up in the slaughter were also a number of innocent Cypriots carrying victuals to the Ottoman camp. Only a few prominent Greeks of Bragadin's party were spared, in an attempt by the Pasha to win over the sultan's new subjects. Bragadin expected to share his companions' fate, but for the time being Mustafa was satisfied with cutting off his ears.

The Ottoman commander had issued strict orders that there should be no more looting in Famagusta, but as soon as news of what had happened spread through the army the soldiers took matters into their own hands. The unfortunate Italians waiting to embark were slaughtered; the Greeks were spared, but many saw their wives and daughters raped in front of them. All those already on board the ships were enslaved, the strongest men being sent straight to the oars. The next day Mustafa entered Famagusta, displaying in the main square the heads of the executed Venetians and hanging a few more found in the city. Some managed to save their skins by pretending to be Greek or through the complicity of Ottoman officials more interested in profit than blood. Count

Ercole Martinengo was hidden by one of Mustafa's dragomans until his master's fury abated, while the French consul, on friendly terms with the Pasha, managed to ransom Alessandro Podocattaro.

Bragadin's fate was the most tragic of all. With other Christians he was forced to clear debris from the ruined walls and carry on his shoulders sacks of earth from the cavalier at the Limassol gate all the way to the arsenal at the opposite end of the city's southern wall. During the ordeal he suffered taunts, insults and physical abuse, his captors attempting to force him into accepting Islam. According to one source, eight days after the fall of the city Bragadin made it known that he wanted to become a Muslim. When an imam arrived, Bragadin asked him which were the first words of the Gospel of St John. The puzzled cleric, possibly a renegade Christian answered, 'In the beginning was the word . . .'

Bragadin, turning towards the Pasha cried, 'So, you treacherous dog, if in the beginning was the word, and the word is God, why, treacherous dog, did you renege on it? But you are a treacherous dog, an enemy of God and of your currish law. Cunning scoundrel, why did you kill those poor Christians? If I offended you, then you should have killed me alone, not all the others. But these are thievish actions worthy of you. Dog, dog, disgusting fucking cuck-old.'

Apparently impassive, Mustafa asked Bragadin if it was true he had said that had their roles been reversed he would have had the Pasha carry on his shoulders all the earth he had piled up in front of Famagusta's walls. The proud Venetian answered that not only had he said that, but also that he would have used Mustafa's beard 'to clean out the shit from latrines'.[24] Whether this story is true or not, there is no doubt that Bragadin's defiant behaviour enraged Mustafa; and there was the added insult, one could argue, of having made the imam an apostate by tricking him into saying the first words of the Gospel of St John, according to many Muslim legal scholars of the time the speaker's intention being irrelevant.[25]

On 15 August the captive Venetian, already seriously ill from the infection deriving from his amputated ears, was taken to the harbour and hoisted to the main yard of a galley so that all could see. Ottoman soldiers below shouted up mockingly, asking if from there he could see Christ. After an hour he was taken down, dragged to the main square and tied to a column. Mustafa, watching the scene from the balcony of a nearby palace, shouted once more the request that Bragadin convert to Islam, but the Venetian's answer was to raise his voice in prayer. Then two executioners started to flay him alive. First they stripped the skin from his skull, then did the same with his back and arms. They had reached his navel when Bragadin shouted, 'In your hands, Lord, I commend my spirit,' and expired. The executioners laid the lifeless body on the ground and proceeded methodically to finish their grisly work. The body was then quartered, and the pieces displayed in various parts of Famagusta. Bragadin's skin was pickled, stuffed with straw, clad in its owner's crimson robes and carried through the town on top of an ox, preceded by a Turk carrying a parasol. Then it was hoisted once more to a galley's main yard and paraded around the coast of Cyprus before being taken to Constantinople with the booty from Famagusta.

Many at the time compared Bragadin's death to Christ's crucifixion. Sokollu Mehmed Pasha – possibly with a keener eye for political expediency than Christian theology – would express his contempt of Mustafa's behaviour to Marcantonio Barbaro, talking about 'the cruel martyrdom inflicted on the most illustrious Bragadin'.[26] Mustafa's brutality towards Famagusta's defenders was widely discussed at the time. The well-informed Venetian historian Paolo Paruta suggested that Mustafa's display of savagery was but a show of force to regain standing with his soldiers, having denied them the opportunity to sack the city. Another possibility is that the Pasha was simply exacting revenge for all his soldiers killed during the ten-month siege – a staggering 80,000 according to one source,[27] although even half that number would have been a terrible toll. Paruta also believed that Mustafa, an extremely choleric man, had been enraged by Bragadin's display of pomp when arriving at his tent, 'as befitted a victor, not a vanquished'.[28] The Venetian historian could have perhaps added another reason. Mustafa was a sworn enemy of Sokollu, and within the *dîvân* a member of the war faction opposed to any deal with Venice. His behaviour at Famagusta can be seen as his way of sabotaging in the immediate future any possible agreement between the Republic of St Mark and the Porte. Whatever his motives, Mustafa's actions would for a long time be cited as an example of Ottoman – indeed Muslim – duplicity, and even today Bragadin's straw-stuffed hide casts a shadow over East–West relations.*

~

Oblivious of the fall of Famagusta the Christian fleet was still in Messina at the end of August, waiting for the arrival of its remaining squadrons. In the meantime Don Juan had been busy inspecting the various forces under his command. He was satisfied with the papal contingent, but could not hide his misgivings about the Venetian ships. In particular he wrote to Don Garcia de Toledo complaining about their lack of men and their indiscipline, with each galley 'doing very much as it pleases', ignoring the fact that when it came to battle the *levantine* method employed by the Venetians, allowing greater independence to individual captains, was as good as any other. Don Juan hoped that the galleys from Crete – which he erroneously believed were from Cyprus – would be in better shape, although he admitted that Ottoman activities in the Adriatic had compelled the republic to concentrate many of its forces in Venice. The young man was also concerned about the best tactical use of firearms, prompting Don Garcia to answer that harquebus fire should be withheld 'until you are near [enough] to the enemy to be splashed with his blood' and that 'the crash of the galleys' rams and the sound of their guns should be heard at the same time'. He added, however, that the artillerymen should not fire until Don Juan ordered them to.[29] Since this last letter was written on 13

---

* Bragadin's skin was eventually recovered by his family, and now rests in the church of SS Giovanni e Paolo in Venice.

September, it is unlikely that Don Juan received it before his departure from Messina. In any case, the number of expert seamen with the fleet more than compensated for Don Juan's ignorance in naval matters.

Giovanni Andrea Doria entered Messina harbour on 1 September with eleven galleys, and the sixty Venetian galleys from Crete turned up the next day, in good shape and well equipped with rowers. Some had a few Cretan archers, and most the normal complement of fifty *scapoli* 'but no other soldiers'. Prospero Colonna had also arrived from Naples with the infantrymen he had managed to recruit in that kingdom. But even with these troops and the 1,200 'bellicose Calabrian soldiers' recruited for Venier by Baron Gaspare Toraldo, the Venetian ships were still short of fighting men. The difficulties experienced by the Venetians in filling their ranks were partly due to the bouts of disease that still afflicted their fleet, but also to the fact that few people were willing to face the apparently invincible Ottoman navy. As a result, the soldiers enlisted were green and, according to the Savoyard admiral Provana de Leynì 'of the worst type seen at sea for a long time'. Wishing all galleys to have at least 100 soldiers on board, Don Juan reiterated to Venier his former offer to provide the necessary troops: 2,000 Germans, 1,500 Italians and 1,500 Spanish. The Venetian captain-general was loath to accept, mistrustful of the Spaniards' real intentions; but thanks to the mediation of Marcantonio Colonna agreed to embark the Italian and Iberian soldiers, on average forty men to each galley. Santa Cruz's thirty galleys made their way into Messina on the 6th, bringing the league's fleet to its full fighting strength.[30]

More or less at the same time Knight Commander Gil de Andrada returned from his scouting mission with news of the Ottoman fleet. He had stopped in Corfu, where the governor Benedetto Orsini informed him that the Ottomans had nearly 300 vessels, but only 150 galleys, the rest being round-ships or galliots with few soldiers on board. From other Venetian outposts the knight commander had also received word that the Ottoman ships were ill-equipped with artillery and riddled with disease. Having delivered his findings, Gil de Andrada set out for some more scouting, leaving Don Juan to ponder what to do next. On the 8th a general review took place, but those who expected an immediate departure were disappointed, for Don Juan told Venier and Colonna that he wished to convene a general conference of all the league's senior officers to decide on a course of action. Don Juan was not just bowing to his advisers' appeals for prudence; he was also aware that any major decision taken by a small council would inevitably arouse the resentment and jealousy of those left out. Indeed, a few days later the Venetian *provveditori* Antonio da Canal and Marco Querini would write to the senate complaining that Venier and Barbarigo were excluding them from the restricted meetings they held with the other commanders.[31]

The general conference took place on 10 September, with some sixty senior officers gathered on the Habsburg flagship. Don Juan postulated two alternative courses of action: seek battle with the enemy or remain on the defensive. The prince's advisers immediately raised a number of objections to any sort of venture in the Levant, arguing that the strength of the Ottoman fleet, the insufficient victuals and soldiers, and the approaching autumn pointed instead to a more profitable attack against Tunis. The other participants, especially the Venetians, rejected this idea out of hand and the discussion shifted to whether battle should be sought or not. Again Don Juan's counsellors expressed objections, despite the fact that later Don Luis de Requesens would maintain that he always advocated fighting.[32] It is easy, as many have done, to accuse the Spanish of sabotaging the league's efforts for their own parochial interests, but it should be remembered that North Africa was among the league's objectives and that the conquest of Tunis had some very sound strategic merits. Besides, the idea of engaging the intact Ottoman fleet in battle was enough in itself to encourage caution.

Shrewdly, Giovanni Andrea Doria approached the problem from a different angle. He did not reject the possibility of a sea battle, but pointed out that 'even if we should be victorious, we would in any case have to retreat and this will allow the Turks to recover their strength'. He suggested instead sailing to Cyprus and trying to relieve Famagusta, thus disrupting the Ottoman war effort.[33] Doria had apparently gone over to the Venetians, but his words belied his real intentions: he understood perfectly the Ottomans' potential for recovery, but also knew that the fleet would never make it to Cyprus before the bad weather set in. By backing the Cyprus option Doria was attempting to erase the accusations of cowardice levelled against him the year before, without exposing his ships, and Philip's, to excessive risks. Other commanders, including Santa Cruz, advocated battle against the Ottoman fleet, and Don Juan concluded the meeting by stating that he was resolved, with the aid of the Venetian and papal squadrons, to seek out the enemy.[34]

The prince could not have done otherwise without a colossal loss of face; the Venetians had made it known that if the league fleet should delay its departure any longer, they would go hunting the Ottomans alone. Colonna was also under pressure from the papal authorities to get moving, and it was more than likely that he would join Venier's venture. Thus, as the Savoyard commander Andrea Provana di Leynì had a few days before informed Duke Emmanuel Philibert, 'not everyone willingly agrees to fight, but nonetheless [is] forced and pressured by shame to do so'.[35] Meanwhile, to be sure that nothing was decided contrary to Spain's interests, Philip II had written to Don Juan ordering him to dismiss the league's non-Spanish contingents and move his own forces into winter quarters in Sicily.[36] But the prince did not receive this letter until the end of October, by which time the situation had changed completely.

On 14 September Don Juan issued the official order of movement and combat. The fleet was to be divided into four squadrons – three front line and one reserve. During the voyage Doria would occupy the vanguard, Don Juan the centre and Barbarigo the rear. Santa Cruz with the reserve was to follow, accompanied by twenty-six ships with 3,000 German infantry. Each front-line squadron was allocated a pair of galleasses, navigating a mile ahead. In the event of battle, Doria would have the right wing, Barbarigo the left and Don Juan the centre, or 'battle', with Santa Cruz placing himself behind the main line with the reserve. The sailing ships' position was on the wings, to avoid the Christian line being outflanked, exploiting the wind to manoeuvre with the galleys. Alternatively, they were to use their boats to feed troops into the fight. The galleasses had the task of disrupting the enemy line with their artillery fire before the two fleets came to blows. It was a well-designed plan, which Doria would later claim as his, although it owed much to Don Garcia de Toledo's suggestions.[37]

Two days later the fleet finally set sail from Messina, with an impressive show of strength, music and colour. Slowly the vessels exited the harbour, blessed one by one by the papal nuncio Giulio Maria Odescalchi, whom Pius V had sent to join the Christian armada with the aim of hastening its departure. In front of the nuncio's eyes passed 207 galleys, six galleasses, twenty-eight round-ships and thirty-two smaller vessels (frigates and brigantines), with on board some 30,000 fighting men and about 50,000 sailors and rowers.[38] Doria's squadron led the way, his flagship displaying at the stern the rich celestial sphere – a gift from his wife – he used as a recognition sign. The galleys under his command were Genoese (his own, plus those of other *asientistas* such as the Lomellini, Negroni, Grimaldi and De Mari), papal, Savoyard and Venetian, the latter making up half his squadron. This is hardly surprising, since Venice provided 50 per cent of all the galleys present. By dividing the various national contingents among the four squadrons Don Juan was insuring himself against the possibility of one contingent deserting en masse. By all accounts Doria's division was a very mixed and ill-balanced formation. The light, plain Genoese galleys contrasted with the heavily armed, refined Venetian vessels.* The papal (Tuscan) galleys, loaded down with ordnance, proudly

---

* The stern of Genoese galleys usually lacked the decorations and gilding typical of these vessels. Cfr. ASF, MP, 2426, n.n.f. (Vincenzo Graffigna to Domenico Pandolfini, 13 November 1650, from Pisa).

flaunted at their sterns the Medici coat of arms. Two of the Savoyard ships, the *Piemontesa* and *Margarita*, were small – with their eighteen rowing benches more galliots than galleys – and the *Margarita* decrepit. Admiral Provana di Leynì had tried to replace her in Naples with a new galley, but had been thwarted by lack of funds.[39]

In the middle of the fleet in the central division stood Don Juan's majestic *Real*, its stern decorated in true humanistic fashion with a mixture of motifs borrowed from both pagan and Christian traditions.[40] It was preceded and followed respectively by Colonna's and Venier's flagships. These were large galleys, with full sets of heavy and light ordnance and fighting contingents of over 200 men each, the *Real* having 400 harquebusiers from the *tercio* of Sardinia. Some of the most important galleys were in the central squadron, although these were not necessarily the strongest. Bunching together well-equipped powerful vessels was a way to archive tactical superiority at a specific point of the line of battle, but often matters of precedence prevailed over military expediency. The *capitana* of Savoy with its twenty-five rowing benches was little more than a glorified *galea sottile*, but Admiral Provana, following Duke Emmanuel Philibert's instructions, had insisted that it should take position immediately to the right of the papal flagship. Previously the Maltese commander Fra' Pietro Giustiniani had tried to usurp Provana's place, causing a diplomatic scuffle. The impenitent Giustiniani tried the same trick again after the fleet left Messina, forcing Don Juan to put his foot down in the Savoyards' favour. Perhaps for this reason the Maltese flagship was placed on the extreme right of the central division, another honourable position.[41]

The three galleys deployed by the Order of Malta belied its real strength within the coalition. All the Knights of St John came from the ranks of the European aristocracy – although the majority were from the petty nobility – and trained as soldiers from birth. Adding this to the traditional religious monastic vows of chastity, poverty and obedience made them formidable fighters, reckoned as among the toughest in Europe. Everyone was keen to exploit the knights' expertise in naval matters, and as a result scores of them could be found throughout the allied fleet, sometimes as galley captains but in many cases simply as volunteers. Gil de Andrada, Pagano Doria (Giovanni Andrea Doria's brother) and Luigi Mazzinghi were just three of the Maltese scattered throughout the galleys, and on more than one occasion during the forthcoming battle their presence would make a significant difference.

Once the whole fleet reached the high seas it spread out in accordance with Don Juan's orders. The vanguard, with fifty-seven galleys, sailed six miles from the coast; the centre, with sixty-four, was four miles from the shoreline; the third division, with fifty-six, two miles. The reserve squadron brought up the rear, keeping the same distance from the coast as the central division. Each squadron was separated from the others by four to six miles. Eight of the best galleys from Doria's and Barbarigo's squadrons scouted ten miles ahead of the vanguard, while the galleasses sailed a mile in front of their respective squadrons. Battle formation could be adopted by halting Doria's division and allowing the others to catch up.[42] Should the van stumble upon the Ottoman armada, there was enough time for the Christian fleet to meet the enemy in an orderly fashion. Don Juan was confident about his chances of success, writing to Don Garcia de Toledo on the day the fleet left Messina that although the Ottoman fleet was superior in numbers, the quality of its ships and of the men on board was not good.[43]

What the league's commanders ignored was that the enemy knew of their whereabouts and probably their planned tactics. By mid-September the Ottoman fleet was at Preveza, where Müezzinzâde Ali Pasha received the latest intelligence about the allied forces. Executing a daring cloak-and-dagger operation, the corsair Kara Hodja had managed to penetrate the port of Messina at night in an all-black galliot in order to assess the strength of the Christian fleet. Not detecting Barbarigo's squadron, at anchor in the inner part of the harbour, Kara Hodja estimated the league galleys at not more than 140. Puzzled by the report, Müezzinzâde Ali decided to retreat to the logistics base of Lepanto to replenish his ships with victuals and men.[44] He may also have managed to obtain one of the broadsheets printed at some point before the fleet's departure from Messina showing the allied battle plan★ – with so many people attending the general conference of the 10th it was inevitable that news should leak out, to the advantage of the efficient Ottoman spy ring present in every port of the Mediterranean.[45] In fact, both sides were under the impression that they were dealing with a numerically inferior enemy, a factor that would crucially influence their subsequent decisions.

Don Juan learnt with displeasure about Kara Hodja's exploit while passing Santa Maria di Leuca, at the tip of Italy's heel. But there was nothing he could do at this point, except stop to embark 500 Calabrian infantrymen and send twelve galleys to Brindisi to take on 1,500 more. When the league's fleet reached Corfu on the 26th it lacked a third of its force, inclement weather and victualling delays accounting for many of the missing galleys. The galleasses had also lagged behind, and a total of thirty-six galleys had to be sent to take them in tow. Once the whole fleet gathered in Corfu there was some talk about attacking Sopot or Margariti, the excuse being that it was late in the season and that little bread remained. Venier would have nothing of it, insisting that the advance be resumed. Corfu's bread supplies would be sufficient for another two months, and Venier was eager to catch the Ottomans before it was too late. Besides, thanks to the liberation of two important Venetian prisoners, exchanged for a high-ranking Ottoman officer, fresh intelligence had become available.

The freed gentlemen had managed to observe closely the Ottoman fleet and reported that it counted more than 300 sail, including 160 galleys, but lacked fighting men. The Venetian commander grudgingly agreed to take on six siege pieces from the

---

★ I have come across two versions of this broadsheet. One, giving the strength and disposition of the allied fleet in great detail, was published in SALIMEI between pages 96 and 97. The other, with the names of the Ottoman squadron commanders, can be found in QUARTI, between pages 568 and 569. I thank Admiral Tiberio Moro for pointing out to me the existence of the latter. Both versions show the Ottoman fleet in a crescent formation.

fortress of Corfu, since Don Juan wanted at the very least to reduce a fortress or two before the end of the campaign. Venier immediately pointed out that landing infantry and artillery with an unbeaten fleet of over 200 sail in the rear was courting disaster. Receiving another demand for pikes and powder, in order to avoid further delay he decided to leave five galleys in Corfu with orders to rejoin the rest of the fleet once they had finished loading the armaments.[46]

The allied armada sailed to Igoumenitsa, where it stopped for water and fuel, Christian troops skirmishing with local Ottoman forces sent to harass the foraging parties. What happened next nearly wrecked the league for good. Ever since the Venetians had agreed to embark Spanish soldiers on their galleys, the tensions already existing between the two nationalities had increased by the day. Tempers were already running high when on 2 October Giovanni Andrea Doria visited Venier's galleys demanding to see if they were in fighting order. The captain-general could hardly contain his ire in the face of such a blatant breach of protocol, his anger worsened by Venier's personal animosity towards the Genoese admiral. Venier, according to his own report, nevertheless allowed the inspection to take place, although other sources state that he flatly refused to receive Doria, agreeing however that the inspection be conducted by Luis de Requesens. Worse was to come.

Around four o'clock in the afternoon a scuffle started on one of the Cretan galleys between crew members and some Italian soldiers in Spanish pay led by one Captain Muzio Alticozzi from Cortona, which quickly degenerated into a fight with dead and wounded. When Venier sent some officers to see what was happening, Alticozzi attacked them, shouting, 'I am not obeying these fucking cuckolded Venetians.' For Venier it was the last straw. Surrounding the Cretan galley with other vessels and threatening to sink anyone who tried to stop him, he managed to capture Alticozzi and four of his accomplices after a stiff fight. Some days before, a similar incident had resulted in the killing of some Venetian crewmen by Spanish soldiers, but the intervention of Don Juan's advisers had got the culprits off scot-free. Venier was determined not to allow such a thing to happen again. Paying lip service to legal niceties, he organized a drumhead court martial which promptly sentenced Alticozzi and three others to death. The punishment was executed immediately, and the four men found themselves dangling from a yardarm.

Don Juan's representative arrived soon after to see what had happened and immediately reported his findings to his master. The prince was understandably enraged. Not only had Venier flouted the commander-in-chief's authority, but Alticozzi held a Spanish commission and thus did not fall under Venetian jurisdiction. Such was Don Juan's fury that, according to some, he swore to hang Venier in reprisal for his dead men. For a few hours everyone thought that a full-blown battle was about to erupt between the Spanish and the Venetians, both contingents standing at the ready with guns loaded and matches lit. It is unlikely that Don Juan would have carried out his threat, if he ever made it in the first place. Executing an allied commander would have had incalculable consequences. Eventually cooler heads prevailed, Marcantonio Colonna and Barbarigo doing much to soothe the prince's ruffled feathers. In any case, as Colonna pointed out, the Spanish would be fighting more than 100 Venetian galleys and six galleasses. Still, Don Juan was not to be appeased so easily, informing Venier that from then on he would only deal with Barbarigo. The captain-general shrugged his shoulders, commenting that if such were His Highness's desires he would not object.[47]

Once the tension between Spaniards and Venetians abated the fleet resumed its voyage south. On reaching Capo Bianco, Don Juan ordered a general rehearsal of the battle formation, with the squadrons taking up their positions along a five-mile front. The squadrons were distinguished by flags of different colours: Doria's ships sported green pennants at the peak of each mainyard; Don Juan's had blue ones at each masthead; Barbarigo's flew yellow banderols from their foreyards; and Santa Cruz's ships hoisted white pennants from a flagstaff over the stern lamp. Gil de Andrada rejoined the fleet, having shadowed the Ottoman armada until forced to retreat by the arrival of a strong enemy squadron. Some Greek locals he had encountered on his way told him that the Ottoman fleet was at Lepanto and assured him that if the Christians attacked they had a good chance of winning. Little did Andrada know that those same Greeks were also keeping the Ottomans informed of the league's movements, assuring them also that victory was at hand. On the afternoon of the 4th the allies reached Kefallonia and received a rude shock. A frigate sent by the *provveditore generale* of Crete Marino Cavalli was in the Bay of Guiscardo, carrying letters of 24 August with news of the fall of Famagusta and the fate of its defenders. When the tidings were made public a wave of indignation swept through the fleet. Old rivalries vanished in a flash, as the Spanish shared the rage of the now vengeful Venetians.[48] If Lala Mustafa had indeed intended by his actions to provoke the allies to battle he had certainly accomplished his goal, but now the Ottomans faced a swarm of angry hornets.

The anger of the rank and file was not shared by all senior officers. Indeed, the fall of Famagusta had to a great extent pulled the strategic rug from under the allies' feet. That evening a restricted conference was held aboard Don Juan's flagship to discuss what to do next. With Cyprus lost any foray into the Levant was now pointless, leaving two possible options open: attack some Ottoman fortresses in the area or continue searching for the enemy. Predictably, most of Don Juan's advisers favoured the first choice, but in the face of the Venetian commanders' opposition it was decided to continue towards Lepanto.

Next day the allies managed to advance twelve miles before being forced to drop anchor due to bad weather. The Spanish were clearly frustrated by the Venetians' stubborn determination to seek battle, especially given the presence of many other juicy, easier targets in the area. That evening Barbarigo went to Venier and told him that Don Juan's advisers had been spreading the rumour that the Venetians had no stomach for a fight, and that all their assertions to the contrary were but a sham. Writing to the doge the captain-general vented his spleen against the Spaniards' attitude: 'for thanks to all these delays the enemy will look after his own business, and Christendom will lose the best chance it has ever had'. He added that he was ready to be relieved, 'believing that those who desire this post will be more suited than myself to be overawed, and see Your Lordship's state destroyed by vain hopes'. In truth Venier was being rather unfair to Don Juan, since a few hours before the prince had discussed with Barbarigo and Colonna the best way to engage the Ottomans. The three had agreed to sail up to the mouth of the Gulf of Lepanto to taunt the enemy fleet into fighting; should this not work, they would capture the two fortresses guarding the entrance to the gulf. When Barbarigo informed Venier of the plan the old man grudgingly agreed, given also that according to recent intelligence Uluç Ali had departed east with eighty galleys. However, the *beylerbey* of Algiers had in the meantime returned to Lepanto unnoticed by the Christians, who believed it unlikely that a heavily outnumbered Ottoman fleet would risk battle.[49]

The bad weather conditions lasted until the evening of the 6th, when 'God showed us a sky and a sea as not to be seen even in the finest day of spring.' Under oars the allied ships started moving south, but slowly in order not to overtire the crews of those galleys towing the galleasses, and hampered in their progress by a headwind. As they directed their prows towards the Curzolaris islands at the entrance to the Gulf of Patras, the galleys of the advanced guard under Juan de Cardona managed to bottle themselves up in a small cove,[50] rejoining the fleet just moments before battle was joined.★ Four of these galleys were part of Doria's squadron, and their absence would have a telling effect on future developments. In fact, the Christian armada had lost rather more than its vanguard. The round-ships, with nearly 5,000 German troops on board, had failed

---

★ In Doria's report (ADP, 79/53, int. 5A, 'Particolare relazione', f. 3) the original phrase 'due to a mistake of their pilots found themselves inadvertently inside a small cove, with no exit except from the entrance', has been deleted and substituted by 'the galleys of the vanguard remained somewhat behind'.

to keep up with the rest of the fleet even before it reached Corfu, and the Venetians' determination to push forward meant that these ships and soldiers would not be available in the event of a fight. Also the temporary loss of Cardona's galleys meant that the original battle plan devised in Messina was now irremediably damaged, with what consequences still remained to be seen.

The Ottomans had been lurking in the shadow of the fortress of Lepanto since 27 September, retreating there after the allied fleet's presence in the Adriatic had forced them to abandon operations against the Venetian port of Kotor. Speculation about the Christians' moves and objectives had been rife throughout the summer, the Ottomans being at one stage convinced that the league's objective was the Dalmatian coast. As a result, reinforcements, victuals and munitions had been sent to various garrisons in the area. The *kapudan paşa* himself was short of supplies and men. Believing the campaign season over, many *sipahis* had been allowed to return home, and the Ottoman ships badly needed repairs after being constantly at sea since March. On receiving the news that the enemy fleet was approaching, the Ottomans had hastily conscripted men from the local fortresses and population.

Müezzinzâde Ali could look back with pride at the accomplishments of his fleet in the last four months, but now he was grappling with the various directives he had been receiving from Constantinople. A message of 19 August had ordered him to 'display all his courage and intelligence' when facing the enemy, and also winter his fleet in the still-unconquered Kotor. The next instruction he received confirmed Kotor as a winter base, but at this point the league's fleet was already approaching Corfu, making it impossible for the *kapudan paşa* to execute the order. In fact, a later directive that Müezzinzâde Ali never received gave him the choice of Kotor or in 'another port after consulting with Pertev Pasha'. The same letter ordered him to attack the Christian armada 'after getting reliable news about the enemy' and consulting the other commanders of the fleet 'all in perfect agreement and unity, in accordance with what is found most suitable'.[51]

Much has been made of Müezzinzâde Ali's alleged slavish adherence to the letter of these orders to explain his subsequent decision to fight – a consequence, it has been suggested, of the Ottoman central authorities trying to micromanage a campaign being fought hundreds of miles from the capital. In fact, the instructions to the *kapudan paşa* allowed him considerable latitude, not least because they specified that all decisions should be taken in accord with the other commanders. The military situation had changed since May, when the sultan had ordered him to seek out and destroy the enemy fleet; besides, Ottoman pragmatism permitted the man on the spot to act according to circumstances. This emerges forcefully from the records of the war council held on 6 October in the castle of Lepanto with the participation of all the most important Ottoman officers, a number of whom would later report the details of the meeting to their Christian captors. Present were the *beylerbey* of Algiers Uluç Ali Pasha; two of Hayreddin Barbarossa's sons, Mehmed Pasha and the corpulent Hasan Pasha; Salihpaşazâde Mehmed, *bey* of Negropont; Pertev Pasha, Kara Hodja and many others.

Kara Hodja, just back from another reconnaissance mission, reported that the Christian armada numbered 150 galleys at most. By interrogating prisoners previously captured near Igoumenitsa he had also discovered that the fleet was short of water, most supplies having remained with the round-ships, and in need of repairs. Pertev Pasha argued against attacking the enemy, pointing out that the Christians were not there for fun. Other reports estimated a force of some 200 galleys, and he worried about the presence of the Venetian galleasses. The Ottoman fleet was admittedly larger, but not in pristine condition. He added that many of the *sipahis* had gone home, the remaining soldiers were inexperienced, and even the veterans had not much practice in sea fights. Moreover, the Christians were heavily armoured and equipped with harquebuses, while the Ottomans had mostly bows and lacked bodily protection. Pertev also suggested that the many enslaved oarsmen in the Ottoman galleys could be a potential source of trouble, should they manage to free themselves during the battle. His conclusion was that although the sultan had ordered the fleet to fight the Christians, he did not wish to see it in ruins.

Salihpaşazâde Mehmed Bey agreed with Pertev Pasha about the perils of an attack, stating that it would be better to find out the enemy's intentions under the shelter of the guns of Lepanto. Şuluç Mehmed Pasha and others also advised prudence, and the North African Abd el-Malik – who would feature as Mulay Maluco in Cervantes' play *Los Baños de Argel*[52] – stressed the foolishness of attacking fresh forces with battle-weary troops. At this point Hasan Pasha intervened, stating that he not only believed Kara Hodja's report, but that it was a known fact that the enemy fleet was riddled with dissension. Besides, as his father had proven, the Christians were no match for the Ottomans. Uluç Ali also wanted battle, but was against the Ottomans attacking first.

Once everyone had given his opinion Müezzinzâde Ali rose to speak. He pointed out that although the enemy fleet was of considerable size, it was nonetheless rent by jealousy and discord. Besides, according to his spies, Giovanni Andrea Doria was still far away escorting the sailing vessels. Dismissing the galleasses as worthless, the *kapudan paşa* stated that it would be better to attack the Christians before the arrival of their round-ships. He admitted that many of his soldiers were green, but they would be fighting alongside veterans; in any case, they had always been victorious, even without armour. Bows were better weapons than harquebuses, having a rate of fire thirty times greater. The Christian slaves were not a problem, since they would be forced on pain of death to lie under their benches once the fleets clashed. Given these favourable circumstances and the sultan's wishes, the Ottomans should not hesitate to fight the Christian armada: 'For what shall the world say if we, used to provoking the others to battle, now challenged by such despicable enemies should refuse to fight?' Besides, should the Ottomans be victorious the whole of Italy would be theirs to invade. With this the meeting broke up, everyone falling in with the *kapudan paşa*'s bellicose proposal 'either because convinced, or in order not to be accused of cowardice'.[53]

Müezzinzâde Ali has been criticized for his decision, which many have attributed to rashness and/or inexperience. Some Turkish historians have even seen Sokollu Mehmed Pasha's Machiavellian hand in this: by appointing Müezzinzâde Ali and Pertev Pasha, both new to naval warfare, the wily grand vizier had created conditions likely to lead to the Ottomans' subsequent defeat. Michel Lesure has dismissed this idea as a mere conspiracy theory, pointing out that if such a plan ever existed it would have been a risky one to implement.[54] Still, Sokollu had already tried before the stratagem of giving someone a difficult task with the hope of discrediting him – Lala Mustafa's appointment as *serdar* in the Yemen expedition of 1567 being a case in point – and according to Marcantonio Barbaro, Müezzinzâde Ali, originally one of Sokollu's protégés, had sided with the grand vizier's enemies over going to war with Venice.[55] If this was indeed the case, then Sokollu had every interest in making the *kapudan paşa*'s life difficult.

It is also possible that Müezzinzâde Ali was acting out of personal ambition. The son of a *muezzin* in Edirne, he had entered the Porte's corps of gatekeepers (*bevvab*), apparently thanks to the patronage of Süleyman I's powerful wife Hürrem. From there he had advanced by merit to become a taster (*çasnigir*), steward of the gatekeepers (*kapıcılar kethudası*), commander of the janissaries (*yeniçeri ağasi*), governor (*beylerbeyi*) of Algiers and grand admiral. However, he was looked down upon as an outsider by those state officials who had been trained in the inner palace service (the *birun* as opposed to the *enderun*, to which the gatekeepers belonged), for not having been recruited through the *devşirme*.[56] From contemporary accounts it is clear that the *kapudan paşa* used the sultan's order to attack in order to silence his opponents, not because he feared Selim's wrath. Indeed, according to Katib Çelebi his attitude was cavalier to say the least: 'Is there no zeal for Islam and for the sultan's wishes?' he is supposed to have cried. 'What does it matter if there are five or ten men missing from every ship?'[57] The same author describes the admiral as being an inexperienced, rash and stubborn man. These are unfair accusations, for while Pertev Pasha had little knowledge of maritime matters, Müezzinzâde Ali had participated in the Djerba and Malta campaigns, acted as Piyale Pasha's deputy and been *kapudan-ı deryâ* since 1567. Clearly he had some understanding of naval affairs, and his decision to attack was also based on the opinion of some of the most distinguished mariners of the time. Given the intelligence at his disposal, taking the offensive was as good a choice as any other.

That evening the Ottoman fleet sailed out of the Bay of Lepanto, galleys, galliots and other smaller vessels making it 300 strong. Many on board were happy that battle was about to be joined 'for they believed that victory was theirs'.[58]

9. THE 7TH OF OCTOBER

~

As the allied fleet moved into the Gulf of Patras, Marcantonio Colonna was sure something big was about to happen. The renowned mariner Cecco Pisano had just returned from a scouting mission, bringing news of the enemy's strength. Not wishing this intelligence to become public – lest Don Juan be swayed by his cautious advisers – he cryptically whispered to Colonna, 'Sir, you will need to bare your claws and fight'. Don Juan, however, had also received fresh information. Requesens' secretary together with Romegas had been spying on the Ottomans, and reported having seen the enemy vanguard sailing out of the port of Lepanto.[1] Still, Don Juan ignored the size of the force he was about to encounter, like his adversaries convinced he was dealing with a weaker foe.

As the first rays of the sun lit up the sky the Christian lead division under Doria was approaching the northernmost of the Curzolaris islands, sailing through a seascape now much altered by nature. Since Harold Edgerton and Peter Throckmorton conducted their pioneering archaeological research at the site of the battle scholars have accepted the fact that the shoreline has changed significantly from what it was in 1571. At the time of the battle the coast was roughly one to three nautical miles north of the present shoreline. The silting of the river Acheloos has since turned the island of Koutsilaris into hills a short distance inland from the coast,

Oxia being the only isle left of the original archipelago.[2] Ignoring this fact, in 1888 the admiral and scholar Jean-Pierre Edmond Jurien de La Gravière reconstructed the Christian approach to the Curzolaris[3] according to the shoreline of his own time, a theory slavishly followed by other authors over the years. According to Jurien de la Gravière's reconstruction, the league's ships sailed north from Kefallonia, then south through some offshore islands which he thought to be the Curzolaris, to pass between today's Point Scropha and the isle of Oxia before deploying in the Gulf of Patras. In reality the allied armada navigated straight from Kefallonia to south of Petala, at least part of it passing through the channel separating the then island of Koutsilaris from the mainland. Given the slowness of its progress, if the fleet had taken the route described by Jurien de la Gravière it would not have managed to arrive in the Gulf of Patras by the morning of 7 October.

Approaching the Curzolaris, Don Juan ordered lookouts to land on the islands and climb the peaks. No sooner had Giovanni Andrea's lead galleys debouched from the narrow channel separating Oxia from Koutsilaris than from the crow's nests sails were sighted to the east. With the increasing light it became clear that the whole Ottoman fleet had exited the Gulf of Corinth, advancing under sail 'like a forest' in no apparent order. Waiting for the news to be confirmed, Don Juan halted his flagship in order to allow the rest of the fleet to catch up. As more reports confirmed the sighting and the increasing strength of the enemy fleet, Don Juan ordered a green banner to be unfurled on the mainmast of his flagship and a gun fired, in this manner signalling the fleet to ready itself for battle.

The prince then called a conference on his flagship to decide the best course of action. Asking Romegas what he thought should be done, the fire-eating Gascon answered, 'What I think? That if the emperor your father had seen such an armada like ours, he would not have stopped until he had become emperor of Constantinople, and done so with ease.' 'You mean we must fight, Monsieur Romegas?' enquired the prince again. 'Yes, sir.' 'Let's fight then.' When asked the same question Marcantonio Colonna answered laconically in Latin, paraphrasing the Gospel, 'Even if I should die, I will not deny you.' Some of Don Juan's advisers, still remembering Philip II's instructions, tried to dissuade the prince from joining battle, pointing out that in the event of defeat the Ottomans could still retire to the haven of Lepanto while the Christians had nowhere to go if beaten. (Sarcastically a contemporary French author described Requesens as 'considering all the possible options, in true Spanish fashion'.) Don Juan, however, was determined to implement the course of action decided upon in Corfu, cutting short the conference with: 'Gentlemen, this is not the time to discuss, but to fight.'[4]

In the meantime the galleys' decks and bridges were being cleared for battle, and some of the rowers' benches covered over with planking to allow the soldiers greater freedom of action. Offensive and defensive weapons were stacked in the prescribed areas of each vessel, as men checked their arms and donned armour. Gunners loaded their pieces with round, chain and canister shot, and prepared anti-personnel fire pots and fire trumpets. Wine, water, cheese, bread 'and other necessities' were stored on the bridges, fighting being a terribly tiring and thirst-inducing activity. Convicts on the *ponentine* galleys were unchained and provided with weapons, Don Juan having promised a general amnesty if victorious; Muslim slaves, on the other hand, found themselves manacled to their oars. In fact the prince's promise was to a degree fraudulent, for although the league's commander-in-chief he only had the power to liberate those convict rowers under his immediate jurisdiction, certainly not those belonging to others.[5]

Don Juan, reputedly following a suggestion of Giovanni Andrea Doria, also ordered the removal of the rams from the bows of the Christian galleys, so that their guns could be depressed to hit the Ottoman vessels at the shortest possible range. William Prescott commented in 1855, 'It may seem strange that this discovery should have been reserved for the crisis of a battle.' Actually, according to one source, the Venetians had already removed their rams sometime before, since they 'do not allow the use of the centreline gun, a much esteemed and feared weapon, and time is needed to remove them'. Captain Pantero Pantera would comment a few years later that in most cases they were but ornamental objects, and in any case it would appear all the Christian galleys managed to cut off their rams before the battle began.[6]

As soon as the conference ended, Doria informed the prince that he would be moving towards the open sea to allow the Christian fleet room to draw up for battle. Still nourishing some doubts about his decision to fight, Don Juan then boarded a frigate and was rowed over to Venier's flagship. A few words exchanged with the Venetian admiral were sufficient to dispel the prince's misgivings and reconcile him to Venier, mutual need dispelling the animosity that had existed between the two men since the troubles at Igoumenitsa. Don Juan remained on the frigate for some time, offering encouragement to each galley as it passed. The ships moved slowly towards their assigned stations, so as not to create confusion, following a more or less south-easterly course. Barbarigo, instead, probably took a more northern route, skirting the shallows at the mouth of the Acheloos. The narrow channels separating the Cuzo-laris only allowed for the passage of a few galleys at a time, making rapid deployment impossible. In any case, the slow-moving galle-asses needed time to reach their battle stations ahead of the fleet, and the galleys had to trim and close their ranks 'to stop the enemy from entering the line and striking them in the flank'.[7] The advance party of eight galleys under Cardona was expected to split in two, half being allotted to Barbarigo and the rest to Doria. In fact, those assigned to Doria never made it to their stations, taking position instead on the right of the Christian centre. Thus Doria was deprived of four galleys, at least two of them heavily armed *bastarde* with strong fighting complements.[8]

Delays and problems also hampered the galleasses' deployment; in fact it is by no means certain that those allotted to Doria's wing actually managed to reach their prescribed battle station in time. Most modern authors, following Jurien de La Gravière's reconstruction, based on Benedetto Veroggio's very biased and imprecise work written to justify Giovanni Andrea Doria's actions, maintain that these galleasses remained behind Doria's line.[9] Contemporary accounts contradict this, and even those most favourable to Doria admit that at least one galleass made it to the front of the Christian right. Due to the contrary wind the galleasses took time to reach their assigned posts a mile ahead of the Christian line, and two of them were so far behind that Don Juan, 'uttering holy curses', ordered the nearer ones to move ahead. Doria himself was concerned about the delay, and sent repeated requests that the galleasses make haste. Eventually it proved necessary to tow them into place, but since it took around three hours for the Christian fleet to complete its deployment the four galleasses allotted to the centre and left wing managed to move into position in time, a mile ahead of their respective divisions. As for the other two they certainly reached the front of the right wing, but probably only a few hundred yards from it.[10] Subsequent events would appear to confirm this.

The Christians' southward movement did not go undetected by the Ottomans, who initially had not spotted the enemy forces in the fast fading darkness. 'Allah, Allah,' they cried, 'these dogs are running. Let's go and catch them.' Under the false impression that the allied fleet was trying to escape towards the open sea, the Ottoman armada adopted a south-west course in an attempt to cut off the imagined Christian escape. As the other Christian ships slowly came into view, Müezzinzâde Ali realized his mistake and quickly realigned his fleet onto a course parallel to the enemy's. He also started to have misgivings about joining battle, but Uluç Ali reassured him that the Christians were craven scoundrels, ready to run at the first chance. The *kapudan paşa*'s doubts derived also from the many crows seen hovering over the fleet when departing from Lepanto, considered an ill omen by the Ottoman mariners. Müezzinzâde Ali had tried to reassure his men that there was nothing to fear, similar signs having been seen on other occasions when the Ottomans had been victorious, but had only partially managed to allay their fears. The *kapudan paşa* was worried that many of his men were unhappy about the prospect of a naval battle, and a number had been tricked on board the galleys while carrying on ammunition and flags. Animosity was also present between the Ottoman commanders. Abd el-Malik was accused behind his back of being a coward and in cahoots with Don Juan of Austria. Discovering this, Abd el-Malik publicly berated his critics: he was no coward or traitor, but a good Muslim descended directly from the Prophet Muhammad, while most of the Ottoman commanders were Christian renegades 'with pork flesh still stuck between their teeth'.[11] Abd el-Malik's words reveal a certain amount of ethnic and social tension, the North African aristocrat looking down on those he considered mere upstarts, often by-products of the *devşirme*.

The Ottomans took roughly the same time as the allies to deploy their fleet, Uluç Ali's Algerian contingent moving out first to face Doria's division. The Christians in turn interpreted their opponents' deployment as an escape attempt 'and because of these erroneous thoughts, each side took heart to fight the other'. To both contenders battle now seemed inevitable. Müezzinzâde Ali called his sons to him and reminded them of who they were and their duty. Having listened with humility, they took their leave with the promise to bring back the papal flagship and the simple words, 'Blessed be the bread and the salt you have given us.' Like their Christian counterparts the Ottomans were getting ready for battle. A large number of the fighting men on each galley took position on the bow platforms, while on the decks, from bow to stern, stood paired archers and harquebusiers in groups of four. Ottoman galleys lacked pavisades (large wooden planks along the sides of the rowing benches) and usually did not reinforce their forecastles with movable ramparts of reinforced timber – both features typical of western Mediterranean galleys – leaving the men on board exposed to firearms.[12]

The Ottoman fleet was now deployed in a crescent shape, apparently a much favoured formation, the right wing under Şuluç Mehmed Pasha with fifty-five galleys and one galliot; the centre, commanded by the *kapudan paşa*, with ninety-one galleys and five galliots; and the left under Uluç Ali with sixty-seven galleys and twenty-seven galliots. A small reserve under Murad Dragut with eight galleys, five galliots and eighteen *fuste* was placed behind the central division. Smaller vessels with extra fighting men stood ready to assist wherever needed, making a total of about 300 ships. There is no doubt that the Ottoman fleet was numerically stronger, many galliots being no different from normal galleys – some of them having up to twenty-five rowing benches – except possibly in the amount of ordnance carried.* In ordnance the league definitely held the stronger hand, and while archival evidence has laid to rest Alberto Guglielmotti's tidy estimate of the guns present (1,815 for the league and 750 for the Ottomans), it is probable that the Christians held a two to one advantage in artillery pieces.[13]

Having disposed his forces for battle, Müezzinzâde Ali issued his orders. The two wings were to advance and envelop the Christian flanks, while his division would tackle the enemy centre. The simple Muslim tactical plan was to break through the enemy line by skilful use of numbers, isolating and destroying the allied ships piecemeal. Şuluç's and Uluç Ali's divisions were to move first, immediately followed by the *kapudan paşa's*. By exercising enough pressure on Don Juan's centre and left the Ottomans calculated that he would be forced to commit his reserve prematurely to aid these divisions. Should this happen, then Uluç Ali could deal unhindered with an outnumbered Doria. The Algerian *beylerbey's* galleys were to pin down the Genoese admiral, allowing his galliots to swing round the allies' right flank and fall upon their rear. Should the manoeuvre succeed, then the hapless allies would be pinned against the shore, and cavalry units had been stationed on the coast with the task of rounding up the stranded Christians.[14] Alternatively, if Don Juan sent Santa Cruz to help Doria, then the *kapudan paşa* would attempt to smash through the enemy centre by sheer weight of numbers causing the disintegration of the Christian line.

---

* This is probably the reason why estimates of the Ottoman fleet vary significantly in the various contemporary sources.

The crescent formation initially adopted by the Ottomans was, in theory, ideal for enveloping manoeuvres, allowing, in the words of a near contemporary, 'in different directions but at the same time to invest the front of the enemy, while the horns on the side surround him, or retreat should there be the need'.[15] Yet the size of the Ottoman fleet meant that the tips of the crescent would come too early into contact with a much stronger enemy and possibly be severely mauled before the rest of the armada could come to their aid. To be successful the *kapudan paşa*'s plan called for good timing and the whole fleet to work in unison for the Ottoman punch to be delivered with full force. Müezzinzâde Ali therefore altered his fleet's formation, dividing it into three divisions mirroring the Christian deployment. He also ordered that no one should overtake his galley on pain of death, reserving the same fate for any enslaved Christian oarsman who should turn his head towards the enemy fleet – something that inevitably would cause a drop in speed. A good psychologist as well as a humane and generous person, Müezzinzâde Ali promised freedom to all his slaves if victorious. Since the Ottomans were convinced that the Christians were lambs to the slaughter, the *kapudan paşa* was banking on having enough prisoners to take the place of the liberated slaves.[16]

Yet the *kapudan paşa* was worried. He could not understand the galleasses' tactical role in front of the enemy line, and was bemused that what he thought were transport vessels had been placed in such an exposed position. It was common knowledge that the Venetians had armed some *galie grosse*, a number of his officers expressing concern about their presence. But prisoners recently captured near Igoumenitsa had told him that these big galleys had only three artillery pieces at the stern and three at the bow, hardly something to be worried about. Müezzinzâde Ali was more anxious about the number and position of the *ponentine* galleys, having little regard for the Venetian ones 'even if there had been a thousand of them'. The *kapudan paşa*'s dismissive attitude may appear strange, but the poor performance of the Venetian fleet during the 1570 campaign should be borne in mind. Müezzinzâde Ali was certainly aware of the many problems still afflicting the republic's ships, including the scarcity of fighting personnel, and was thus puzzled to discover that the allies had intermixed *ponentine* and *levantine* galleys. His decision to strike Barbarigo's wing first and with the same number of galleys as his adversary could also have resulted from the belief that the Venetians represented, in every sense, the league's soft underbelly.[17]

Not everyone approved of Müezzinzâde Ali's plan. As he watched the Ottoman fleet deploy, Uluç Ali was unable to hide his concerns from the *kapudan paşa*. In particular he had serious misgivings about Şuluç's wing being placed so near to the coast, urging his commander-in-chief to move the fleet towards the open sea. Otherwise, not only would the Ottoman right have little manoeuvring space, but the crews would also be tempted to make for the shore should the tide of battle turn against the Turks. Müezzinzâde Ali stubbornly stuck to his plan, causing Uluç Ali to tear at his beard crying in despair, 'Why don't those who learnt their trade with Hayreddin and Dragut speak out?'. This story may have been concocted at a later date and with the benefits of hindsight, but the contemporary Genoese author Foglietta would also stress that by deploying near the coast the Ottomans had provided their crews with an irresistible escape route.[18]

The Christian fleet was now fully arrayed. On the left stood the fifty-seven galleys of Barbarigo's division, four placed behind the front line as an immediate reserve, the Venetian commander having moved as close to the shore as he dared to avoid envelopment. But Barbarigo, not knowing the coast well and wary of sandbanks, made the mistake of leaving a gap between the left of his squadron and the shore wide enough to allow a few galleys at a time to slip through. The central division under Don Juan of Austria numbered sixty-two galleys, two at the stern of the prince's *capitana*, many being the flagships of the various contingents. Doria with fifty-three galleys was to the right, still lacking four of Cardona's vessels. Seeing that the opposing Ottoman division under Uluç Ali far outnumbered his own, Doria extended himself to the south, thinning his ranks and creating a gap between the Christian right and centre. But the Genoese admiral sent word to Don Juan not to commit his reserve unless the Ottomans managed to break through in force, it being more advantageous to meet any threat with fresh forces than having to do so with battle-weary galleys and men. Doria's suggestion was sound given that the absence of the round-ships and of Cardona's group had weakened the whole Christian front, but he still believed that the vanguard would eventually reach its assigned position, and was probably counting on the galleasses to plug the hole developing to the right of the allied main division. Behind the main line stood Santa Cruz's reserve with thirty galleys, plus some forty brigantines and frigates, each loaded with ten harquebusiers and a couple of small guns, whose job was to tackle the enemy's light craft 'doing as much damage possible'.[19]

The centre of both fleets was heavily larded with *capitane* and *padrone*, eighteen on the allied and twenty-two on the Ottoman side, all lantern galleys. John F. Guilmartin in his seminal study of galley warfare describes the latter as not necessarily larger than ordinary galleys – nor were *bastarde* necessarily lantern galleys – but as 'invariably exceptionally heavily armed and . . . [playing] an important role as tactical focal points in battle'.[20] While the second part of this statement is to an extent true, the first assertion is debatable. As we have seen, the *capitana* and *padrona* of the Lomellini family, both lanterns, were small and carried limited amounts of ordinance. The same was true of the twenty-five-bench *capitana* of Savoy, but in the Christian battle array it occupied the place immediately to the right of the papal flagship. The Lomellini *capitana* also occupied a particularly exposed position on the extreme left of the central division, where one would have expected to find a more powerful vessel. The answer to this riddle lies in the complicated system of precedence, typical of the age. Significantly, Doria's and Barbarigo's galleys stood on the extreme flanks of their respective divisions, Cardona's flagship should have been placed at the extreme left of Doria's wing, and the flagship of the contingent provided by the Genoese republic was beside Venier's galley – all these dispositions proving how tactical needs had to take into consideration social conventions. This was not limited to the West, the Ottomans also having to deal with problems of hierarchy when deploying their fleet, although they tended to group together the galleys of the various contingents making up their armada. Nor were the Ottoman lantern galleys necessarily all *bastarde*; for many independent captains the lantern was a status symbol, even if their command be just one vessel.[21]

The exact number of soldiers on each side remains a matter of debate. Alfonso Salimei, writing in 1931, estimated 34,000 Christian soldiers present, a figure accepted by some Turkish historians as proof that the Ottomans were quantitatively inferior in troops. However, Salimei, while undoubtedly a thorough researcher, based his estimates on theoretical calculations and overtly attempted to claim the so-called battle of Lepanto as an Italian victory 'with Spanish help'. Salimei, after all, wrote during the Fascist period, glossing over the fact that in the Early Modern age – and to an extent today – Italy was but a cultural and geographical expression, and also that many of the Italians participating in the 1571 campaign were Neapolitans, Sicilians and Milanese, all subjects of the king of Spain.[22] Contemporary documents show the league having between 28,000 and 31,000 soldiers, and the Ottomans fielding 25,000 *sipahis* and janissaries. To the latter should be added a few thousand Algerian, Tunisian and Tripoli corsairs, plus an unknown number of garrison soldiers taken from nearby fortresses. A few years after the battle Mario Savorgnan estimated the fighting complement of the standard Ottoman galley present as on average 120 'swordsmen', lantern galleys boasting up to 300, yet we know that the crews of a number of Ottoman galleys were under strength. In reality, calculating the exact number of fighting men is virtually impossible: not only were Venetian and Ottoman sailors and free rowers trained combatants, it was also customary for commanders facing a difficult situation to augment their forces by unchaining and arming *buonevoglie* (on *ponentine* galleys) and convict oarsmen.

Thus, it is safe to say that the two forces were more or less equal as to fighting men, although the Ottomans probably had more seasoned veterans.[23]

Both sides aimed to reduce the enemy's combat strength by the use of artillery before the fleets came into contact. Since the Ottomans relied more on hand-to-hand fighting, they preferred to load their naval ordnance with stone balls, 'considering that by shattering into pieces, smashing the timber and sending splinters flying through the air they do more damage than iron balls, that pass clean through the wood'. For this reason the Ottomans preferred firing their guns at close range in one single volley, leaving their boarding parties to finish off a stunned and decimated foe. Western tactics emphasized damaging vessels as much as crews, galley ordnance being loaded with different types of shot and discharged at various moments during a battle. In his fighting orders Don Juan allowed every captain 'to fire when they believe it will most damage the enemy' but ordered them to reserve at least one piece for the final clash.[24] Events would prove which of the two philosophies was best.

On his flagship Don Juan donned a suit of mirror-polished armour and then, crucifix in hand, climbed on a swift frigate. Marcantonio Colonna and Requesens also boarded frigates, each of the three men travelling to one of the divisions division to ascertain that the galleys were in fighting order and to encourage those on board. Back on his galley, Don Juan heard mass, and on both sides men bowed their heads in prayer, asking God to aid them in their cause. On Christian vessels priests, many from the new Jesuit and Capuchin orders, heard confessions, while the Muslims performed ritual ablutions. Pius V's bull of general indulgence and absolution for all those who should happen to die in battle against the infidels was read aloud on each of the league's ships. The Muslims did not need such reassurance, believing that dying in battle for their faith would automatically allow them into heaven.[25]

It was now about eleven in the morning, and the two fleets had slowly been moving towards each other for at least three hours, the allies still hampered in their movements by a headwind. The league's fleet had taken up position, its extreme left wing close to the northern shore of the Gulf of Patras, and it now awaited the enemy onslaught. As soon as Müezzinzâde Ali was sure his fleet was ready he ordered a blank shot to be fired in the direction of the enemy, formally challenging his opponent to battle. Immediately the *Real* answered with a shot loaded 'with ball'. To confirm his intentions, the *kapudan paşa* had another blank shot fired, and again Don Juan answered with a fully loaded artillery piece. In this way not only did the prince signal to his opponents the position of the allied flagship – since the Ottomans' vision would soon be impeded by the sun shining in their faces – but the water columns produced by the impacting balls allowed him to adjust his guns' elevation for maximum effect. Trumpets sounded, and the great banner of the league, displaying Christ crucified accompanied by the coats of arms of Habsburg Spain, the pope and the republic of Venice, was hoisted on the *Real*'s mainmast.[26]

At a signal the whole Ottoman fleet advanced towards the Christian array. It was an impressive and daunting sight, enough to make even the bravest man quake, made of multicoloured banners, robes and turbans, accompanied by the sound of drums, horns and other instruments. From the mainmast of Müezzinzâde Ali's flagship (called in the west the *Sultana*) flew the Ottoman battle standard, on which the name of Allah was embroidered 29,800 times. The Ottomans moved at a leisurely pace, exploiting the favourable wind to advance without having to tire their crews, galleys using oars only to keep in line. Suddenly the wind changed, a breeze starting to blow in the Ottomans' faces. Hastily the *kapudan paşa* ordered all sails furled and the fleet to continue under oars. The Christians were quick to see the change in weather as a sign of divine favour and took fresh heart. Apparently calm and relaxed, Don Juan watched from the poop deck of the *Real* the Ottoman fleet pause. Calling for his musicians, he went to the *arrembata* and there, in a supreme example of what the Italians call *sprezzatura*, he danced a galliard together with two other Spanish gentlemen.[27] But very soon everyone would be dancing to the tune of the Totentanz.

~

It was nearly midday, and the Ottomans were about a mile and a half from the Christian line, galleys oars dipping into the sea in constant, long strokes, the beating of drums giving the rhythm to thousands of free and forced rowers.[28] The Christian galleasses lay in the middle of the sea like sleeping castles, but the men on board were awake and alert, impatiently waiting near their guns or at the pavisades for the enemy to approach. Tension was evident on the face of Master Gunner Zaccaria Schiavina, the inventor of a new aiming system 'to shoot at the enemy creating the outmost damage'.[29] Now the moment of truth had arrived, the Ottomans being little more than half a mile away and steadily moving in for the kill. Francesco Duodo, commanding the galleasses, uttered a brisk order and the Venetian gunners' lit matches struck the touchholes.

The effect of the galleasses' fire on the advancing Ottomans was devastating, the last thing many of them saw being the flash and the smoke of the Christian bow pieces. Most did not even hear the thunder of the guns before being hit. The flying iron balls easily found targets in the formation of densely packed Muslim ships, smashing through timber and flesh. Shouts of '*mavna, mavna!*' rose from the Ottoman vessels, mingling with the screams of the wounded and the sound of splintering wood. 'God allow us to get out of here in one piece,' cried Müezzinzâde Ali, seeing a shot carry away the central lantern of his flagship.[30] Beholding the destruction around him, Pertev Pasha tugged at his beard in consternation. In one case, the impact of Venetian shot lifted a galley out of the water, its oars waving helplessly like the legs of a wounded centipede, before sending it to the bottom with all hands. In another, a galley was blown sky-high after a ball penetrated its ammunition magazine. At least two other ships were lost to the galleasses' fire, and many more damaged. Other galleys, their coxswains dead, caused havoc by colliding with those adjacent to them.

Scores of Ottomans were crushed or torn apart; masts toppled into the sea; water poured into smashed hulls. The drums on the Muslim ships stopped beating, and a number of galleys started to backwater; others instinctively converged towards the galleasses, discharging their guns as they did. Slowly Duodo's six ships made a half-turn, oars moving the vessels in unison as if in a pirouette, before delivering another volley from the port side. Again the gentle manoeuvre, and the process was repeated with the aft and starboard artillery, the relentless Venetian fire making the galleasses look like 'all one flame'.[31] Duodo had dealt the Ottomans a dizzying upper-cut; not yet a knockout, it was a blow that brought the enemy to his knees. Acting quickly, Müezzinzâde Ali barked out orders, and the rowers on the Ottoman vessels increased their stroke rate in an attempt to get away as quickly as possible from the hellish galleasses. But as the Ottoman fleet pushed on, full speed ahead, formation was irremediably lost; many galleys, at sea for too long now, lagged behind. The *kapudan paşa*'s plan lay in ruins, together with its formation the Ottoman fleet having lost much of its punch. However, with grim determination it pressed ahead towards the waiting Christian galleys to see what the remainder of the battle would bring.

Attempting to avoid the devastating Venetian heavy ordnance the Ottoman right and centre had to run the gauntlet of swivel guns and harquebuses fired by the men posted on top of the galleasses. The galleys passing nearest to the big vessels were the worst hit, single leaden balls and grapeshot opening gaping holes on the densely packed decks and forecastles. No sooner were they free of the galleasses' steely claws than the Ottomans started being pounded by the allied galleys' centreline guns. By this point nearly a third of the Muslim ships had been sunk or damaged to a greater or lesser degree; worse still the smoke from the league's ordnance was blowing in the Ottomans' faces, hiding the Christian fleet from sight and impeding the aim of archers and gunners. But despite its losses the Ottoman armada still had plenty of fighting spirit in it, as the allies were soon to find out.

No sooner had the galleasses opened fire than the allied fleet began slowly to advance towards the now broken enemy line. The unhurried pace had the purpose of keeping a tight formation, although according to one source the Christian fleet would have done better fighting closer to the galleasses 'which could have been of greater aid in the battle'.[32] Because of the fleet's size, perfect alignment proved impossible, much to Venier's chagrin. The *capitana* of Malta moved 'the length of two galleys' ahead of the line, as did Marco Querini's group on the extreme right of Barbarigo's wing. From a nearby galley Count Ferrante Caracciolo noticed Querini's escapade, potentially very dangerous for the whole allied fleet, and immediately sent a message to Barbarigo allowing him to redress the situation in time by ordering Querini to fall back into line.

In an attempt to avoid the galleasses' murderous fire, Şuluç Mehmed Pasha swung his division towards the coast. To an extent he managed to get out of the range of the Venetian heavy guns, but the *beylerbey* of Alexandria's move also had another purpose. Exploiting the knowledge of the Genoese renegade Caur Ali, Şuluç passed under the promontory of Malcantone, braving the shallows at the mouth of the river Acheloos with the intention of turning Barbarigo's flank. The Venetian commander saw the peril and reacted quickly. The four Venetian galleys of Cardona's vanguard had just reached the Christian left and had positioned themselves to the rear of Barbarigo's flagship. Being the nearest at hand, Barbarigo ordered them to stop the Muslim outflanking manoeuvre. It was a timely decision. As the Ottomans rounded Malcantone, they found their way blocked by the first of these vessels, the *Santa Maria Maddalena* under Marino Contarini. Counting on superior numbers they attacked it immediately, and very soon Contarini's men were fighting for their lives. Barbarigo understood that if he did not stop the advancing Muslims in their tracks all would be lost. Turning his flagship – easily recognizable because of its sides painted Venetian red, the colour of ordinary Venetian galleys being brown – towards the coast, he signalled to the nearest galleys to follow him. With guns blazing he headed for the flank of the advancing enemy galleys and then placed himself squarely in their path 'so that not even a small boat could pass'.[33] It was an act of desperate courage, for now he was pitted against a far superior foe.

It did not take long for the *Santa Maria Maddalena* to resemble a charnel house. Marino Contarini himself was killed almost immediately by a harquebus shot, the same fate befalling many of the galley's officers. Colonel Paolo Orsini, in command of the Venetian infantry on board, received a ball in the right shoulder and burns all over his body from a fire pot. Then *Il Sole* captained by Vincenzo Querini emerged from the smoke, crashing into the Ottoman ships and relieving the pressure on Contarini. Thanks to their plentiful small-calibre artillery firing at point-blank range the Venetians managed to keep the Muslims at bay, but *Il Sole* in its turn suffered grievous losses from Ottoman harquebusiers, archers and swordsmen. Querini was killed, and for more than a hour the Venetians desperately tried to push back their Ottoman assailants. Nevertheless, with their determined stand Contarini and Querini's men had bought precious time for the rest of the Christian left wing.

Seeing Barbarigo's galley approaching, Şuluç had swung his galleys round to confront the Venetian. Hit by the withering fire of eight Ottoman galleys, Barbarigo's ship was soon in the centre of a maelstrom. Muslim soldiers poured over the gunwales and the forward platform, pushing back the Venetian defenders. Barbarigo himself was in the thick of the fight, constantly encouraging his men and leading them in one counter-attack after another. More Venetian galleys joined the fray, fresh troops allowing Barbarigo to push back his attackers. Şuluç realized that he had to finish the job quickly, lest he lose his chance of turning the Christian left flank. Exploiting local tactical superiority he redoubled his efforts to capture Barbarigo's flagship, hoping that this would lead to the collapse of organized resistance in that sector. But for the *beylerbey* of Alexandria time was running out fast, more and more Christian galleys engaging the Muslim vessels or helping the ships thus occupied by feeding troops into the fight.

Meanwhile, below Malcantone, the two Venetian galleys protecting Barbarigo's left flank had prevailed over their enemies. Locked together side by side they had provided mutual support to each other, repulsing attack after attack with the aid of the galleys *Santa Caterina* and *Nostra Donna*, all originally part of the vanguard. As the Alexandrian galleys attempted to prise apart *Santa Maria Maddalena* and *Il Sole*, Paolo Orsini exploited a momentary lull in the fighting to organize a counter-attack with his surviving men. Taken by surprise, the Ottomans attempted to resist, but suddenly, having somehow managed to break open their shackles and grabbing the weapons of the fallen, Christian slaves attacked their former masters from all sides. Caught unawares the Muslims quickly succumbed, the Ottoman galleys near Malcantone falling one by one to the Christians. The *Santa Caterina* and *Nostra Donna* now turned to Barbarigo's aid.

More help was on its way. Santa Cruz, already engaged with the Ottomans in the centre, had sent ten galleys of the reserve to plug the potential gap developing on the left wing. Meanwhile, Provveditore Marco Querini was also coming, having on his own initiative swung his detachment towards the coast. The *Santa Caterina* and *Nostra Donna* joined the hard-pressed Barbarigo, but nearly immediately their *sopracomiti* Marco Cicogna and Pier Francesco Malipiero were struck down. To make matters worse, an Ottoman galley under the cover of thick smoke managed to round Malcantone and ram Barbarigo's galley at the stern. Once again the Christian left was at risk, the Ottomans still having enough advantage in numbers to execute a breakthrough, with potentially incalculable consequences for the battle's outcome. Marco Querini's manoeuvre had also opened a large gap to the left of the Christian central division. Should Müezzinzâde Ali be able to exploit this chance and unite with Şuluç's forces at the rear of the allied battle line, all would be lost for the league.

A hail of arrows fell on Barbarigo's ship as the Ottomans once again tried to take it by storm. Rallying his men Barbarigo raised the visor of his helmet to make himself heard. His aides warned him of the peril. 'Better to be hit than not heard,'[34] answered the feisty Venetian. No sooner had he uttered these words than an arrow pierced his left eye. Collapsing into the arms of his secretary Andrea Suriano, he was hastily carried below with the help of Colonel Silvio da Porcia. Dismay struck the defenders, and the Ottomans exploited the confusion to board the galley, fighting their way up to the mainmast. It was now up to Barbarigo's deputy Federico Nani to repel the Ottoman assault – Nani himself having been wounded several times – but luckily for the Venetians relief was at hand. With all guns firing, the galley *Dio Padre e la Trinità* under Giovanni Contarini del Zaffo struck Şuluç's galley at the stern, carrying away its rudder. Behind this vessel was the galley of Provveditore Antonio da Canal, who having just dispatched an enemy vessel went straight for the *capitana* of Alexandria, ramming it amidships. But immediately da Canal was in turn attacked from the rear, and it was left to Nicolò Avonal's Cretan vessel and to the galleys of the vanguard to fight off the ships attacking Barbarigo's galley.

Slowly the tide was swinging in the allies' favour. Marco Querini had reached his beleaguered companions, and the ten galleys from the reserve led by Martin de Padilla were bearing down on the wavering enemy line. The Neapolitan and papal galleys of both Querini's and Barbarigo's squadrons – *ponentine* with strong fighting contingents – engaged Şuluç's front and right, the Spanish harquebusiers pouring pounds of lead into the Ottoman ranks. The galleasses of Antonio and Ambrogio Bragadin also joined the fray, their heavy guns disabling one galley after another. But the Ottomans were not prepared to give up, and scores of impatient Venetians fell trying to board the enemy vessels.

Exploiting a gap in the Muslim line created by galleass fire, the Tuscan *Elbigina* charged through followed by a number of other galleys. Swinging to the right they went for a contingent of Anatolian vessels commanded by Salihpaşazâde Mehmed Bey. On one of the allied galleys, the *Marchesa* owned by Giovanni Andrea Doria, lay the ailing Miguel de Cervantes. Rising from his sick bed to join the fight for the Anatolian galleys, his left hand was permanently crippled by a harquebus shot. 'For the glory of the right one,' he would later comment, proudly showing his wound.[35] The *Elbigina* and her companions intercepted a group of about thirty Ottoman galleys escaping from the centre,* and after a stiff fight captured the *capitana* of Rhodes, commanded by Hasan Bey, with a fighting contingent of 250 men. On board, the victorious soldiers found rich booty, including four falcons and as many greyhounds. Salihpaşazâde Mehmed was also captured, and now the Neapolitans of Padilla's squadron were busy wrapping things up on the left.

By now the Ottomans in this sector of the battle were thoroughly demoralized. As a small group of slow and undermanned Turkish galleys approached the battle, the crews realized that the game was up. Believing discretion the better part of valour, they headed straight for the shore, abandoning their galleys without a fight. The rest of the Ottoman right was likewise being pushed towards the coast by the allied galleys, some of the latter running aground in their haste to come to grips with the enemy. A shot from Giovanni Contarini's ship sent Şuluç's galley to the bottom, but it didn't sink far, the sea at that point being less than two metres deep. Badly wounded, Şuluç was dragged from the water onto Contarini's galley. Antonio da Canal, dressed in a quilted cotton jacket and hat, had meanwhile donned a pair of rope shoes so as not to slip on the blood-soaked planks and was busy clearing the enemy decks with a two-handed sword. Hundreds of Ottomans jumped into the sea in an attempt to reach the safety of the nearby coast. Many got trampled by their comrades and drowned in the shallow waters; others were chased and killed by the pitiless Venetians; others still, wounded or not knowing how to swim, surrendered, trusting in their enemies' mercy. The Venetians had little, but the soldiers of the other contingents were happy to take as many prisoners as possible. The slaughter on the Christian left had been

---

* This could explain why Ferrante Caracciolo states that Şuluç had seventy galleys with him. (CARACCIOLO: 37. Cfr. ADRIANI: 885).

great, but was nothing compared to what was still happening else-where.

~

Rowing furiously and in some disorder, the Ottoman main division hit the allied centre just after midday. Accompanied by a group of powerful *lanterne*, the *Sultana* went straight for the *Real*. As they approached the enemy line, the Ottomans had been subjected to a continuous bombardment from the Christian vessels, some of which managed to shoot up to five times at the advancing Muslims. The latter, having retained their galleys' rams, could not depress their guns sufficiently to reply, in most cases the Turkish shots sailing clean over the decks of the Christian ships. Besides, the allied artillery fire had been mainly directed at the front of the advancing Ottoman galleys, killing many gunners before they could fire their pieces, a number being found still loaded at the end of the battle. But still the Ottomans came on, until the fleets clashed with an ear-splitting cacophony of sound. Giovanni Battista Contarini has left us a vivid image of the scene:

> There happened a mortal storm of harquebus shots and arrows, and it seemed that the sea was aflame from the flashes and continuous fires lit by fire trumpets, fire pots and other weapons. Three galleys would be pitted against four, four against six, and six against one, enemy or Christian alike, everyone fighting in the cruellest manner to take each other's lives. And already many Turks and Christians had boarded their opponents' galleys fighting at close quarters with short weapons, few being left alive. And death came endlessly from the two-handed swords, scimitars, iron maces, daggers, axes, swords, arrows, harquebuses and fire weapons. And besides those killed in various ways, others escaping from the weapons would drown by throwing themselves into the sea, thick and red with blood.[36]

The air was dense with gunpowder smoke, which engulfed all combatants without distinction. Often men knew that they were

273

under attack only when they felt their galley struck by an enemy vessel, seconds before being hit by a storm of arrows, harquebus or artillery fire. In the confusion it was difficult to distinguish friend from foe, although the league's ships displayed sheep's fleeces as field signs.[37] It would be wrong to think that the combatants were only intent on boarding each other's vessels. Storming an enemy galley was not easy, unless its fighting crew had been substantially reduced in numbers. The Ottomans were more inclined to employ boarding tactics, after thinning the enemy ranks with guns, bows, flaming pots and fire tubes. Muslim archers were particularly active, one source describing the Christian galleys as being so studded with arrows as to resemble hedgehogs.[38] The allies preferred to keep the Muslims at a distance with a continuous barrage of grapeshot and small-arms fire: at close range one well-directed harquebus volley was enough to clear an opponent's bridge, even if in the confusion many fell victim to friendly fire.[39]

With banners fluttering in the wind, Müezzinzade Ali's galley now descended on the *Real*, striking it diagonally at the bow. The *Sultana*'s guns thundered, one ball smashing through the *Real*'s *arrembata*, wounding and killing a number of rowers; another went wide and the third sailed clean over the gunwales. The *Real*'s artillery also did considerable damage to the enemy flagship, the advantage gained from having no ram being evident. Shouting like madmen, the *Sultana*'s janissaries leapt onto the *Real*'s foredeck, trying to storm the *arrembata* and engaging Don Juan's soldiers in a furious hand-to-hand fight. Marcantonio Colonna moved his galley in to assist Don Juan, but was hit by Pertev Pasha's vessel. The blow caused the papal flagship to turn sharply to its left and in turn strike the *Sultana* at the second bench from the bow, just as another Ottoman galley crashed into Colonna's stern. On Don Juan's left, Sebastiano Venier also attempted to engage the *Sultana*, counting on the support of Genoa's *capitana* commanded by Ettore Spinola. But seeing Spinola already engaged with four other enemy galleys and himself about to be intercepted by a group of Ottoman vessels, he sent for two Venetian galleys of Santa Cruz's squadron. As

Venier pushed forward a small mastless boat managed to reach undetected the starboard side of the Venetian flagship, slipping under its oars to prevent the galley from moving. Never lacking initiative, Venier ordered all his men to the starboard side, tilting his galley onto the boat until it sank.

Meanwhile on the *Real* the harquebusiers had repulsed the Ottomans, and now counter-attacked under the command of Maestre de Campo (Colonel) Don Lope de Figueroa. His 400 Sardinian harquebusiers were augmented by a number of gentlemen volunteers and their retainers, bringing the *Real*'s fighting complement to 800 men. Battling furiously they boarded the *Sultana*, pushing back the Ottomans to its mainmast. With the arrival of Muslim reinforcements from the galleys coming up behind Müezzinzâde Ali's flagship, the allies were in turn forced to retreat as the Turks once more gained a foothold on the *Real*. From the Christian galleys at Don Juan's stern came more troops in support of their hard-pressed companions, and again the allies boarded the *Sultana* only to be pushed back once more. This deadly see-saw continued for some time, neither side managing to gain the upper hand as more and more men were pushed into the battle, often to their deaths. The bridges of both flagships had makeshift pavisades at three different places, and were covered with fat and oil to cause assailants' to slip and fall.

Having managed to free his vessel, Venier headed once more for the *Sultana*. En route, he noticed four enemy galleys moving to intercept him but 'thank God they all went by my stern'.[40] Pushing ahead, Venier struck the *Sultana* amidships but was in turn hit in the prow by a Turkish lantern galley, and by another towards the stern. Now Venier had to fend off attacks from two sides, and to make matters worse the four galleys which had previously failed to intercept him reversed course, heading for his stern. Luckily the two galleys Venier had sent for arrived just in time to stop the Ottoman vessels in their tracks, engaging them in furious combat. Both their *sopracomiti*, Cattarin Malipiero and Giovanni Loredan, were killed, with their sacrifice saving Venier from almost certain destruction. But in the meantime other Ottoman galleys were attacking the allied command squadron, one of them striking the *Real* at its stern. The Christian centre had been pierced, and should the gap in the line become wider the Ottomans could still exploit their superiority in numbers to stage a major breakthrough.

Malipiero and Loredan's galleys were followed by Santa Cruz's whole squadron. Whether the leader of the Christian reserve simply followed the two vessels or made a deliberate decision to engage his division is unclear. He had been ordered 'with the greatest attention and care to see which section be the weakest, where his intervention be necessary, and with what number of galleys . . . leaving every decision to the aforesaid marquis's prudence, only if it coincides with what we expect and confide he shall do'.[41] Santa Cruz had been given complete freedom of action, but he knew that he had to use it shrewdly. Committing the reserve too soon or unnecessarily could mean having nothing left to stop the Ottomans should they manage to turn one of the allied flanks. On the other hand, Santa Cruz could not stand by idly while the Christian centre was penetrated and possibly annihilated. In the event, seeing the Ottomans pierce the allied line, the marquis moved his galleys forward and pushed back the enemy – something for which his political adversary Requesens would later criticize him.[42] Santa Cruz soon had his hands full, and was saved from a bullet only thanks to his buckler. For others even the strongest armour was no protection. Virginio Orsini died when a ball sailed clean through his buckler and breastplate – which speaks volumes about the poor quality of both. Don Bernardino de Cardenas was hit in the chest by a shot fired from a swivel gun, and although his armour withstood the blow the unfortunate gentleman died from shock.

Marcantonio Colonna had meanwhile forced Pertev Pasha to pull back, but was still faced by other Ottoman galleys. On his right the *capitana* of Savoy had been fending off the attacks of one commanded by Mustafa Esdey, paymaster general of the Ottoman fleet, and another vessel. The Savoyard galley was nearly overwhelmed, and its commander, Provana di Leynì, received a harquebus ball in his helmet that left him stunned for half an hour – he was still suffering from headaches a few days later when he wrote his report to Duke Emmanuel Philibert. The timely arrival of one of Santa Cruz's galleys restored the situation, allowing Provana to repulse his assailants.[43] On the left of the *Real* Sebastiano Venier was busy encouraging his men, shooting with a crossbow at enemy soldiers. Standing on his bridge he received an arrow in the leg but refused to leave his post.

To the right of the *capitana* of Savoy was the *Grifona*, one of the galleys leased by Cosimo I de' Medici to Pope Pius V. It was a powerful vessel and had been given to the grand duke by Ugolino Grifoni, a rich and powerful Medici supporter. Captained by Alessandro Negroni, it had on board also Onorato Caetani and Bartolomeo Sereno, who later would leave detailed accounts of the fight. Kara Hodja and the galley of the corsair Kara Deli attacked the *Grifona* head on, meeting the stiffest of resistance. The papal soldiers poured harquebus and artillery fire into the Muslim ranks, already depleted since the Ottoman galleys had already fought two Venetian vessels. True to his reputation, Kara Hodja led his men from the front until shot by an Italian harquebusier. The arrival of a Venetian galley from the reserve commanded by the confusingly named Giovanni Loredan (a relation of his recently killed namesake) put an end to the matter, allowing the capture of the Turkish vessels. Onorato Caetani paid tribute to the Ottomans' fighting spirit, writing that between the two galleys 'no more than six Turks remained alive'.[44]

Leaving other galleys to deal with Colonna's, Pertev Pasha sailed round to the stern of the *Sultana* with the intention of bringing aid to the *kapudan paşa*. It was a mistake, for Pertev had already suffered considerable losses at Colonna's hands and now found himself subjected to devastating fire from Venier's *capitana*. Already in bad shape, Pertev's galley was also set upon by the *capitana* of the Lomellini under Paolo Giordano Orsini (son-in-law of Cosimo I) and a Venetian vessel from Sebinik commanded by Cristoforo (or Michele) Lucich. Still, it took some time for the Christians to subdue their adversaries, Orsini suffering a leg wound from a spent arrow. In the end Pertev, having lost his rudder and nearly all his men, badly burnt in the shoulder by a fire trumpet and 'berating the folly of the rash, and cursing [Müezzinzâde] Ali's obstinacy', abandoned ship together with his son. Climbing into a boat rowed by a Bolognese turned Muslim the two men passed unscathed among the allied ships, the Italian renegade shouting 'Don't shoot. We also are Christians.'[45]

Harquebus and cannon fire was slowly turning the battle in the Christians' favour. The gunpowder smoke prevented the Ottoman archers from aiming properly, and fatigue made their shooting weaker by the minute. To the left of the *Real* Ettore Spinola had managed to drive away his assailants after a fierce fight during which he had been struck three times in the leg by arrows, one of which 'was my saving grace, for while stooping to pull out the arrow, a harquebus shot passed over my head grazing my morion; and if I had been standing I would have been in great peril'.[46] Under oars he moved nearer to the *Real* so as to provide Don Juan with assistance. By now Christian galleys were converging on the *Sultana* in numbers, while the stream of reinforcements sent by the other Ottoman vessels to their flagship was rapidly declining to a trickle. Allied gunfire had effectively stopped men from reaching the *Sultana* by boat, and those who tried to do so by swimming were shot as soon as they attempted to climb the ship's sides. The galleasses allotted to the centre were now fighting the rearmost Ottoman vessels, effectively preventing them from assisting their flagship. On the papal *capitana* Romegas turned to Colonna, who had just finished dealing successfully with an enemy ship. 'That galley is ours,' he said. 'Shall we seek another one, or help our still embattled *Real*?' 'Let's help our *Real*,' answered Colonna. Personally taking the tiller, Romegas directed the galley against the *Sultana*'s stern.[47]

For the Ottoman flagship the end was approaching fast, even if a number of Turkish galleys tried to interpose themselves between the *Sultana* and the advancing Christian vessels. Allied soldiers poured onto the *kapudan paşa*'s galley, pushing the defenders back towards the poop deck. There the remaining janissaries managed to throw up a makeshift barrier made of satin mattresses, from behind which they shot arrows at the Christian soldiers to slow down their advance. Seeing this, Filippo Venier loaded one of the Venetian flagship's *petriere* with canister shot and fired it at the resisting Ottomans. The barrier went down in a flurry of fabric, blood and bone, as the allies once more surged forward. Müezzinzâde Ali fought to the last, discharging arrow after arrow until killed, the circumstances of his death constituting one of the minor mysteries of the battle. Did he die outright from a harquebus ball in the head? Was he wounded and then beheaded by a Spanish soldier – who is supposed to have brought the head to Don Juan, only to receive a frosty rebuke? Did he commit suicide by slitting his throat after throwing his valuables into the sea? Whatever the truth, his head was stuck on a pike and raised high for everyone to see, while from the *Sultana*'s mainmast the Ottoman standard was taken down and replaced with a Christian banner. At these sights Ottoman resistance started to crumble, as the shout of 'Victory! Victory!' rang from the Christian galleys.

But Nike's price was to be hefty, and had not yet been paid in full.

~

Advancing towards the Christian right wing Uluç Ali started receiving shots from the two galleasses placed in front of Doria's division. As the balls from the heavy Venetian guns starting finding targets among his ships, the *beylerbey* of Algiers quickly changed course, pushing his force south towards the open sea. Giovanni Andrea Doria noticed the move and immediately took a course parallel to his adversary's. Their galleys slowly rowing towards the south, each commander, 'attempting to catch out (*uccellarsi*) the other',[48] kept a constant eye on his opponent's movements, the gap between the Christian right and centre increasing to roughly a mile. Uluç Ali was careful to stay out of the range of the *galie grosse*,[49] but every now and then stopped to exchange gunfire with the Christian galleys. The heavily outnumbered Doria was successfully managing to keep Uluç Ali at a distance, relying on his galleasses' firepower to thwart any outflanking movement and buying precious time by keeping his opponent from joining the battle. Uluç Ali's movements appear incomprehensible if one excludes, as many have done, the galleasses' presence in front of the Christian right. Without their presence, it would have been easy for Uluç Ali to surround and destroy Doria, as subsequent events would prove.

Doria's actions would afterwards be the subject of much discussion and recrimination, the Order of Malta and his old enemy Marcantonio Colonna – rather than the Venetians, despite what is usually believed – accusing him of having behaved with suspiciously excessive prudence.[50] The accusation that he was reluctant to risk his galleys is disproved by the fact that more than half were serving in the other two divisions. As for the suggestion of a secret agreement between him and Uluç Ali – Doria being part of Philip II's secret plan to bribe the *beylerbey* of Algiers into switching his allegiance from the Ottomans to the Spanish – first suggested by Cesareo Fernandez Duro at the end of the nineteenth century,[51] it ignores the fact that the two commanders could not possibly have known in advance they would be facing each other; indeed, according to Ottoman intelligence Doria was not even supposed to be present. Given the circumstances, the Genoese admiral could not have acted differently faced with Uluç Ali's outflanking attempt. Still, his southward move worsened his numerical disadvantage vis-à-vis the Algerian, since a number of galleys, largely Venetian, became separated from the division's main body. It is uncertain whether this happened because they were unable to keep up with the rest of Doria's ships, Venetian oarsmen having to row wearing armour, or because their recalcitrant captains had decided to join the fight in the centre. Whatever the truth, these vessels were now scattered along a mile-long front. It was a chance that no commander worthy of the name would let slip through his fingers, and 'the most cunning' (*furbaccio*)[52] Uluç Ali seized it with both hands.

Suddenly reversing course, the Algerian headed straight for the stragglers. It would appear that Doria did not notice the move immediately, possibly because Ali was moving behind a screen of smoke, but when at last the Genoese admiral realized what was going on, he reacted with energy. Hoisting sail, Doria with twelve of his swiftest galleys swung towards the east – in the process leaving behind the galleass of Piero Pisani – exploiting the wind to increase the speed of his ships as he attempted to catch up with Uluç Ali's rearguard. Meanwhile the Algerian was moving north-west, his vessels taking hits from the guns of Andrea da Pesaro's galleass as they passed its port side. For the Algerian it was a necessary price to pay, and his force smashed into the ships spread out between the Christian right and centre. The fight that developed was of the sort that the Ottomans had in vain sought until then. Each of the isolated Christian galleys found itself pitted against four or five enemy vessels and quickly succumbed to overwhelming numbers. Uluç Ali's galliots were all corsair ships, most of them of the large North African type, with experienced fighting crews. Against these men, the defenders of the beleaguered Christian galleys could do little except sell their lives as dearly as possible.

Losses were heavy on both sides. Benedetto Soranzo's galley went down with all on board, including the Ottomans who had captured it, when the ammunition magazine blew up. Captains fell with their crews: Girolamo Contarini, Marcantonio Lando, Marcantonio Pasqualigo, Giacomo di Mezo, Giorgio Corner and Pietro Bua. Alvise Cipico was lucky to survive with seven wounds in his body, surrendering his galley with only six of his men standing. Twelve remained alive on the *Piemontesa* of Savoy, her captain Ottaviano Moretto dying in the company of Cesare Provana di Leynì, a kinsman of the Savoyard admiral. One by one the allied galleys fell to the enemy, who started to tow away what had become floating coffins. Venier would later acidly comment that 'the galleys behind did not aid them', adding however that he had received this information from the survivors of the debacle 'for being at a distance did not see it myself'.[53] It is unclear whether Venier was pointing the finger at Santa Cruz, or at those galleys of Doria's squadron nearest to the action. His attitude was typical of many in the league and his suspicions unfair, the allied rearguard being already heavily engaged and Doria coming to the rescue as fast as he could.

Uluç Ali's plan was to keep Doria busy with the remainder of his command while he attacked the Christian centre with about thirty vessels. The first enemy galley he encountered was the *capitana* of his old enemies the Knights of Malta, sitting in the middle of the sea after having driven off two enemy ships. For Uluç Ali the standard of the Hospitallers had the effect of a red rag to a bull, and the temptation to repeat the previous year's capture of the order's galleys at Montechiaro must have been irresistible.

Four Ottoman galleys surrounded the already battle-worn Maltese flagship, boarding parties invading it from all sides. The Knights of St John fought desperately to save the sacred banner of the order, until only the captain Fra' Pietro Giustiniani and a handful of defenders remained alive. The extraordinary bravery and tenacity of the knights is exemplified by the Aragonese Don Martin de Ferrera, who defended the standard until his left arm was nearly hacked off at the shoulder and his face cut in two. The epic fight on the *capitana* became part of the order's lore, fact merging into legend. According to the latter, Giustiniani's Muslim slave saved his master by dragging him below deck and blocking a door with coats and blankets. As a token of gratitude he was presented with his freedom and money to return home, but chose instead to remain with his master for the rest of his life. In fact Giustiniani and the other knights saved their skins by bribing the Algerians with cash and silverware – something that a Barbary corsair would find much more profitable than blood – and the Ottomans' task was made easier by the revolt of the vessel's Muslim slaves. Uluç Ali also captured the order's standard, despite the knights' later claim that it was but a ceremonial banner – the real standard having been previously hidden. Myth-making was not unique to the Hospitallers. Uluç Ali made the most of his exploit, claming falsely that he had taken two Maltese galleys. Seventy years later the polymath Khatib Çeleby could even write that the *beylerbey* of Algiers had personally decapitated Giustiniani.[54]

Seeing the *capitana* of Malta under attack, Don Juan de Cardona came to its rescue accompanied by the flagship of the Imperiale family. Cardona had a reputation as a skilled commander, and his action forced Uluç Ali to stop and deal with this new foe. Once more, superior ordnance and Spanish harquebusiers proved crucial, even if the Ottomans managed to board Cardona's galley to the mainmast. On the Imperiale *capitana* losses were also heavy, the fighting contingent being nearly wiped out although the vessel was not taken. The same fate befell the isolated Tuscan galley *Fiorenza*, only the severely wounded captain Tommaso de' Medici, a kinsman of Cosimo I, and fourteen men remaining alive. With eight or so prizes in tow, Uluç Ali's force swung behind the Christian centre, mauling a number of scattered and ill-equipped Venetian galleys. Had he arrived half an hour earlier, the outcome of the battle could have been reversed.

But for the Ottomans it was now too late. All Muslim resistance in the centre had collapsed and Don Juan, Santa Cruz, Colonna and Venier turned their bows, guns firing, towards the new menace. In the meantime Doria was approaching fast, picking up on the way Andrea da Pesaro's galleass, but in his path were between fifty and sixty of Uluç Ali's still unconquered vessels, busy gobbling up isolated Christian galleys. The Ottomans tried to block Doria's advance, but with the arrival of the galleys from the allied centre the Muslim ships found themselves in turn isolated and attacked from all sides. But for the allies it was no picnic, the Muslims giving them a good run for their money. The Tuscan *San Giovanni*, riddled with bullets and cannonballs, suffered sixty killed and 150 wounded, including her captain, Knight of St Stephen Agnolo Biffoli, who received two harquebus shots in the throat.* Doria himself did not shrink from battle, fourteen oarsmen on his flagship – about 7 per cent of the total – becoming fatalities. The Genoese admiral would later remember the cacophony – the rumbling of guns, the cracking of harquebuses, the beating of drums and the shrill sound of trumpets 'that made the sea rumble and vessels shake'.[55]

Uluç Ali, behind the Christian line and under attack, realized that all was lost and decided wisely that it was time to go. But the allies' galleys were closing in on him, forcing many of his ships back towards the shores of the Curzolaris. Uluç Ali now abandoned his prizes – the Venetian galley *Aquila Nera e D'Oro* under the slain Pietro Bua had already been towed back to Lepanto – by severing the tow ropes. With a handful of vessels he passed through the channel between Koutsilaris and Oxia and aided by the rising south-south-easterly wind managed to sail to Modon. Don Juan wished to give chase, but was dissuaded by the other commanders and it was left to Onorato Caetani to go after the Algerian with a small force. By now it was after half past two in the afternoon and there was still plenty left to be done.

The Ottomans may have been defeated, but many still possessed plenty of fighting spirit. Girolamo Diedo described how those who had not taken refuge on land or were unwilling to jump into the sea obstinately refused to surrender. Lacking arrows and shot, they threw oranges and lemons at the attacking Christians, who proceeded to fling them back. 'And many of these fights happened at the end of the battle, a sight that made everyone laugh.' Amusing incidents happened everywhere. An unnamed gentleman was hit by a small wooden splinter when a shot from his harquebus hit one of his galley's flag poles, but for two months afterwards he went around with his head bandaged and later doctored the insignificant

---

* Biffoli is usually included among the fallen, although Bernardino Antinori clearly states in his letter that he was recovering. In any case, he was still alive and active in 1576 (ANTINORI: 2r. ASF, *MP*, 695, f. 341r (Piero Tiragallo to Francesco I de' Medici, 12 May 1576)).

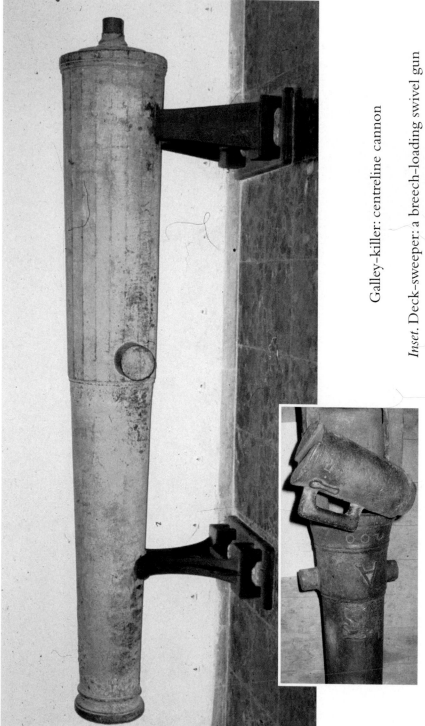

Galley-killer: centreline cannon

Inset. Deck-sweeper: a breech-loading swivel gun

The League's soldiers
Left to right: Venetian
Galeotto di Libertà;
Italian galley captain;
Spanish junior officer
(drawings by Bruno
Mugnai)

Ottoman soldiers
Left to right:
North African corsair;
janissary on naval duty;
topçu (artilleryman)
(drawings by Bruno
Mugnai)

The galley's 'muscle': rowers on a Tuscan vessel

Saint Mark's marines:
Venetian *scapolo*

The core of the matter:
the Holy League's Banner
as reproduced in a
contemporary pamphlet

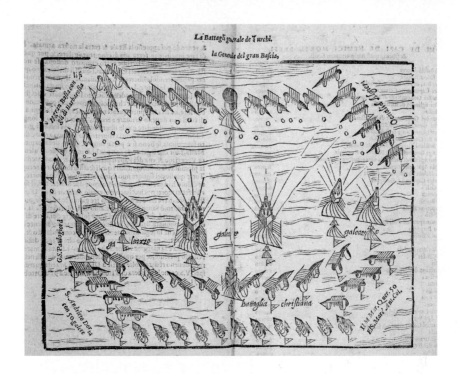

Crude but clear:
a contemporary sketch
of the Battle of the
Curzolaris

A better view:
Genoese print of the
battle showing the fleets'
initial disposition and
Uluç Ali's manoeuvre

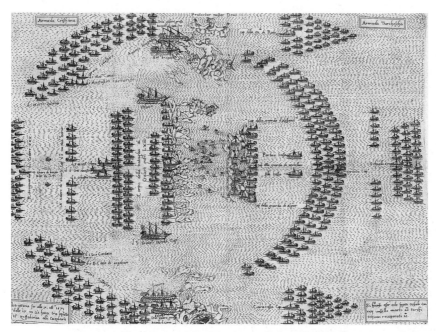

Winning tactics: the galleasses' opening barrage

Gruelling match: galley melee at the Curzolaris

High noon: the climax of the battle

Sadness in victory: Agostino Barbarigo's death

Privilege of holiness:
Pius V's vision

Half-hearted
celebration: Philip II of
Spain offering the infant
Don Fernando
to victory

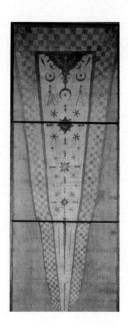

Full-blown celebration:
Francesco Maria della
Rovere with his gilded
victory armour

Surviving trophy:
standard taken from
Müezzinzâde Ali's *Sultana*

Breaking the news:
one of the many
contemporary pamphlets
describing the league's
victory

COPIA
D'VNA LETTERA SCRITTA
DAL SIGNOR CAVALIERE
ANTINORI.
Alli Signori Suoi Fratelli.

Qual narra la Felice, & Gloriosa Vittoria, che hà hauuto l'Armata
Christiana cõtro alli nemici perfidi della Fede di Gieſu Chriſto.

Con il numero de' Signori, & Principi Chri-
ſtiani, & gran prodezze loro che hanno
fatto à queſta felice, & honorata
impreſa.

Con il numero delle Galere preſe, & rouinate
dell'Armata Turcheſcha.

Et il numero de' Signori Caualieri, & Capitani morti, & feriti.

IN FIORENZA.
Nella Stampa di Lor'Altezze Sereniſſime. Adi vltimo d'Ottobre.

scar to make it look like a bullet wound.[56] But death and destruction were nothing to laugh about, and both abounded in the bloody waters of the Gulf of Patras. Hundreds of bodies floated and men struggled in the sea, galleys hardly being able to move for the corpses blocking their way. The wounded Ottomans in the water were left to their fate or used for target practice by the allied harquebusiers.

The battle was still raging when the looting started, for 'as soon as the Christians knew that they were victorious and masters of the enemy, they preferred to sack and bind, than fight and kill'. Onorato Caetani bitterly commented that he 'had not come to steal, but instead to fight and serve Our Lord' after some Venetians sacked the galleys he had defeated. Sebastiano Venier wrote that 'to us has befallen to fight, die and be wounded; to others to carry away booty', adding that 'from such a victory I have gained 505 ducats, two lire and six shillings, some knives, a coral necklace, and two blackamoors hardly fit to row in the middle of a gondola'. Everywhere sailors were busy fishing Ottoman bodies out of the water in order to despoil them. It was the rank and file that benefited most from the looting, pocketing money and jewels often with their officers' complicity. In fact, sailors, soldiers and *forzati* went on looting and ransacking for another two hours after the battle had ended, and only with the greatest difficulty did galley officers manage to get their unfettered convicts to return to their benches and take the captured Ottoman galleys in tow. Prisoners were also considered valuable items, for slaves or for ransom, even if the vengeful Venetians were less keen on sparing those who surrendered.[57]

Dusk was approaching fast, and with it heavy rain clouds. Don Juan sent his fleet to find refuge for the night in a number of havens along the coast, a wise decision since a few hours later the whole area was hit by a violent thunderstorm. That evening a meeting was convened on the *Real* at which Don Juan warmly received Venier and Colonna even to the point of embracing the crusty old Venetian. The prince also thanked Francesco Duodo, stating unequivocally that the allies owed their victory to the galleasses. Don Juan was not wrong, although there were also other reasons for the success.[58] But ultimately many believed that the real winner was not of this world.

10. THE PHOENIX'S ASHES

~

On the morning of 8 October the sun shone once more on the Gulf of Patras, the previous night's storm having cleansed from the waters the blood of the fallen. Corpses littered the shores; more floated among the waves; others still had drifted out to sea, some allegedly turning up as far away as Crete. The early light accompanied a strong allied force to the site of the slaughter. The rank and file were looking forward to looting more Ottoman bodies, but their commanders sought prizes of greater importance. Presently, two stranded Ottoman galleys were sighted on the coast, one of them nearly completely burnt out, the other wedged between some rocks. Marcantonio Colonna tried to tow away the latter, but since it would not budge the allies removed its artillery and other useful items, before handing it over to looting and fire. At one point some thirteen enemy galleys came into view, probably with the intention of aiding those Ottomans who had sought refuge on the coast, but seeing the Christian array quickly turned tail towards Lepanto. Less lucky was the crew of a small Ottoman vessel which sailed unawares straight into the allies' arms.

Having scoured the whole coast, the reconnaissance force returned to Petalas. There a war council was held to decide on the next objective. The Venetians were in favour of recapturing one of their former possessions; Don Juan wanted to attack Lepanto, believing it devoid of troops as Müezzinzâde Ali had embarked its garrison on his galleys. Others thought that due to the advanced season and the condition of the fleet it was time to go home. In the end it was agreed to capture the island of Levkás (Santa Maura), on the way to Corfu. The Christian armada sailed there on the 12th, towing the captured Ottoman galleys, together with those friendly ones too damaged to move under their own power. However, it soon became apparent that at least a fortnight would be necessary to take Levkás and eventually the decision was taken to postpone all further operations to the following spring.[1]

For the victorious allies it was time to count their gains and losses. A total of 117 galleys and thirteen galliots had been captured, being divided as follows: nineteen galleys and two galliots went to the pope; to the Spanish went fifty-eight and a half and six and a half of each; thirty-nine and a half and four and a half went to the Venetians. Between eighty and ninety enemy vessels had sunk or been wrecked on the shore, around forty or fifty managing to escape. Of the captured ordnance, Venice, Spain and the pope received as many centreline pieces as galleys, and proportional shares of the remaining 256 small guns and seventeen *petrieri*. The pope got 881 prisoners, Spain 1,742 and Venice 1,162. All these numbers are open to question, various sources giving sometimes significantly different totals and portions. Besides, not all the guns were accounted for, and not just the small pieces – in John Guilmartin's words, 'light enough to manhandle out of their mounts and carry off as loot'. In fact, the Venetians (and probably not just they) managed to surreptitiously remove at least eleven large and medium-sized guns, something about which Requesens would complain to Philip II; Venier for his part would protest about the Spaniards wanting more than the lion's share of the booty. The pope had placed a ban of excommunication on anyone who illegally held on to spoils of war, but this had little effect on these hard-bitten warriors. Similarly, not all the prisoners were accounted for, 'many having been left to die, and others hidden by their captors'. Şuluç Mehmed Pasha, concealed by the Venetians on board Marco

Querini's galley, died of his wounds a couple of days after the battle.* It is unclear how many men the Ottomans lost dead, captured or missing, but including oarsmen their casualties can't have been less than 35,000, including most of their senior officers.[2]

Disagreements arose over the division of forty important prisoners, and in the end it was decided to entrust them to the pope's care. Among these were Müezzinzâde Ali Pasha's sons, Salihpaşazâde Mehmed Bey, Caur Ali and Hindī Mahmūd, who would later write, 'While fighting for the faith, I was taken prisoner on the sea – I fought hard but I was overcome.' The Ottoman prisoners appear to have accepted their fate with remarkable fortitude. One day the seventeen-year-old Ahmed Bey, Müezzinzâde Ali's eldest son, saw Don Bernardino de Cardena's son in tears, and enquiring what had happened was told that the boy's father had been killed in battle. 'So,' answered the Turk, 'I know someone who lost his father, property and freedom, yet does not cry.' Don Juan treated the two youths with the respect due to royalty, their father being related to the sultan by marriage, allowing their old tutor to return to Constantinople to inform their mother that they were still alive. Don Juan was genuinely sad about Müezzinzâde Ali's death, not only for his value as a prisoner but also because he believed the *kapudan paşa* to have been a worthy and chivalrous person 'more loved than feared' by his own slaves.[3]

Allied losses were also heavy, an approximate count giving 7,650 killed and 7,800 wounded on the Venetian, papal and Spanish ships. The Venetians had paid the highest price with 4,836 dead and 4,604 wounded, including oarsmen, a witness to the savagery of the hand-to-hand fighting, 'where swords proved particularly effective, and harquebuses little used'. On the papal galleys 800 died and some 1,000 were wounded; on the Spanish, 2,000 and 2,200 – the *Tercio de Sicilia*'s total casualties alone amounting to 600 hundred men. To these numbers should be added the losses suffered by the Maltese,

---

* This may be the reason why there are so many different versions of his death: fallen in battle, drowned, captured and immediately executed, or dispatched to spare him from more suffering.

Genoese (private and public), Savoyard and Tuscan crews. Given the majority of forced oarsmen on *ponentine* galleys, it is only possible to make an educated guess at how many of them died on the benches or fighting with weapon in hand. Giovanni Andrea Doria's eleven galleys lost a total of seventy-four rowers killed, roughly seven each. Thus probably at least 700 rowers were killed in the approximately 100 *ponentine* galleys present at the battle, probably more if one takes into account the larger crews of the *bastarde*. It should be remembered that the complements of some galleys, for example the Maltese *capitana*, the Tuscan *Fiorenza* and the Savoyard *Piemontesa*, were all but wiped out. In contrast, the commander of Genoa's state contingent Ettore Spinola, after stating in his report that on his galleys 'blood flowed from stern to bow', admitted nonetheless that while a number of sailors had been wounded he had lost only one oarsman.[4]

Of the officers, sergeants and gentlemen present only a few hundred died or suffered wounds, thanks to the fact that many wore bulletproof armour. A record of the losses incurred by two Spanish *tercios*★ lists a total of fifty-seven, including Don Lope de Figueroa and Pagano Doria. Don Juan himself received a dagger wound in the ankle, something he would later report to his brother in an off-hand manner. Of the roughly 100 knights of St Stephen involved, fifteen died. At least forty knights of St John lost their lives, the majority on Giustiniani's *capitana*. Some fifty Venetian officers and gentlemen were killed, including Barbarigo, or seriously injured. The galleasses also had their share of casualties, some of them the result of an explosion of a powder magazine which killed nearly fifty men. Thus, between dead, wounded and captured (the few taken by Uluç Ali), allied casualties must have been around 20,000 men. In addition, the Christians lost between twelve and sixteen galleys – according to Bartolomeo Sereno, 'thanks to those who refused to fight', – an incorrect and unfair comment – including those sunk, captured or so badly damaged that they had to be destroyed. Among the latter was the *Fiorenza*, which after being stripped of everything

---

★ *Tercios* were Spanish infantry units roughly equivalent to regiments.

useful served as a bonfire during the celebrations held at Levkás. Thus was fulfilled the prophecy that in 1571 the Medici would lose Florence.[5]

True to his promise, Don Juan liberated all the convict oarsmen under his authority who had fought during the battle. He also ordered that all Christian slaves on the Ottoman galleys be immediately freed, possibly fearing someone would try to hold on to some extra 'booty'. The Venetians, despite the pope's objections, treated as slaves all captured Ottoman subjects, including non-Muslims. Between 12,000 and 15,000 Christians were liberated, the Ottomans having compensated for their end-of-campaign shortage of free rowers by chaining to galley benches the prisoners taken during their raids the previous summer. Venier also tried to free eighty of the bravest convicts on his galleys, but had his request turned down by the Venetian authorities. Although not bound by Don Juan's promise, Cosimo I de' Medici later liberated a number of his own *forzati*. One who did not regain his freedom was the musician Aurelio Scetti, despite the fact that 'he had captured two Moors and brought them to his galley saying, "If not in the other way, at least for this I shall be free."' Scetti was probably lying, since it is difficult to see how he could have accomplished such a deed with his crippled leg, although it could also be that in his memoirs he exaggerated his lameness. Given that he clearly enjoyed the protection of someone at the Tuscan court, had Scetti's claim been true he would certainly have reaped the benefit of his actions. Quite a few unfettered convicts deserted in the heat of the battle or immediately afterwards. Giovanni Andrea Doria lost to desertion the same number of oarsmen as killed in battle – the equivalent of the rowing crew of one of his galleys. Scetti would attribute these desertions to the *forzati*'s mistrust of their commanders' promises, but one should also keep in mind that many convicts had acquired booty and were unwilling to share their new-found wealth with anyone else.[6] Scetti's account is also disingenuous in other ways, since it is impossible to know how many 'deserters' lay instead on the seabed of the Gulf of Patras.

The harmony between the Christian commanders did not last long, factional interests soon raising their ugly heads once more. Venier had immediately insisted that news of the victory be sent to the various governments. Three days later, seeing that nothing had been done, he took matters into his own hands and dispatched to Venice the galley of Onfrè Giustinian. When he found out Venier's escapade Don John was positively livid, considering this behaviour a breach of protocol and an attack on his own prerogatives as commander-in chief. In the meantime the supply problem was becoming acute. Provisions found on the captured Ottoman galleys had come in handy but were hardly enough for a prolonged campaign. The allied fleet sailed from Levkás on the 21st, reaching Corfu three days later. On the way it ran into three other Venetian galleasses and thirteen galleys, stranded in the port of Paxoi by contrary winds. Their crews stated that on the day of the battle they had heard the rumbling of the guns from the Gulf of Patras. Once in Corfu the division of prizes was finally settled, although not without problems. Venier protested bitterly about the Spaniards' claims, even accusing Don Juan of intercepting and reading letters sent to him by his government. In the end, thanks once more to Colonna's mediation, Venier agreed to sign the document concerning the division of spoils. Don Juan gave the Order of Malta thirty slaves to replace their losses during the battle, encouraging the other confederates to do the same. Prisoners were allotted also to various officers and officials, and it was decided at the same time that any future claims would be resolved in Messina It was high time for Don Juan to go, having finally received Philip II's orders about wintering in Sicily. On the 27th he took his leave of Venier, who had been instructed by the Venetian government to remain in Corfu, and set off for Italy.[7]

By now news of the Christian victory was common knowledge. Onfrè Giustinian had arrived in Venice on the 19th, finding the city in a state of shock over the loss of Famagusta. However, people immediately realized that something important had happened when they saw Giustinian's galley trailing in the water

Ottoman banners, and in their hundreds rushed to the port to hear the news. As soon as Giustinian delivered his report to the Senate, the whole of Venice exploded in spontaneous rejoicing. Bells were rung, bonfires lit and masses celebrated. Mourning was forbidden, even for close relatives. The festivities continued for three days and nights, the city a fantasy of colours, banners and music. Turkish carpets, standards and turbans were displayed on the Rialto bridge for all to see. The only people who did not take part in the celebrations were those Ottoman subjects still at liberty in Venice. Fearful of being stoned by the crowds, they locked themselves in their quarter, displaying their grief by beating their breasts, shaving their moustaches and scratching their faces and bodies.[8]

In Rome there was also much rejoicing. Pius V had miraculously known about the outcome of the battle since the evening of 7 October (evidence of this being later used during his beatification trial), but he nonetheless prudently waited for the arrival of official reports before starting any celebration. The dispatch from the nuncio in Venice was brought by fast courier on the night of the 21st, and Pius reportedly exclaimed, quoting the Gospel, '*Nunc dimittis servum tuum, Domine . . . quia viderunt oculi mei salutare tuum*' (Now, Lord, you can take your servant, for my eyes have seen your salvation). As soon as the news became public the populace lit bonfires, accompanying the flames with artillery salvos, although the pope considered this cannonading a waste. Pius was also concerned that the victory would count for nothing should the allies not press home their advantage, but realized that nothing could be done before the spring. The pontiff was soon busy with thanksgiving celebrations, and as more details of the battle arrived his joy only increased. Referring to Don Juan's role in the victory, he is supposed to have quoted from the Gospel, '*Fuit homo missus a Deo, cui nomen erat Johannes*' (God sent a man by the name of John). More significant was his decision to dedicate 7 October, the feast of St Justine, to Our Lady of Victory. Later, his successor Gregory XIII would change the dedication to Our Lady of the Rosary, thus recognizing the role played by this devotion in the Christians' success.[9]

Philip II received news of the battle on 2 November, at the same time as the Venetian ambassador Leonardo Donà. No sooner had the latter read his dispatches from Venice than he rushed to the royal chapel where the king was attending vespers, appropriately arriving as the Magnificat was being intoned. Philip waited for the end of the service to hear Dona's report in full, and then asked him to participate in the recital of the Te Deum. Don Lope de Figueroa arrived with more news on the 22nd, the king questioning him closely about Don Juan, the prince's health and the battle. In the meantime festivities were held all over Spain, particularly in Seville, in honour of the Christian victory, while Philip graciously bestowed honours, benefices and monetary rewards on those officers and men who had most distinguished themselves in the battle. The king also ordered the dean and chapter of Toledos cathedral to institute a service to be performed in perpetuity every 7 October.

Despite his apparent elation over the Christian victory, the king was not totally happy about the league's success. Don Juan had put the Habsburg galleys and soldiers at considerable risk by deciding to join battle – a rash decision to say the least, especially for *el rey prudente*, and according to a number of Philip's councillors the prince could only thank God if he had come out of it alive. Significantly, the king commissioned only one work of art to commemorate the victory – Titian's *Philip II, after the victory of Lepanto, offers the prince Don Fernando to victory*, now in the Prado – and to celebrate more the continuity of the Habsburg line than the Ottoman defeat. The six large canvases of the battle by Luca Cambiaso, now in the Escorial, were probably gifts of Giovanni Andrea Doria to the royal secretary Antonio Pérez, acquired by the king at a later date.[10] One has the distinct impression that for Philip the league victory represented a potential source of political trouble, possibly because by weakening the Porte's navy it had altered the balance of power in the Mediterranean and loosened Spain's grip on Italy.

Things were seen differently by the veterans of the 1571 campaign. Many celebrated their participation in the battle of the Curzolaris (although the name Lepanto was used almost immediately – and misleadingly, since Lepanto was forty miles away from where the battle was fought) by commissioning paintings, sculptures and literary works – the latter, according to Sereno, much favoured by those whose fighting achievements were somewhat doubtful. The Barbarigo family had a hall of its country villa near Vicenza frescoed with scenes exalting their kinsman's role in the battle. So did the relatives of Ascanio Della Corgna, in their palace on Lake Trasimene. The marquis of Santa Cruz had the battle painted on one of the walls of his palace at El Viso – sadly these frescoes were destroyed by an earthquake in the eighteenth century. The popes after Pius V were also active proponents of the battle's artistic merits, the Vatican palaces and the church of Santa Maria Maggiore, for example, receiving their share of images commemorating the league and the victorious fight. Works of art on the same topics are scattered in churches all over Italy, some of them ex-voto offerings by those who had managed to bring their skins back home. Similarly, the various Italian rulers commissioned works exalting their involvement in the battle. Ferdinando I de' Medici, Cosimo I's son and successor, added a scene from it to the paintings exalting the deeds of the knights of St Stephen in the order's church in Pisa. Francesco Maria della Rovere had himself portrayed proudly wearing a splendid suit of gilded 'victory' armour.

Marcantonio Colonna outdid everyone, commissioning celebratory frescoes for his castle of Paliano and entering Rome in a triumphal procession worthy of ancient Rome. In reality Colonna would have preferred to enter the city privately, fearing that the envy of his adversaries at the Spanish court could endanger his future preferment, but the pope was adamant about giving Marcantonio his due. Accordingly, on 4 December 1571 a long cavalcade entered Rome from the San Sebastiano gate, passing under the arches of Constantine, Titus and Septimius Severus. Skirting the Capitol, it proceeded to Monte Giordano and then St Peter's, where the pope was waiting to celebrate a solemn Te Deum. Along the route were inscriptions comparing Marcantonio to the great Roman generals of the past; the sound of musical instruments and the booming guns of Castel Sant'Angelo accompanying 'an exhibition of barbaric and exotic opulence'. The whole Colonna clan participated in the event, including those related by marriage like Onorato Caetani. Marcantonio brought up the rear, mounted on a white horse and wearing a simple black robe. The triumph differed from classical Roman parades in that it lacked carts filled with the spoils of victory, this 'for respect of the most serene Don Juan of Austria', although a few Ottomans in chains were included in the procession. Conspicuous was the absence of most of the Roman nobility, unwilling to pay even token homage to their successful peer – something that Don Luis de Requesens, always Colonna's enemy, would not fail to report to Don Juan in Messina. Philip II, evidently irritated by Colonna's elevation, found it expedient to wait a while before sending him a brief note of thanks for his role in the allied victory.[11]

~

While much of Christian Europe rejoiced for the league's success – even Charles IX of France, despite his worries about Spain's power in the Mediterranean and the alliance treaty between France and the Porte, having a Te Deum sung in thanksgiving for the victory – in Constantinope the mood was very different. Selim II is supposed to have received official news of his fleet's destruction on 23 October while in Edirne, thanks to a special courier sent to him by Uluç Ali. There is evidence that the sultan had already found out about the disaster a few days before, at least according to some chronicles.[12] Information sent by Jews in Constantinople to their brethren in Venice would appear to confirm this.

> The Great Turk [Selim II] one night having heard much wailing and screaming coming from the city, the next day asked about the noise. It was answered that some important citizens had died,

and that their relatives had done what was appropriate in these cases. The next night having heard greater commotion and louder crying, he enquired again about the reason for such a din. It was answered that rumours had it that his fleet had joined battle with ours [the allied], and in the fight both had been badly mauled with great loss of life on each side, although the details were unknown. The third night, with the whole city wailing and screaming because no one could hide any more the grief for such a loss, the Great Turk, concerned and irked by all the moans and tears, demanded to hear the truth. It was answered that it was impossible now to hide the news that his fleet had been all burnt, sunk and taken by the Christians, with the death of all his great soldiers, captains and his General [Müezzinzâde Ali Pasha]. Hearing this he gave a deep sigh and said, 'So, these treacherous Jews have deceived me!' And having the Lord's utterance spread through the palace and the streets, everyone started shouting, 'Death to the Jews; death to the Jews!' and there was much fear that this would degenerate in a general massacre.[13]

In mentioning Jews, was Selim referring to Joseph Nassi? Certainly the fortunes of the duke of Naxos declined after 1571, and maybe the sultan made him a convenient scapegoat for the losses sustained in the war. In any case, while we may doubt the details of this particular report, there is no doubt that the debacle shook the Porte. Dimitri Cantemir, writing 150 years after the event, would describe how the downcast Selim refused to eat for three days, until he found consolation and encouragement in a passage of the Koran: 'it may be that you dislike a thing while it is good for you'. But the sultan could not afford to grieve for too long; in fact he decided to return to Constantinople in some haste, according to one source covering in less than a week the roughly 250 kilometres separating Edirne from the capital, entering it on 28 November.[14] In the meantime, the imperial *dîvân* was taking energetic measures to address the crisis.

There were a number of matters that needed to be settled

urgently. The reconstruction of the fleet was top priority, and a new *kapudan paşa* was needed. The fact that Uluç Ali had managed to salvage part of the Ottoman fleet helped solve the second problem. Many were convinced that having survived the battle, the *beylerbey* of Algiers would be executed for his share in the rout. But Uluç Ali not only had fifty vessels with him, but also – equally important from a psychological point of view – the Maltese standard. As a result, the Algerian not only retained his master's favour, but was also made *kapudan paşa* with the new name of Kılıç Ali – Ali the Sword – although shrewd and malicious observers would comment that Uluç Ali's elevation to grand admiral had less to do with his abilities than to the fact that nobody else was available for the job. The sultan would later order the captured banner of the Knights of Malta hung in the old cathedral (now mosque) of Hagia Sophia, in an attempt to minimize the extent of the defeat. The arrival on 3 November of sixteen ships loaded with the booty of Famagusta further aided Selim's propaganda efforts: after all, by conquering Cyprus the Ottomans had attained what, ostensibly, had caused them to go to war in the first place. As for the disaster at the Curzolaris, the sultan could write to Pertev Pasha, 'the results of a war are uncertain. God's will manifests itself in these occasions, as appears in destiny's mirror.' For the Ottomans the Curzolaris would simply be *sıngın donanma* – 'the dispersed fleet'.[15]

But if misinformation could to an extent appease the populace, the military emergency could not be ignored. Sokollu Mehmed Pasha's well-known exchange with Marcantonio Barbaro was an admission of uneasiness despite the grand vizier's apparent confidence. Sokollu acknowledged that the Christians had given the Ottomans 'a close shave', adding however that by losing Cyprus the Venetians had been deprived of an arm. The fleet, like a beard, could grow again thicker and stronger 'if the forests don't fail us', but a lopped-off arm would never do so.[16] The simile was only partially apt. Cyprus was an extremely important commercial centre in the Levant, and by the loss of its ports, produce and salt mines Venice's economy suffered a serious blow. However, by holding on to Crete and Corfu the Venetians could still imperil Ottoman maritime routes towards the west. Rather than an arm, for Venice the Porte's conquest of Cyprus was more akin to the loss of a couple of fingers. Besides, certain beards could take time to grow again; and, if thicker, were not necessarily stronger for that.

Words could not rebuild fleets: material resources and resolve were needed, both of which the Porte possessed in abundance.[17] Kılıç Ali had been ordered to gather together all the surviving ships and stay on guard in the Aegean, but once the allied fleet moved to its winter quarters in Messina he returned to Constantinople. The historian Selânikî Mustafa Efendi was there when he arrived on 19 December, at the head of forty-two vessels including *bastarde*, galleys and galliots all firing their guns in salute 'as if they had been two hundred'. The salvos also served to drown the wailing of the many who had come to the port looking in vain for a husband, a father or a brother.[18] The rebuilding of the fleet had been in progress since the end of October, orders having been sent out to various governorships to cut the necessary timber with the utmost haste. Wood abounded in the Ottoman empire – Sokollu had not been wrong to mention the forests – and so did oakum, pitch, hemp, sailcloth, awnings, nails and other iron parts. The losses in artillery incurred at the Curzolaris were quickly made good, orders for the production of enough thirty-pounder cannon to arm 100 galleys being issued as early as 24 October. The bronze necessary for the casting appears to have been obtained by melting down a number of church bells previously stored in Trebizond.[19]

Despite their abundance, the huge demands for all these materials imposed a severe strain on the Porte's resources. Kılıç Ali expressed his concerns about this to the grand vizier: 'Building the hulls is feasible, but to find 500 or 600 anchors, the materials of war and the sails for 200 ships is impossible'; to which Sokollu Mehmed is supposed to have glibly retorted, 'My dear Pasha. You do not yet know this state. Trust in God. This is such a state that if desired there would be no difficulty in making all the anchors in the fleet of silver, the ropes of silk and the sails of satin. For whatever materials of war or sails are lacking from any ship, ask me.' Then Kılıç Ali answered, 'I now know that if anyone can complete this fleet, you can.'[20] Although Sokollu was clearly boasting for rhetorical purposes, he was not exaggerating the Porte's resources. On 5 January 1572 Marcantonio Barbaro would inform the Venetian government that the Ottomans had eighty-one galleys ready, old and new, and another thirty-eight in various stages of construction.[21] The many arsenals along the Anatolian coast allowed for the simultaneous building of large numbers of vessels, the imperial arsenal in Istanbul only adding the artillery and final fittings. However, the demand for timber was such that builders were forced to use green wood, meaning that the new vessels were susceptible to rot and infestation, making them slow, difficult to steer and short-lived. Cordage was another problem, the only material in short supply. Orders to the hemp officials in Sinop produced only partial results, demand being greater than supply, and even at the end of March 1572 the ships at Amasra and Kefken lacked their rigging.

The Ottomans had been deeply impressed by the volume of fire produced by the Venetian galleasses at the Curzolaris, and were soon busy on their own version of the new weapon.[22] Apparently this would not be too difficult since the Ottomans already knew how to build the large merchant galley from which the galleass had originated. Yet in building these vessels the Ottomans made the erroneous assumption that they were simply modified *galie grosse* with all-round shooting capabilities. Instead, as we have seen, Venetian galleasses were the product of a long tradition of naval engineering debates and experiments, and not of a single stroke of genius. By April 1572 the Porte could field half a dozen modified *maone*, but their construction left much to be desired and the Ottomans soon found that they lacked the necessary naval skills to operate them. The Curzolaris veteran and engineer Pompeo Floriani could write around 1580 that the Ottomans 'don't know how to fabricate galleasses'. In this they were not alone. The battle inspired the Tuscans to build their own galleasses, even creating a special arsenal for them on the isle of Elba, only to discover that they did not know how to handle them. When they tried the experiment again in the 1630s, the sailors and pilots had to be brought in from Venice. The Spanish appear to have been more successful in copying the new Venetian vessel, the English being much impressed by the performance of four Spanish galleasses during the Armada campaign of 1588.[23]

Manning the new Ottoman fleet proved to be the biggest problem of all. The heavy losses in manpower suffered by the Porte during the previous year meant that naval personnel was in short supply. Those *sipahis* who had survived the Curzolaris were tired, dispirited and naturally unwilling to face another maritime campaign. Eventually the government managed to find 4,396 *sipahis* and some 3,000 janissaries to serve at sea, a far cry from the roughly 20,000 troops required by the fleet. The only alternative was to enlist volunteers, something that had already been done in the years before the Cyprus war. Learning from the abundant crop of lives reaped by the repeated allied harquebus volleys, the government's intention was to raise as many men possible armed with bows or firearms. The plan was to have 150 soldiers for each galley, placing between each thwart two harquebusiers and one bowman. Firearms were distributed to the *sipahis*, but despite the Porte's efforts it would appear that the traditionally minded *timariots* were more than reluctant to accept the new weapons. This would explain the increase in the number of volunteers in the years ahead. Certainly the number of soldiers now equipped with firearms struck European observers. On 10 June 1572, François de Noailles, bishop of Dax and the French envoy in Istanbul, wrote that the Ottomans were putting 20,000 harquebusiers aboard their fleet − an exaggerated number, perhaps, but evidence of the Ottomans' shift in naval tactics.[24]

Oarsmen were also in short supply. The navy needed some 20,000 every year, normally raising them through conscription from the ranks of the non-military population. It was a much-resented blood tax, made worse by the terrible losses suffered by rowing crews at the Curzolaris. Each new galley required a force of about 150 oarsmen, but raising them through traditional means proved an impossible task. Some local notables managed to exchange the levy for a cash payment, the resulting money being used to raise volunteer rowers at ninety *akçe* a month. But even with this method results proved disappointing, while in some cases oarsmen already recruited never made it to the capital due to the negligence of their overseers. Resistance to the levy was such that the Porte was forced to look elsewhere for the necessary manpower. War prisoners were one source, but with not enough available the government took the unprecedented step of sending large numbers of criminals to the galleys. *Kadis* (judges) from all over the empire were ordered to send to Constantinople all convicts whose crimes did not carry the death penalty. It was not a measure the government took willingly, since rowing gangs made up of convicts or war prisoners were more likely to mutiny than crews of conscripts or volunteers. Still, extreme situations call for extreme means, and there is no doubt that in the winter of 1571–2 maritime affairs looked grim for the Porte.

However, thanks to the energy and administrative skills of Sokollu Mehmed Pasha and Kılıç Ali's maritime experience, by the beginning of spring 1572 the Ottomans could field a fleet of 134 galleys plus a number of large galliots owned by Muslim corsairs from Anatolia and Rumelia, with more vessels being added each day. The effort to accomplish this had been enormous in every sense, and all those in positions of power had been asked to share in the endeavour: 'The leading viziers . . . committed themselves as their wealth permitted', in the historian Selânikî's succinct words.[25] One captain volunteered to build two *bastarde*, and the grand vizier's chief clerk paid out of his own pocket for the construction of a galliot. In less than six months the Porte had managed the impossible – although Giovanni Andrea Doria had predicted that such a thing could happen – and like a phoenix the Ottoman navy was rising from its ashes. Admittedly, its ships were poorly built, undermanned and no match for the Western vessels. Nonetheless, it was a fleet in being, and that's what ultimately mattered.

~

While the Porte was busy rebuilding its naval forces, the Venetians were taking measures to nip in the bud a resurgence of Ottoman maritime power. On 22 October 1571 the Council of Ten ordered the captain-general of the Venetian fleet that 'with the utmost caution, deft and secret manner he immediately kill first Captain Şuluç'. On the same day the council wrote to Venier to make sure that no 'prisoner of importance, galley captain or corsair' be freed or ransomed without the Ten's authorization, and ordering him to execute immediately those already in Venetian hands 'so that they will no more be able to inflict damage on Christendom'.[26] Şuluç was already beyond the council's reach, having died of his wounds four days after the battle. Still not happy the Ten harassed the pope and Don Juan of Austria to kill the Ottoman captives in their custody. Ostensibly the Venetians ordered the executions because they did not trust their own galley captains not to accept ransom money 'since everyone desires profit', although they admitted that they were taking revenge for what had happened at Famagusta. But if the papal nuncio in Venice was perturbed by the Ten's decision, Pius V was positively shocked: it was one thing killing an armed enemy in battle, quite another murdering powerless prisoners. The pope adamantly refused to have anything to do with the matter, while Don Juan answered that one should take pity on a defeated enemy; besides, given the fickleness of the fortunes of war, there was always the possibility of being captured oneself and so it was better not to invite reprisals. Don Juan could have also pointed out the foolishness of eliminating potential bargaining chips, and in any case the Ottoman captives were worth quite a bit of ransom money. In the end it would appear that the only important prisoner the Venetians managed to execute was the renegade Dimo Baffo, although it is possible that some other unnamed captives also lost their lives. As for the other Ottoman prisoners of rank, the papacy treated them with all due honour and respect, housing them in a palace in Rome.[27]

For the whole of the winter of 1571–2 the Venetians were active on the Dalmatian coast, Venier managing to recapture Sopot and Margariti and giving support to the rebellions which had flared up in various parts of Albania and Greece. These revolts were partly religious in nature but had also a material side, the rebels for instance refusing to pay taxes or provide oarsmen for the new Ottoman fleet. Ultimately, the disturbances were settled by the Porte by the use of carrot-and-stick policies, aided by the fact that the league could not support the rebels in any significant way. The Venetians lacked enough men and resources to exploit their temporary advantage after the Curzolaris, and had to settle for limited goals. The Spanish, on the other hand, did not have a clear idea of what to do next. Their primary objective was the Barbary Coast, but they were afraid that any such proposal would rekindle the pope's suspicions about Spain not having the 'general interest' of Christendom at heart. Don Juan was of the opinion that it would be best first to capture and fortify some strategic positions in the Levant to keep the Ottomans distracted, and then take Algiers. In Western capitals there was much discussion of the league's future plans – the Venetians, rather too optimistically, going as far as contemplating the capture of Constantinople – but everyone agreed that it was vital not to allow the Ottomans any respite. As it happened, when the league's capitulations were renewed in Rome on 10 February, the Spanish agreed that in 1572 all military operations should take place in the Levant with a force of 250 galleys, nine galleasses and 32,000 men.[28]

The superficially friendly dealings barely hid the deep suspicions and resentments existing between the allies, not just on a national but also on a personal level. Giovanni Andrea Doria was the first victim of a smear campaign. Already on 13 November 1571 Giovanni Andrea had complained to Marcantonio Doria, prince of Melfi, that in Rome and elsewhere 'for the evil of this world' somebody was trying to diminish his role in the victory; he hoped Philip II had been informed of the truth. Likewise, writing to Donna Costanza d'Avalos, Doria begged her not to believe all the malicious gossip circulating in Rome that 'he had been the last to fight, and the first to run'.

The whole anti-Doria campaign owed much to Marcantonio Colonna, who in his various reports to Pius V had done everything to boost his own role, at the same time lambasting the Genoese admiral for his – according to Colonna – overcautious behaviour during the battle, prompting the misinformed pontiff to comment that Doria had behaved 'more like a corsair than a captain'. Pius's secretary of state, Cardinal Girolamo Rusticucci, on 16 December wrote to the papal nuncio in Madrid that Doria had 'tried more to save himself than fight the enemy', implying also that he had chosen the right wing in order to escape more easily. The Spanish faction in Rome rushed to Giovanni Andrea's aid, Luis de Requesens writing to Don Juan on 15 December that he had defended Doria as much as possible, and eventually nobody dared to speak ill of him in his presence. However, Requesens added, the pope had already made up his mind, and since 'His Holiness sometimes speaks freely', Giovanni Andrea had been advised not to show his face in Rome. In order to avoid friction within the league the Genoese commander left the allied fleet, his place being taken by his cousin Antonio Doria.[29]

Venier's head was the next to roll. Don Juan had never forgiven him for the Igoumenitsa hangings, nor for his breach of protocol after the battle. The Spanish wanted Venier to go – Cardinal Granvelle describing him as an old fool with no more brains than an ape – and, *pro bono pacis*, so did the pope. But understandably the Venetians were loath to recall their captain-general – after all, he had defended Venice's interests within the league, and he enjoyed wide popularity within the city. Instead, the Venetians chose a dual-command solution, nominating a second captain-general in the person of the *provveditore generale* of Dalmatia, Giacomo Foscarini.

Furthermore, in an attempt to sweeten the bitter pill for Venier, the Venetian senate offered to entrust him with an independent force of ten galleys.[30]

Dramatic changes were also about to take place on the international scene. On 1 May 1572 Pius V died after a brief illness. With him disappeared the driving force that had kept the league in existence, the new pope Gregory XIII, while committed to the anti-Ottoman alliance, not possessing his predecessor's charisma and austerity. The cracks that had always existed in the alliance became more apparent. Philip II was worried about the prospect of war with France over Flanders, the French Protestants' active support for the Flemish rebels being an open secret. Rumours were circulating that Charles IX – or at least his Huguenot subjects – were about to launch a military campaign in the Netherlands, something the Ottomans were hoping would occur. Should war erupt on the Franco-Spanish border, Philip could not afford to have nearly 20,000 men somewhere in the Levant. For this reason, Philip II wrote to Don Juan in Messina on 17 May, ordering him to delay his departure for the east using as much secrecy and deceit as possible. In the meantime he could busy himself by collecting victuals and munitions for the fleet. Don Juan, who had spent the whole winter 'looking over old papers and passed life feeling more and more lonely each day', was none too happy. In other letters to Granvelle and Juan de Zuñiga, the king wrote that in the event of the pope's death it would be better to strike at Algiers, so as to get something back for the huge sums spent on the league. A few days later he informed Don Juan that with Pius dead he intended to attack Bizerte and Algiers. The king was not inspired exclusively by selfish reasons, since in Western diplomatic circles there was a widespread belief that Uluç Ali was ready to go over to the Christians. Despite Philip's orders that lips remain sealed about the planned Barbary expedition, it did not take long for his intentions to become common knowledge. The Venetians were deeply alarmed by this apparent Spanish volte-face, while the new pope sent the king a stiff reminder of his duties. Cosimo I de' Medici was of the opinion that the French threat should not stop Philip from joining forces with the Venetians, believing that giving the Ottomans another licking was the best way to keep the Valois at bay. But at this point, with reports coming in about the Ottoman fleet's activities, the king had already written to Don Juan giving him the green light to sail for Corfu, taking with him part of the force assembled in Messina.[31]

What happened next can only be described as a series of misunderstandings and blunders. Marcantonio Colonna had received express orders from the pope to go to Messina and convince – or order if necessary, using the league's clauses – Don Juan to give him the necessary galleys for a Levant expedition. Cardinal Granvelle had the new pope in his pocket, and was actively manoeuvring to discredit the Roman admiral in every possible way. Colonna, with an eye to future employment with the Spanish, reluctantly obeyed, and managed to convince Don Juan to let him go to Corfu with fifty-seven galleys, the prince caving in to allay Venetian suspicions about the Spaniards' endless delaying tactics. Colonna departed east on 6 July, while Don Juan, having not yet received his brother's most recent instructions, sailed west towards Palermo with twenty-six galleys, twenty-two other ships and most of his infantry, still convinced that Philip II wanted him to attack a Muslim base in North Africa. Indeed, Cosimo I de' Medici, always good at guessing which way the wind was blowing, on the 17th had written to the pope attempting to convince him of the need to take Algiers.

No sooner did Don Juan arrive in Palermo than he received the king's message with orders to depart for the Levant. Meanwhile, Colonna had sailed for Otranto with the intention of embarking the infantry waiting there, but since the necessary orders from Cardinal Granvelle had not yet arrived the papal admiral continued on towards Corfu empty-handed. En route he met Santa Cruz, who added four more galleys to his fleet. Colonna arrived at his destination on the 13th, joining forces with Foscarini's seventy-four galleys, six galleasses and twenty-five galliots. From there the allied armada moved in the direction of Igoumenitsa, where the commanders received a letter from Don Juan ordering them to wait for him in Corfu. The Venetians were unwilling to agree to this since it would delay even further an encounter with the Ottoman fleet, while Colonna wished to enhance his reputation with another victory that would silence his enemies at home. For these reasons the decision was taken to disobey the prince's orders and seek the enemy instead.[32]

Receiving some reinforcements on the way, on 7 August the allied fleet of 145 galleys, twenty-two round-ships, six galleasses and twenty-five galliots and *fuste* finally met the Ottoman armada, 200 sail strong, off the Venetian-held island of Kythira. The Christian order of battle followed the one used at the Curzolaris. Colonna, with fifty-eight galleys and two galleasses, took the centre; on the left and right wings, flanked by eleven round-ships, were forty galleys and two galleasses each; a mere seven galleys made up the reserve. Kılıç Ali, although possessing a numerically superior fleet, refused to close with the enemy, employing instead hit-and-run tactics in an attempt to break the allied formation. Hampered by the slow galleasses, Colonna was unable to catch his crafty opponent, and at nightfall the Ottomans withdrew towards the Gulf of Lakonia. Two days later the allies left for Corfu, and on the morning of the 10th again encountered the Muslim armada off Cape Matapan (Akra Tainara). This time the eagerness of Giacomo Soranzo, commanding the Christian right, to come to grips with the enemy nearly cost him his life when the apparently retreating Ottomans pounced on his exposed force of eleven galleys and one galleass. Superior Venetian firepower managed to keep the Ottomans at bay long enough for Colonna to bring up the remaining galleasses. Again Kılıç Ali refused to engage in a full-scale battle, retreating under cover of a smoke screen with the loss of seven galleys. The Ottomans had suffered a tactical defeat, but strategically for them it was at worst a draw. With news that Kılıç Ali's fleet was growing daily, after further debate the allies decided to sail to Corfu, reaching it on 31 August.[33]

In Corfu Colonna and Foscarini found Don Juan, furious that

his orders had been disobeyed. Colonna tried to blame the Venetians, but by now his stock with the Spanish had plummeted. Don Juan waited only long enough to repair and resupply his fleet before setting out in search of the enemy. Arriving off Navarinou on 16 September, the allies found that the Ottomans were now in the securer haven of Methoni. Attempts to force the latter harbour resulted in nothing, and the rest of the campaign was spent in desultory skirmishing, with the Christians finding the enemy forces becoming increasingly strong. The only bright spot was the capture outside Methoni, on the anniversary of the Curzolaris, of an Ottoman lantern galley. But by now the campaign season was over, and on 26 October the allied fleet dropped anchor in Messina.[34]

The Venetians were exhausted and eager to reach a deal with the sultan. The victory at the Curzolaris had in no way offset their huge military expenses, since it was apparent that it would be impossible to dislodge the Ottomans from Cyprus. Also in Constantinople the political situation was ripe for peace talks. The sultan had gained territory but his losses in military personnel and war materiel over the past two years had buried any Ottoman chances of conquering more Venetian possessions in the short run, and a plan to attack Crete was shelved in consequence. Besides, the possibility of war between Spain and France was appearing more and more remote. On 17 July a Huguenot force had crossed the border between France and the Netherlands, only to be routed by the Spanish, who also discovered evidence of Charles IX's involvement. The French king quickly distanced himself from the enterprise, and the mass killings of the Huguenots in Paris on the night of 24 August (the St Bartholomew's Day massacre) radicalized religious divisions in France. The Valois now had too many domestic problems to think about fighting Spain. The Venetians knew that with France out of the way the Ottomans were diplomatically isolated in the Mediterranean; and despite the fact that both the Holy Roman Emperor and the king of Poland had refused to join the league, should war break out in Hungary the Porte would be in a very sticky position, given also the enormous sums spent on its new fleet. In addition, Sokollu Mehmed had prevailed over his adversaries within the Imperial *dîvân*, and was now in a position to negotiate unhindered a treaty with Venice.[35]

Diplomatic feelers had been put out practically on the morrow of the Curzolaris. In September 1571 the bishop of Dax had appeared in Venice on his way to Constantinople, ostensibly to secure the release of the Ottoman ambassador but really to try and sabotage the league by brokering peace between the Venetians and the Porte. Dax was unsuccessful in his efforts, but on his arrival in Constantinople the following March he had immediately started exploring the possibility of a settlement by meeting both Barbaro and Sokollu. In Venice the Council of Ten was also working behind the scenes, on 6 June instructing the imprisoned *bailo* to investigate the possibility of a deal with the Porte. On 22 August the Ten wrote again to Barbaro, ordering him to work secretly with Dax towards this goal, and on 19 September, at the height of military operations in the Levant, the *bailo* was given a free hand to negotiate a peace treaty with the Ottomans.

The republic was working behind its allies' back, but the Spaniards' procrastinations over the previous months had made the Venetians suspicious of their intentions, while Gregory XIII's openly pro-Spanish stance was far from reassuring. By starting peace talks the Council of Ten was bowing to the mercantile lobby in Venice, and by employing secrecy it was acting in the republic's best interests. Keeping things completely confidential was not easy, however. Already at the end of June the papal nuncio in Venice had an inkling of an imminent Venetian–Ottoman rapprochement, a suspicion that became more and more pronounced during the following months. By the beginning of 1573 an agreement between the Porte and Venice was considered imminent in European diplomatic circles.[36]

The ensuing treaty had been negotiated by the *bailo* with Sokollu through his Jewish doctor Solomon Ashkenazi, always very well disposed towards the Venetians. Dax was not present at the beginning of the talks, having left the Ottoman capital on 20 September 1572. He returned the following February, after learning in Dubrovnik of the St Bartholomew's Day massacre, but arrived too late to influence the negotiations. However, he had managed to talk the sultan out of an offensive against Corfu and attacking Venice's home territory, since this would have meant passing through the Holy Roman Emperor's possessions. The last thing the French wanted was a military alliance between the two branches of the Habsburg dynasty.[37]

It took some time to hammer out an agreement satisfactory to both Venice and Istanbul, due in part to the slowness of communications between the two capitals, but also because the Ottomans' initial requests included the surrender of the fortresses of Kotor and Corfu. Barbaro refused outright, knowing that accepting would have turned the Adriatic into an Ottoman lake. Sokollu backed off a bit, requesting Sopot plus an indemnity of 300,000 ducats, but even this the *bailo* found unacceptable. Both parties were trying not to appear weak, since the warmongers in Venice and Istanbul were still active. When Kılıç Ali was informed of the negotiations he asked Sokollu why he had not yet hanged Ashkenazi, flying into a rage when the latter suggested that the Ottomans were no match for the allied fleet. Sokollu then suggested reconfirming the territorial boundaries of the treaty of 1567, with the exception of Cyprus and the other recently captured territories, the surrender of Sopot and the 300,000-ducat indemnity. At this point Dax intervened in the negotiations, although by now the treaty was virtually a done deal. The *bailo* had initially welcomed the bishop's efforts, believing that with the French as guarantors any settlement would carry greater weight, but later he would write off Dax as a meddlesome pest. The treaty between Venice and the Porte was finally settled on 7 March 1573. The Venetians regained most of their lost territories in Albania and Dalmatia. Ulcinj and Bar remained in Ottoman hands, and the Venetians agreed to pay 1,500 ducats a year for the possession of the island of Zakynthos. Arrangements were made for the exchange of prisoners; merchants were to be released, and their goods restored or compensation paid.[38]

These terms may seem harsh on Venice, but should be considered in context. The Ottomans had gained Cyprus and other territory, but the republic had saved Crete, Corfu and Kotor, regained its commercial rights, and become once more the Porte's privileged trading partner. The loss of possessions may have been hard to swallow, but at least now Venice did not have to pay for their defence and the 300,000-ducat indemnity was a fraction of the republic's war costs. It is significant that the peace treaty was ratified in Venice with little opposition.[39]

Having signed a separate treaty with the Porte in blatant violation of the league's terms, it was now up to the Venetians to get their allies to swallow it. When informed of the deal by the republic's ambassadors Leonardo Donà and Lorenzo Priuli, Philip II took it with good grace, listening to them without showing any emotion except for a slight twist of his lips. He had been expecting the news for some time and was probably sympathetic to the Venetians' excuse that the peace had been done 'out of need and to avoid greater damage'. After listening carefully to the diplomats, the king dismissed them saying that he needed to meditate on the matter before giving an answer. Philip had no reason to be unhappy. For the Spanish crown the league had been a financial liability – although its costs had been partly covered by the Church – producing little in return, since the Venetians had reaped most of the benefits. In any case, with Ottoman naval power humbled and trouble brewing in Flanders, Philip was happy to close this chapter of his Mediterranean policy. Gregory XIII's reaction to the news was far more heated. When the Venetian ambassador Paolo Tiepolo told him about the deal, the pope rose screaming from his chair and ordered the diplomat out, cursing the Venetians and threatening excommunications left, right and centre. But apart from this there was little Gregory could do, except take away the subsidies granted to the republic by his predecessor. Excommunication is a serious matter, but sixteenth-century Catholic politicians saw it as a risk intrinsic to their job.[40]

The Venetian defection killed the league, but the Spanish still had a substantial military force in the Mediterranean. In October a fleet under Don Juan took Tunis and Bizerte practically unopposed, effectively blocking Ottoman access to the western Mediterranean. But the new acquisitions could not be defended without huge monetary investment, something the Spanish could ill afford. Besides, their capture was a challenge the Ottomans could not ignore, as the Curzolaris veteran Pompeo Floriani noted. Sure enough, nine months later a huge armada under Kılıç Ali arrived off Tunis, capturing it in two months together with the island of La Goleta, a Spanish possession since 1535. By now Philip II was embroiled in Flanders, and by 1580 Spain and the Porte had agreed on a truce that, despite its ups and downs, was destined to become permanent.[41]

～

For many of those present, the battle of the Curzolaris was an experience never to be repeated. Many would have agreed with Cervantes's comment on the event,* some to the point of paying ghost writers to describe their real, or imaginary, participation in the fighting, or would claim that some wound on their body dated back to that bloody October day. Others did not need to feign, their reputation assured by three gory hours of fighting over crimson waters.[42]

After Tunis, Don Juan of Austria served as viceroy of Naples, and there was even talk of him marrying Mary, queen of Scots; Philip II was not interested in the match, however. In 1576, following the death of Luis de Requesens, he was sent to Flanders as governor-general. He tried to pacify the region through a combination of force and clemency. Some of the insurgents were appeased, but many others, led by William of Orange, refused to

* See page vii.

lay down their arms. On 31 January 1578 Don Juan routed a rebel army at Gembloux, regaining the southern portion of the Netherlands for the Spanish crown. But by now his health was failing, and intrigues in Madrid had deprived him of Philip II's trust. After another, useless attempt to settle the Flanders rebellion peacefully, he died, a broken man, on 31 October 1578. He was first buried at Namur, but a year later his body was taken to Spain and interred in the Escorial, where he lies to this day.[43]

Marcantonio Colonna's political fortunes nose-dived after 1572. The league's collapse made his military position redundant, and the intrigues of his many political enemies in Rome, Naples and Madrid prevented him for some time from finding employment with the Spanish crown. Don Juan never forgave Colonna for challenging his leadership, and the Roman nobleman's offers to join the Tunis expedition were met with cold refusals. However, he was still grand constable of Naples, and for some time Philip II employed him to raise troops and inspect fortresses in that kingdom. At last, Colonna's endless nagging got him in 1577 the job of viceroy of Sicily, but he soon managed to get embroiled in a running fight with part of the Sicilian ruling elite. Accused of mismanagement and of usurping the king's authority, Colonna was on his way to Madrid to justify his actions when he died of a fever in Medinaceli on 1 August 1584.[44]

Sebastiano Venier was finally recalled to Venice at the end of 1572. He remained fiercely anti-Ottoman, adamantly opposing all peace deals with the Porte to the point of offering his personal fortune to help the war effort. Although considered something of a crank, he was also a national hero and one of those selected to receive King Henry III of France during his visit to Venice in 1574. Three years later, following the death of Alvise Mocenigo, he was unanimously elected doge. During his short term of office he displayed all the virtues and defects he had been known for during his spell as captain-general – a proud patriot who ignored protocol and showed little regard for political niceties. He died nine months after his election, some say from grief after a fire nearly burnt the ducal palace to the ground. True to his simple lifestyle, he was originally buried in a modest tomb on the island of Murano. With him was interred a rosary, made from the coral necklace he had won at the Curzolaris. In 1907 his body was solemnly moved to its present resting place in the church of SS Giovanni e Paolo in Venice.[45]

Giovanni Andrea Doria never lost the king of Spain's favour. He participated in the Tunis expedition and was one of those who advocated a negotiated solution of the Genoese civil war of 1577. In 1582 he ceded most of his galleys to Philip II – managing at the same time to retain control over them – and a year later the king chose him for the prestigious post of captain-general at sea. Also a member of the *Consejo de Estado*, Doria asked to retire in 1594, claiming ill health, but his request was turned down. In 1601 he planned and organized an expedition against Algiers, but the enterprise was sabotaged by bad weather. Finally allowed to retire, he spent the last years of his life augmenting the already considerable family fortune. He died in 1606, possibly the last of the great Italian sea captains of the sixteenth century. Nonetheless, doubts about his behaviour at the Curzolaris followed him to the grave and beyond, despite all the efforts to clear his name.[46]

Don Álvaro de Bazan, marquis of Santa Cruz, also remained persona grata with Philip II, having to his credit a continuous record of victories. He commanded the Spanish fleet during the invasion of Portugal in 1580, and two years later won a brilliant naval battle against a combined French and (unofficial) English fleet off Punta Delgada, in the Azores islands. A superb administrator, as well as a brilliant tactician, in 1587 Santa Cruz was chosen to lead the Armada being put together to invade England the following year. His death, on 9 February 1588, possibly changed the course of European history, for who can say what the Armada might have accomplished had Santa Cruz, and not the uninspiring duke of Medina Sidonia, been in command?[47]

Kılıç Ali, Doria's old adversary, remained *kapudan paşa* until his death. Under his energetic leadership by 1576 the Ottoman fleet was completely back to its pre-Curzolaris strength, the sultan now having 300 galleys plus a number of smaller boats at his disposal, while the pool of expert naval officers had been replenished thanks to the arrival of many corsairs from North Africa. Ottoman galleys now had also more artillery and men. In 1582 Kılıç Ali sailed to the Crimea to install the Ottoman-appointed khan of this vassal state, before going into semi-retirement. Like many Ottoman officials he spent the last years of his life erecting and endowing religious buildings. He died in July 1587, the last of the great Ottoman admirals from the school of Barbarossa and Dragut, and was buried in Constantinople near the Tophane – the cannon foundry – at the side of a mosque allegedly erected by the great architect Sinan. In 1989 a monument to him was erected in his native town of Le Castella in Calabria.[48]

Pertev Pasha, the other major Ottoman commander to survive the Curzolaris, was not so lucky. Returning to Constantinople, he was employed for a while during the emergency period following the battle, but having disgraced himself his life was now in jeopardy, and he owed his survival to his many connections at the Ottoman court. Dismissed from his position of second vizier, he died in obscurity in 1574. Barbaroszâde Hasan Pasha, reported to have died in the fight, actually managed to escape, being appointed *beylerbey* of Algiers in place of Kılıç Ali. Already sick, possibly as a result of wounds received at the Curzolaris, he never managed to occupy the post, expiring at the beginning of 1572. Abd-el Malik also survived the battle, participating in Kılıç Ali's 1574 Tunis campaign. Later with the aid of Ottoman troops he managed to become sultan of Morocco by capturing the city of Fez.[49]

Fortune distributed her favours unevenly to other veterans. Francesco Maria della Rovere was recalled by his father to Urbino in 1572, succeeding him two years later. His marriage on the rocks, the duke spent the rest of his life administering his state and collecting works of art, becoming more and more devout as the years went by. His only son (from his second wife) turned out a debauched individual, expiring because of his own excesses at the age of eighteen. Francesco Maria survived him by eight years, and on his death the duchy of Urbino was incorporated into the papal territories.[50]

Onorato Caetani's later history was grim. Received by Philip II into the Order of the Golden Fleece, he had nonetheless incurred Marcantonio Colonna's displeasure for the shoddy way he had handled the recruitment of soldiers in 1571. Colonna had him replaced as general of the papal infantry with Pius V's nephew Michele Bonelli, a veteran of the Curzolaris. With the election of Gregory XIII Caetani's fortunes went further downhill, the new pope distrusting Onorato partially because he was at loggerheads with the latter's uncle Cardinal Sermoneta. Without employment and faced with increasing family expenses, by the time of his death in 1592 Caetani had been forced to sell much of his property to pay his debts.[51]

Romegas got embroiled in the internal politics of the Order of Malta, in 1581 heading a revolt against the then grand master Jean de La Cassière. Called to Rome to answer to the Pope for his actions, he died there in November of the same year. After recovering from his wounds Miguel de Cervantes remained a soldier for some time. In 1575 he was captured by Muslim corsairs while on his way to Spain, spending five years as a slave in Algiers until ransomed. Cervantes spent the rest of his life eking out a living by working for the Spanish government, suffering bankruptcy and imprisonment. He died poor in 1616, but not before having acquired international fame with his immortal *Don Quixote*. Bernardino Antinori, another soldier-writer, was not so lucky. Some time after his return to Florence he got embroiled in a passionate love affair with Eleonora de Toledo 'the younger', wife of Cosimo I de' Medici's son Pietro. Eleonora was allegedly murdered by her enraged husband, and Grand Duke Francesco I had Antinori strangled in prison soon after. The same week as Eleonora's death, the Medici suffered another family tragedy when Isabella, Cosimo I's daughter, was murdered by her husband, the Curzolaris veteran Paolo Giordano Orsini, who suspected her of adultery. Orsini then embarked on a long affair with Vittoria Accoramboni, who was married to Francesco Mingucci, a nephew of the future Sixtus V. Paolo Giordano duly arranged the murder of Vittoria's husband – or at least so it was believed at the time – and eventually married his lover. Orsini died in Venetian territory in 1585 and Vittoria joined him soon after, murdered in Padua by one of her first husband's kinsmen.[52]

Others fared better, and indeed connections made during the campaigns of 1570–2 helped many a career. Pompeo Floriani became sergeant major general of infantry in the Holy Roman Empire, and in 1573 was entrusted by Antonio Doria, on the suggestion of Paolo Sforza, with devising ways to defend the newly captured Tunis. Returning home, Floriani held a number of military/administrative posts all over Italy, gaining a reputation as an expert in fortifications. He died in 1600, his fame as an engineer subsequently eclipsed by that of his son Pietro Paolo. Francesco Duodo also enjoyed fame and public employment, crowning his career in 1587 when elevated to the dignity of *procuratore di San Marco*. He died in November 1592 while inspecting fortifications on the Venetian mainland. Juan de Cardona continued in command of the Sicilian galley squadron for some years before returning to Spain. In 1587 he was viceroy and captain-general of the kingdom of Navarre, dying some time at the beginning of the seventeenth century. For a number of Ottoman survivors of the Curzolaris, career advancement was due as much to ability as to the battle leaving many places vacant. Ahmed ben Sinan rose to the rank of galley captain after serving as helmsman on the *Sultana* and distinguishing himself with an harquebus during the fight.[53]

The important Ottoman prisoners were not liberated until some years after the battle. Müezzinzâde Ali's elder son died in captivity, while the younger regained his freedom after his sister sent a written plea to Don Juan of Austria. Eventually most were exchanged for high-ranking Christians captured at Famagusta or Tunis. Not many of the lesser captives had such luck, most facing a life of toil, often on a galley bench, away from their families and homes. Count Silvio da Porcia brought back two slaves whom he employed as masons and bricklayers for his home. In time they became Christians, and the count threw a party (costing him a substantial amount of money) to celebrate their baptism. In 1610 the Venetian authorities liberated three Ottomans enslaved after the battle, housing them in hospices on the mainland.[54]

By then all the main protagonists in the Cyprus war had died: Philip II in 1598, Selim II in 1574 and Cosimo I' de Medici the same year. Mehmed Sokollu was stabbed by an assassin in 1579, his power by now on the wane. His old enemy Lala Mustafa managed to become grand vizier after his demise, but died after only a few months in office. Joseph Nassi, often thought the villain of the piece, did not retain his influence under the new sultan, and when he passed away in 1579 Murad III seized all his possessions. As for the thousands of common soldiers on both sides, after their brief moment in the spotlight they quickly slid back into obscurity.

EPILOGUE

~

The league was finished, Tunis recaptured, the Ottoman fleet rebuilt, the Porte still firmly entrenched in Europe; the Christian effort, the innumerable deaths, the economic drain, had been for nothing. Indeed Voltaire would comment that it seemed as if the Turks had been the real victors at the Curzolaris. But how much of this is true? Fernand Braudel would appositely remark that instead of scoffing at the battle's apparent lack of consequences, one should look instead at what the situation was before: Cyprus captured, Crete, Corfu, southern Italy, Spain, Venice, Vienna and ultimately a way of life threatened by the Muslim advance.[1] Now the Ottoman onslaught had been stopped in its tracks; its rebuilt fleet was unable to dominate the Mediterranean as before, the recapture of Tunis, brilliant as it may appear, being due more to Spain's mistakes than Kılıç Ali's ability. The Ottoman beard had indeed grown again at lightning speed, but was no stronger. It was not so much the lack of skilled personnel – North African corsairs and ransomed prisoners could plug that gap – as the Porte's not having a long-term naval policy. Even more important, the battle of the Curzolaris had not just been a psychological success; it had also confirmed the viability of Western military strategy and tactics.

The reasons for the Christian victory at the Curzolaris include: galleass fire, better tactical use of artillery, harquebusiers, body protection and Ottoman overconfidence. Most important was that the allies largely succeeded in stopping the Ottomans from exploiting their skill in hand-to-hand fighting, something at which they were the undisputed masters. The Europeans had realized that they could not win in a sword fight with the Ottomans and that in the long run it was not worth trying. In the Hungarian war at the beginning of the seventeenth century, Western field tactics forced the Ottomans to adapt their war machine, not always successfully, to the changed situation. Military initiative was now in European hands, although ultimate success was not assured. Western military superiority would not be a confirmed fact until the end of the eighteenth century, and until then the Ottomans remained a formidable foe.

Christian Europe would find other allies in its struggle against the Porte. In the 1580s the Ottoman empire was hit by a serious economic crisis, in the long term producing much political and social unrest. By the beginning of the seventeenth century the financial burden of maintaining simultaneously a numerous army and a large fleet had become intolerable. Something had to give, and that was the navy. In 1600 *kapudan Paşa* Cigalazâde Sinan (originally captured at Djerba with his father, Visconte Cigala) was going to sea with a mere sixteen galleys 'and then more as a corsair than as the sultan's admiral'. The Ottomans would not be the only ones forced to make such a choice. By 1650 Tuscany had sold or scrapped two thirds of its fleet to meet the costs of a substantial army.[2] Long wars between Constantinople and Persia did not help a situation made worse by the crisis in leadership that plagued the Porte in the first half of the seventeenth century, with sultans, grand viziers and government continually toppled and killed by palace conspiracies and army revolts. To many Western observers, by 1640 the Ottoman empire appeared on the verge of collapse.

But the Porte was more resilient than people thought, the Ottoman state still capable of functioning with the right people at its helm. These were the grand viziers of the Köprülü 'dynasty', who ran the empire for nearly half a century. Thanks to them, the Porte was able to resume its role in Europe, indeed make the continent shudder once more. In 1645 the Ottomans attacked Crete, and although the city of Irakleio resisted until 1669 it was clear from the beginning that the Venetians would eventually lose the island. True, whenever the Ottomans encountered the Venetians at sea they invariably came off worse, but they proved unbeatable when it came to amphibious operations. On land the Porte suffered a few defeats at the hands of the Habsburgs, but in 1683 a huge Ottoman army penetrated Austria and besieged Vienna. The timely arrival of a makeshift army of Saxons, Poles and Austrians restored the situation, the Ottomans suffering a major defeat and in the years to come losing most of Hungary to Austria and large chunks of Greece to the Venetians.[3] But Venice was no longer the military power it had been, and in 1718 a whirlwind Ottoman offensive recaptured nearly all the lost territories in Greece. The Porte also made headway in the Balkans, in 1738 retaking Belgrade from the Austrians.

By now in the West the Ottoman Empire had become an intellectual curiosity, seen within the frame of the Enlightenment as an exotic culture. Mozart would compose a 'Turkish March' and write the score for the opera *The Abduction from the Seraglio*. Coffee houses, an idea imported from the east, sprang up everywhere in Europe, and Turkish objects were eagerly sought after by collectors. From a military standpoint the Ottomans now faced not only Austria but also a resurgent Russia, as attempts to reform the state apparatus failed in the face of internal resistance. Sultan Selim III tried to modernize the army, navy and public administration, with partial success.[4]

In 1797, Venice, by now only a shadow of its former greatness, fell to Napoleon's revolutionary army practically without a fight. The following year it would be Malta's turn, the knights cowering from the French fleet behind their hitherto impregnable fortifications. Having overrun Italy and Malta, Napoleon now attacked Ottoman Egypt, defeating the army sent against him but then unable to advance further after a British fleet under Horatio Nelson destroyed a French one at the battle of the Nile. Now at war with

France, the Ottoman empire joined forces with the Austrians and Russians. In 1799 Ottoman soldiers fought side by side with papal troops near Ancona, collaborating also with a Russian contingent to rid Rome of its French-sponsored republican government. Turkish units fought alongside anti-French Tuscan insurgents, who advanced to the battle cry of 'Viva Maria'; others operated in the south of Italy with the army of the Catholic/Bourbon 'Army of the Holy Faith'. The wheel had come full circle. The Ottomans were now allies of those very forces they had always opposed as enemies of their religion, but by recognizing the heathen French Revolution, that monstrous offspring of Western civilization, as the enemy of both Christianity and Islam they had acknowledged Europe's true soul.

~

The battle of the Curzolaris is still very much a presence in the Mediterranean. Many palaces, houses, churches and museums, especially in Italy and Spain, display relics, real or alleged, of the fight – weapons, banners, pieces of Turkish cloth. The Turks, understandably, prefer to remember the epic exploits of people like Hayreddin Barbarossa, the Turkish navy celebrating as its own day the anniversary of the battle of Preveza. In the naval museum in Istanbul one can admire some well-preserved seventeenth-century rowing vessels, the only ones in such a state left in the world. The same institution holds the banners captured by the papal contingent at the Curzolaris, and returned in 1965 by Pope Paul VI. One of the standards from Müezzinzâde Ali's flagship is still to be seen, together with many other Muslim banners, in the church of Santo Stefano in Pisa. The great Ottoman banner sent to Spain by Don Juan of Austria was destroyed by fire at the end of the seventeenth century. Marco Antonio Colonna's much frayed standard is still visible in the Pinacoteca Comunale of Gaeta.

By taking the ferry from Brindisi to Patras it is possible to follow more or less the route of the league's fleet in 1571, passing Corfu, Igoumenitsa and Kefallonia. Entering the Gulf of Patras, the boat skirts the southern tip of the isle of Oxia, the only one of the original Curzolaris not to have been consumed by the silt of the Acheloos, and crosses over what once was the battlefield. The ferry's wake appears profane, stirring as it does the waters where so many fell. But the depths of the gulf placidly guard the eternal resting place of all the brave men who lost their lives on a distant October day, fighting for their beliefs and a way of life.

APPENDIX 1. BATTLE ARRAYS

~

A — HOLY LEAGUE

LEFT WING

State/Owner	Number	Guns	Lanterns
Genoa (private)	3	9	0
Naples	10	30	0
Tuscany (Papal)	1	5	0
Venice	43	215	3
Total	57	259	3

NOTE: Included the four Venetian galleys of the vanguard.

GALLEASSES OF THE LEFT WING

Name/Captain	Guns
Bragadina (Antonio Bragadin)	32
Bragadina (Ambrogio Bragadin)	27
Total	59

NOTE: Originally positioned one mile ahead of the division.

CENTRE

State/Owner	Number	Guns	Lanterns
Genoa (private)	9	27	5
Genoa (public)	2	10	2
Malta	3	15	1
Naples	3	11	1
Savoy	1	3	1
Sicily	4	16	2
Spain	9	35	4
Tuscany (Papal)	7	35	1
Venice	26	130	1
Total	64	268	18

NOTE: Included the three Sicilian and one Genoese (private) galleys of the vanguard, originally allotted to Doria's division.

GALLEASSES OF THE CENTRE

Name/Captain	Guns
Guora (Jacopo Guoro)	23
Duoda (Francesco Duodo)	28
Total	51

NOTE: Originally positioned one mile ahead of the division.

RIGHT WING

State/Owner	Number	Guns	Lanterns
Genoa (private)	13	39	7
Genoa (public)	1	3	0
Naples	7	21	0
Savoy	2	2	0
Sicily	1	3	0
Tuscany (Papal)	2	10	0
Venice	27	135	0
Total	53	213	7

NOTE: Many of the Venetian galleys appear to have been undermanned, and possibly with less ordnance than usual.

GALLEASSES OF THE RIGHT WING

Name/Captain	Guns
Pesara (Andrea da Pesaro)	26
Pisana (Piero Pisani)	23
Total	49

NOTE: Supposed to be one mile in front of the division, but probably positioned just ahead of the line.

RESERVE

State/Owner	Number	Guns	Lanterns
Naples	11	33	1
Sicily	2	6	0
Spain	3	9	0
Tuscany (Papal)	2	10	1
Venice	12	60	0
Total	30	118	2

NOTE: Ten galleys were sent to aid Barbarigo, soon after the initial clash.

BREAKDOWN OF HOLY LEAGUE'S FORCES

Division	Galleys	Galleasses	Lanterns	Guns
Left	57	2	3	318
Centre	64	2	18	319
Right	53	2	7	262
Reserve	30	0	2	118
Total	204	6	30	1,017

B — OTTOMAN

RIGHT WING

Provenance	Number	Guns	Lanterns
Alexandria	21	63	2
Istanbul	11	33	2
Tripoli (Syria)	8	24	1
Anatolia	13	39	0
Negropont (Evvoia)	1	3	1
Galliots, Alexandria	2	4	1
Total	56	166	7

NOTE: Probable estimate. Some galleys from the Ottoman battle may have joined the right trying to escape the galleasses' cannonade.

CENTRE

Provenance	Number	Guns	Lanterns
Istanbul	41	120	15
Rhodes	11	33	2
Napulia	12	36	1
Gallipoli	10	30	1
Mytilene	10	30	1
Tripoli (Libya)	6	18	1
Avlona	1	3	1
Galliots, Istanbul	5	5	0
Total	96	275	22

NOTE: The Ottoman battle was on two lines. The first, with 62 galleys; the second, with 29 galleys and 8 galliots. At least six lanterns were bunched together in the middle of the division.

LEFT WING

State/Owner	Number	Guns	Lanterns
Avlona	2	6	1
Anatolia	12	3	0
Istanbul	26	72	2
Algiers	7	15	4
Negropont	13	6	0
Tripoli (Syria)	6	18	1
Izmir	1	3	1
Galliots, Avlona	8	16	0
Galliots, Algiers	9	9	0
Galliots, Anatolia	10	25	0
Total	94	173	9

NOTE: The Ottoman left was on two lines. The first, with 67 galleys; the second, with 27 galliots.

RESERVE

State/Owner	Number	Guns	Lanterns
Chios	1	3	1
Istanbul	6	18	3
Tripoli (Libya)	1	3	1
Galliots, Istanbul	3	3	0
Galliots, Tripoli (Libya)	2	2	0
Total	13	29	5

NOTE: The Ottoman reserve included also 18 *fuste*.

BREAKDOWN OF OTTOMAN FORCES

Division	Galleys	Galliots	Lanterns	Guns
Left	67	27	9	173
Battle	91	5	22	275
Right	54	2	7	166
Reserve	8	5	5	29
Total	220	39	43	643

The number of artillery pieces is a rough estimate, give or take 5–6 per cent, and includes only the main gun batteries. As explained in the text, lantern galleys were not necessarily more heavily armed than other vessels of the same type, their function being more command centres of a particular unit. The large number of Ottoman lantern galleys is due to the fact that they were also a symbol of rank, befitting the many dignitaries of the Porte present at the Curzolaris. It should be stressed, however, that, despite some recent, admirable attempts to produce the exact order of battle of the two forces,★ the precise strength of the two opponents is likely to remain a mystery. For instance, the League departed from Messina with 207–208 galleys, but apparently a couple of those sent to Apulia to embark troops did not manage to rejoin the allied fleet in time for the battle. Other two were disarmed in Corfu to allow, at Don Juan's request, the loading of the siege artillery taken from the fortress. As for the Ottomans, we have estimates ranging from 180 to nearly 300 fighting vessels. Guido Antonio Quarti would sum up the matter by commenting: 'The confusion is such, that we don't know whom to believe.'†

★ BICHENO: 306–318. GARGIULO: 189–197.
† QUARTI: 590–591. 616–617. Citation: 591.

APPENDIX 2

~

A — GALLEY ARMAMENT

Country	Main Battery★	Secondary Armament†	Weight of Shot, Centreline Gun(s)‡	Equivalent, UK/USA pounds
Algiers, *sottile*	1–3	2+	–	15.0–30.0
Algiers, *bastarda*	1–3	2+	–	30.0–35.0
Algiers, *galliot*	1	2+	–	15.0–30.0
Florence, *sottile*	5	4+	40–50 pounds	30.0–37.5
Florence, *bastarda*	5	10+	40–50 pounds	30.0–37.5
Genoa, *sottile*	3	2+	20–40 pounds	13.5–27.5
Genoa, *bastarda*	3–5	4+	30–50 pounds	20.5–34.5
Malta, *sottile*	5	4+	50–60 pounds	29.0–35.0
Malta, *bastarda*	5	10+	50–60 pounds	29.0–35.0
Naples, *sottile*	3	2+	20–50 pounds	14.0–35.0
Naples, *bastarda*	3–5	10+	40–50 pounds	28.0–35.0
Ottoman, *sottile*	1–3	2+	9–11 *okka*	25.5–31.0
Ottoman, *bastarda*	3	2+	11–21 *okka*	31.0–60.0
Ottoman, *galliot*	1–3	2+	9–11 *okka*	25.5–31.0
Savoy, *sottile*	1–3	2+	20–40 pounds	14.0–20.5
Sicily, *sottile*	3	2+	25–60 pounds	15.5–35.0
Sicily, *bastarda*	3–5	10+	50–60 pounds	29.0–35.0
Spain, *sottile*	3	2+	15–30 pounds	15.5–30.5
Spain, *bastarda*	3–5	10+	30–40 pounds	30.5–40.5
Venice, *sottile*	5	10+	40–50 pounds	27.5–34.5
Venice, *bastarda*	5	15+	50–60 pounds	34.5–40.0
Venice, *galleass*	12–18	5–22+	20–60 pounds	13.0–40.0

★ The fixed artillery of the galleys or galleasses.
† Swivel guns and anti-personnel light artillery.
‡ For Algiers the estimate is based on captured artillery pieces.

It would appear that at this date *ponentine* galleys had a main battery of three guns with the exception of the Maltese and Florentine/Tuscan galleys, specifically designed for hunter/killer operations against Muslim shipping.* The normal Spanish, Neapolitan, Sicilian and Genoese galley had the same number of guns as its Ottoman counterpart, and mounted lighter pieces than those found on Venetian vessels. For this reason they often beefed up their hitting power by mounting a pair of heavy *falconete* swivel guns.† In general Venetian galleys sported more and heavier artillery, between main and secondary armament, than *ponentine*, to compensate for their lack of fighting men. Only in the 1590s did the five-gun main battery become the standard armament of western galleys,‡ although to generalize would be risky: galleys were armed with whatever was available, standardization not being a feature of early-modern warfare.

From the above chart it is clear that every country in the Mediterranean employed guns of more or less equivalent calibre, as shown by the table below. The only exception would seem to be that of the Ottomans with their gargantuan 60-pounder. But this particular piece weighed only 4,782 Venetian "heavy" pounds (other two Turkish 35-pounders weighing 4,799 pounds each), which suggests it was intended to fire stone balls, and may have been one of the 20-*okka* (1 *okka* =2.83 UK/USA pounds) guns cast for naval use in 1538.§ What made the difference at the Curzolaris was not the size or the number of guns, but instead the tactical use of firearms in general. The concentrated bombardment of the Venetian galleasses, the long-range shooting of the other western galleys, swivel guns and massed harquebus volleys proved superior to the Ottoman short-range artillery fire, arrow barrage and hand-to-hand fighting.

---

* ASF, *MP*, 220, f. 33rv (Cosimo de' Medici to Francesco di Ser Jacopo, 19 April 1564).
† *CN*, VIII, 14, ff. 114r-118r. (1580).
‡ Cfr. PANTERA. CRESCENZO. *CN*, VIII, 23, ff. 156r-157r. (1590).
§ ASV, *CX, Parti Comuni*, filza 122, n.n. f. (25 February 1575). ÁGOSTON: 77.

B — THE SOUTHERN EUROPEAN POUND

Country	'Heavy' Pound (kg)	Ounces	'Light' Pound (kg)	Ounces
Genoa	0.317664	12	0.31675	12
Florence	–	-	0.339542	12
Malta	–	-	0.26447	12
Naples	–	-	0.32076	12
Rome	–	-	0.339072	12
Savoy (Nice)	–	-	0.311628	12
Sicily	–	-	0.26447	12
Spain	0.4601	16	–	-
Venice	0.476999	12	0.30123	12

Where the division between 'heavy' (*libbra grossa*) and 'light' (*libbra sottile*) pounds existed, the former was usually employed for metals, and sometimes spices. In Venice, however, 'heavy' pounds were used to establish the weight of artillery pieces, but 'light' ones for shot, possibly because in origin ordnance was supposed to fire stone balls. The Spanish pound is equivalent to the standard UK/US one: 0.4536 kg. (16 ounces). The Spanish also had the *libra carnicera* ('butcher's pound') of 32 ounces, used for meat.

GLOSSARY

~

a scaloccio Italian (probably from *scala* = ladder) referring to the rowing arrangement on a galley (q.v.) with one oar per bench handled by several rowers.

ağa Head servant of a household. Also commander of certain military units.

akçe Silver coin, the main unit of currency in the Ottoman empire.

akinci Light cavalryman from Rumelia (q.v.) engaged in permanent warfare along the Habsburg–Ottoman frontier in the Balkans.

alla sensile Italian (from the Spanish *sencillo* = simple) referring to the rowing arrangement on a galley (q.v.) with more than one oar per bench each handled by an individual rower.

arrembata Italian (Spanish *arrumbada*) for the elevated forecastle at the bow of a *ponentina* (q.v.) galley (q.v.).

askerî Military, in the Ottoman empire all those, with their retainers and families, not part of the *reaya* (q.v.) class.

azab Galley (q.v.) officer under a *reis* (q.v.); provincial soldier on garrison duty.

bagno Corral-type building for housing galley convicts and slaves.

bailo Venetian, a resident diplomat.

bastarda A galley (q.v.) with more than twenty-six rowing benches on each side (from the Italian for mongrel).

Bektaşi Dervish sect, its beliefs incorporating elements of Islam, Christianity, Buddhism and pre-Muslim Turkish paganism.

bey See *sancak bey*.

beylerbeik Ottoman province.

beylerbey Governor of a *beylerbeik* (q.v.).

buonavoglia Volunteer oarsman, especially on a ***ponentina*** (q.v.) galley (q.v.).

capitana Galley (q.v.) designed as a flagship, usually but not invariably a *bastarda* (q.v.) and a *lanterna* (q.v.).

çavuş Official of the Ottoman *dîvân* (q.v.).

cebelü Armed retainer in the service of a *timar*-holding *sipahi* (q.v.).

chief mufti (Turkish *şeyhü'l-islam*) The mufti (q.v.) of Constantinople, in the sixteenth century the highest religious and legal authority in the Ottoman empire.

condottiere (plural *condottieri*) Italian military entrepreneur.

culverin Artillery piece, approximately one third longer than a cannon.

darülharb The world not under Muslim rule.

darülislam The world under direct Muslim rule.

devşirme The forced recruitment of Christian youths for service, after conversion to Islam, in the *kapıkulu* (q.v.) corps or the Ottoman administration.

dîvân Council.

dîvân-ı hümâyûn The sultan's council, meeting under the presidency of the grand vizier (q.v.).

fanale See *lanterna*.

fatwa In Islamic law an opinion, given by a competent religious authority.

forzato (plural *forzati*) Convict oarsman on a galley (q.v.).

fusta Small galley (q.v.) with between twelve and fifteen rowing benches.

galeotto Galley (q.v.) oarsman.

galia grossa *See* galleass.

galley The standard vessel of the Mediterranean for many centuries, powered by oars and sail and with approximately twenty-five rowing benches.

galleass Large and heavily armed galley (q.v.) also known as a *galia grossa*, created by the Venetians by modifying transport galleys.

galliot Smaller galley (q.v.) with between sixteen and twenty-three rowing benches

gaza Raid, an alternative term for jihad.

gente de cabo Spanish for the artillerymen, sailors and guards on board a galley (q.v.).

grand vizier (Turkish *sadr-ı azam*) The chief vizier and the sultan's deputy.

harquebus Portable gun fired from the shoulder shooting a ball of approximately half an ounce.

has The largest fief within the Ottoman system, with a revenue of more than 100,000 *akçe* (q.v.).

imam Muslim prayer leader in a mosque; Muslim doctor of divinity.

janissary (Turkish *yeniçeri*) Ottoman infantry soldier recruited through the *devşirme* (q.v.) and part of the *kapıkulu* (q.v.) corps.

jihad Islamic term (Arabic *jahd* = effort) for holy war against the infidels.

kadi Ottoman judge.

kapıkulu ('slave of the Porte') In the Ottoman empire an individual recruited through the *devşirme* (q.v.) and employed in the sultan's army, administration or palace.

kapudan-ı deryâ Ottoman title for the grand admiral of the Mediterranean fleet.

kapudan paşa The *kapudan-i deryâ* (q.v.) when entrusted with a *beylerbeik* (q.r.)

küreçi azab Ottoman levied oarsman.

lanterna (also *fanale*; Venetian *fanò*) The lantern at the stern of certain galleys (q.v.); galley acting as a command vessel, usually a *capitana* (q.v.) or a *padrona* (q.v.).

levantina Type of galley (q.v.) used mainly in the eastern Mediterranean.

maona Vessel akin to a transport galley (q.v.) (Turkish *mavna*); Ottoman name for a galleass (q.v.); in Chios under Genoese rule, the body ruling the island.

mariol Ottoman volunteer oarsman.

mavna See *maona*.

moschetto da zuogo Small artillery piece used on Venetian ships.

moschetto da braga Venetian type of swivel gun.

mufti Religious authority with the power to issue a fatwa (q.v.).

padişa Official Ottoman title for the sultan.

padrona Galley (q.v.) designed as a deputy flagship, usually but not invariably a *bastarda* (q.v.) and a *lanterna* (q.v.).

Pasha/*paşa* Ottoman title given to viziers and major provincial governors.

piece of eight (Spanish *peso de ocho*) Spanish silver coin worth eight *reales*, and the standard medium of exchange in the Mediterranean of the sixteenth century.

ponentina Type of galley used mainly in the western Mediterranean.

Porte The Ottoman government and state.

provveditore Term used mainly in Venice to indicate the chief administrator of a certain body or place.

reaya In the Ottoman Empire all those, with their retainers and families, not part of the *askerî* (q.v.) class.

reis Ottoman naval captain.

Rumelia The part of Europe under Ottoman rule

sancak Subdivision of a *beylerbeik* (q.v.), comprising a number of *timar* (q.v.).

sancak bey Governor of a *sancak* (q.v.)

Safavid The dynasty ruling Persia in the sixteenth and seventeenth centuries.

scapolo Venetian term for a marine.

Schmalkaldic Bund Defensive league of German Lutheran princes.

serdar Ottoman commander with extensive powers in charge of a military expedition.

şeyhü'l-islam *See* chief mufti.

sharia The body of Islamic law.

sipahi Cavalryman; cavalryman holding a *timar* (q.v.) in exchange for military service.

Sipahi of the Porte Member of one of the Six Cavalry Divisions (q.v.).

Six Cavalry Divisions Mounted units of the *kapıkulu* (q.v.) military corps.

sopracomito Captain of a Venetian galley (q.v.).

tercio Spanish infantry unit akin to a regiment, with between twelve and fifteen companies and a theoretical strength of 3,000 men.

timar Ottoman military fief worth less than 20,000 *akçe* (q.v.) a year.

uomini da spada In Venice an alternative name for *scapoli* (q.v.); all fighting individuals (i.e. other than rowers) on board a galley.

vizier One of the sultan's ministers, with both military and political authority, and a member of the *dîvân-ı hümâyûn* (q.v.).

wagenburg Field fortress of fortified carts joined together.

yeniçeri *See* janissary.

yeniçeri ağasi The officer in command of the janissaries.

zeamet Military fief valued at more than 20,000 *akçe* (q.v.) a year.

NOTES

~

ABBREVIATIONS

ADP: Archivio Doria-Pamphilij, Rome

AFMC: Archivio Floriani, Macerata

AGF: Archivio Guicciardini, Florence

AGS: Archivo General de Simancas, Simancas (Valladolid)

   SE: Secretaría de Estado

ASF: Archivio di Stato di Firenze, Florence

   CS: Carte Strozziane

   DGA: Depositeria Generale, parte antica.

   GCS: Guicciardini-Corsi-Salviati

   MM: Miscellanea Medicea

   MP: Mediceo del Principato

   SFF: Scrittoio delle Fortezze e Fabbriche

ASG: Archivio di Stato di Genova, Genoa

   NA: Notai Antichi

ASTr: Archivio di Stato de Trieste, Trieste

   TT: Torre e Tasso

ASV: Archivio di Stato di Venezia, Venice

   CCX: Capi del Consiglio dei Dieci

   CM: Cariche da Mar

   CLS: Collegio Lettere, Secreta

   CR: Collegio Relazioni

CX: Consiglio dei Dieci
MC: Miscellanea Codici
MdM: Milizia da Mar
SAPC: Secreta, Archivi Propri Contarini
ScMN: Scritture Miste Motabili
SD: Senato Dispacci
SDM: Senato Deliberazioni Mar
SM: Senato Mar
SMMN: Secreta, Materie Miste Notabili
SS: Senato Secreta
ST: Senato Terra
BAV: Biblioteca Apostolica Vaticana, Rome
BMCCV: Biblioteca del Museo Civico Correr, Venice
BMrF: Biblioteca Moreniana, Florence
BNCF: Biblioteca Nazionale Centrale, Florence
BNMV: Biblioteca Nazionale Marciana, Venice
BOA: Basbakanlık Osmanlı Arşivi, Istanbul
  MD: Mühimme Defterleri
CLDSP: *Calendar of Letters, Despatches, and State Papers, relating to the negotiations between England and Spain*
CN: *Colección de documentos y manuscriptos compilados por Fernandez de Navarrete*
CODOIN: *Colección de documentos inéditos para la historia de España*
CSPV: *Calendar of state papers and manuscripts, relating to English affairs, existing in the archives and collections of Venice*
DBI: *Dizionario Biografico degli Italiani*
EI²: *Encyclopaedia of Islam*, 2nd edition
f.: folio
MS.: manuscript
n.: number
n.n.f(f.): non numbered folio(s)
r: recto
RBM: Real Biblioteca, Madrid
  EBG: Ex Bibliotheca Gondomariensi
reg.: registro

SOCSS: Statuti, capitoli, et constitutioni, dell'Ordine de' Caualieri di Santo Stefano.

v: verso

PROLOGUE

1 SELÂNIKÎ: I, 84. BNMV, Ms It. VII, 11, c. 204r. 'Lettera di Sultan Selim imperator de' Turchi, presentata alla Signoria di Venetia, 1570 a' 28 marzo'.

2 Venier's report, in: MOLMENTI, (1899): 311.

3 ARROYO: 61r.

4 MONGA: 59.

5 *Intiero, e minuto ragguaglio*: f. 1v.

6 CATENA: 215–16.

1. THE WAXING CRESCENT

1 ASF, *MP*, 1171, ins. 5, f. 235 (Lorenzo Pagni to Pierfrancesco Riccio, undated, but early February 1545).

2 MACHIAVELLI (1524): Act III, Scene 3.

3 EMMERT. ATIYA.

4 BABINGER (1978). INALCIK (1960).

5 BARBARO. PERTUSI.

6 SIRE.

7 LAGGETTO. FONSECA.

8 E. TYAN (1965). KHADDURI.

9 INALCIK (1980).

10 BARTUSIS.

11 IMBER (2002): 194–8. INALCIK (2003): 113.

12 MACHIAVELLI (1994): 14.

13 KÁLDY-NAGY (1977). MATUZ: 177.

14 MÉNAGE (1965). MÉNAGE (1966). MÉNAGE (1956). repp. wittek.

15 GOFFMAN: 68.

16 ALBERI (1844a): 48–58. UZUNÇARŞILI (1984). AKGÜNDÜZ. For the

strength of the janissaries, as well as for other troops, I have relied on: MURPHEY (1999): 43–9, Table 3.5. IMBER (2002): 257–67. For an example of rewarding troops in the field, see: GIOVIO (1564): II, 580–1.

17 *Ibid.*: 8.

18 *Ibid.*: 134.

19 *Ibid.*: 39.

20 FISHER: 45.

21 *Ibid.*: 52.

22 ALLOUCHE.

23 BIRGE: 66–7.

24 FISHER: 88.

25 TEKINDAĞ. FISHER: 90–1.

26 HESS (1973).

27 FODOR (2000**b**): 119.

28 LABIB.

29 Quoted in: KÁLDY-NAGY (1974): 55.

30 FODOR (2000**b**): 119–20.

31 KNOLLES: I, 404.

32 PERJÉS: part II. NEGYES. Süleyman's retreat baffled his contemporaries, as well as future historians. For a discussion of the problem, see: FODOR, (2000**b**): 119–20.

33 SEYYD MURAD.

34 GIOVIO (1564): II, 423–6.

35 GULLINO. TURAN.

36 KHALILIEH: 133–48. SANTILLANA: I, 421. BRAUDEL (1976): I, 103. ROSSI.

37 BELLINGERI. GOKBILGIN: 57–9. KÜTÜKOLU: 148–9.

38 PRYOR: 165–74.

39 ÖZBARAN (1978).

40 KATIB ÇELEBI (1911): 159. ALBERI, (1844**a**): 291–5.

41 IMBER (2002): 298–302.

42 IMBER (1996**a**): 23–33.

43 PRYOR: 176–7.

44 See on this problem: FODOR (2002).

45 BRUMMETT. HESS (1970).

46 LUFTI PAŞA: 31–2.

47 ÖZBARAN (1994).

48 ALBERI (1844**b**): 100.

49 FODOR (2000**b**): 131–43.

50 BEBINGER.

51 IMBER (2002): 53–4.

52 INALCIK (2003): 37.

53 ALBERI (1844**b**): 98.

54 For a summary of the Djerba operation, see: GUILMARTIN (2003): 137–48.

55 IMBER (1996**a**): 48–9.

56 AGS, SE, 1325, n. 122 (Garcia Hérnandez to Philip II, from Venice, 23 November 1565). KATIB ÇELEBI (1697): 149.

2. A HOUSE DIVIDED

1 PARISOT DE LA VALLETTE: 71–3.

2 AGS, *SE*, 1325, n. 117 (García Hernández to Philip II, 29 September 1565, from Venice).

3 GUICCIARDINI (1949): 41.

4 MACHIAVELLI (1994): 45.

5 EVERT-KAPPESOVA: 245.

6 BROQUIERE: 149.

7 PIUS II: 11–12.

8 BISAHA.

9 See, for example: RUNCIMAN: 467–8.

10 For the Italian Wars, see: PIERI.

11 BOCCACCIO: 33.

12 For Savonarola, see: RIDOLFI.

13 ERASMUS: 319.

14 LUTHER (1957): 91–2. LUTHER (1967): 205.

15 LUTHER (1961): 47. See also: SETTON: III, 189–90.

16 For Hadrian VI, see: PASOLINI.

17 *CLDSP*, III, 2: 201–2.

18 For the Pontificate of Clement VII, see: GOUWENS AND REISS.

19 For the Schmalkaldic Bund, see: SCHLÜTTER-SCHINDLER.

20 MSETTON: III, 484, 502−4.

3. MEDITERRANEAN MEDLEY

1 *CSPV*, VI-2, n. 791, pp. 907−8.

2 PEPPER: 43−4.

3 *Ibid.*: 52−3.

4 PRETO (1975): 36−45.

5 PRETO (2002): 3.

6 CAPASSO.

7 PAOLETTI: 49.

8 BORNATE. ORESTE (1953).

9 MANFRONI (1898): 757−82, 809−56.

10 BASSO: 1−2.

11 *Ibid.*: 4.

12 PICCINO: 5−6.

13 HALICZER.

14 HESS (1968): 1−7.

15 OLESA MUÑIDO: I, 364.

16 MICCIO.

17 CANTAGALLI: 14−15.

18 TOGNARINI: 32−3.

19 SETTON: IV, 635.

20 NORES: 35−43.

21 ALBERI (1846): 389.

22 For the papal−Spanish war, see: PAOLETTI: 63−8.

23 SETTON: IV, 672.

24 The bishop of Lodève, French ambassador in Venice, to Henry II, in: RIBIER: II, 673−5.

25 NORES: 481−500.

26 DUMONT: 10−13.

27 BAZZANO: 74−6.

28 For the text of the treaty, see: DUMONT: 34−57.

29 MALLETT.

30 ASF, *MP*, 5, f. 194rv (Cosimo I de' Medici to Francisco Alvarez de Toledo, 4 July 1543).

31 AGLIETTI: 60.

32 CAMERANI: 86.

33 ASF, *MP*, 186, f. 46rv (Cosimo I de' Medici, to Alfonso Berardi, 16 September 1547).

34 ANGIOLINI (1996): ch. 1.

35 ASF, *MM*, 264, ins. 29, 'Ristretto delle Entrate Ordinarie e Straordinarie di S.A. Ser.ma, si come di tutte le Uscite Calculate dall'anno 1625 a tutto l'anno 1650', n.n. ff.

36 For the Spanish espionage ring in Istanbul, see: FLORistan imizcoz: 579–737.

37 AGS, *SE*, 485 (Francesco Franchis to Philip II, 21 January 1559); (Memorandum of Gonzalo Pérez to Philip II, 5 March 1559); (Philip II to the duke of Sessa, from Brussels, 6 March 1559).

38 GUILMARTIN (2003): 145–6.

39 AGS, *SE*, 1068, doc. 5, 'La respuesta del Duque de Terranova sobre el estrado que quedan las cossas del Reyno de Siçilia' (1576).

40 ASP *Segretari del Regno – Ramo Protonotaio*, 47, n.n.f. (30 June 1565).

41 GUILMARTIN (2003): 203–5.

4. BUILD-UP TO DRAMA

1 I have taken most of the information concerning the Ottoman take-over of Chios from: ARGENTI (1949); ARGENTI (1958).

2 DOUAIS: I, 61–2. For the Corsican rebellion, see: BRAUDEL: II, 1001–4.

3 BORNATE (1939).

4 BOSIO: III, 757.

5 See on this matter: MILLER.

6 BRAUDEL: 625. Many thanks to Gabor Ágoston for pointing this out to me.

7 The struggle for Süleyman's succession is described in detail in: TURAN.

8 cfr. IMBER (2002): 108.

9 IMBER (1997).

10 DOUAIS: I, 49.

11 ZRINYI.

12 This section is based mainly on: HAMMER: VI, 149–58.

13 ALBERI (1844a): 360–1.

14 CHARRIERE: III, 259.

15 ALBERI (1844a): 401.

16 WOODHEAD (1995): 131–2.

17 KRAMER: 720.

18 OSLARAM: 571–2.

19 ALBERI (1844a): 299. HAMMER: 156. BABINGER (1993b): 316.

20 See, for instance: PEDANI (2003): 287.

21 CHARRIERE: II, 735–7; III, 80–4. ROMER.

22 CHARRIERE: III, 14–15, and notes.

23 KRAMER: 720–1.

24 SERRANO (1914): I, 87.

25 GRENTE.

26 For the Council of Trent, see: JEDIN.

27 SERRANO (1914): I, 28–30.

28 GOODMAN: 56.

29 SERRANO (1914): I, 152–4, 187.

30 AGS, SE, 530 (Margaret of Parma to Philip II, 18 August 1566).

31 For the Flanders revolt, see: PARKER (1977).

32 SERRANO (1918): 57–9.

33 SERRANO (1914): II, 132–3, 180.

34 Ibid.: II, 524–5.

35 MARRANA-ROSSI.

36 ASF, MP, 5040, f. 199 (Bernardetto Minerbetti to Cosimo I, from Madrid, 28 December 1561).

37 ANGIOLINI (1999).

38 AGLIETTI: 62–3.

39 ASF, MP, 211, f. 59r (Cosimo I de' Medici to Albertaccio degli Alberti in Constantinople, 11 July 1560). Ibid., f. 60r (Cosimo I de' Medici to Angelo Biffoli, 11 July 1560).

40 ASF, Manoscritti 127 'Settimanni vol. III:' ff. 272r–273v.

41 ASF, *MP*, 2077, ff. 347r–352r. FONTANA: 31–2. GUARNIERI (1960): 99–100.

42 AGLIETTI: 71–3. GOODMAN: 55–6.

43 Quoted in: SETTON: IV, 823.

44 FRIEDA: 47–9.

45 DIAZ: 187–8.

46 AGLIETTI: 85.

47 ASF, *MP*, 615, ins. 3, f. 528rv (Cosimo I de' Medici to Queen Catherine de' Medici, 15 September 1570).

48 The whole Don Carlos affair can be found in: GACHARD.

49 ELLIOT: 231–6. KAMEN: 128–9. HESS (1968): 13.

50 For the Morisco revolt see: CARO BAROJA. DOMINGUEZ ORTIZ, VINCENT.

51 AGS, SE, K 513 (Francés de Alava to Philip II, from Paris, 9 December 1569). HESS (1968): 13–16. CARO BAROJA: 188.

52 KAMEN: 130–2. VINCENT.

53 HAËDO: 78v–79v. BRAUDEL: II, 1068.

5. CYPRUS

1 ASV, *CCX*, *Lettere da Costantinopoli*, 3, n.n.f. (Vettore Bragadin to the Council of Ten, 13 January 1566).

2 ASV, *SS*, reg. 75, ff. 28v–29r (26 July 1567). STELLA (1963): 255.

3 PRETO (1986): 80–4.

4 I am grateful to Professor Maria Pia Pedani for this information.

5 SETTON: IV, 934–5.

6 ASV, *CX*, *Parti Secrete*, reg. 8, ff. 118v–119r (4 June 1568). BNMV, Ms. It., VII (390), *Copialettere di Marc'Antonio Barbaro*, (19 December 1569).

7 PEDANI (2003): 288–9.

8 FAROQHI: 7–10.

9 PEDANI (2003): 289.

10 PARUTA: 11–17. HAMMER: 196. FODOR (2000d): 201.

11 STELLA (1972): 124–5. PARUTA: 21–3. TOSI.

12 CHARRIÈRE: III, 84, 87.

---

13 ASV, *SD*, *Costantinopoli*, 4 (Marcantonio Barbaro to the Venetian Senate, 31 January 1570). STELLA (1972): 187–8.

14 Quoted in: FODOR (2000c): 218.

15 HAMMER: 197.

16 PEDANI (1994): 199–203. CANOSA: 59–62.

17 QUARTI: 110–11; quote: 111. MACCHI: III, 9.

18 CONTI: II, 74r–75v. On Salomon Ashkenazi's influence, see: ASF, *MP*, 4274, ins. 1, f. 23rv (Bongianni Gianfigliazzi to Francesco I de' Medici, 14 September 1578, from Constantinople).

19 STELLA (1972): 215–16.

20 PIOT, POULLETT: IV, 51–2.

21 SERRANO (1914): III, 248–50, 275–7.

22 DRAGONETTI DE TORRES. SERRANO (1918): 82–115. SERRANO (1914): III, 295–9.

23 VARGAS-HIDALGO (2002): 656.

24 SERRANO (1914): III, 335–51.

25 SERENO: 393ff. SERRANO (1918): 85–94. SETTON: IV, 962–3. GATTONI: 626–8.

26 PIOT, POULLETT: IV, 81. BAZZANO: 129–31.

27 ASV, *CLS*, 25 n.n.f. (The collegio to Michele Surian in Rome, 6 June 1570). ASV, SS, reg. 76, f. 121r (Alvise Mocenigo to Gerolamo Zane, 22 July 1570). SERRANO (1914): III, 446–7.

28 HALE (1990): 353.

29 CARRIERE: III, 113. SERENO: 51.

30 GUGLIELMOTTI (1887): VI, 30–1. DUMONT: V (1), 192b. DRAGONETTI DE TORRES: 104–5. SERRANO (1914): III, 479.

31 STELLA (1965): 383, and note 27.

32 ADP, 69/32, 3, ff. 12v–14r (Giovanni Andrea Doria to the Prince of Melfi (Marcantonio Doria del Carretto), 8 August 1570). ADP, 69/32, 3, f. 22rv (Giovanni Andrea Doria to Philip II, 11 August 1570, from Messina). AGS, *SE*, 1399, n. 74 (Diego Guzmán de Silva to Philip II, 28 July 1570, from Genoa). ADP, 69/32, 3, f. 19rv (Giovanni

33 Andrea Doria to Stefano De' Mari, 11 August 1570, from Messina).

34 BOSIO: III, 855–65.

35 BMCCV, 3596, G. SOZOMENO, *Della Presa di Nicosia*.

36 GUILMARTIN (2003): 204.

37 QUARTI: 263. Quote in: PARUTA: 101.

38 PROMIS: 410. Quote in: FARA: 45.

39 HAMMER: VI, 205.

40 KALDY-NAGY.

41 CONTI: 87v.

42 QUARTI: 319–20. KATIB ÇELEBI (1911): 88.

43 HALE (1990): 298.

44 ASV, SM, reg. 39, f. 149v (4 April 1570). PARUTA: 128.

45 ASV, *Annali*, 1566–70, f. 501r. SERRANO (1914): III, 447. Quote in: PARUTA: 73–4.

46 DOGLIONI (1598): 826.

47 GUGLIELMOTTI: 29.

48 ADP, 69/32, 3, f. 25r (Giovanni Andrea Doria to Count Giuseppe Francesco di Landriano, 22 August 1570, from Otranto).

49 CAMPANA: I, 56.

50 LO BASSO: 279–80.

51 ASV, CM, *Processi*, 4, f. 18r.

52 ASV, *Annali*, 1566–70, f. 523r (8 September 1570). PARUTA: 128. CONTARINI: 14r.

53 IBÁÑEZ DE IBERO.

54 GUGLIELMOTTI: 58–64. SERENO: 67.

55 ADP, 69/32, 3, f. 26rv (Giovanni Andrea Doria to the viceroy of Sicily, 17 September 1570, from Crete).

56 AGS, SE, 1133, n. 107 (Marcantonio Colonna to Philip II, 29 September 1570, from Crete). ASV, CM, *Processi*, 4, ff. 39v–40v.

57 DORIA: 359. ASV, CM, *Processi*, 4, ff. 37v–38r. SETTON: IV, 984–5. ADP, 70/25, int. 8 (Giovanni Andrea Doria to the viceroy of Sicily, 17 October 1570, from Cape Spartivento).

58 CONTARINI: 12r.

59 GUGLIELMOTTI: 91.

60 TUCCI.

61 PARUTA: 133.

62 GUGLIELMOTTI: 107. CONCINA: 127. SERENO: 72.

6. A LEAGUE OF MISTRUST

1 BAZZANO: 133–5. PIOT, POULLETT: IV, 81. CAETANI, DIEDO: 151.

2 ADP, 69/32, 3, f. 42v (Giovanni Andrea Doria to the viceroy of Sicily, 14 November 1570, from Genoa). STELLA (1966): 391. MOLINI: 481–4.

3 SETTON: IV, 990–1.

4 SERRANO (1914): IV, 21–5.

5 AGLIETTI: 85–7. FRIEDA: 104.

6 SETTON: IV, 994. WANDRUSZKA.

7 ASF, MP, 4901, 'Instruttione al Cavaliere de Nobili sopra 'l negozio delle galere' (17 March 1569). Ibid, (Crown Prince Francesco de' Medici to Leonardo de' Nobili in Madrid, 14 August 1570).

8 AGLIETTI: 88, 90–1.

9 SERRANO (1914): IV, 175–85.

10 GATTO: 45. ASV, Annali, 1571, f. 460r (25 January 1571).

11 SERENO: 124. CONTARINI: 22r.

12 ASV, SM, I reg. 39, f. 256r.

13 TENENTI (1972).

14 BNMV, cl. VII, 391, f. 116r (Report by Marcantonio Barbaro to Venice, 8 January 1571).

15 ASV, CX, Secreta, reg. 9, f. 144v (7 March 1571). ASV, SD, Costantinopoli, reg. 4, c. 27rv (4 March 1571). STELLA (1972): 456–7.

16 BNMV, cl. VII, 391, c. 136v (Giacomo Ragazzoni to the Venetian Senate, 7 May 1571).

17 QUARTI: 406–11.

18 ASV, SS, Deliberazioni, Costantinopoli, 1569–75, I. f. 29.

19 KAMEN: 134–5.

20 PIOT, POULLETT: IV, 50–1. CAETANI, DIEDO: 155–9.

21 BRUNETTI, VITALE: i, 176–7. AGS, SE, 917, n. 36 (Cardinal Granvelle to Philip II, 9 March 1571, from Rome).

22 BAZZANO: 143.

23 Quote in: GÓMEZ-CÉNTURION: 57.

24 cfr. PARKER (1998): 123.

25 BAZZANO: 143.

26 STELLA (1972): 490–1. AGS, SE, 1329, n. 34 (Diego Guzmán de Silva to Philip II, 24 April 1571, from Venice).

27 AGS, SE, 914, n. 318 (Philip II to Juan de Zuñiga, 24 September 1570, from Madrid). ASF, MP, 4901 (Cosimo I de' Medici to Leonardo de Nobili, 13 February 1571, from Pisa).

28 AGLIETTI: 106–12. The text of the *asiento* is in: ASF, MP, 2131, ins. 5.

29 SERRANO (1914): IV, 183–4.

30 GATTONI: 631. ASF, MP, 3596, n.n.f. (Piero Usimbardi to Cosimo I de' Medici, 18 May 1571).

31 SERRANO (1914): IV, 272–3. QUARTI: 423–5.

32 The text of the treaty was widely publicized, both in manuscript and print, and translated into many languages. The original Latin text may be found in: SERRANO: IV, 299–309.

33 *La batalla naval*: 194.

34 For this section I have relied on the accounts by: MARTINENGO; AGOSTINO DA FAMAGOSTA; GATTO; VISINONI; FOGLIETTA; plus large sections of the account by Pietro Valderio transcribed and translated by SETTON: IV, 1027–36.

35 ASV, MC, 100, f. 130r (Marcantonio Bragadin to the doge, 8 October 1570, from Famagusta).

36 AGOSTINO DA FAMAGOSTA: 20.

7. THE CUTTING EDGE

1 PANTERA: *proemio*, n.n.p.

2 See on this matter: BOTTI.

3 'R.C.' GUILMARTIN (2003): 210–14, 219. RODGERS: 232.

4 PRYOR: 210.

5 See for instance: ASF, MP, 5153, ins. 1, f. 126rv (Grand Duke Ferdinando I de' Medici to Don Giovanni de' Medici, 16 August 1597).

6 ASF, *Guidi*, 97, n.n.f. (Cammillo Guidi to Grand Duke Cosimo III de' Medici, beginning of March 1703).

7 ASV, CR, 57 'Arsenale', n.n.f. (Report by Andrea Morosini, 12 March 1628).

8 ASF, *MP*, 2131, part I, n.n.f. (Inventory of the Florentine galleys, 20 May 1558). FODOR (2000a): 186. *ASF*, MP, 2426, n.n.f. (Vincenzo Graffigna to Domenico Pandolfini, 13 November 1650, from Pisa). ÇIZAKÇA: 777. Cfr LANE: 264.

9 GUILMARTIN (2003): 231.

10 ALBERI (1844**b**): 335–8. ALBERI (1855): 152–3, 191–4. ASV, *CR*, 57, *Arsenale* (Report by Andrea Querini, 1580). GOODMAN: 112.

11 ASV, *CX*, *Parti Comuni*, reg. 27, f. 165v (11 January 1566); reg. 31, f. 95v (30 December 1573). ADP, 76/21, int. 2 'Inventarii delle due galere di S. Altezza Santa Caterina e Santa Margherita, fatto alla fine di febraro 1588'. cfr VIOLA: 4. Cfr. also ASV, SCMN, 13, 'Scritture diverse di Giulio Savorgnan', ff. 16v–17v (13 January 1588).

12 ADP, 70/25, int. 9 bis 'Inventari delle galere' (1582).

13 ASG, *NA*, 3150 (Notary Domenico Tinello, deed of 23 April 1575).

14 COLOMBINA: 470–3. SARDI.

15 MORIN (2004): 74. HALL: 85–7. RUSCELLI: 215.

16 MORIN (2004): 71–2. OLESA MUÑIDO: 318–21.

17 PANTERA: 87.

18 ÁGOSTON (2005): 53, Table 2.3. ALBERI (1844**b**): 100. BELHAMISSI: 59. AGS, *SE*, *Napoles*, 1049, n. 175, in: CONIGLIO: II, 363–70.

19 ASV, *CX*, *Parti Comuni*, reg. 30, f. 156v (28 November 1572). ASV, *SDM*, 689, n.n.f. (20 January 1690). ASV, *CX*, *Parti Comuni*, 122, n.n.f. (25 February 1574).

20 ÁGOSTON: 187.

21 ASV, *SM*, 95, n.n.f. (26 May 1587).

22 BNCF, *Magliabechiano*, cl. XIX, 12, *Armar d'una galea sottile, di Giovanni Brandimarte Franconi Fiorentino*, f. 14v.

23 HUGHES: 36. MORIN (2004): 73.

24 GIOVIO: II, 55.

25 PEDROSA: 331. PANTERA: 90.

26 See for example: ASF, *SSF*, *Fortezze Loronesi* 1928, ins. 38, n. 58, n.n.f. (Michele Grifoni to Alessandro Nomi, 1 April 1643).

27 ASV, *SM*, 226, n.n.f. (Petition of Antonio Surian's son to the Senate, 20 August 1616).

28 ASF, MP, 238, f. 67v (Cosimo I de' Medici to Bartolomeo Concini, 27 February 1572). Many thanks to Dr Maurizio Arfaioli for this document.

29 ASV, *SDM*, reg. 39, f. 180r (April 1570).

30 ASV, *ScMN*, 18 bis, n.n.f. (1570).

31 Unless otherwise indicated, for this section I have relied on Luca Lo Basso's excellent study on galley oarsmen. See: LO BASSO.

32 ALBERI (1844**b**): 100.

33 IMBER (1996**a**): 53–4.

34 ASF, *MP*, 2084, part 1, n.n.f. (Admiral Lodovico da Verrazzano to First Secretary Andrea Cioli, 29 June 1630, from Livorno).

35 ADP, 70/25, int. 24 'Notta de le chiusme che vi sono datte per la rassegna delle undice galere dell'Ill.mo Sig. Giovanni Andrea . . .' (no date, but early 1560s).

36 DORIA: 19, 185.

37 ASF, *MP*, 2077 f. 396r.

38 MAFRICI: 196–8.

39 ASF, *MP*, 627, ff. 25, 36, 56 (Inventory of the Florentine galleys, April–May 1555).

40 ALBERI (1855): 192.

41 FONTENAY. DAVIS.

42 IMBER (1996**a**): 54. SOCSS: 242. Cfr. Table 5.

43 ASV, *MdM*, 707 'Carattade diverse de galeotti fatte in diversi tempi . . .' Census of 1545. Again many thanks to Luca Lo Basso for this document.

44 IMBER (1996**a**): 52–3. ALBERI (1855): 152.

45 DA CANAL.

46 ASF, MP, 627, ff. 25v–62r (April–May 1555).

47 ASF, MP, 638, f. 199rv (Cosimo I de' Medici to Pier Francesco del Riccio, 3 March 1548).

48 FRATTARELLY FISCHER. FRIEDMAN.

49 HAEDO (1612): 42.

50 ASF, *MP*, 2426, n.n.f. (Giuseppe Orsati to Secretary Domenico Pandolfini, 2 August 1645, from Livorno). CANAVAGGIO: 77–97. DAVIS: 129. ASF, *MP*, 211, f. 110rv (Cosimo I de' Medici to Piero Machiavelli, 29 May 1561).

51 ASF, MP, 695, f. 264r (Cara Assam Reis of Istanbul to Francesco I de' Medici, 9 September 1576, from Algiers).

52 BOSIO: III, 213.

53 ASF, GCS, 128, ins. 1 (Luigi della Stufa to Agnolo della Stufa, 5 February 1569, from Rome); Ibid (Luigi della Stufa to Lena Strozzi-della Stufa, 10 July 1571, from Rome).

54 ASF, Urbino, Iᵃ, X, n. 6/22, 'Vita di Francesco Maria 2° da Montefeltro della Rovere, Duca Sesto et ultimo di Urbino, signore di Pesaro', ff. 625r–627v.

55 ASF, MP, 3596, n.n.f. (Piero Usimbardi to Cosimo I de' Medici, 1 April 1570, from Rome).

56 CASTANI, DIEDO: 11. BRUNELLI: 39. DE CARO.

57 TESTA: 126. DAL POZZO: I, 11.

58 TESTA: 46–8, 63. VIANELLO.

59 SOUCECK.

60 SAGREDO: 396.

61 ADAMI: 333. BNCF, Passerini, 47: 'Antinori', 97–101. SOCSS: 269–73.

62 CANAVAGGIO: 14–53.

63 MEREDITH-OWENS: 456–61.

64 PASERO: 35–44.

65 LO BASSO: 357–8. MONGA: 107.

66 GUILMARTIN (2003): 264 note 6.

67 HALE (1983): 312–13.

68 ASF, MP, 2355, Capitoli della Nuova Militia Marittima. Nuovamente Stabilita da Sua Altezza Serenissima, Firenze 1586, ff. 305r and 306v. FERRETTI: II, 69. GUILMARTIN (2003): 145. IMBER (1996a): 46–50. IMBER (2002): 303–4. ÁGOSTON: 53.

69 CAETANI, DIEDO: 83–8. CODOIN: III, 8–10. ERCAN: 3. HALE (1990): 44, 154.

70 SOCSS: 242. ADP, 76/21, int. 2, 'Inventarii delle due galere di S. Altezza Santa Caterina e Santa Margherita' (1588). ASG, NA, 3150 (Notary Domenico Tinello, deed of 23 April 1575). CN, XII, 83, f. 311v. cfr. PARKER (1990): 274–6.

71 GUILMARTIN (2003): 160–1. PARKER (1996): 19–20.

72 ALBERI (1841): 131–2.

73 ÁGOSTON (2005): 57–8. GUILMARTIN (2003): 161–4. BNCF, *Magliabechiano*, cl. XIX, 12, *Armar d'una galea sottile*, f. 11r.

74 STANLEY: 350–2. OLESA MUÑIDO: 793.

75 FODOR (2002**a**): 174. MURPHEY: 93–100.

76 ASF, *MM*, 264, ins. 29, 'Ristretto delle Entrate Ordinarie e Straordinarie di S.A. Ser.ma, si come di tutte le Uscite Calculate dall'anno 1625 a tutto l'anno 1650', nn.ff. PARKER, THOMPSON: 15–16.

77 ASF, *MP*, 1802, part. 2, 'Instrutione delle parti si danno al Generale, Commissario, Capitani, e tutti li altri offitiali di Galera, e in che consistono' [1601], n.n.f.

78 ALBERI (1841): 134. BNCF, *Rossi-Cassigoli*, 199: ff. 132–45. ASF, *mp*, 49, f. 102r (note dated 16 June 1558). GUILMARTIN (1993): 121–2.

79 ADP, 79/37, int. 1, 'Copia della relazione delle vettovaglie che furono date alle galere del sig. Giovanni Andrea Doria il 1571, 1572' (16 June 1573), n.n.f. BNCF, *Magliabechiano*, cl. XIX, 12, *Armar d'una galea sottile:* f. 9v. LO BASSO: 126. ASF, MP, 2131 (Register dated 1572 on galley provisions), c. 44r. ADP, 22/40, int. 7 (Paolo de Guirardi to Giovanni Andrea Doria, 18 March 1571, from Palermo).

80 BNCF, *Magliabechiano*, cl. XIX, 12, *Armar d'una galea sottile:* f. 17v.

8. BRAGADIN'S HIDE

1 CAETANI, DIEDO: 86–95. SERENO: 115–18. MOLMENTI (1899): 80–1, 353–5.

2 MOLMENTI (1899): 1–30.

3 STELLA (1964): 49–50.

4 ASV, *Secreta, Archivi Propri Contarini*, reg. 25. ff. 3v–4r.

5 Venier's report to the Senate (29 December 1572), in: MOLMENTI (1899): 295–9.

6 cfr. SETTON: 1019–22.

7 SERRANO (1914): IV, 429–30. VANDERHAMMEN: 42–4.

8 BAZZANO: 148.

9 Don Juan of Austria to Ruy Gómez de Silva (8 July 1571), and Philip II (12 July 1571), in STIRLING-MAXWELL: II, 376–83.

10 FERNÁNDEZ-ARMESTO: 1–4. ADP, 22/40, int. 7 (The Marchioness of Pescara to Giovanni Andrea Doria, 30 July 1571 from Palermo). ADP, 22/40, int. 7, (The Count of Landriano to Giovanni Andrea Doria, 3 August 1571, from Palermo). *Batalla Naval*: 120. CAETANI, DIEDO: 116.

11 AGLIETTI: 114–23. See also: PANICUCCI.

12 ASF, *Urbino*, Iª, 112, f. 199rv (Francesco Maria della Rovere to the duke of Urbino, 27 August 1571, from Messina).

13 Venier's report in: MOLMENTI (1899): 207. *Batalla naval*: 121. CAETANI, DIEDO: 120.

14 CODOIN: III: 8–10, 11–15.

15 BAZZANO: 144–6, 152, 381 note 120. Marcantonio Colonna to Francisco Borja, 4 September 1571, from Messina, in: GUGLIELMOTTI: 180.

16 INALCIK (1974): 187–9. QUARTI: 446.

17 SERENO: 126. CONTARINI: 29r. PARUTA: 103.

18 SERENO: 128. LESURE: 81–2. INALCIK (1974): 187–8. SELÂNIKÎ: 81.

19 STELLA (1977): 72–3.

20 For this section I have relied mainly on: GATTO: BNMV, MS. It. VIII, 399 ff 236r – 240r. 94–101. AGOSTINO DA FAMAGOSTA: 24–8. MARTINENGO. VISINONI: 35–42. *Il crudelissimo assedio*. TOMITANO. CONTARINI: 30r–31r. SETTON: IV, 1030–43.

21 PEÇEVÎ: I: 490–1. CONTI: 131.

22 ASV, *Annali*, 1571, f. 204r.

23 PEDANI (2003): 295.

24 AGOSTINO DA FAMAGOSTA: 25–6.

25 Cfr. IMBER (1996c): 220.

26 BNMV, MS. It, VII, 391 f. 426r. (Marcantonio Barbaro to the doge of Venice, 27 March 1573).

27 GATTO: 54–7.

28 PARUTA: 260–1.

29 CODOIN: III, 15–18, 21–6.

30 CAETANI, DIEDO: 125. COSTO: 24. SEGRE: 134.

31 ASV, *Annali*, 1571, ff. 196v–197v (Dispatch from Messina, 13 September 1571).

32 Don Luis de Requesens to Pedro Fajardo, 28 December 1571, in: MARCH: 19–21.

33 VENTURINI: II, 130–2.

34 SERENO: 190. STIRLING-MAXWELL: 383.

35 QUARTI: 490.

36 VARGAS-HIDALGO (2002): 768.

37 CONFORTI: 40. CARACCIOLO: 18. SALIMEI: 51. *L'Ordine che ha tenuto l'armata*: ff. 1r–3v. ADP, 79/53, int. 5A, 'Particolare relazione del viaggio e della vittoria dell'armate della Lega contro gl'Infedeli', ff. 1–2.

38 Numbers deduced from various sources, including: CODOIN: 26–7, III, 203–15. ADP, 79/53, int. 5A, 'Particolare relazione', f. 1. CARACCIOLO: 24. SALIMEI: passim.

39 CAETANI, DIEDO: 210. GUILMARTIN: 255. MANUELE: 46.

40 CALANDRIA.

41 GUILMARTIN: 256. SALIMEI: 89. ALBERI (1841): 131. MANUELE: 52.

42 *L'Ordine che ha tenuto l'armata*: ff. 1r–3v. *Ordine che si debbe tenere*: f. 5r. ADP, 79/53, int. 5A, 'Particolare relazione', f. 2. SETTON: IV, 1047–8, note 16. CONTARINI: 37r–39r. SEGRE: 136.

43 Don Juan of Austria to Don Garcia de Toledo, 16 September 1571, in: CODOIN: III, 27.

44 MONGA: 110. QUARTI: 497–8.

45 IPSIRLI: 471.

46 ASV, *Annali*, 1571, f. 216r, (Sebastiano Venier to the senate, 29 September 1571). Venier's report in: MOLMENTI (1899): 307.

47 ASV, *Annali*, 1571, f. 219r, (Sebastiano Venier to the Senate, 3 October 1571). TORRES Y AGUILERA: 64r. CARACCIOLO: 25. Venier's report in: MOLMENTI (1899): 308–10. CAETANI, DIEDO: 130–1, 184. VANDERHAMMEN: 173. ROSELL: 92.

48 ADP, 79/53, int. 5A, 'Particolare relazione', f. 3. CONTARINI: 40r. ROSELL: 93. TORRES Y AGUILERA: 63rv.

49 Venier's report in: MOLMENTI: ASV, *Annali*, 1571, f. 221v (Sebastiano Venier to the doge, 5 October 1571). *Il Successo della nauale vittoria christiana*: f. 1. CAETANI, DIEDO: 192–3.

50 ADP, 79/53, int. 5A, 'Particolare relazione', f. 3. ASF, *Urbino*, C, ff. 1525r–1526r, 'Per lettere d'Anibal Protetico da Corfù, li 3 di ottobre 1571'.

51 INALCIK (1974): 188. LESURE: 80–1.

52 CERVANTES (1984).

53 There are many versions of what happened during the meeting, but, with the exception of Uluç Ali's position, they differ only in detail. My reconstruction is based on: *Intiero e minuto ragguaglio*: ff. 1–2. CAETANI, DIEDO: 184–92. SERENO: 170–82. TORRES Y AGUILERA: 55r–62r. ADP, 79/53, int. 5A, 'Particolare relazione', ff. 3–4. HERRERA: 30–1. SAGREDO: 396. CARACCIOLO: 31. CONTI: 138v–141v. KATIB ÇELEBI (1911): 93. PEÇEVÎ: 496. SELÂNIKÎ: 82.

54 DANIŞMEND (1948): 402–20. LESURE: 64–5.

55 ALBERI (1844a): 299.

56 PEÇEVI: I, 443. UZUNÇARSILI (1995): 182.

57 CONTARINI: 44r. KATIB ÇELEBI (1911): 93. Cfr. SELÂNIKÎ: I, 82.

58 *Del successo dell'armata*: f. 4.

9. THE 7TH OF OCTOBER

1 SERENO: 188. *Il successo della navale vittoria*, n.n.f.

2 EDGERTON, THROCKMORTON, YALOURIS. MORIN (1985): 210. PIERSON: 13–14. CONTARINI: 50r.

3 See for example: CARRERO BLANCO.

4 BRÂNTOME: II, 112–13.

5 CONTARINI: 48v–49r.

6 PRESCOTT: I, 622. HERRERA: 30. COLLADO, f. 50. APARICI: 98, note 38. PANTERA: 71.

7 ADP, 79/53, int. 5A, 'Particolare relazione', f. 4.

8 CAETANI, DIEDO: 133. SERENO: 192. *Ordine che si debbe tenere*: f. 5r. CARACCIOLO: 37.

9 JURIEN DE LA GRAVIÈRE: II, 150–210 VEROGGIO. GUILMARTIN (2003): 258.

10 ADP, 79/53, int. 5A, 'Particolare relazione', f. 4. *Copia d'una lettera*: f. 2. FOGLIETTA: 349, 361. *Del successo dell'armata*: f. 2. ADRIANI: 884. CAETANI, DIEDO: 133. ASV, MC, 670, 'Relazione Particolare delli successi dell'armata cristiana dell'anno 1571', f. 97. ORESTE (1962): 228.

CONTARINI: 51r. LESCAUT DE ROMEGAS: f. 2r. SERENO: 193. RBM, EBG, II/2211, n. 56 (Nicolás Augusto de Benavides to Lope de Acuña, from Portofigo, 10 October 1571). BNMV, *Ms. It.*, cl. VII 2582, f. 25r. *Discorso sopra due grandi battaglie navali*: 30. APARICI: 31. CODOIN: III, 242. *Batalla naval*: 190.

11 *Avvisi Particulari*: f. 1. CARACCIOLO: 33. SAVORGNANO: 221. HERRERA: 31.

12 CARACCIOLO: 36–7. GUILMARTIN (2003): 163.

13 CONTARINI: 40r–44r, 49r. *Ordine che si debbe tenere*: f. 6r. SORANZO: 12. GUGLIELMOTTI: 211–12.

14 CONTARINI: 52r.

15 PANTERA: 355.

16 SORANZO: 14. *Ragguaglio particolare*, n.n.f. ROSELL: 101. MONGA: 115.

17 *Intiero, e minuto ragguaglio*: f. IV. CARACCIOLO: 33. FIGUEROA: f. 2v.

18 PEÇEVÎ: 497. FOGLIETTA: 357.

19 CONTARINI: 37r–40r. FOGLIETTA: 347–8. CONTI: 144. *Ordine che si debbe tenere*: f. 6v.

20 GUILMARTIN (2003): 87.

21 *L'Ordine che ha tenuto l'armata*: ff. 1r–4r. *Ordine che si debbe tenere*: ff. 1r–4v. CONTARINI: 37r–40r. ASTr, TT, 264, n. 1 (Anonymous report about the Ottoman navy; no date, but beginning of the seventeenth century. Again; many thanks to Luca Lo Basso for this document.) n.n.f.

22 SALIMEI: 57–63. ERCAN: 7.

23 CODOIN: III, 203–15, 250. *Del successo dell'armata*: 4. CAETANI, DIEDO: 126. SAVORGNANO: 220. FOGLIETTA: 357. Cfr. PARKER (1996): 50–1.

24 FIRPO: 622. *Ordine che si debbe tenere*: f. 6r.

25 CONTARINI: 49v. CARACCIOLO: 33. *Il successo della navale vittoria*, n.n.f.

26 CAETANI, DIEDO: 202–3.

27 CARACCIOLO: 36. CODOIN: III, 270–2.

28 Since any description of the battle requires an endnote for practically every other phrase, I have limited notations to quotes, or when discussing specific points. Among the many sources used to reconstruct the event, see in particular: ADP, 69/32, ff. 146r–147r (Giovanni Andrea Doria to Stefano di Mare, 13 November 1571, from Naples). ADP, 79/53, int. 5A, 'Particolare relazione', ff. 4–6. ASF, *Manoscritti*,

127 'Settimanni, vol. III', ff. 541r–550v. ASF, CS Iᵃ, 137, ff. 138r–140r
(Fra Luigi Mazzinghi to Fra Emilio Pucci, from Messina, 15 November 1571). ASF, CS Iᵃ, 145, 'Imprese delle galere', f. 11r. ASF, CS Iᵃ, 254,
ff. 129r–130r (letter of 29 November 1571). ASF, *Urbino*, Iᵃ, 112, f. 110r
(Francesco Maria della Rovere to the duke of Urbino, 8 October
1571, from the Curzolaris). ASV, *ANNALI*, 1571: ff. 224r–228v. ASV,
MC, 670. BAV, *Barb. Lat.* 5367, f. 108r. *Relazione dell'Ucciali.al Gran
Turco della rotta della sua armata l'anno 1571*. RBM, EBG, II/2211, n. 56
(Nicolás Augusto de Benavides to Lope de Acuña, 10 October 1571).
AMMIRATO: XI, 329–36. ANTINORI: IV–2v. *Ritratto d'una lettera*: ff.
1r–2v. CARACCIOLO: 38–43. CONTARINI: 49r–54v. FOGLIETTA: 352. F.
HERRERA: 350–82. ILLESCAS: 353r–355r. KATIB ÇELEBI: 94. LÓPEZ DE
TORO: 18–20. ORESTE (1962): 227–33. PEÇEVÎ: 495–9. SAGREDO:
396–401. SELÂNIKÎ: 84. SERENO: 194–216.

29 ASV, CX, *Parti comuni*, 138, n.n.f. (Testimony of Paolo Orsini, 20
November 1579).

30 *Discorso su due grandi battaglie*: 40. *La batalla naval*: 180.

31 SAGREDO: 397.

32 FOGLIETTA: 353.

33 CONTARINI: 51v.

34 CAETANI, DIEDO: 205.

35 CERVANTES (1980): f. 5v.

36 CONTARINI: 52r.

37 TESTA: 140, note 21.

38 FOGLIETTA: 361.

39 CARACCIOLO: 39. ASF, CS Iᵃ, 145, 'Imprese delle galere', f. 11r.

40 Venier's report in: MOLMENTI (1899): 311–12.

41 *Ordine che si debbe tenere*: f. 6r.

42 MARCH: 52–3.

43 Provana's report in: SALVO: 78.

44 CAETANI, DIEDO: 135.

45 VANDERHAMMER: 181. SERENO: 199. CARACCIOLO: 38.

46 Spinola's report in: SPINOLA 7.

47 CARACCIOLO: 38.

48 FOGLIETTA: 355.

49 CONTI: 150v. CAETANI, DIEDO: 210.

50 cfr. ASF, *CS* I^a, 137, f. 139r (Fra Luigi Mazzinghi to Fra Emilio Pucci). DAL POZZO: I, 25–7. SAVORGNANO: 222. CAETANI, DIEDO: 210–11. CONTARINI: 51v. cfr. LESURE: 139.

51 FERNANDEZ DURO: 184.

52 *Ritratto d'una lettera*: f. 2r.

53 Venier's report in: MOLMENTI (1899): 313–14.

54 DAL POZZO: I, 26. ASF, *CS* I^a, 137, f. 139r (Fra Luigi Mazzinghi to Fra Emilio Pucci). SAFVET: 561, doc. III. KATIB ÇELEBI (1911): 43r.

55 ADP, 79/53, int. 51, 'Morti et fuggiti nelle galere di Gio. Andrea d'Oria al di 7 Ottobre 1571', n.n.f. ADP, 69/32, f. 146v.

56 CAETANI, DIEDO: 212. SERENO: 214.

57 CONTARINI: 52v. CAETANI, DIEDO: 136. Venier's report, in MOLMENTI (1899): 314. SERENO: 216. CARACCIOLO: 44. TORRES Y AGUILERA: 76v. BMrF, 269, *Priorista della città di Firenze a Tratte*, 'Rotta del Turco nel Golfo di Lepanto', f. 367v.

58 CARACCIOLO,: 45.

10. THE PHOENIX'S ASHES

1 SERENO: 216–20. CARACCIOLO: 47–51. ADP, 69/32, ff. 138r–139r (Giovanni Andrea Doria to unidentified recipient ['Molto Maggior Signore'], 28 October 1571, from Levkás).

2 CONTARINI: 55rv. CODOIN: III, 227–30. GUILMARTIN (2003): 245. ASV, cx, *Parti Comuni*, 122, n.n.f. (25 February 1575). SERRANO (1914): 684–5. AGS, *SE*, 1501, n. 201 (Decree by Don Juan of Austria, 15 October 1571). Venier's report in: MOLMENTI (1899): 316–17. ADRIANI: 887.

3 CARACCIOLO: 39, 52, 56. MEREDITH-OWENS: 462. *L'ordine che ha tenuto l'armata*: f. 4v.

4 CONTARINI: 55r. QUARTI: 725. *Copia d'una lettera*: f. 2r. AGS, *SE*, 1135, n. 70, n.n.f (Juan de Cardona to Philip II, 8 October 1571, from Petalas). ADP, 79/53, int. 51 'Morti et fuggiti nelle galere di Gio. Andrea d'Oria', n.n.f. Spinola's report in: SPINOLA: 8.

5 ADP, 70/25, int. 13 n.n.f. (List of Spanish officers, sergeants and

gentlemen killed and wounded). APARICI: 27. GUARNIERI (1965): 193–6. DAL POZZO: I, 26. CONTARINI: 55r. ASV, *ST*, 237, n.n.f. (Petition by Girolamo d'Adorno to the senate, 12 November 1577). QUARTI: 726. SERENO: 217. *La batalla naval*: 194.

6 AGS, *SE*, 1501, n. 201 (Decree by Don Juan of Austria, 15 October 1571). ASV, *SS*, reg. 78, f. 51v (The senate to Sebastiano Venier, 29 December 1571). Da Canal's report in: PRASCA: 128. Venier's report in: MOLMENTI (1899): 316–17. MONGA: 118. ADP, 79/53, int. 51 'Morti et fuggiti nelle galere di Gio. Andrea d'Oria', n.n.f.

7 SERENO: 220–4. Venier's report in: MOLMENTI: 315–18. CODOIN: III, 230–5. BRUNETTI, VITALI: I, 360. TORRES Y AGUILERA: 78rv.

8 BENEDETTI.

9 STELLA (1977): 121. SETTON: IV, 1062–4. SERRANO (1914): IV, 493. ASCF, *MANOSCRITTI*, 127 'SETTIMANNI, VOL. III' F. 550V. CAETANI, DIEDO: 223. CARACCIOLO: 54.

10 BRUNETTI, VITALI: I, 372–5. ROSELL: 208–10. MULCAHY.

11 BAZZANO: 158–61. ALBERTONI. TASSOLO. ROSELL: 208–10.

12 SELÂNIKÎ: 84.

13 ASF, *Urbino*, Iª, 217, f. 935rv (Don Cesare Carafa to the duke of Urbino, 19 November 1571, from Venice).

14 CANTEMIR: 224. KORAN: II, 216. SELÂNIKÎ: 88–90. FOGLIETTA: 384–5.

15 *L'ordine che ha tenuto l'armata*: f. 4v. BRÂNTOME: 59. BOA, *MD*, 16: 316, n. 559 (Order to the *kapudan paşa*, 29 October 1571). FOGLIETTA: 384–5. INALCIK (1974): 192. TESTA: 132. BOA, *MD*, 16: 323, n. 568 (Order to Pertev Pasha, 28 October 1571).

16 CANTEMIR: 224, note 20.

17 Unless otherwise indicated, for this section I have relied mainly on Colin Imber's study of the reconstruction of the Ottoman fleet. See: IMBER (1996**b**).

18 SELÂNIKÎ: 84. PEDANI-FABRIS (1996): 167.

19 BOA, *MD*, 16: 75, n. 151 (Order of 24 October 1571). ALBERI (1844**a**): 421.

20 PEÇEVÎ: I, 498–9.

21 BNMV, MS. It. 391, f. 244r (Marcantonio Barbaro to the doge, 5 January 1572).

22 BAV, *Barb. Lat.* 5367, f. 108r, *Relazione dell'Ucciali*.

23 ALBERI (1855): 222. AFMC, 0002/004/534, segn. 17 'In due modi le forze
delli Principi Cristiani sono superiori a quelle del Turco' (n.d. but early
1580s). FARA: 20. ASF, *MP*, 238, ff. 67r–68r (Cosimo I de' Medici to
Bartolomeo Concini, 27 February 1572). ASF, *MP*, 1803, segn. 64, n.n.f.
'Condizioni accordate con il Comito Giorgio Condocali, Veneziano,
che partì alli 22 novembre 1631 per andare a servire S.A. Ser.ma'. ASF,
DGA, 658, n. 1097, n.n.f. (Muzio degli Agli to Ferdinando II de' Medici,
7 January 1633, from Pisa). AGS, SE, 1134, n. 150, n.n.f. (Don Juan of
Austria to Philip II, 21 November 1571, from Messina).

24 CHARRIÈRE: III, 271–3.

25 SELÂNIKÎ: 85.

26 ASV, *CX*, *Parti Secrete*, reg. 9, f. 182v (22 October 1571). ASV, *CX*, *Parti
Secrete*, 15, n.n.f. (The Council of Ten to Sebastiano Venier, 22
October 1571).

27 STELLA (1977): 123–5. CANOSA: 189, note 266. LESURE: 152. PRETO
(2004): 26.

28 Venier's report in: MOLMENTI (1899): 315–27. LESURE: 191–211.
ROSELL: 217–29. CANOSA: 188. ASV, *SS*, reg. 78, ff. 24r–25r (The senate
to Sebastiano Venier, 22 October 1571). SERRANO (1914): 656–9.

29 ADP, 69/32, f. 148r (Giovanni Andrea Doria to the prince of Melfi, 13
November 1571, from Naples). ADP, 69/32, f. 149r (Giovanni Andrea
Doria to Donna Costanza d'Avalos, 15 November 1571, from Naples).
PARUTA: 292. ROSELL: 223. VARGAS-HIDALGO (2002): xxx–xxxi.

30 AGS, *SE*, 1328, n. 62, n.n.f. (Cardinal Granvelle to Diego Guzmán de
Silva, 31 October 1571, from Naples). SETTON: IV, 1073–4.

31 FRIEDA: 246–7. MANFRONI (1893): 395–7, 402. SERRANO (1918): I,
294–300, 363–70. DORIA PAMPHILI: 27. LESURE: 226–7. CHARRIÈRE: III,
287–9, 363. GUARNIERI (1960): 296–7. DONÀ: II, 473–6, 500–13.

32 BAZZANO: 163–8. AGS, *SE*, 1505, n. 102, n.n.f. (Don Juan of Austria to
Philip II, 6 July 1571, from Messina). GUARNIERI: 297–8. AGS, *SE*, 1331,
n. 77, n.n.f. (Diego Guzmán de Silva to Philip II, 14 July 1572, from
Venice).

33 CODOIN: XI, 372–7. SERRANO (1918): II, 35–46. SERENO: 285–91.
LONGO: 35–40. MANFRONI (1893): 427–32.

34 SERRANO (1918): II, 47–60. SERENO: 291–327. AGS, *SE*, 1138, n. 183 (Marcantonio Colonna to Philip II, 18 August 1572).

35 IMBER (1996**b**): 85. FRIEDA: 246–75. INALCIK, QUATAERT: 94.

36 CHARRIÈRE: III, 175–9. AGS, *SE*, 1329, n. 94, n.n.f. (Diego Guzmán de Silva to Philip II, 15 September 1572, from Venice). AGS, *SE*, 1332, n. 6, n.n.f. (Diego Guzmán de Silva to Philip II, 2 January 1573, from Venice). ASV, CX, *Parti Secrete*, 16, n.n.ff. (The Council of Ten to Marcantonio Barbaro, 6 June 1572; 22 August 1572). TENENTI: 405–7. STELLA (1977): 225–7, 318–19, 329–30, 369–75.

37 BNMV, MS. It. VII, 391, f. 261r. CHARRIÈRE: III, 261 and note, 286–7.

38 BNMV, MS. It. VII, 391, ff. 372r–417r. SETTON: 1091. ROSI (1901): 29–32.

39 SETTON: 1092–3.

40 DONÀ: II, 677–80. GARCÍA HERNÁN, GARCÍA HERNÁN: 81–155. SERRANO (1918): II, 413–14.

41 FLORIANI. BRAUDEL: 1143–85.

42 SERENO: 213–14.

43 PETRIE: 260–329.

44 BAZZANO: 182–333.

45 MOLMENTI (1899): 221–59. MOLMENTI (1915).

46 SAVELLI: 371–5. VARGAS-HIDALGO (2002): XXXI–XXXIV.

47 cfr. IBÁÑEZ DE IBERO.

48 PEDANI-FABRIS (1996): 197–8. SOUCEK: 811.

49 BABINGER (1993**a**): 296. LESURE: 182. BNMV, MS. It. VII, 391, ff. 233v–234r. LE TOURNEAU, ORHANLU: 252. HESS (1972): 65.

50 AGS, *SE*, 1483, n. 167, n.n.f (Duke of Urbino to Philip II, 28 May 1572). ASF, *Urbino*, Iª, X, n. 6/22 'Vita di Francesco Maria 2° da Montefeltro della Rovere, Duca Sesto et ultimo di Urbino, signore di Pesaro'. PIERACCINI: 453–4, 459–70.

51 BRUNELLI: 42–3. CAETANI, DIEDO: 70.

52 BNCF, *Passerini*, 47: 'Antinori', 101. PIERACCINI: 163–87. LITTA: tav. XXIX.

53 AFMC, 0001/001/053 (Letter patent to Pompeo Floriani as sergeant major general, 25 August 1574). ADAMI: 335–6. GULLINO (1993): 31–2. SCICHILONE: 794–5. IMBER (1996**a**): 39–40.

54 ROSELL: 237–9. ROSI (1897). ROSI (1901). DE PELLEGRINI. ASV, SDM, reg. 69, f. 88rv (7 June 1610).

EPILOGUE

1 BRAUDEL: 1088.
2 ALBERI (1840a): 429. N[iccolò] CAPPONI (2004).
3 EICKHOFF.
4 SHAW. ARTAN, BERTKAY.

BIBLIOGRAPHICAL NOTE

~

Much has been written on the battle of the Curzolaris, and tackling the various sources can be risky without adequate historiographical skills. Indeed, in this particular case the well-known quote attributed to the Duke of Wellington about the impossibility of accurately describing battles and balls, rings as somewhat of an understatement. The encounter of 7 October 1571 was fought on a front of nearly ten kilometres, the main clash lasting roughly ninety minutes with the two opposing fleets engulfed in smoke. Thus, witnesses had a limited vision of what was happening, and for this reason the letters and reports written immediately after the battle provide few details. Yet all those present immediately understood the importance of the event and within a few weeks detailed descriptions of the battle were circulating in print or as manuscripts. Unfortunately, the political or personal bias of some of these accounts means that they have to be taken with more than a grain of salt. Even the battle's name was not immune from distortion, the original 'Curzolaris' being quickly replaced by 'Lepanto' (forty miles to the east), possibly giving the impression that the allied fleet had penetrated deeper into Ottoman waters than in reality.

Amongst the earliest printed reports the most complete is by Girolamo Diedo, written a couple of months after the battle and based on the recollections of survivors on both sides. The *Discorso sopra due grandi e memorabili battaglie navali*, published a little later, is less comprehensive but also relies on eyewitnesses' testimony. The account by Giovanni Andrea Doria's secretary provides some interesting details, one suspects to justify his master's behaviour. Doria, trying to counter Marco Antonio Colonna's accusations, prepared his own version of the 1571 campaign, apparently it never went to print. It is preserved in the Doria-Pamphilij archive in Rome, catalogued under *scaffale* 79/53, int. 5A. Giacomo Contarini published in 1572 a detailed description of the previous year's military operations against the Ottomans, a fountain of information from which many would drink. In the years following the Curzolaris a number of the participants divulged their own accounts of the event, including Ferrante Caracciolo, Fernando de Herrera and, in an original manner, Miguel de Cervantes. The war of 1570–3 found its place in general histories of the time, the various authors usually emphasizing aspects relevant to their country. For instance, Uberto Foglietta's work has a strong Genoese slant, whilst Giovan Battista Adriani exalts Florence's role. Pro-Venetian, but nonetheless an excellent piece of historiography, is Paolo Paruta's *Storia della guerra di Cipro*, the author having access to the official documentation of the Venetian Republic. Natale Conti's *Istorie* is valuable not just for the details it includes, but also for the author's understanding of the military/political situation of the time. Several other histories of the Cyprus War still remain in manuscript form, a number being preserved in the Biblioteca Nazionale Marciana in Venice.

From the Ottoman side information is scant and sketchy, the Porte being unwilling to remember a defeat. Still, the works of Kâtib Çelebi, Peçevî Ibrahim Efendi, Selânikî Mustafa Efendi and Dimitri Cantemir provide some useful information. Unfortunately, most of these sources are not available in a western language. There is an early Italian edition of Kâtib Çelebi's historical chronology, whilst James Mitchell translated the first four chapters of his *Thufat al-Kibar fi Asfar ad-Bhihar* into English under the title *The History of the Maritime Wars of the Turks* (London, 1831). Mitchell's version stops in 1560, but is useful for an overall picture of Ottoman naval organization before the Cyprus War. Some time after the Curzolaris Western chanceries managed to obtain Uluç Ali's alleged report on the battle, and more Ottoman documents ended up in Venetian hands. It is quite possible that writings like Seyyd Murad's biography of Hayreddin Barbarossa may still be gathering dust in some unknown repository. One may hope that in the future more translations of Ottoman sources will be available in print.

The advent of Romanticism in the nineteenth century, often coupled with a growing national sentiment across Europe, produced a renewed historical attention to the struggle between East and West. From the 1840s onwards the Cyprus War became a hot topic amongst historians, greatly aided by the steady publication of archival documents. Unfortunately, the prevailing nationalistic feeling pervading the Western world caused historians to focus on their fellow countrymen's role, conversely undermining everyone else's. Instead of treating original sources as elements of a complex jigsaw puzzle, most writers used them as one employs letters in a game of scrabble.

This was not apparent initially. In 1853 Cayetano Rossell published *Historia del combate naval de Lepanto*, the first comprehensive monograph on the Curzolaris and perhaps the most balanced account of the battle itself. The author relied heavily on primary sources, not just Spanish ones, and although understandably partial to Philip II's subjects tried to give everyone his due. Sadly, mainly thanks to Italian historians, this example was not followed. In 1862 father Alberto Guglielmotti published his *Marcantonio Colonna alla battaglia di Lepanto*, which over the years went through a number of reprints. Guglielmotti's work on Colonna was an integral part of his history of the papal navy. A Dominican friar living in a time when the papacy was politically and culturally under constant attack from the most nationalistic elements of Italian society, Guglielmotti, by an extensive – if somewhat arbitrary – use of archival sources, argued instead that without Rome's commitment and Colonna's ability Italy would have been lost to the Ottomans. In order to do this he purposely diminished everyone else's contribution to the League's victory, with the notable exclusion of the Venetians, given their general good relationship with Colonna. The villain of the piece was, of course, Giovanni Andrea Doria (the Spanish, Doria's employers, getting a respectable second place), whom Guglielmotti squarely accused of cowardice and treachery for his behaviour at the Curzolaris.

The popularity of Guglielmotti's work ignited a heated row between Doria's detractors and supporters. Prominent amongst the latter was Benedetto Veroggio, a retired Genoese army officer, whose *Giannandrea Doria alla battaglia di Lepanto* was little less than Guglielmotti's argument turned on its head. For Veroggio the Christian victory could only be attributed to Doria and, to an extent, the Spanish. Belittling Colonna and the Venetians' contribution, he also created the myth that the two galleasses allotted to Doria never reached their battle stations. Veroggio was a polemicist not a historian, and as a result his book is of little worth. Unfortunately, its influence would have long-standing consequences, thanks to another serviceman turned historian. In 1889 Jean Pierre Edmond Jurien de la Gravière published his *La guerre de Chypre et la bataille de Lépante*, destined to become the main reference source on the Curzolaris outside Italy. Jurien de la Gravière's authority derived from being an admiral, as well as a hydrographs expert. His reconstruction of the Curzolaris was the result of this, but La Gravière wrongly assumed the coastline around the Acheloos was the same as in 1571, ignoring the extent of the silting at the river's mouth. As a result he moved the battlefield a couple of miles to the south, thus altering the structure of the fight. This, and his use of Veroggio as a *bona fide* source (evidently trusting a fellow military man), effectively marred Jurien de la Gravière's conclusions. In particular, he perpetuated the myth that the two galleasses of Doria's division did not arrive in time, ignoring all other evidence to the contrary. Despite these mistakes La Gravière's book was a solid piece of scholarship, and since it was written in French (a language which the majority of the educated classes in the West understood), his account of the Curzolaris became internationally accepted and, with a few variations, repeated to this day. Even more telling, his reconstruction of the 1571 campaign became the official version in Spain after the civil war of 1936–9. In 1948 Luis Carrero Blanco published *La victoria del Christo de Lepanto* (reissued in 1971 with the more sober title *Lepanto, 1571–1971*), to all intents and purposes La Gravière all over again, maps included, and with an even more pronounced Spanish slant. For Carrero Blanco Europe's civilization had been saved at the Curzolaris thanks to the Spanish and Don Juan de Austria, a resounding victory like the Nationalists one in the Spanish Civil War (dubbed the *cruzada*) under the leadership of Francisco Franco.

As befitted their parochial nature, few Italians bothered to publish anything equivalent to La Gravière's account, concentrating instead on publishing the exploits of particular individuals during the Cyprus War: Neapolitans, Sardinians, Sicilians, Romans, Lombards, Tuscans, and others, received their share of attention, and so did some key characters like Sebastiano Venier. Most of these studies contained useful information, and many included original documents in full. But nobody attempted to weave all this material together, until the publication in 1935 of Guido Antonio Quarti's *La guerra contro il turco in Cipro e a Lepanto*. Whilst mirroring the nationalistic psychology of its times, there is no doubt that Quarti's work was an impressive piece of research. Ploughing through libraries and archives, the author added greatly to the historical knowledge of the Cyprus War. In particular he challenged, although without mentioning him directly, La Gravière and his interpretation of the battle, but at the same time criticized Guglielmotti and gave a balanced assessment of Doria's behaviour. Quarti's main limitation was that he relied nearly exclusively on Italian primary sources, and often was careless in his footnoting. Besides, his study never circulated in sufficient numbers to make a real historiographical impact.

Following the end of the Ottoman Empire after World War I,

a few scholarly works appeared in Turkish on the 1570–3 conflict. Most of these consisted of published documents with a commentary, but only in 1973 did Halil Inalcik produce an article in English on the battle of the Curzolaris based on Ottoman documents. At the same time Michael Lesure came out with his *Lepante et la crise de l'empire ottoman*, in which Ottoman archival sources figured prominently. With the voice of the vanquished now available to Western scholars, the Ottomans' strategic and political goals became clearer. Lesure structured his book as a collection of original accounts interspaced by a commentary, which sometimes makes it difficult to follow the sequence of events. Besides, one is puzzled by the author's theory that the defeat at the Curzolaris shook the Ottoman Empire at its roots, and that the Holy League failed to exploit the situation. Colin Imber's essay *The Reconstruction of the Ottoman Fleet after the Battle of Lepanto*, also based on Ottoman documents, makes it clear instead that the Porte had little difficulty making good its material losses, something impossible to do in a situation of chaos.

Lesure added new fuel to the historical debate (as old as Voltaire) about the long-term effects of the Curzolaris' outcome. The most often repeated story dismisses the League's victory as nothing more than a psychological success – for Carrero Blanco, quoting Cervantes, it showed that the Ottomans were no longer invincible – given that the Venetians lost Cyprus while the Ottoman fleet was rebuilt within six months, and after the Western powers had incurred huge expenses. Echoes of this attitude can still be found in Andrew C. Hess's article *The Battle of Lepanto and its Place in Mediterranean History* (1972), and Geoffrey Parker's essay *Lepanto (1571): The Cost of Victory*, (1978). Turkish historians, understandably, tend to agree. However, already Fernand Braudel in his *The Mediterranean and the Mediterranean World in the Age of Philip II* had pointed out the obvious: instead of looking at the situation after the battle, one should look at the one before: to all extents and purposes the League's victory at the Curzolaris helped to stop the Ottoman advance in the Mediterranean. As a historian of economics, Braudel understood that war is made of men and materiel, and both cost money. Despite their conquest of Cyprus, the destruction of their fleet imposed a heavy strain on the Ottomans' war effort that could not be sustained indefinitely (Braudel also pointed out that Spain's many military commitments had been the cause of the League's inability to exploit its victory).

In his 1974 study *Gunpowder and Galleys*, John Guilmartin took Braudel's argument one step further, underscoring how the huge losses incurred by the Ottomans in skilled naval personnel had lasting effects on the efficiency of the Porte's fleet for many years afterwards. While Guilmartin's book contained a chapter on the Curzolaris its focus was not so much on the fighting itself, but instead discussed the logistics, technology and tactics peculiar to galley warfare (these matters had already been tackled a few year before by Francisco Fernando Olesa Muñido in his encyclopaedic *La organización naval de los estados mediterráneos*). Although Guilmartin's description still followed La Gravière's outline, his book laid the ground for a reinterpretation of the battle. The survey of the site done in 1971–2 by Throckmorton, Edgerton and Yalouris successfully challenged the acquired knowledge about the battlefield's outline, thus clarifying the movements of the contending fleets. Marco Morin added to this in his 1985 article *La battaglia di Lepanto*, which included some pointed criticism of previous scholarship. In particular, Morin made clear that without a profound knowledge of the weaponry involved it was impossible to understand what had happened at the Curzolaris. He also took to task those who had written about the battle without making proper use of primary and archival sources. Despite Morin's warning, some recent monographs on the Curzolaris still repeat the dated story popularized more than a century ago by Jurien de La Gravière. But such a historical attitude is not limited to the battle of 'Lepanto'.

BIBLIOGRAPHY

~

For abbreviations used in the Bibliography see the list at the start of the Notes on page 340–42.

ARCHIVAL SOURCES

Archivio Doria-Pamphilij, Rome
  Scaffale: 22/40, 38/32, 69/32, 70/25, 76/21, 79/17, 79/37, 79/53, 93/37
  Bancone: 72/5, 72/6
Archivio Floriani, Macerata
  001/001/053
  002/004/534
Archivio Guicciardini, Florence
  Miscellanea, II, n. 24
Archivo General de Simancas, Simancas (Valladolid)
  Secretaría de Estado: 485, K 512, 530, 914, 917, 1049, 1058, 1068, 1133, 1134, 1135, 1325, 1328, 1329, 1332, 1399, 1483, 1501, 1505
Archivio di Stato di Firenze, Florence
  Carte Strozziane: Iª serie, 137, 145, 254
  Depositeria Generale, parte antica: 658
  Guicciardini-Corsi-Salviati: 128

Guidi: 97

Manoscritti: 127

Miscellanea Medicea: 264, 370

Mediceo del Principato: 211, 238, 615, 627, 638, 695, 2077, 2084, 2131, 2355, 2426, 3596, 4274, 4901, 5040, 5153

Scrittoio delle Fortezze e Fabbriche: Fortezze Lorenesi 1528

Urbino: Iᵃ serie X, 112, 132, 201, 217; C

Archivio di Stato di Genova, Genoa

Notai Antichi: 3150

Archivio di Stato di Trieste, Trieste

Torre e Tasso: 264

Archivio di Stato di Venezia, Venice

Annali: 1566–70, 1571

Capi del Consiglio dei Dieci: Lettere da Costantinopoli, 3

Cariche da Mar: Processi, 4

Collegio Lettere, Secreta: 25

Collegio Relazioni: 57

Consiglio dei Dieci:

   Parti Comuni: reg. 27, 30, 31; filza 122, 138

   Parti Secrete: reg. 8, 9; filza 15, 16

Miscellanea Codici: 100, 670

Milizia da Mar: 707

Scritture Miste Motabili: 13, 18 bis

Senato Dispacci: Costantinopoli, 4

Secreta, Archivi Propri Contarini: reg. 25

Senato Deliberazioni Mar: reg. 39, 40, 69; filza 689

Senato Mar: I, reg. 39, filza 95, 226

Senato Secreta: reg. 39, 75, 76, 78; Deliberazioni Costantinopoli I

Senato Terra: filza 237

Başbakanlık Osmanlı Arşivi, Istanbul

Mühimme Defterleri: 12, 16

Biblioteca Apostolica Vaticana, Rome

Barberiniani Latini 5367

Biblioteca del Museo Civico Correr, Venice

Ms. 3596

Biblioteca Nazionale Centrale, Florence
  Magliabechiano, classe XIX, 12
  Passerini, 47
  Rossi-Cassigoli, 199
Biblioteca Nazionale Marciana, Venice
  Ms. Italiani, classe VII: 11, 390, 391, 2582
Real Biblioteca, Madrid
  EGB: Ex Bibliotheca Gondomariensi: II/2211

PRINTED PRIMARY SOURCES

ADRIANI, G. *Istoria de' suoi tempi di Giouambatista Adriani gentilhuomo fiorentino* (Florence, 1583).

AGOSTINO DA FAMAGOSTA (Fra) *La perdita di Famagosta e la gloriosa morte di M. A. Bragadino. Nozze Lucheschi-Arrigoni*, ed. A. MOROSINI (Venice: Ferrari, 1891).

A. AKGÜNDÜZ, (ed.) *Kavanin-i Yeniçeriyan-i Dergah-I Ali*, in A. AKGÜNDÜZ, *Osmanli kanunnâmeleri ve hukukí tahlilleri*, vol. 9, (Istanbul, 1996): 127–367.

ALBERI, E. (ed.) *Relazioni degli Ambasciatori veneti al Senato raccolte, annotate ed edite da Eugenio Alberi*, 15 vols. (Florence, 1839–66): vol. 2, 1st series (Florence, 1840), vol. 3, 2nd series (Florence, 1846), vol. 6, 3rd series (Florence, 1844**a**); vol. 7, 3rd series (Florence, 1844**b**); vol. 9, 3rd series (Florence, 1855).

ALBERTONI, F. *Lentrata che fece l'ecellentissimo signor Marc'Antonio Colonna in Roma alli 4 di decembre 1571* (Viterbo, 1572).

AMMIRATO, S. *Istorie fiorentine*, 11 vols. (Florence, 1824–27).

ANTINORI, B. *Copia d'una lettera scritta dal sig. cavaliere Antinori ai suoi fratelli. Qual narra la felice, et gloriosa vittoria, che ha hauuto l'armata christiana contra alli nemici perfidi della fede di Giesù Cristo* (Florence, 1571).

APARICI, J. *Colección de Documentos Inéditos relativos a la célebre Batalla de Lepanto sacados del Archivo de Simancas* (Madrid, 1847).

ARGENTI, P. P. *Chius vincta* (Cambridge, 1941).

– *The occupation of Chios by the Genoese and their administration of the Island 1346–1566* (Cambridge, 1958).

ARROYO, M. A. *Relacion del progresso de la Armada de la Santa Liga . . . con un breve discorso sopra el accrescentamiento de los turcos* (Milan, 1576).

AVENA, A. *Memorie Veronesi della guerra di Cipro e della battaglia di Lepanto* (Venice, 1912).

BARBARO, N. *Diary of the Siege of Constantinople, 1453,* J. R. JONES (trans.) (New York, 1969).

La batalla naval del señor don Juan de Austria: Según un manuscrito anónimo contemporáneo. Homenaje del Instituto Histórico de Marina. IV Centenario de Lepanto (Madrid, 1971).

BENEDETTI, R. *Ragguaglio delle allegrezze, solennità e feste fatte in Venetia per la felice vittoria* (Venice, 1571).

BERGENROTH, G. A., GAYANGOS, P. DE, HUME, M. A. S., TYLER, R., (eds.) *Calendar of Letters, Despatches, and State Papers, relating to the negotiations between England and Spain, preserved in the Archives at Simancas and elsewhere,* 12 vols. (London, 1862–1916).

BOCCACCIO, G. *The Decameron,* G. WALDMAN (trans.), J. USHER (ed.) (Oxford, 1999).

BOSIO, G. *Dell'istoria della sacra religione et ill.ma militia di San Giouanni gerosolimitano,* 3 vols. (Rome, 1594–1602).

BRÂNTOME, P. DE BOURDEILLE, SEIGNEUR DE *Oeuvres complètes: publiées d'après les manuscrits avec variantes et fragments inédits pour la Société de l'histoire de France,* L. LALANNE (ed.), 11 vols. (Paris, 1864–68).

BROQUIERE, B. DELLA *Le voyage d'outremer de Bertrandon de La Broquiere,* ed. C. SCHEFER (Paris, 1892).

BROWN, R., BROWN, H. F., HINDS, A. B. (eds.) *Calendar of state papers and manuscripts, relating to English affairs, existing in the archives and collections of Venice and in other libraries of Northern Italy,* 38 vols. (London 1864–1947).

BRUNETTI, M., VITALE, E. (eds.) *La corrispondenza da Madrid dell'ambasciatore Leonardo Donà: (1570–1573),* preface by F. BRAUDEL, 2 vols. (Venice & Rome, 1963).

CAETANI, O., DIEDO, G. *La battaglia di Lepanto, 1571* (Palermo, 1995).

CAMPANA, C. *Volume primo, che contiene libri dieci: ne' quali diffusamente si narrano le cose avvenute dall'anno 1570 fino al 1580. Nuovamente stampate, con gli argomenti a ciascun libro. Con una tavola de' nomi proprii, e delle materie* (Venice, 1599).

CANTEMIR, D. *The history of the growth and decay of the Othman empire,* 2 vols. N. TINDAL, (trans.) (London, 1734–35).

CARACCIOLO, F. *I commentarii delle guerre fatte co' turchi da D. Giouanni d'Austria, dopo che venne in Italia, scritti da Ferrante Caracciolo conte di Biccari* (Florence, 1581).

CATENA, G. *Vita del gloriosissimo papa Pio quinto . . . Con una raccolta di lettere di Pio 5. a diversi principi, e le risposte, con altri particolari. Et i nomi delle galee, et de capitani, cosi christiani, come turchi, che si trovarono alla battaglia navale* (Mantua, 1587).

CERVANTES SAAVEDRA, M. DE *Los Baños de Argel,* J. CANAVAGGIO (ed.) (Madrid, 1984).

– *Viaje del Parnaso: facsimil de la primera edicion Madrid, Viuda de Alonso Martin, 1614* (Madrid, 1980).

CHARRIÈRE, E. *Négociations de la France dans le Levant,* 4 vols. (Paris, 1848–60; repr. New York, 1965).

Colección de documentos inéditos para la historia de España, 113 vols. (Madrid, 1842–95).

Colección de documentos y manuscriptos compilados por Fernandez de Navarrete, 33 vols. (Madrid, 1946).

COLLADO, L. *Pratica manuale di arteglieria; nella quale si tratta della inventione di essa, dell'ordine di condurla, e piantarla sotto a qualunque fortezza, fabricar mine da far volar in alto le fortezze* (Venice, 1586).

COLOMBINA, G. B. 'Origine, eccellenza, e necessità dell'arte militare', in B. GIUNTA (ed.) *Fucina di Marte, nella quale con mirabile industria, e con finissima tempra d'instruzioni militari, s'apprestano tutti gli ordini appartenenti a qual si voglia carico, essercitabile in guerra. Fabbricata da' migliori autori e capitani valorosi, ch'abbiano scritto sin'ora in questa materia, i nomi de quali appaiono doppo la Lettera a' lettori* (Venice, 1641): 440–92.

CONFORTI, L. *I napoletani a Lepanto: ricerche storiche. Lettera di Bartolommeo Papasso* (Naples, 1886).

CONIGLIO, G. (ed.) *Il viceregno di Napoli e la lotta tra Spagnoli e Turchi nel Mediterraneo*, 2 vols. (Naples, 1987).

CONTARINI, G. P. *Historia delle cose successe dal principio della guerra mossa da Selim Ottomano a' Venetiani, fino al di della gran giornata vittoriosa contra Turchi* (Venice, 1572).

CONTI, N. *Delle historie de' suoi tempi di Natale Conti. Di latino in volgare nuouamente tradotta da m. Giouan Carlo Saraceni. Aggiunteui di piu e postille*, 2 vols. (Venice, 1589).

Copia d'una lettera del Signore Secretario dell'Illustrissimo Signore Giovanni Andrea Doria. Con il vero disegno del luogo dove è seguita la giornata, che fu il dì de S. Marco Papa, e confessore il dì 7 Ottobre 1571, 40 miglia sopra Lepanto (Rome, 1571).

COSTO, T. *Del compendio dell'istoria del regno di Napoli, di Tomaso Costo napolitano. Parte terza* (Venice, 1613).

CRESCENZIO, B. *Nautica Mediterranea* (Rome, 1607).

Il crudelissimo assedio, et nova presa della famosissima fortezza di Famagosta (Milan, 1571).

DAL POZZO, B. *Historia della sacra religione militare di S. Giovanni Gerosolimitano detta di Malta, del signor commendator Fr. Bartolomeo Co. Dal Pozzo veronese, cavalier della medesima*, 2 vols. (Verona, 1703–15).

Del successo dell'armata della Santa Lega dell'anno 1571 (Rome, 1571).

Discorso sopra due grandi e memorabili battaglie navali fatte nel mondo, l'una di Cesare Augusto con M. Antonio, l'altra delli sig. venetiani, e della santissima Lega con sultan Selim signor di Turchi (Bologna, 1572).

DOGLIONI, G. N. *Historia venetiana scritta breuemente da Gio. Nicolo Doglioni, delle cose successe dalla prima fondation di Venetia sino all'anno di Christo 1597* (Venice, 1598).

DORIA, G. A. *Vita del Principe Giovanni Andrea Doria scritta da lui medesimo*, V. BORGHESI (ed.) (Genoa, 1997).

DORIA PAMPHILJ, A. *Lettere di D. Giovanni d'Austria a D. Giovanni Andrea Doria* (Rome, 1896).

DOUAIS C. (ed.) *Lettres de Charles IX. à M. de Fourquevaux ambassadeur en Espagne, 1565–1572; publiées pour la première fois*, 2 vols. (Paris, 1897).

DRAGONETTI DE TORRES, A. *La Lega di Lepanto nel carteggio diplomatico inedito di Don Luys De Torres nunzio straordinario di S. Pio 5. a Filippo 2* (Turin, 1931).

DUMONT, J. *Corps universel diplomatique du droit des gens contenant un recueil des traitez d'alliance, de paix, de treve, de neutralite . . .* vol. 5 (Amsterdam & The Hague, 1728).

ERASMUS OF ROTTERDAM 'On the War against the Turks', in E. RUMMEL (ed.) *The Erasmus Reader* (Toronto, 1990): 316–32.

FERRETTI, F. *Della osservanza militare del capitan Francesco Ferretti d'Ancona, cavallier dell'Ordine di San Stefano . . .* (Venice, 1577).

FIGUEROA, L. DE *Relatione fatta in Roma a sua santità dal s. maestro di campo del terzo di Granata Don Lopes di Figheroa imbasciatore del signor don Giovanni d'Austria mandato alla catolica maestà del re Filippo* (Florence, 1571).

FIRPO, L. (ed.) *Relazioni di ambasciatori veneti al Senato: tratte dalle migliori edizioni disponibili e ordinate cronologicamente. Vol. 13: Costantinopoli, 1590–1793* (Turin, 1984).

FLORIANI, P. *Discorso della goletta, et del forte di Tunisi . . .* (Macerata, 1574).

FLORISTAN IMIZCOZ, J. M. *Fuentes para la política oriental de los Austrias. La documentación griega del Archivo de Simancas (1571–1621)*, vol. II (León: Universidad de León, 1988).

FOGLIETTA, U. *Istoria di Mons. Uberto Foglietta nobile genovese della sacra lega contra Selim, e d'alcune altre imprese di suoi tempi, cioe dell'impresa del Gerbi, soccorso d'Oram, impresa del Pignon, di Tunigi, & assedio di Malta, fatta volgare per Giulio Guastauini nobile genovese* (Genoa, 1598).

FONTANA, F. *I pregi della Toscana nelle imprese più segnalate de' cavalieri di Santo Stefano* (Florence, 1701).

GATTO, A. *Narrazione del terribile assedio e della resa di Famagosta nell'anno 1571 da un manoscritto del capitano Angelo Gatto da Orvieto*, P. CATIZZANI (ed.) (Orvieto, 1895).

GIOVIO, P. *Delle Istorie di Mons. Giovio*, 2 vols. (Venice, 1564).

GÖKBILGIN, M. T. (ed.) *Osmanlı İmparatorluğu medeniyet tarihi çerçevesinde Osmanlı paleografya ve diplomatik ilmi* (Istanbul, 1979).

GUEVARA, A. DE *Arte de marear*, R. O. Jones (ed.), (Exeter, 1972).

GUICCIARDINI, F. *Ricordi*, N. H. THOMSON (trans.) (New York, 1949).

HAËDO, D. DE *Topographia, e historia general de Argel, repartida en cinco tratados, do se veran casos estranos, muertes espantosas, y tormentos exquisitos* . . . (Valladolid, 1612).

HERRERA, F. *Relación de la guerra de Cipre y sucesso de la batalla Naval de Lepanto*, in *Colección de documentos inéditos para la historia de España*, vol. XXI: 243–382.

HERRERA Y TORDESILLAS, A. *Segunda parte de la historia general del mundo, de 15. anos del tiempo del senor rey don Felipe 2. el prudente, desde el ano de 1571. hasta el 1585* (Valladolid, 1606).

ILLESCAS, G. DE *Segunda parte de la historia pontifical, y catholica: en la qual se prosiguen las vidas, y hechos, de Clemente Quinto, y de los demas pontifices sus sucessores hasta Pio Quinto. Contienese ansi mismo la recapitulacion de las cosas, y reyes de Espana* . . . (Madrid, 1613).

Intiero e minuto ragguaglio della vittoria contra Turchi, con alcuni versi sopra il signor Don Giovanni d'Austria (Rome, 1571).

KATIB ÇELEBI *Cronologia historica scritta in lingua turca, persiana, e araba, da Hazi Halife Mustafa, e tradotta nell'idioma italiano da Gio. Rinaldo Carli nobile justinopolitano* . . . (Venice, 1697).

—— *Thufat al-Kibar fi Asfar ad-Bhihar* (Istanbul, 1911).

KNOLLES, R. *The Turkish history, from the original of that nation, to the growth of the Ottoman Empire: with the lives and conquests of their princes and emperors, by Richard Knolles* . . . 3 vols. (London, 1687).

KÜTÜKOGLU, M. S. *Osmanlı belgelerinin dili (diplomatik)* (Istanbul, 1994).

LA BROCQUIERE, B. DE *Le voyage d'outremer de Bertrandon de La Broquiere*, C. SCHEFER (ed.) in *Recueil de voyages et de documents pour servir a l'histoire de la Geographie depuis le XIIIe jusqu'a la fin du XVIe siecle*, vol. 12 (Paris, 1892).

LAGGETTO, G. M. *Historia della Guerra di Otranto nel 1480, Come fu presa dai Turchi e martirizzati li suoi fedeli Cittadini* (Maglie, 1924).

LECHUGA, C. *Discurso del capitan Cristoual Lechuga, en que trata de la artilleria, y de todo lo necessario a ella. Con un tratado de fortification, y otros advertimento* . . . (Milan, 1611).

LESCAUT DE ROMEGAS, M. *Relatione della giornata delle Scorciolare, fra l'armata Christiana e Turchesca alli 7 d'Ottobre 1571, ritratta dal Commendator Romagasso* (Siena, 1571).

LESURE, M. *Lepante et la crise de l'empire ottoman* (Paris,1972).

LONGO, F. *Successo della guerra fatta con Selim Sultano Imperator de' Turchi e giustificazione della pace con lui conclusa di M. Francesco Longo, fu di M. Antonio a M. Manco Antonio Suo fratello*, in *Archivio Storico Italiano*, 17, appendice al tomo IV (1847): 3–58.

LÓPEZ DE TORO, J. *Lepanto y su héroe en la historia y en la poésia: José Lopez de Toro. Hallazgo de la crónica inédita de un soldado en la batalla de Lepanto*, J. GUILLÉN TATO (ed.) (Madrid, 1971).

LUFTI PASHA, *Das Asafname des Lufti Pasha*, R. TSCHUDI (ed. and trans.) (Berlin, 1910).

LUTHER, M. *Luther's Works*, vol. 31: *Career of the Reformer I*, H. J. GRIMM (ed.) (Philadelphia: Muhlenberg Press, 1957); vol. 46: *The Christian in Society III*, R. C. SCHULZ (ed.) (Philadelphia, 1967).

—— *Martin Luther: Selections From His Writing*, J. DILLENBERGER (ed.) (Chicago: Quadrangle Books, 1961).

MACHIAVELLI, N. *Comedia facetissima intitolata Mandragola et recitata in Firenze* (Rome, 1524).

—— *The Prince*, G. BULL, (trans.) introduction by A. GRAFTON (London, 1999).

MARCH, J. M. *La batalla de Lepanto y Don Luis de Requesens, lugarteniente general de la mar: con nuevos documentos historicos* (Madrid, 1944).

MARTINENGO, N. *L'Assedio et presa di Famagosta doue s'intende minutissimamente tutte le scaramuccie, batterie, mine & assalti dati ad essa fortezza: et quanto valore habbiano dimostrato quelli signori, capitani, soldati: popolo: e infino le donne . . .* (Brescia, 1571).

MICCIO, S. *Vita di Don Pietro di Toledo*, in *Archivio Storico Italiano*, 9 (1846): 1–143.

MOLINI, G. *Documenti di storia italiana copiata su gli originali autentici e per lo più autografi esistenti in Parigi*, 2 vols. (Florence, 1836–37).

MONGA, L. (ed.) *Galee toscane e corsari barbareschi. Il diario di Aurelio Scetti, galeotto fiorentino 1565–1577* (Fornacette, 1999).

NORES, P. *Storia della guerra di Paolo IV, sommo pontefice, contro. gli Spagnuoli*, in *Archivio Storico Italiano*, 12 (1847): 1–303.

L'ordine che ha tenuto l'armata della Santa Lega, cominciando dal di che si partì da Messina, con li nomi di tutte le galere, e di tutti li capitani di esse.

Aggiuntavi ancora la relatione, che ha fatta a sua Beatitudine il signor don Lope Fighuerola nel passar per Roma, portando lo Stendardo della Reale del Turco, a sua Maestà Cattolica in Spagna (Rome, 1571).

L'ordine che si debbe tenere per il serenissimo don Giovanni d'Austria generale dell'armata della s.lega nel navigare in dar la battaglia all'armata del Turco. Col numero delle galere, e nomi, e capitani d'esse, e del modo tenuto nell'accompagnarle nelle squadre a tutte le nationi di detta lega (Florence, 1571).

ORESTE, G. 'Una narrazione inedita della battaglia di Lepanto', *Atti della Società Ligure di Storia Patria*, 76, 2 (1962): 209–33.

PANTERA, P. *L'armata nauale, del capitan Pantero Pantera gentil'huomo comasco, e caualliero dell'habito di Cristo. Diuisa in doi libri* . . . (Rome, 1614).

PARRISOT DE LA VALLETTE, J. 'An Unpublished Letter of Jean de La Valette', B. C. WEBER (ed.), *Melita Historica*, 3, 1 (1960): 71–3.

PARUTA, P. *Storia della guerra di Cipro libri tre di Paolo Paruta* (Siena, 1827).

PEÇEVÎ İBRAHIM EFENDI *Tarih*, 2 vols. (Istanbul, 1864).

PEDANI-FABRIS, M. P. (ed.), *Relazioni di ambasciatori veneti al Senato*, vol. XIV, *Costantinopoli. Relazioni inedite (1512–1789)*, (Padua, 1996).

PEDANI-FABRIS, M. P., BOMBACCI, A. (eds.) *I 'documenti turchi' dell'archivio di Stato di Venezia* (Rome, 1994).

PIOT, C., POULLET, E., (eds.) *Correspondance du cardinal de Granvelle, 1565–1586*, 12 vols. (Bruxelles, 1877–96).

PIUS II (AENEAS SILVIUS PICCOLOMINI) *Epistola ad Mahomatem II (Epistle to Mohammed II)*, A. R. BACA (ed. and trans.) (New York, 1990).

PRASCA, E. *Nuovi documenti sulla battaglia di Lepanto* (Padova, 1909).

RIBIER, G. *Lettres et mémoires d'estat, des roys, princes, ambassadeurs, et autres ministres, sous les regnes de François premier, Henri 2. & François 2*, vol. II (Paris: Clousier, 1666).

Ritratto d'una lettera scritta dall'Ill.mo et Ecc.mo Ambasciatore Cesareo dalla Armata. Donde si hanno molti nuovi, belli e particolari ragguagli circa la Vittoria avuta contra Turchi (Rome, 1571).

SAGREDO, G. *Memorie istoriche de monarchi ottomani* (Venice, 1673).

SANSOVINO, F. *Gl'Annali ouero le Vite de' principi et signori della casa Othomana di m. Francesco Sansouino. Ne quali si leggono di tempo in tempo tutte le guerre particolarmente fatte dalla nation de' Turchi, in diuerse prouincie del mondo contra i christiani* (Venice, 1571).

SARDI, P. *L'artiglieria di Pietro Sardi romano divisa in tre libri* . . . (Venice, 1621).

SAVORGANO, M. *Arte militare terrestre e marittima* (Venice: Francesco de' Franceschi, 1599).

SELÂNIKÎ MUSTAFA EFENDI, *Tarih-i Selânikî*, M. İPŞIRLI (ed.), 2 vols. (Istanbul, 1989).

SERENO, B. *Commentari della guerra di Cipro e della lega dei principi cristiani contro il turco, di Bartolomeo Sereno; ora per la prima volta pubblicati da ms. autografo con note e documenti per cura de' monaci della Badia Cassinese* (Monte Cassino, 1845).

SERRANO, L. *Correspondencia diplomatica entre España y la Santa Sede durante el pontificado de S. Pio V*, 4 vols. (Rome, 1914).

—— *La liga de Lepanto entre Espana, Venecia y la santa sede: (1570–1573): ensayo historico a base de documentos diplomaticos* (Madrid, 1918).

SEYYD MURAD *La vita e la storia di Ariadeno Barbarossa*, G. BONAFFINI (ed.) (Palermo, 1993).

SPINOLA, E. *Lettera sulla battaglia di Lepanto*, A. NERI (ed.) (Genoa, 1901).

Statuti, capitoli, et constitutioni, dell'Ordine de' Cavalieri di Santo Stefano, fondato e dotato dall'illustr. e eccell. S. Cosimo Medici, duca 2. di Fiorenza, e di Siena, riformati dal sereniss. Don Ferdinando Medici, terzo Gran duca di Toscana, & Gran maestro di detto ordine. Et approvati, & pubblicati nel capitolo generale di detto ordine, l'anno 1590 (Florence, 1595).

STELLA, A. (ed) *Nunziature di Venezia*, F. GAETA (general editor), vol. VIII (Rome, 1963); vol. IX (Rome, 1972); vol. X (Rome, 1977).

Il Successo della navale vittoria christiana, contra l'armata turca; occorsa (mercé divina) al golfo di Lepanto; di nuovo ristampato, e aggiontovi più particolarità secondo varij riporti (Venice & Brescia, 1571).

TASSOLO, D. *I Trionfi feste, et livree fatte dalli Signori Conservatori, e Popolo Romano, e da tutte le arti di Roma, nella felicissima, & honorata entrata dell'illustrissimo signor Marcantonio Colonna* (Venice, 1571).

TOMITANO, B. *Resa di Famagosta e fine lagrimevole di Bragadino e di Astorre Baglioni, Per le faustissime nozze Marcello Zon* (Venice, 1858).

TORRES Y AGUILERA, G. DE *Chronica, y recopilacion de varios successos de guerra a que ha acontescido en Italia y partes de leuante y Berberia, desde que el turco Selin rompio con venecianos . . .* (Caragoca, 1579).

TOSI C. O. (ed.) *Dell'incendio dell'Arsenale di Venezia nel 1569: due nuovi documenti inediti pubblicati da Carlo Odoardo Tosi* (Florence, 1905).

VANDERHAMMEN Y LEON, L. *Don Juan de Austria, historia* (Madrid, 1627).

VARGAS-HIDALGO, R. *Guerra y diplomacia en el Mediterráneo: Correspondencia inédita de Felipe II con Andrea Doria y Juan Andrea Doria* (Madrid, 2002).

—— *La battalla de Lepanto: segun cartas ineditas de Felipe 2, Don Juan de Austria y Juan Andrea Doria e informes de embajadores y espias* (Santiago, 1998).

VENTURINI, T. N. *Storia, grandezze, e miracoli di Maria Vergine del Santissimo Rosario secondo il corso delle domeniche, e feste di tutto l'anno* (Venice, 1732).

VISINONI, L. A. (ed.) *Del successo in Famagosta, 1570–71: diario d'un contemporaneo, Nobili nozze Gozzi-Guaita* (Venice, 1879).

ZRINYI, M. *Szigeti veszedelem. Az torok afium ellen valo orvossag* (Budapest, 1997).

PRINTED SECONDARY SOURCES

ABOU-EL-HAJ, R. A. *Formation of the modern state: the Ottoman Empire, sixteenth to eighteenth centuries* (Albany, 1991).

ADAMI, G. 'Floriani, Pompeo', in *DBI*, XLVIII (Rome, 1997) 49–52.

AGLIETTI, M. *La partecipazione delle galere toscane alla battaglia di Lepanto*, in D. MARRARA (ed.) *Toscana e Spagna nell'età moderna e contemporanea* (Pisa, 1998) 55–145.

ÁGOSTON, G. *Guns for the Sultan. Military Power and the Weapon Industry in the Ottoman Empire* (Cambridge, 2005).

ALLOUCHE, A. *The Origins and Development of the Ottoman–Safavid Conflict: 906–962/1500–1555*, in *Islamkundliche Untersuchungen*, vol. 91 (Berlin, 1983).

R. C. ANDERSON, 'The "Mahona"', *The Mariner's Mirror*, 5, 3 (1919): 59.

—— *Naval Wars in the Levant* (Liverpool, 1952).

ANGIOLINI, F. *I cavalieri e il principe. L'Ordine di Santo Stefano e la società toscana in età moderna* (Florence, 1996).

—— *Il Granducato di Toscana, l'Ordine di S. Stefano e il Mediterraneo (secc. XVI–XVIII)*, in *Ordens Militares: guerra, religião, poder e cultura – Actas do III Encontro sobre Ordens Militares*, vol. I (Lisbon, 1999) 39–61.

ARENAPRIMO DI MONTECHIARO, G. *La Sicilia nella battaglia di Lepanto* (Pisa, 1886).

ARTAN, T., BERTKAY, H. 'Selimian times: a reforming grand admiral, anxieties of re-possession, changing rites of power' in *The Kapudan Pasha: His Office and His Domain* (Rethymnon, 2002) 7–45.

ATIYA, A. S. *The Crusade of Nicopolis* (London, 1934).

BABINGER, F. *Mehmed the Conqueror and His Time* (trans.) R. MANN-HEIM (trans.)(Princeton, 1978).

—— 'Pertew pasha', in *EI²*, vol. VIII (Leiden, 1993**a**) 295–6.

—— 'Piyâle pasha', in *EI²*, vol. VIII (Leiden, 1993**b**) 316–17.

BARTUSIS, M. C. *The Late Byzantine Army: Arms and Society, 1204–1453* (Philadelphia, 1992).

BASSO, E. 'L'ochio drito de la città nostra de Zenoa: il problema della difesa di Chio negli ultimi anni del dominio genovese' in *Le armi del sovrano: armate e flotte nel mondo tra Lepanto e la Rivoluzione francese, 1571–1789* (Rome: Assostoria, 2001): 1–9. http://www.assostoria.it/Armisovrano/Basso.pdf

BAZZANO, N. *Marco Antonio Colonna* (Rome, 2003).

BELHAMISSI, M. *Histoire de la marine algérienne, 1516–1830* (Algiers, 1986).

BELLINGERI, G. 'Il Golfo come appendice: una visione ottomana', in *Mito e antimito di Venezia nel bacino adriatico (secoli XV–XIX)*, S. GRACIOTTI (ed.) (Rome, 2001) 1–21.

BENZONI, G. (ed.) *Il Mediterraneo nella seconda metà del '500 alla luce di Lepanto* (Florence, 1974).

BERENGER, J. 'La Collaboration Militaire Franco-Ottoman a l'Epoque de la Renaissance', *Revue Internationale d'Histoire Militaire*, 68 (1987) 51–70.

BICHENO, H. *Crescent and Cross: The Battle of Lepanto, 1571* (London, 2003).

BIRGE, J. K. *The Bektashi Order of Dervishes* (London, 1996).

BISAHA, N. 'Pius II's Letter to Sultan Mehmed II: A Reexamination', *Crusades*, 1 (2003) 183–200.

BONO, S. *Corsari nel Mediterraneo. Cristiani e musulmani fra guerra, schiavitù e commercio* (Milan, 1993).

BORGHESI, V. 'Le galere del Principe Giovanni Andrea Doria (1540–1606)' in *Le navi di legno. Evoluzione tecnica e sviluppo della cantieristica nel Mediterraneo dal XVI secolo a oggi* (Grado, 1998) 91–100.

BORNATE, C. 'La missione di Sampiero Corso a Costantinopoli', *Archivio Storico di Corsica*, 15, 3 (1939) 472–502.

—— 'I negoziati per attirare Andrea D'Oria al servizio di Carlo V', *Giornale Storico e Letterario della Liguria*, XVIII, II, (1942) 63–84.

BOTTI, F. 'Come non ci si prepara a una guerra', *Storia Militare*, 2 (4) 1994: 42–50.

BRAUDEL, F. *The Mediterranean and the Mediterranean World in the Age of Philip II* (New York, 1976).

BRUMMETT, P. *Ottoman Seapower and Levantine Diplomacy in the Age of Discovery* (Albany, 1994).

BRUNELLI, G. *Soldati del Papa. Politica militare e nobiltà nello Stato della Chiesa (1560–1644)* (Rome, 2003).

CALANDRIA, E. C. 'Nuevos Datos Sobre Pintores Españoles y Pinturas Mitológicas en el Siglo XVI. La Galera Real de Don Juan de Austria', *Goya*, 286 (2002) 15–26.

CAMERANI, S. 'Contributo alla storia dei trattati commerciali fra la Toscana e i Turchi', *Archivio Storico Italiano*, XCVII, 4, (1939) 83–101.

CANAVAGGIO, J. *Cervantes*, J. R. Jones (trans.) (New York, 1990).

CANOSA, R. *Lepanto: storia della Lega santa contro i turchi* (Rome, 2000).

CANTAGALLI, R.3 'LA GUERRA DI SIENA', IN L. ROMBAI (ED.) *I MEDICI E LO STATO SENESE, 1555–1609. STORIA E TERRITORIO* (ROME, 1980).

CAPASSO, C. 'Barbarossa e Carlo V', *Rivista storica italiana*, 49 (1932) 169–209.

CAPPONI, N[eri] 'Il Sacro Militare Ordine di Sa. Stefano Papa e Martire e il Sacro Militare Ordine Costantiniano di S. Giorgio quali enti canonici' in *Gli Ordini dinastici della I.E.R. casa granducale di Toscana e della reale casa Borbone Parma* (Pisa, 2002) 39–60.

CAPPONI, N[iccolò] 'Strategia marittima, logistica e guerra navale sotto

Ferdinando II de' Medici, 1621–1670' in *L'Ordine di Santo Stefano e il Mare* (Pisa, 2001) 114–29.

CARO BAROJA, J. *Los moriscos del Reino de Granada: ensayo de historia social* (Madrid, 1985).

CARRERO BLANCO, L. *Lepanto, 1571–1971* (Madrid, 1971).

CHIAVARELLO, G. *La Battaglia di Lepanto (7 ottobre 1571): apporto decisivo della tecnica del fuoco napoletana; localizzazione dello specchio d'acqua ove avvenne lo scontro* (Naples, 1976).

CIRAKMAN, A *From the 'Terror of the World' to the 'Sick Man of Europe': European Images of Ottoman Empire and Society from the Sixteenth Century to the Nineteenth* (New York, 2002).

ÇIZAKÇA, M. 'Ottomans and the Mediterranean: An Analysis of the Ottoman Shipbuilding Industry as Reflected by the Arsenal Registers in Istanbul' in R. Ragosta (ed.), *Le genti del mare Mediterraneo*, vol. II (Naples, 1981) 773–88.

CONCINA, E. *Navis: l'umanesimo sul mare, 1470–1740* (Turin, 1990).

DANIŞMEND, I. H. *Izahlı Osmanlı tarihi kronolojisi*, vol. II (Istanbul, 1948).

DAVIS, R. C. *Christian Slaves, Muslim Masters: White Slavery in the Mediterranean, the Barbary Coast and Italy, 1500–1800* (London, 2003).

DE CARO, G. 'Caetani, Onorato' in *DBI*, XVI (Rome, 1973) 205–9.

DIAZ, F. *Il Granducato di Toscana: i Medici* (Turin, 1987).

DOMINGUEZ ORTIZ, A., VINCENT, B. *Historia de los moriscos: vida y tragedia de una minoria* (Madrid, 1985).

EDGERTON, H. E., THROCKMORTON, P., YALOURIS, E. 'The Battle of Lepanto. Search and survey mission 1971–2', *International Journal of Nautical Archeology*, 2, 1 (1973) 121–30.

EICKHOFF, E. *Venezia, Vienna e i turchi: bufera nel sud-est europeo, 1645–1700* (Milan, 1991).

ELLIOTT, J. H. *Imperial Spain, 1469–1716* (New York, 1966).

EMMERT, T. A. *Serbian Golgotha: Kosovo, 1389* (New York, 1990).

ERCAN, Y. *Power balance between east and west: the Lepanto naval battle*, paper presented at the international conference: *Le armi del sovrano: armate e flotte nel mondo tra Lepanto e la Rivoluzione francese, 1571–1789*, Rome, 5–8 March 2001.

EVERT-KAPPESOVA, H. 'Le tiare ou le turban', *Byzantinoslavica*, 14 (1953) 245–57.

FARA, A. *Portoferraio. Architettura e urbanistica, 1548–1877* (Turin, 1997).

—— *Il sistema e la città. Architettura fortificata dell'Europa moderna dai trattati alle realizzazioni, 1464–1794* (Genoa, 1989).

FAROQHI, S. *Pilgrims and sultans: the Hajj under the Ottomans, 1517–1683* (London & New York, 1996).

FERNÁNDEZ ARMESTO, F. *The Armada Campaign. The Experience of War in 1588* (Oxford, 1988).

FERNÁNDEZ DURO, C. *Armada española desde la unión de los reinos de Castilla y de Aragón*, 9 vols. (Madrid, 1896).

FISHER, S. N. *The Foreign Relations of Turkey, 1481–1512*, in *Electronic Journal of Middle East Studies*, III, 3 (originally published in *Illinois Studies in the Social Sciences*, XXX, 1, 1948).

FODOR, P. 'An Anti-Semite Grand Vizier? The Crisis in Ottoman–Jewish Relations in 1589–1591 and its Consequences' in *In Quest of the Golden Apple: Imperial Ideology, Politics and Military Administration in the Ottoman Empire* (Istanbul, 2000d) 191–206.

—— 'Between Two Continental Wars: The Ottoman Naval Preparations in 1590–1592' in *In Quest of the Golden Apple: Imperial Ideology, Politics and Military Administration in the Ottoman Empire* (Istanbul, 2000a) 171–90.

—— 'The Organization of Defence in the Eastern Mediterranean (end of the 16th Century)' in *The Kapudan Pasha: His Office and His Domain* (Rethymnon, 2002) 87–94.

—— 'Ottoman Policy Towards Hungary, 1520–1541' in *In Quest of the Golden Apple: Imperial Ideology, Politics and Military Administration in the Ottoman Empire* (Istanbul, 2000b) 105–69.

—— 'Sultan, imperial Council, Grand Vizier: Changes in the Ottoman Ruling Elite and the Formation of the Grand Vizieral Telhis' in *In Quest of the Golden Apple: Imperial Ideology, Politics and Military Administration in the Ottoman Empire* (Istanbul, 2000c) 207–27.

FONSECA, C. D. (ed.) *Otranto 1480: atti del Convegno internazionale di studio promosso in occasione del 5°centenario della caduta di Otranto ad opera dei turchi. Otranto, 19–23 maggio 1980* (Galatina, 1986).

FONTENAY, M. 'Chiourmes turques au XVIIᵉ siècle' in R. Ragosta (ed.) *Le genti del mare Mediterraneo*, 2 vols. (Naples, 1981) 877–903.

FRATTARELLI-FISCHER, L. 'Il bagno delle galere in 'terra cristiana'. Schiavi a Livorno fra Cinque e Seicento', *Nuovi Studi Livornesi*, 8 (2000) 69–94.

FRIEDA, L. *Catherine de Medici* (London, 2003).

FRIEDMAN, E. 'Christian Captives and "Hard Labor" in Algiers, 16th–18th Centuries', *The International Journal of African Historical Studies*, 13 (1980) 616–32.

GACHARD, L. P. *Don Carlos et Philippe II*, 2 vols. (Brussels, 1863).

GARCÍA HERNÁN, D., GARCÍA HERNÁN, E. *Lepanto: el día después* (Madrid, 1999).

GARDINER, R. (ed.), *The Age of the Galley: Mediterranean Oared Vessels Since Pre-classical Times* (London, 1995).

GARGIULO, R. *La battaglia di Lepanto* (Pordenone, 2004)

GATTI, L. *Navi e cantieri della Repubblica di Genova (secoli XVI–XVIII)* (Genoa, 1999).

GATTONI, M. 'La spada della croce: la difficile alleanza ispano-veneto-pontificia nella Guerra di Cipro. Politica estera e teoremi filosofica nei documenti pontifici', *Ricerche Storiche*, 29 (3) 1999 611–50.

GOFFMAN, D. *The Ottoman Empire and Early Modern Europe* (Cambridge, 2002).

GÓMEZ-CÉNTURION, C. *Felipe II, la empresa de Inglaterra y el comercio septentrional 1566–1609* (Madrid, 1988).

GOODMAN, D. C. *Spanish naval power, 1589–1665: reconstruction and defeat* (Cambridge & New York, 1997).

GOUWENS, K., REISS, S. (eds.) *The Pontificate of Clement VII: History, Politics and Culture*, 2 vols. (London, 2005).

GRENTE, G. *San Pio 5, 1504–1572* (Alba, 1932).

GUARNIERI, G. *I Cavalieri di Santo Stefano* (Pisa, 1960).

—— *L'Ordine di Santo Stefano nei suoi aspetti organizzativi tecnici-navali sotto il gran magistero mediceo*, vol. I (Pisa, 1965).

GUGLIELMOTTI, A. *Marcantonio Colonna alla battaglia di Lepanto, 1570–1573* (Florence, 1887).

GUILMARTIN, J. F. *Gunpowder and Galleys: Changing Technology and Mediterranean Warfare at Sea in the 16th Century* (London, 2003).

—— 'The Logistics of Warfare at Sea in the Sixteenth century: The Spanish Perspective' in J. A. LYNN (ed.) *Feeding Mars: Logistics in Western Warfare from the Middle Ages to the Present* (Boulder, 1993) 109–37.

GULLINO, G. 'Duodo, Francesco' in *DBI*, XLII (Rome, 1993): 30–2.

—— *Le frontiere navali* in *Storia di Venezia. Dalle origini alla caduta della Serenissima*, vol. IV, *Il Rinascimento. Politica e cultura* (Rome 1996) 13–111.

HALE, J. R. 'Men and Weapons: The Fighting Potential of Sixteenth Century Venetian Galleys', in J. R. Hale (ed.) *Renaissance War Studies* (London, 1983) 309–32.

—— *L'organizzazione militare di Venezia nel '500* (Rome, 1990).

HALICZER, S. *The Comuneros of Castile: The Forging of a Revolution 1475–1525* (Madison, 1981).

HALL, B. S. *Weapons and Warfare in Renaissance Europe: Gunpowder, Technology and Tactics* (Baltimore, 2002).

HAMMER, J. V. *Histoire de l'empire ottoman, depuis son origine jusqu'à nos jours*, vol. 6 (Istanbul, 1999).

HESS, A. C. 'The battle of Lepanto and its Place in Mediterranean History', *Past and Present*, 57 (1972): 53–73.

—— 'The Evolution of the Ottoman Seaborne Empire in the Age of Discovery', *American Historical Review*, 75, 7 (1970) 1892–1919.

—— *The Forgotten Frontier: A History of the Sixteenth Century Ibero-African Frontier* (Chicago, 1978).

—— 'The Moriscos: an Ottoman Fifth Column in Sixteenth-Century Spain', *American Historical Review*, 74 (1968) 1–25.

—— 'The Ottoman Conquest of Egypt (1517) and the Beginning of the Sixteenth Century World War', *International Journal of Middle East Studies*, 4, 1 (1973) 55–76.

HILL, G. *A History of Cyprus. Volume III: The Frankish Period, 1432–1571* (Cambridge, 1972).

IBÁÑEZ DE IBERO, C. *Santa Cruz, primer marino de España* (Madrid, 1946).

IMBER, C. 'Four letters of Ebu's-su'ud', *Arab Historical Review for Ottoman Studies*, 15–16 (1997) 177–83.

— '"Involuntary" Annulment of Marriage and Its Solutions in Ottoman Law', in *Studies in Ottoman History and Law* (Istanbul, 1996c): 217–251.

— 'The Navy of Süleyman the Magnificent' in *Studies in Ottoman History and Law* (Istanbul, 1996a) 1–69.

— The Ottoman Empire, 1300–1650. The Structure of Power (Basingstoke & New York, 2002).

— 'The Reconstruction of the Ottoman Fleet after the Battle of Lepanto' in *Studies in Ottoman History and Law* (Istanbul, 1996b) 85–101.

— *Studies in Ottoman History and Law* (Istanbul: The Isis Press, 1996).

INALCIK, H. 'Lepanto in the Ottoman Documents' in G. BENZONI (ed.) *Il Mediterraneo nella seconda meta` del '500 alla luce di Lepanto* (Florence: L. S. Olschki, 1974) 185–92.

— 'Mehmed the Conqueror and His Time', *Speculum*, 35, 3 (1960) 408–27.

— *The Ottoman Empire. The Classical Age, 1300–1600* (London, 2003).

— 'The Question of the Emergence of the Ottoman State', *International Journal of Turkish Studies* 2 (1980) 71–9.

INALCIK, H., QUATAERT, D. (eds.) *An Economic and Social History of the Ottoman Empire*, 2 vols. (Cambridge, 1997).

İPŞIRLI, M. 'Observations on the Ottoman Secret Service during World War I (organization and activities)' in *Military Conflicts and 20th Century Geopolitics* (Athens, 2002) 471–4.

JEDIN, H. *A History of the Council of Trent*, 2 vols. (London, 1957–61).

JURIEN DE LA GRAVIÈRE, J. P. E. *La guerre de Chypre et la bataille de Lépante*, 2 vols. (Paris, 1888).

KÁLDY-NAGY, G. 'The First Centuries of the Ottoman Military Organization', *Acta Orientalia Academiae Scientiarum Hungaricae*, 31 (1977) 147–83.

— Szulejmán (Budapest, 1974).

KAMEN, H. A. F. *Philip of Spain* (New Haven, 1997).

KHADDURI, M. 'Harb. 1 – legal aspects', EI^2, vol. III (Leiden, 1971) 180–1.

KHALILIEH, H. S. *Islamic Maritime Law: An Introduction* (Leiden-Boston-Cologne 1998).

KRAMERS, J. H. 'Mustafa Pasha, Lala', *EI²*, vol. VII (Leiden, 1991) 720–1.

LABIB, S. 'The Era of Suleyman the Magnificent: Crisis of Orientation', *International Journal of Middle East Studies*, 10, 4 (1979) 435–51.

LANE, F. C. *Venetian ships and shipbuilders of the Renaissance* (Baltimore, 1992).

LE TOURNEAU, R., ORHANLU, C. 'Hasan Pasha', *EI²*, vol. III (Leiden, 1971) 251–2.

LITTA, P. *Orsini di Roma* (Turin, 1847–8).

LO BASSO, L. *Uomini da remo: galee e galeotti del Mediterraneo in età moderna* (Milan, 2004).

MACCHI, M. *Storia del Consiglio dei Dieci*, 9 vols. (Milan, 1864).

MAFRICI, M. *Mezzogiorno e pirateria nell'età moderna, secoli XVI–XVIII* (Naples, 1995).

MALLETT, M. E. *The Florentine Galleys in the Fifteenth Century: With the diary of Luca di Maso degli Albizzi, Captain of the Galleys, 1429–1430* (Oxford, 1967).

MANFRONI, C. 'La Lega cristiana del 1572', *Archivio della Reale Società romana di storia patria*, 16 (1893) 412–32; 17 (1894) 38–54.

—— 'Le relazioni fra Genova, l'Impero Bizantino e i Turchi', *Atti della Società Ligure di Storia Patria*, XXVIII, 3 (1898) 577–858

—— *Storia della Marina italiana, dalla caduta di Costantinopoli alla Battaglia di Lepanto* (Turin, 1897).

MANTRAN, R. 'L'écho de la bataille de Lépante à Constantinople', in G. BENZONI (ed.) *Il Mediterraneo nella seconda metà del '500 alla luce di Lepanto* (Florence: L. S. Olschki, 1974): 243–56.

—— *L'Empire ottoman du XVIe au XVIIIe siècle: administration, économie, société* (London, 1984).

MANUEL, J., BLECUA, A. (eds.) *Cervantes y Lepanto* (Barcelona, 1971).

MANUELE, P. *Il Piemonte sul mare. La Marina sabauda dal Medioevo all'unità d'Italia* (Cuneo, 1997).

MARRARA, D., ROSSI, C. 'Lo stato di Siena tra Impero, Spagnae Principato Mediceo (1554–1560): questioni giuridiche e istituzionali' in D. MARRARA (ed.) *Toscana e Spagna nell'età moderna e contemporanea* (Pisa, 1998) 5–53.

MASALA, A. *La banda militare ottomana (Mehter), con l'aggiunta di testi musicali e di uno studio di Cinucen Tanrikorur sulla musica classica ottomana* (Rome, 1978).

MATUZ, J. *Das Osmanische Reich: Grundlinien seiner Geschichte* (Darmstadt, 1985).

MÉNAGE, V. L. 'Devshirme', *EI²*, vol. II (Leiden, 1965) 210–13.

—— 'Sidelights on the *Devshirme* from Idris and Sa'duddin', *Bulletin of the School of Oriental and African Studies* (1956) 181–3.

—— 'Some Notes on the *Devshirme*', *Bulletin of the School of Oriental and African Studies*, 29 (1966) 64–78.

MEREDITH-OWENS, G. M. 'Traces of a Lost Autobiographical Work by a Courtier of Selim II', *Bulletin of the School of Oriental and African Studies*, 23 (3) 1960 456–63.

MILLER, W. *The Latins in the Levant: a history of Frankish Greece, 1204–1566* (New York, 1979).

MOLMENTI, P. *Sebastiano Veniero dopo la battaglia di Lepanto* (Venice, 1915).

—— *Sebastiano Veniero e la battaglia di Lepanto* (Florence, 1899).

MORI UBALDINI, U. *La marina del Sovrano militare ordine di San Giovanni di Gerusalemme, di Rodi e di Malta* (Rome, 1971).

MORIN, M. 'La battaglia di Lepanto: alcuni aspetti della tecnologia navale veneziana' in M. SBALCHIERO (ed.) *Meditando sull'evento di Lepanto. Odierne interpretazioni e memorie* (Venice, 2002) 69–77.

—— 'La battaglia di Lepanto' in *Venezia e i Turchi: scontri e confronti di due cività* (Milan, 1985) 210–31.

MULCAHY, R. 'To celebrate, or not to celebrate: Philip II and representations of the Battle of Lepanto', paper presented at the Renaissance Society of America annual conference, Cambridge, 7–9 April 2005.

MURPHEY, R. *Ottoman warfare, 1500–1700* (New Brunswick, 1999).

MUSCAT, P. B. J. *Food and Drink on Maltese Galleys* (Valletta, 2002).

NANI MOCENIGO, M. *Storia della Marina veneziana, da Lepanto alla caduta della Repubblica* (Rome, 1935).

NEGYESI, L. 'A Mohacsi Csata', *Hadtortenelmi Kozlemenyek*, 107, 4 (1994) 62–79.

OLESA MUÑIDO, F. F. *La organización naval de los estados mediterráneos y en especial de España durante los siglos XVI y XVII*, 2 vols. (Madrid, 1968).

ORESTE, G. 'Genova e Andrea Doria nella fase critica del conflitto francoasburgico', *Atti della Società Ligure di Storia Patria*, LXXII, 3 (1950) 2–71.

ÖZBARAN, S. 'Kapudan Pasha', *EI²*, IV (Leiden, 1978) 571–2.

—— *The Ottoman Response to European Expansion: Studies on Ottoman – Portuguese Relations in the Indian Ocean and Ottoman Administration of the Arab Lands during the Sixteenth Century* (Istanbul, 1994).

PAOLETTI, C. *Gli italiani in armi: cinque secoli di storia militare, 1494–2000* (Rome, 2001).

PARKER, G. *The Army of Flanders and the Spanish Road, 1567–1659* (Cambridge, 1990).

—— *The Dutch Revolt* (London, 1977).

—— *The Grand Strategy of Philip II* (New Haven & London, 1998).

—— *The Military Revolution: Military Innovation and the Rise of the West, 1500–1800* (Cambridge, 1996).

PARKER, G., THOMPSON, I. A. 'Lepanto (1571): The Cost of Victory', *The Mariner's Mirror*, 64 (1978) 13–21.

PASERO, C. *La partecipazione bresciana alla guerra di Cipro e alla battaglia di Lepanto: 1570–1573* (Brescia, 1954).

PASOLINI, G. *Adriano VI* (Rome, 1913).

PEDANI, M. P. 'Tra economia e geo-politica: la visione ottomana della Guerra di Cipro', *Annuario dell'Istituto Rumeno di Cultura e Ricerca Umanistica di Venezia*, 5 (2003) 287–97.

PEDROSA, F. G. 'A artilharia naval portuguesa no século XVI', in *A Guerra e o Encontro de Civilizações a partir do Século XVI* (Lisbon, 1999).

PELLEGRINI, A. DE, *Di due turchi schiavi del conte Silvio di Porcia e Brugnera dopo la battaglia di Lepanto* (Venice, 1921).

PERJÉS, G. *The Fall of the Medieval Kingdom of Hungary: Mohács 1526–Buda 1541*, M. D. Fenyö (trans.) in *War and Society in East Central Europe*, vol. 26 (1989).

PEPPER, S. 'Fortress and Fleet: The Defence of Venice's Mainland Greek Colonies in the Late Fifteenth Century' in D. S. CHAMBERS, C. H. CLOUGH, M. E. MALLETT (eds.) *War, Culture and Society in Renaissance Venice. Essays in Honour of John Hale* (London, Rio Grande, Ohio, 1993) 30–55.

PERTUSI, A. *La caduta di Costantinopoli*, 2 vols. (Milan, 1976).

PETRIE, C. *Don Juan of Austria* (New York, 1963).

PICCINNO, L. 'I rapporti commerciali tra Genova e il Nord Africa in età moderna: il caso di Tabarca', *Quaderni di ricerca della Facoltà di Economia dell'Università degli Studi dell'Insubria*, 15 (2003) 1–21.

PIERACCINI, G. *La stirpe de' Medici di Cafaggiolo. Saggio di ricerche sulla trasmissione ereditaria dei caratteri biologici*, vol. II (Florence, 1986).

PIERI, P. *Il Rinascimento e la crisi militare italiana* (Turin, 1952).

PIERSON, P. 'Lepanto', *MHQ: The Quarterly Journal of Military History*, 9 (1997) 6–19.

PILONI, G. *I bellunesi a Lepanto. Episodi tratti dalle storie inedite* (Belluno, 1892).

PRESCOTT, W. H. *History of the Reign of Philip the Second, King of Spain*, 3 vols. (Boston, 1855–58).

PRETO, P. 'La guerra segreta: spionaggio, sabotaggi, attentati', in M. REDOLFI (ed). *Venezia e la difesa del Levante. Da Lepanto a Candia: 1570–1670* (Venice, 1986) 79–85.

—— *Venezia e i Turchi* (Florence, 1975).

—— 'Venezia, i Turchi e la guerra di Cipro', in M. SBALCHIERO (ed.) *Meditando sull'evento di Lepanto. Odierne interpretazioni e memorie* (Venice, 2002).

PRYOR, J. H. *Geography, Technology and War. Studies in the Maritime History of the Mediterranean* (Cambridge, 1992).

QUARTI, G. A. *La guerra contro il turco in Cipro e a Lepanto 1570–1571: storia documentata* (Venice, 1935).

RANKE, L. V. *The Ottoman and the Spanish empires in the sixteenth and seventeenth centuries*, W. K. KELLY (trans.) (New York, 1975).

'R. C.' 'Sull'impiego economico delle nostre navi da guerra', *Rivista marittima*, 8 (9) (1875) 238–9.

REDOLFI, M. (ed.) *Venezia e la difesa del Levante: da Lepanto a Candia 1570–1670* (Venice,1986).

REFIK, A. 'Kıbrıs seferine aid resmi vesikalar', *Istanbul Universitesi Darül-fünun Edebiyat Fakültesi Mecmuası*, 5 (1927): 29–75.

REPP, R. C. 'A Further Note on the *Devshirme*', *Bulletin of the School of Oriental and African Studies*, 31 (1968): 137–9.

RIDOLFI, R. *Vita di Girolamo Savonarola* (Florence, 1997).

RODGERS, W. L. *Naval warfare under oars: 4th to 16th centuries: a study of strategy, tactics and ship design* (Annapolis, 1967).

ROMBAI, L. (ed.) *I Medici e lo Stato Senese, 1555–1609. Storia e territorio* (Rome, 1980).

ROMER, C. 'A Firman of Suleyman the Magnificent to the King of France preserved in an exercise book of the "K. K. Academie Orientalischer Sprachen" in Vienna, 1831', *Turcica*, 31 (1999) 461–70.

ROSELL, C. *Historia del combate naval de Lepanto y Juicio de la Importancia y Consecuencias de aquel suceso* (Madrid, 1853).

ROSI, M. 'Alcuni documenti relativi alla liberazione dei principali prigionieri turchi presi a Lepanto', *Archivio della Reale Società Romana di storia patria*, 21 (1898) 141–220.

—— 'Nuovi documenti relativi alla liberazione dei principali prigionieri turchi presi a Lepanto', *Archivio della Reale Società Romana di storia patria*, 24 (1901) 5–47.

ROSSI, E. 'La leggenda turco-bizantina del pomo rosso', *Studi bizantini e neo-ellenici*, 5 (1939) 542–53.

ROSSI, E., ALBERANI, M., FELLER, A. M. *Le galee: storia, tecnica, documenti* (Trento, 1990).

RUNCIMAN, S. *A History of the Crusades: Volume 3, The Kingdom of Acre and the Later Crusades* (Cambridge, 1987).

SAFVET, A. 'Sıngın donanma harbi üzerine bazi vesikalar', *Tarih-i Osmani Encümeni Mecmuası*, 2 (1926–27) 558–62.

SALIMEI, A. *Gli italiani a Lepanto: 7 ottobre 1571* (Rome, 1931).

SALVO, U. *Alpignano e Andrea Provana: le straordinarie imprese del conte di Alpignano il grande ammiraglio Andrea Provana nel quarto centenario della sua morte 1592–1992* (Susa, 1992).

SANTILLANA, D. *Istituzioni di diritto musulmano malichita con riguardo anche al sistema sciafiita*, 2 vols (Rome, 1926–38).

SAVELLI, R. 'Doria, Giovanni Andrea' in *DBI*, XLI (Rome, 1992) 361–75.

SCARSELLA, A. (ed.) *Quixote/Chisciotte, MDVC-2005* (Venice, 2005).

SCHLÜTTER-SCHINDLER, G. *Der Schmalkaldische Bund und das Problem der causa religionis* (Frankfurt-am-Main & New York, 1986).

SCICHILONE, G. 'Cardona, Giovanni', in *DBI*, XIX (Rome, 1976) 792–6.

SEGRE, A. 'La Marina Militare Sabauda ai tempi di Emanuele Filiberto e l'opera politico-navale di Andrea Provana di Leyni' in *Memorie della Reale Accademia delle Scienze di Torino*, second series XLVIII (Turin, 1899).

SETTON, K. The Papacy and the Levant, 1204–1571, vols. III, IV (Philadelphia, 1984).

SHAW, S. *Between Old and New: The Ottoman Empire under Sultan Selim III, 1789–1807* (Cambridge, Massachusetts, 1971).

SIRE, H. J. A. *The Knights of Malta* (New Haven, 1994).

SOUCECK, S. 'Ulûdj 'Alî', in *EI²*, vol. X (Leiden, 1998) 810–11.

STANLEY, T. 'Men-at-arms, hauberks and bards: military obligations in The Book of Ottoman Custom' in Ç. BALIM-HARDING, C. IMBER *The Balance of Truth: Essays in Honour of Professor Geoffrey Lewis* (Istanbul, 2000) 331–63.

STELLA, A. 'Barbarigo, Agostino', in *DBI*, VI (Rome, 1964) 49–52.

—— 'Gian Andrea Doria e la Sacra Lega prima della battaglia di Lepanto', *Rivista di Storia della Chiesa in Italia*, 19 (1965) 5–29.

STIRLING-MAXWELL, W. *Don John of Austria, or Passages from the History of the Sixteenth Century, 1547–1578*, 2 vols. (London, 1883).

TAMBORRA, A. *Gli stati italiani, l'Europa e il problema turco dopo Lepanto* (Florence, 1961).

TEKINDAĞ, Ş. 'Şah Kulu Baba teseli ispani', *Belgelerle Türk Tarih Derisi*, 3 (1967) 34–9; 4 (1967) 54–9.

TEMIMI, A. 'Le gouvernement Ottoman face au problème morisque' in *Les Morisques et leur temps, U.E.R. des Langues, Littératures et des Civilisations de la Méditerranée (4–7 juillet 1981)* (Paris, 1983) 297–311.

TENENTI, A. 'La Francia, Venezia e la Sacra Lega' in G. BENZONI (ed.) *Il Mediterraneo nella seconda metà del '500 alla luce di Lepanto* (Florence, 1974) 393–408.

TESTA, C. *Romegas* (Sta Venera, 2002).

TOGNARINI, I. 'La guerra di Maremma' in L. ROMBAI (ed.) *I Medici e lo Stato Senese, 1555–1609. Storia e territorio* (Rome, 1980) 23–34.

TUCCI, U. 'Il processo a Girolamo Zane, mancato difensore di Cipro' in G. BENZONI (ed.) *Il Mediterraneo nella seconda metà del '500 alla luce di Lepanto* (Florence, 1974) 409–33.

TURAN, Ş. *Türkiye-Italya ilişkileri, I Selçuklular'dan Bizans'ın sona erişine* (Istanbul, 1990).

TYAN, E. 'Djihad', *EI²*, vol. II (Leiden, 1965) 538–40.

UZUNÇARSILI, I. H. *Acemi ocagi ve Yeniçeri ocagi* (Ankara, 1984).

—— *Izahlı Osmanlı tarihi kronolojisi*, vol. 5 (Istanbul, 1975).

—— 'Kıbrıs Fethi ile Lepant (İnebahtı) muharebesi sırasında Türk Devletiile Venedik ve Müttefiklerinin Faaliyetine dair bazı Hezine-i Evrak Kayıtları', *Türkiyat Mecmuası*, 3 (1935) 257–92.

UZUNÇARŞILI, I. H., KARAL, E. Z. *Osmanli Tarihi*, 9 vols. (Ankara, 1947–73).

VEROGGIO, B. *Giannandrea Doria alla battaglia di Lepanto* (Genoa, 1886).

VINCENT, B. 'L'expulsion des morisques du royaume de Grenade et leur répartition en Castille (1570–1571)', *Mélanges de la Casa de Velázquez*, 6 (1970) 211–46.

VIOLA, O. *Il governo delle galere e la guerra di corsa sulle coste di Barberia nel secolo XVI illustrati da un ms. della Biblioteca civica di Catania* (Catania, 1949).

WANDRUSZKA, A. 'L'Impero, la casa d'Austria e la Sacra Lega' in G. BENZONI (ed.) *Il Mediterraneo nella seconda metà del '500 alla luce di Lepanto* (Florence, 1974): 435–43.

WITTEK, P. '*Devshirme* and *Shari'a*', *Bulletin of the School of Oriental and African Studies*, 17 (1954) 271–8.

WOODHEAD, C. 'Selim II', *EI²*, vol. IX (Leiden, 1995) 131–2.

INDEX

~

For reasons of space the index has been limited to people, places or events of importance. For clarity, Ottoman names have been indexed with their given name first, instead of last. For instance: Sokollu Mehmed Pasha, instead of the more correct Mehmed Pasha, Sokollu.

INDEX

PICTURE CREDITS

~

Section 1. *Devirme*: Topkapi Library, Istanbul; *Lala Mustafa*: Topkapi Library, Istanbul; *Sultan Süleyman*: from J. SCHRENCK, *Augustissimorum imperatorum* . . . (Innsbruck, 1601); *Sultan Selim II*: Topkapi Library, Istanbul; *Pius V*: copy after El Greco, private collection; *Grand Vizier Sokollu Mehmet Pasha*: from J. SCHRENCK, *Augustissimorum imperatorum* . . . (Innsbruck, 1601); *Cardinal Granvelle*: print by Martin Rota, 1543; *Marcantonio Colonna*: anonymous print, 1569; *Giovanni Andrea Doria*: from D. CUSTOS, *Atrium heroicum Caesarum* . . . (Augsburg, 1600–02); *Cosimo I de' Medici*: from A. MANNUCCI, *Vita di Cosimo I de' Medici* . . . (Bologna, 1586); *Don Juan of Austria*: from J. SCHRENCK, *Augustissimorum imperatorum* . . . (Innsbruck, 1601); *Sebastiano Venier*: print by Cesare Vecellio, 1572; *Francesco Duodo*: from J. SCHRENCK, *Augustissimorum imperatorum* . . . (Innsbruck, 1601); *Uluç Ali Pasha*: print by G. Guzzi, 19th century; *Marcantonio Bragadin*: from G. HILL, *A History of Cyprus*, vol. III (Cambridge, 1948); *Müezzinzâde Ali Pasha*: print by Martin Weigel, c. 1572; *Álvaro de Bazan*: painting by Rafael Tejeo (1528), from an anonymous portrait; Museo Naval, Madrid; *Sultana*: after a print by Melchior Lorch (1572); *galleass*: drawing by Ignazio Fabbroni, Biblioteca Nazionale Centrale, Florence.
Section 2. *centreline cannon*: Museo Storico Navale, Venice; photo by M. Morin. *swivel gun*: Museo Storico Navale, Venice; photo by M. Morin; *League's soldiers*: illustration by Bruno Mugnai (2006); *Ottoman soldiers*: illustration by Bruno Mugnai; *Rowers*: drawing by Ignazio Fabbroni, Biblioteca Nazionale Centrale, Florence; *Venetian scapolo*: from C. VECELLIO, *Degli habiti antichi et moderni* (Venice, 1598); *Banner*: from a contemporary pamphlet, 1571; *sketch*: from a contemporary pamphlet, 1571. *Better view*: anonymous print, 1571; *Barrage*: anonymous print, 1571; *melee*: print by Jacques Callott, c. 1615; *High noon*: arras, Palazzo de Principe, Genoa; copyright Arti Doria Pamphilj s.r.l; *Sadness in victory*: Fresco, Villa Barbarigo, Comune di Noventa Vicentina; photo by M. Morin. *Privilege of holiness*: painting by Lazzaro Baldi (1673), Collegio Ghislieri, Pavia; photo by M. Morin; *Half-hearted celebration*: painting by Titian (1572–75), Museo del Prado, Madrid; *Francesco Maria della Rovere*: painting by Federico Barocci (1572); Galleria degli Uffizi, Florence; *Ottoman standard*: Church of Santo Stefano, Pisa; *Breaking the news*: from a contemporary pamphlet, 1571.